# Road to Power

STEVEN G. MARKS

# Road to Power

The Trans-Siberian Railroad and
the Colonization of Asian Russia
1850–1917

Cornell University Press

ITHACA, NEW YORK

First published 1991 by Cornell University Press.


Library of Congress Cataloging-in-Publication Data

Marks, Steven G. (Steven Gary). 1958–
    Road to power : the Trans-Siberian railroad and the colonization of Asian Russia, 1850–1917 / Steven G. Marks.
        p.  cm.
    Includes bibliographical references and index.
    ISBN 0-8014-2533-6 (alk. paper)
    1. Siberia (R.S.F.S.R.)—History.   2. Velikaia Sibirskaia magistral'—History.
3. Soviet Union—Economic conditions—1861–1917.   4. Vitte, S. IU. (Sergeĭ
IUl'evich), graf, 1849–1915.   I. Title.
DK766.M36   1991
957.08—dc20                                                                                  90-55734


Printed in the United States of America

  ⊗ The paper in this book meets the minimum requirements
of the American National Standard for Information Sciences—
Permanence of Paper for Printed Library Materials, ANSI Z39.48-1984.

TO CINDY

# Contents

# Illustrations

# Maps

ix

# Illustrations

# Preface

The road to power for nation-states in the nineteenth and twentieth centuries lay along the path of technological advance. By the late nineteenth century the Industrial Revolution had transformed western Europe and endowed it with the machine superiority that enabled it to gain control over previously unyielding territories in distant corners of the globe. The age was marked by grandiose undertakings in the quest for wealth, glory, and power—Cecil Rhodes in the Cape Colony, Leopold II in the Congo, Ferdinand de Lesseps in the Suez and Panama, and large-scale railroad building everywhere.

Railroads were tangible symbols of prestige, progress, and power. Along with many other nations, Russia admired the transcontinental railroads of the United States and Canada and kept abreast of plans for railroads that would cut swaths through Brazil and Africa and span Eurasia from England to India. It seemed that nothing less than Russia's strength at home and standing in the world depended on the successful completion of its own transcontinental, the Siberian Railroad.

The construction of the Trans-Siberian was the most ambitious venture of late imperial Russia and one of the most extensive peaceful projects ever undertaken in the history of the world. This is the biography of that railroad, whose history tells us something about the era in which it was born. It also adds a new dimension to our understanding of the great statesman of turn-of-the-century Russia, Minister of Finance Sergei Witte, the individual most responsible for bringing the railroad into existence.

The book has its origins in my desire to understand the place of

Siberia in Russian political and economic life. As a glance at the map will show, Siberia was (and still is) the largest territorial entity of the Russian empire; yet relatively little is known about it or its role in Russian history. The book's second purpose is to contribute to an understanding of the characteristics of Russian economic development, which in many respects seem to diverge from those apparent in Europe and America. The two goals are conjoined, for Siberia was the experimental ground for the first comprehensive economic development scheme in Russian history. The key to the scheme was the Siberian Railroad, one of the major undertakings of the state in the process of modernization.

This volume is the only history of an individual tsarist industrial enterprise. A narrative case study of this sort seems better able to reveal the nature and quality of Russian economic activity than a statistical work that infers from Russia's high growth rates and other indices a pattern of development similar to that of the West. Rather than look at an impressively stocked display case, as quantitative studies tend to do, I have stepped inside the store—and found it barren.

Despite Witte's propaganda, this railroad in the Siberian frontier was surrounded by none of the romance that still clings to the transcontinentals in the United States. The Trans-Siberian was a shabby bureaucratic affair, and its cost, for a poor country, was staggering. Historians have often portrayed the Russian state as vigorous and singularly effective in developing the country. But I have found the opposite to be closer to the truth. The findings of this investigation compel us to reassess the performance of both the state and Witte in the drive to modernize Russia.

The story of the railroad reveals that economic development was to serve first and foremost a political purpose: it was intended to maintain the external and internal power of Russia's autocracy. Commerce, industry, and economic growth were not ends in themselves; they were subordinated to the necessities of state. The reason had to do with the weight of historical tradition, but also with the particular task at hand—the necessity of filling the vacuum of vast Siberia.

Because of Russia's distinctive geography, its economic history was cast in a different mold from that of densely populated western Europe. Economic development fulfilled a more rudimentary function in Russia than it did in the West. Its purpose, in Asian Russia especially, was to colonize, to settle "empty" territory, something that Europe

had accomplished centuries earlier. In this sense the Trans-Siberian project was a continuation of the colonizing process that the pre-revolutionary historian V. O. Kliuchevskii portrayed as the main thrust of Russian history.

The files pertaining to the Committee of the Siberian Railroad are located in the Central State Historical Archive (TsGIA) in Leningrad and remain off limits to Western scholars, despite glasnost. Fortunately, many of the sources in these files are located in other repositories, which willingly made their holdings available to me. For providing me with crucial unpublished sources I thank the Institute for Scientific Information in the Social Sciences (INION) in Moscow and the Scientific-Technical Library of the Leningrad Institute of Transport Engineers (LIIZhT), where I had the pleasure of working for six weeks. I also found valuable materials in Moscow in the Central State Historical Archive of the October Revolution (TsGAOR) and the Lenin Library, and in Leningrad in the Library of the Academy of Sciences (BAN) and the Saltykov-Shchedrin Library. I am grateful to the staffs of all these institutions for their assistance.

American institutions also deserve credit for their significant contributions to the book. I was fortunate to be able to make use of the outstanding collections at Harvard's Widener Library, the Harvard Law Library, the Library of Congress, and the University of Illinois Library in Urbana. The efficient interlibrary loan office of Clemson University helped to lessen the distance between the Blue Ridge foothills and the major libraries of the country. My research could not have been done without the financial support of the International Research and Exchanges Board (IREX).

My work benefited greatly from the advice and assistance of Harley and Marjorie Balzer, Jane Burbank, Lawrence Estaville, Loren Graham, Paul Vladimir Gregory, Patricia and David Herlihy, Sergei Lebedev (Institute of History, Academy of Sciences, Leningrad), Michael Ochs, Patricia Polansky, and A. I. Solov'eva (Institute of History, Academy of Sciences, Moscow). Susan Mefferd drew the maps.

I am deeply indebted to the people who read the manuscript in its various guises and gave me constructive criticism: Richard M. Haywood, Frederick Suppe, David Nicholas, Aviel Roshwald, Robert N. North, Walter M. Pintner, John J. Stephan, and Robert Valliant. John G. Ackerman and his staff at Cornell University Press, especially Barbara Salazar, strengthened the book considerably.

Finally, I thank my colleagues in the Department of History at Clemson University for their encouragement, and Richard Pipes for the unfailing guidance he has given me over the past ten years.

STEVEN G. MARKS

*Seneca, South Carolina*

# Abbreviations

| | |
|---|---|
| BAM | Baikal-Amur Main Line |
| BAN | Biblioteka Akademii Nauk |
| Barabash | "Zapiska o Man'chzhurii General'nogo Shtaba Polkovnika Barabasha," in General'nyi Shtab, *Sbornik geograficheskikh, topograficheskikh i statisticheskikh materialov po Azii*, vol. 1 (1883) |
| Evtiugin | "Zapiska o poezdke G. Sh. Shtabs-Kapitana Evtiugina iz Blagoveshchenska v Tsitsikar v 1884 g.," in General'nyi Shtab, *Sbornik po Azii*, vol. 14 (1885) |
| Grulev | "Izvlechenie iz otcheta Gener. Shtaba Sht.-Kap. Gruleva o rekognostsirovke magistral'nogo sibirskogo puti v predelakh Zabaikal'skoi oblasti," in General'nyi Shtab, *Sbornik po Azii*, vol. 50 (1892) |
| *IIRGO* | *Izvestiia imperatorskogo russkogo geograficheskogo obshchestva* |
| INION | Institut Nauchnoi Informatsii Obshchestvennykh Nauk |
| *ISIPS* | *Izvestiia sobraniia inzhenerov putei soobshcheniia* |
| LIIZhT | Leningradskii Institut Inzhenerov Zheleznodorozhnogo Transporta |
| Medem | "Vsepoddaneishii otchet o proizvedennoi s 30 maia 1910 goda po 29 fevralia 1912 goda po vysochaishemu poveleniiu senatorom grafom Medem revizii material'noi sluzhby i khoziaistva sibirskoi zheleznoi dorogi" |
| MPS | Ministerstvo Putei Soobshcheniia |

| | |
|---|---|
| OKIPP | "Otchet vysochaishe uchrezhdennoi komissii dlia issledovaniia prichin pereraskhodov po sooruzheniiu sibirskoi i perm'-kotlasskoi zheleznykh dorog" |
| PSZRI | *Polnoe sobranie zakonov rossiiskoi imperii* |
| SP | Soedinennoe Prisutstvie |
| TIRTO | *Trudy kommissii* [sic] *imperatorskogo russkogo tekhnicheskogo obshchestva po voprosu o zheleznoi doroge cherez vsiu Sibir', 1889–1890 gg.* |
| TKIM | "Trudy vysochaishe uchrezhdennoi komissii dlia issledovaniia na meste dela sooruzheniia sibirskoi zheleznoi dorogi" |
| TKIM(VP) | "Trudy vostochnoi podkomissii vysochaishe uchrezhdennoi komissii dlia issledovaniia na meste dela sooruzheniia sibirskoi zheleznoi dorogi" |
| TOSRPT | *Trudy obshchestva dlia sodeistviia russkoi promyshlennosti i torgovle* |
| TsGAOR | Tsentral'nyi Gosudarstvennyi Arkhiv Oktiabr'skoi Revoliutsii |
| zas. | zasedanie |
| ZhdD | *Zheleznodorozhnoe delo* |
| ZhKSZhD | "Zhurnaly komiteta sibirskoi zheleznoi dorogi" |
| ZhMPS | *Zhurnal ministerstva putei soobshcheniia* |

# Note on Transliteration
# and Dates

In transliterating Russian words I have sacrificed consistency for familiarity by using the Library of Congress system (without diacritical marks) in general but spelling well-known names and terms (such as Reutern, Witte, and oblast) in accordance with popular usage.

Dates given in the text conform to the Julian or old-style calendar in use before February 1918, when the Soviet government adopted the Gregorian calendar. The Russian calendar lagged twelve days behind that of the West in the nineteenth century, thirteen days by 1917.

# Russian Measurements

| | | |
|---|---|---|
| 1 desiatin | = | 2.7 acres |
| 1 pud | = | 36.11 pounds |
| 1 ruble | = | 50 U.S. cents in 1900 |
| 1 verst | = | 0.66 mile |

# Cast of
# Major Characters

Only relevant offices and dates of tenure are given.

**A. A. Abaza**   State Comptroller, 1871–1874; chairman of State Council's Department of the State Economy, 1874–1880 and 1884–1892; Minister of Finance, 1880–1881.

**Alexander I**   Emperor, 1801–1825.

**Alexander II**   Emperor, 1855–1881.

**Alexander III**   Emperor, 1881–1894.

**M. N. Annenkov**   Chief of War Ministry's Department for Rail Transport of Troops and Military Freight; administrator of Baranov Commission, 1876–1884; chief of construction, Transcaspian Railroad, 1880–1888.

**D. G. Anuchin**   Governor General of Eastern Siberia, 1879–1885.

**N. Kh. Bunge**   Minister of Finance, 1881–1887; chairman of Committee of Ministers, 1887–1895; vice chairman of Committee of Siberian Railroad, 1893–1895.

**Catherine II (the Great)**   Empress, 1762–1796.

**N. M. Chikhachev**   Minister of the Navy, 1888–1896.

**I. N. Durnovo**   Minister of the Interior, 1889–1895; chairman of Committee of Ministers, 1895–1903.

**A. S. Ermolov**   Minister of State Domains (after 1894 Agriculture), 1893–1905.

**T. I. Filippov**   State Comptroller, 1889–1899.

**N. K. Giers**   Director of Foreign Ministry's Asian Department, 1875–1882; Minister of Foreign Affairs, 1882–1895.

**A. I. Giubbenet**   Deputy Minister of Transport, 1880–1885; Minister of Transport, 1889–1892.

xix

**P. D. Gorchakov**   Governor General of Western Siberia, 1836–1851.

**I. L. Goremykin**   Minister of the Interior, 1895–1899.

**S. A. Greig**   State Comptroller, 1874–1878; Minister of Finance, 1878–1880.

**A. P. Ignat'ev**   Governor General of Eastern Siberia (renamed Irkutsk after 1887), 1885–1889.

**A. P. Izvol'skii**   Minister of Foreign Affairs, 1906–1910.

**E. F. Kankrin**   Minister of Finance, 1823–1844.

**K. P. Kaufman**   Governor General of Turkestan, 1867–1882.

**M. I. Khilkov**   Minister of Transport, 1895–1905.

**V. N. Kokovtsov**   Minister of Finance, 1904–1905, 1906–1914.

**A. N. Korf**   Governor General of Priamur'e, 1884–1893.

**A. K. Krivoshein**   Minister of Transport, 1892–1894.

**A. N. Kulomzin**   Administrator of Committee of Ministers, 1883–1902; administrator of Committee of Siberian Railroad, 1893–1902; chairman of Committee of Siberian Railroad's Auxiliary Enterprises Commission.

**A. N. Kuropatkin**   Minister of War, 1898–1904.

**V. N. Lamzdorf**   Minister of Foreign Affairs, 1900–1906.

**M. T. Loris-Melikov**   Minister of the Interior, 1880–1881.

**P. P. Mel'nikov**   Minister of Transport, 1865–1869.

**D. A. Miliutin**   Minister of War, 1861–1881.

**M. N. Murav'ev**   Minister of Foreign Affairs, 1897–1900.

**N. N. Murav'ev (-Amurskii)**   Governor General of Eastern Siberia, 1847–1861.

**N. V. Murav'ev**   Minister of Justice, 1894–1905.

**Nicholas I**   Emperor, 1825–1855.

**Nicholas II**   Chairman of Committee of Siberian Railroad, 1893–1905; Emperor, 1894–1917.

**M. N. Ostrovskii**   Minister of State Domains, 1881–1893.

**G. E. Pauker**   Minister of Transport, 1888–1889.

**V. K. Plehve**   Minister of the Interior, 1902–1904.

**K. P. Pobedonostsev**   Procurator of the Holy Synod, 1880–1905.

**A. A. Polovtsov**   State Secretary (State Council), 1883–1892.

**K. N. Pos'et**   Minister of Transport, 1874–1888.

**G. A. Potemkin**   Viceroy of New Russia, 1775–1791.

**M. Kh. Reutern**   Minister of Finance, 1862–1878; chairman of Committee of Ministers, 1881–1887.

**N. K. Schaffhausen**   Minister of Transport, 1906–1909.

**J. J. Sievers**   Viceroy of Novgorod province, 1776–1781; Viceroy of Pskov province, 1777–1781.

**D. S. Sipiagin**  Minister of the Interior, 1899–1902.

**D. M. Sol'skii**  State Comptroller, 1878–1889; chairman of State Council's Department of the State Economy, 1893–1905.

**M. M. Speranskii**  State Secretary (State Council), 1810–1812; Governor General of Siberia, 1819–1821.

**D. I. Subbotich**  Army Chief of Staff in Kwantung region, 1899–1901; Governor General of Priamur'e, 1902–1903.

**F. G. Terner**  Deputy Minister of Finance, 1887–1892.

**D. A. Tolstoi**  Minister of the Interior, 1882–1889.

**P. F. Unterberger**  Governor General of Priamur'e, 1905–1910.

**P. A. Valuev**  Minister of the Interior, 1861–1868; chairman of Committee of Ministers, 1879–1881.

**P. S. Vannovskii**  Minister of War, 1881–1898.

**I. A. Vyshnegradskii**  Minister of Finance, 1887–1892.

**S. Iu. Witte**  Director of Ministry of Finance's Department of Railroad Affairs, 1889–1892; Minister of Transport, 1892; Minister of Finance, 1892–1903.

# Road to Power

# Introduction

Alexander III devoted his reign to strengthening the presence of the state within its own territory by acting to counter both revolutionary activity and the empire's centrifugal tendency. His remedies for what conservatives had diagnosed as a national illness were large doses of Russification and curtailment of the Great Reforms. Essential for the nation's recovery was the construction of a railroad through Siberia. Although Alexander did not live to see its completion, that railroad came to symbolize his reign: incised on his monument was the epithet "Builder of the Trans-Siberian Railroad."[1]

As a political railroad, the Trans-Siberian was a product of its times. Other nations dreamed up whole railroad networks to serve political purposes. Railroads were essential to the organization and unification of the territories of the United States, Canada, Germany, Italy, and Turkey.[2] The colonial masters of India and Africa turned to railroads

1. V. V. Shulgin, *The Years: Memoirs of a Member of the Russian Duma, 1906–1917*, trans. Tanya Davis (New York, 1984), 84.
2. On the United States and Canada, see L. Girard, "Transport," in *The Cambridge Economic History of Europe*, vol. 6, pt. 1, ed. H. J. Habakkuk and M. Postan (Cambridge, 1965), 231–232, 254; Leonard Bertram Irwin, *Pacific Railways and Nationalism in the Canadian-American Northwest, 1845–1873* (Philadelphia, 1939). On railroads and German unification, see S. Iu. Witte, *Printsipy zheleznodorozhnykh tarifov po perevozke gruzov*, 3d ed. (St. Petersburg, 1910), 83–84, 219. On Cavour's nationalism and Italian railroads, see Andrew Wingate, *Railway Building in Italy before Unification*, Centre for the Advanced Study of Italian Society, Occasional Papers no. 3 (Reading, 1970), 5–6, 12–14. On Turkey, see Orhan Conker, *Les Chemins de fer en Turquie et la politique ferroviaire turque* (Paris, 1935). That Russians viewed the Canadian-Pacific Railway in purely political terms is obvious from the sources. See, e.g., *TIRTO* 6:11.

1

partially to consolidate their political control.[3] In none of these cases, however, was the nonpolitical or "private-industrial character of railroads," to quote Sergei Witte, subordinated to state purposes as it was in Russia by the time of Alexander III. The Siberian Railroad in particular was built for "military-political reasons."[4] In Alexander's reign economic policy was characterized by the increasing intervention of the state in the nation's economy, which the tsar came to consider almost exclusively in political terms.[5]

The predominance of the state in Russian economic life had historical roots. Russia was endowed with a large but inaccessible and unproviding terrain, whose resources were scattered on the periphery. The needs of the military thwarted the development of autonomous social forces that might have competed for these scarce resources. Serfdom strengthened the state's hand in the economy, limiting as it did the internal market and requiring the state to stimulate market demand and create an industrial labor supply. As a long-

---

3. See Daniel R. Headrick, *The Tools of Empire: Technology and European Imperialism in the Nineteenth Century* (New York, 1981), chaps. 13 and 14. See also J. N. Westwood, *Railways of India* (London, 1974), and Charles Miller, *The Lunatic Express: An Entertainment in Imperialism* (New York, 1971).

4. S. Iu. Witte, "Nekotorye soobrazheniia o prichinakh defitsitnosti russkoi zhelezno-dorozhnoi seti," *ZhdD*, 1910, nos. 17–18: 90, 92. As Robert William Fogel points out, although political motives were important in the creation of the American transcontinentals, economic considerations were primary (*The Union Pacific Railroad: A Case in Premature Enterprise* [Baltimore, 1960], 232–235).

5. Surprisingly, the Trans-Siberian has received little attention from historians. In the West the only previous historical work on the subject is Harmon Tupper's *To the Great Ocean: Siberia and the Trans-Siberian Railway* (Boston, 1965), an indiscriminate, if entertaining, ramble through Siberian history. Where the railroad is concerned, Tupper uncritically accepts the word of official sources. For my purposes, his book was most valuable for its assimilation of a great deal of the literature on the construction of the railroad. An earlier article by P. E. Garbutt devotes but a few pages to the railroad before the revolution, based on one official source ("The Trans-Siberian Railway," *Journal of Transport History* 1 [November 1954]: 238–249). The Trans-Siberian does have a Soviet historian, V. F. Borzunov, who has published his research on the early projects for the railroad, its economic impact, and its work force. He has also written a massive three-volume doctoral dissertation that is more comprehensive ("Istoriia sozdaniia trans-sibirskoi zheleznodorozhnoi magistrali XIX–nachala XX vv.," 3 vols. [Tomskii Gosudarstvennyi Universitet, 1972]). Fully half of the dissertation is devoted to the "struggle" for building and supply contracts on the railroad, which he details in apocalyptic tones; I see in this conflict the more mundane bidding that normally accompanies a construction job in the capitalist world. His world view does not permit him to see how capitalist enterprise works or what is unique about this railroad. He has made some valuable comments, which I do not hesitate to accept, and he brings to light important archival materials. But his dissertation, like his other works, is clothed in an ungainly suit of Marxism-Leninism, which does not do justice to the actual dimensions of the subject.

term result, the state's active involvement in industrialization was essential to make up for the lack of capital available in the country.[6]

With Russia's defeat in the Crimean War by a coalition of European powers, a crisis of confidence struck the Russian polity, and major changes were called for in its political and economic life. With the emancipation of the serfs and the Great Reforms introduced by Alexander II, Russia entered a period of economic ferment and growth, fueled by a new, if short-lived, laissez-faire attitude toward the economy. The economic life of the country in this period was presided over by the liberal ministers of finance M. Kh. Reutern, S. A. Greig, and A. A. Abaza, who believed that government ought to stabilize the currency, improve the balance of payments, and maintain strict budgetary rules, but otherwise should interfere only minimally with private enterprise to avoid stifling it. These ministers ran the Ministry of Finance cautiously rather than aggressively, in accordance with their temperaments as political moderates. Their policies found expression in the establishment of the State Bank, in their encouragement of private railroad building in the 1860s and 1870s, and in low import tariffs—all intended to create conditions in which private initiative could flourish.[7]

Doubts about the new liberal policies of the government began to surface almost as soon as they were announced. Events within the country—the attempted assassination of the tsar, the growth of revolutionary activism in the universities, peasant unrest, and the Polish revolt—brought out the instinctive conservatism of Russian officials, who reacted by watering down the reforms and attempting to curb the autonomous political life of the country.[8]

From Europe, too, came a shock that affected Russia almost as profoundly as had the Crimean War. At the Congress of Berlin in 1878

6. Olga Crisp, *Studies in the Russian Economy before 1914* (London, 1976), 7–12; W. O. Henderson, *The Industrial Revolution in Europe: Germany, France, Russia, 1815–191*. (Chicago, 1961), 2, 229.

7. Crisp, *Studies*, 22–23; Gerhart von Schulze-Gävernitz, *Volkswirtschaftliche Studien aus Rußland* (Leipzig, 1899), 175; L. E. Shepelev, *Tsarizm i burzhuaziia vo vtoroi polovine XIX veka: Problemy torgovo-promyshlennoi politiki* (Leningrad, 1981), 68–133; P. A Zaionchkovskii, *The Russian Autocracy in Crisis, 1878–1882*, trans. Gary M. Hamburg (Gulf Breeze, Fla., 1979), 159.

8. Zaionchkovskii, *Russian Autocracy*, 304–305; Dietrich Geyer, *Russian Imperialism: The Interaction of Domestic and Foreign Policy, 1860–1914*, trans. Bruce Little (New Haven, 1987), 22–23. The extent to which the doctrine of free trade ever actually informed policy has been questioned by I. F. Gindin in his *Gosudarstvennyi bank i ekonomicheskaia politika tsarskogo pravitel'stva (1861–1892 goda)* (Moscow, 1960), 47–48, 73.

Russia was forced to renounce the advantageous Treaty of San Stefano, which it had imposed on the Ottoman Empire after the Russo-Turkish War. Humiliation and isolation followed, breeding resentment of Europe in general and of Germany in particular. The tsar described the congress as "a European coalition against Russia under the leadership of Prince Bismarck."[9] Russia seemed to have lost control at home and abroad. As Minister of the Interior P. A. Valuev wrote, "the organism of the state either develops or decays; there is no middle course."[10] In other words, if order and authority were not restored, the realm would soon fall apart.

The assassination of Alexander II in 1881 only confirmed what was already in process: the rejection of the liberal, Westernizing ethos of the Great Reforms. Under Alexander III, bureaucratic Russia would attempt to return to the conservative, centralizing principles of governance that had been at the heart of Nicholas I's reign.[11] Nationalism became the official direction of policy after the war. The government and its conservative ideologues rejected liberal, European values for the supposedly less atomistic, more communal and authority-based values that they saw as specifically Russian. They repudiated economic individualism and unhindered competition on the same grounds.[12]

Like Nicholas I after the Decembrist revolt, Alexander III was determined to assert his absolute personal control over every aspect of his country's life. One by one, Alexander III removed members of his father's cabinet and replaced them with extreme conservatives. The only credential required was approval by the quartet of K. P. Pobedonostsev, V. P. Meshcherskii, M. N. Katkov, and D. A. Tolstoi.[13] These were no Slavophile conservatives with a romantic yearning for a return to the ways of pre-Petrine Muscovy; the reactionaries of Alex-

9. Quoted in C. J. H. Hayes, *A Generation of Materialism, 1871–1900* (New York, 1941), 34.

10. Quoted in S. Frederick Starr, *Decentralization and Self-government in Russia, 1830–1870* (Princeton, 1972), 341.

11. Starr contends that this development was influenced by Bismarck's unification of Germany, which had its admirers in the Russian government, and by the contemporary perception, best expressed by the philosopher Nikolai Danilevskii and the Pan-Slavs, that unification and internal strength were necessary if Russia was to prevail in the fierce competition between nation-states (ibid., 340–342).

12. Schulze-Gävernitz, *Volkswirtschaftliche Studien*, 174–191.

13. Zaionchkovskii, *Russian Autocracy*, 190–240, and *Rossiiskoe samoderzhavie v kontse XIX stoletiia* (Moscow, 1970), passim. Zaionchkovskii shows that if these four men did not exert the direct influence they are reputed to have had, they at least set the tone for the era of reaction and developed its program.

Alexander III. From Ministerstvo Finansov, *Ministerstvo finansov, 1802–1902* (St. Petersburg, 1902).

ander's reign demanded rigid adherence to the principles of Sergei Uvarov, the ideologist of Nicholas I: orthodoxy, autocracy, and nationality. Their aim was to integrate the borderlands with Russia by imposing cultural and political uniformity.[14] Gone was the late tsar's emphasis on public participation, private initiative, and a loosening of the grip of the state; his son aimed to tighten the state's hold over society, in economics as well as in politics.

In the realm of economic policy, a trend in this direction had already started earlier, most notably in railroad affairs. The *Gründerzeit* of the 1860s and 1870s had not been satisfactory. The state had given generous guarantees to private railroad companies in an effort to attract investment at a time when the state's financial resources were straitened. As long as the state stood ready to bail out unprofitable ventures, companies had no need to concern themselves with profit and loss. The resulting waste and abuse imposed serious strains on the Treasury when the Russo-Turkish War was already draining its resources.[15] The state's role in this period of "private" railroad construction was thus preeminent if not apparent.

Once he realized that the Treasury was paying for the railroads while private builders profited, even the liberal Abaza called for more regulation. The policy of *vykup*, or Treasury purchase of private railroad lines, was initiated during his administration. The state began systematic construction of railroad lines soon thereafter. By the end of the 1880s, a quarter of all railroads, including the most important lines, belonged to the state, and by 1900 more than 60 percent were state enterprises. Under Alexander III and Nicholas II a process that initially was viewed as a necessary evil came to be a deeply held principle: the state would shape economic affairs toward its political ends, if necessary in opposition to the interests of free enterprise.[16]

---

14. On the development and implementation of these policies, see Edward C. Thaden, ed., *Russification in the Baltic Provinces and Finland, 1855–1914* (Princeton, 1981), and Zaionchkovskii, *Rossiiskoe samoderzhavie*, 117–138. Rabid Russian chauvinism first reared its head in the 1860s and 1870s. See Geyer, *Russian Imperialism*, 49–63.

15. A. P. Pogrebinskii, "Stroitel'stvo zheleznykh dorog v poreformennoi Rossii i finansovaia politika tsarizma (60–90-e gody XIX v.)," *Istoricheskie zapiski* 47 (1954): 156–161, 173–175, 179. The debt of private railroads to the state reached 1.1 billion rubles by 1880. With nationalization, by the end of the 1890s, 1.5 billion rubles of railroad-company debts to the state had simply been written off.

16. Pogrebinskii, "Stroitel'stvo," 156–157, 173–176; J. N. Westwood, *A History of Russian Railways* (London, 1964), 75–78; A. M. Solov'eva, *Zheleznodorozhnyi transport Rossii vo vtoroi polovine XIX v.* (Moscow, 1975), 178–179; see also chaps. 4–6 below for the conflict between the ministries of transport and finance over this issue and the resulting limitations on coordinated policy. According to one scholar, the government's assertion of its right to inspect the accounts of private railroad companies over the

The process can be seen clearly in the reorganization of the nation's railroad administration. In 1885, after years of ministerial bickering, the Committee of Ministers resolved to enact the "General Statute for Russian Railroads" and to form the Council for Railroad Affairs under the Ministry of Transport, with the goal of standardizing railroad operations. In the same spirit, the government took actions to regulate railroad tariffs. Until 1886, tariffs were in a chaotic state, each railroad firm attempting to undercut the competition by lowering its rates. These rate wars caused traffic flows to take unnatural routes and interfered with the distribution of goods. In 1887 the state took up the issue and in 1888–1889 gave the Ministry of Finance exclusive power to set tariffs by enacting the "Temporary Regulation on Railroad Tariffs and Tariff Institutions" and by creating several new departments, including the Department of Railroad Affairs. To force down the rates for long-distance transport, a unified tariff was introduced on all railroads. Poor harvests in 1881–1882 and again in 1884–1885 demonstrated the wisdom of encouraging grain shipments from the borderlands to the center.[17]

Sergei Witte—the "Speranskii of railroad legislation," as one newspaper called him[18]—was appointed chief of the new department. Witte's pioneering work on the subject of railroad tariffs, *Printsipy zheleznodorozhnykh tarifov po perevozke gruzov* (Principles of railroad tariffs for freight transport), first published in 1883, expressed the political aspect of Treasury-sponsored railroad purchases and tariff regulation. Reflecting the era's wariness of free enterprise, Witte justified state intervention in the economy as a means to counter the vagaries of supply and demand and to harmonize the interests of the individual with those of the community. By protecting the "interests of the weak," the state served its own needs.

It is beyond any doubt that state operation of Russian railroads is in principle highly desirable, for in the operation of railroads, the Russian

course of the 1880s marked the real beginning of railroad nationalization (Everett Bruce Hurt, "Russian Economic Development, 1881–1914, with Special Reference to the Railways and the Role of the Government" [Ph.D. diss., University of London, 1963], 145–146).

17. Solov'eva, *Zheleznodorozhnyi transport*, 153–158; Pogrebinskii, "Stroitel'stvo," 166–168, 179; Westwood, *History*, 83–86; Shepelev, *Tsarizm*, 134.

18. The paper *Kievlianin* in 1888; quoted in B. V. Anan'ich and R. Sh. Ganelin, "I. A. Vyshnegradskii i S. Iu. Witte—korrespondenty 'moskovskikh vedomostei,' " in *Problemy obshchestvennoi mysli i ekonomicheskaia politika Rossii XIX–XX vekov: Pamiati prof. S. B. Okunia*, ed. N. G. Sladkevich (Leningrad, 1972), 22.

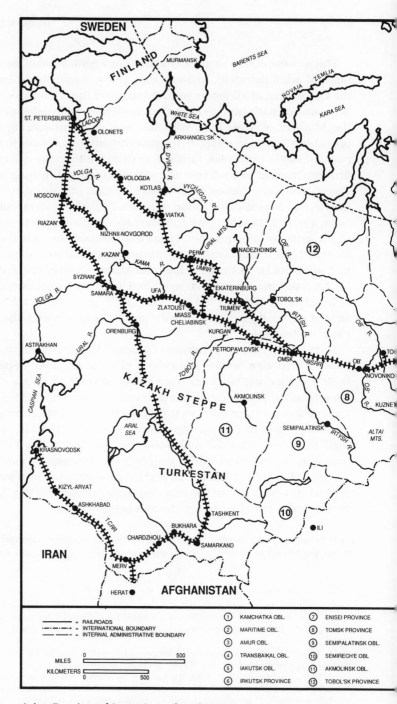

Asian Russia and its major railroads, 1916

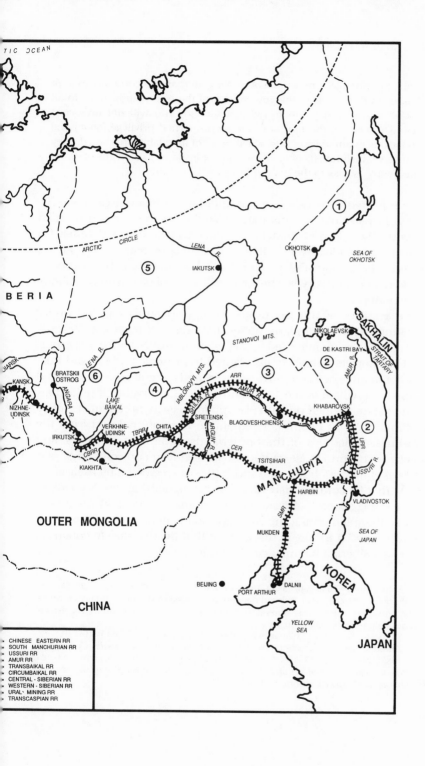

ARCTIC OCEAN

ARCTIC CIRCLE

LENA R.

OKHOTSK

SEA OF
OKHOTSK

IAKUTSK

SIBERIA

STANOVOI MTS.

NIKOLAEVSK

SAKHALIN

DE KASTRI BAY

①

②

STRAIT OF TARTARY

BRATSKII
OSTROG

KANSK

NIZHNE-
UDINSK

ANGARA R.

LENA R.

LAKE
BAIKAL

⑥

④

IABLONOVYI MTS.

SHILKA R.

ARR

AMUR R.

③

KHABAROVSK

②

AMUR R.

UFR

IRKUTSK

VERKHNE-
UDINSK

TBRR

CHITA

SRETENSK

ARGUN R.

BLAGOVESHCHENSK

CBRR

KIAKHTA

CER

TSITSIHAR

MANCHURIA

USSURI R.

VLADIVOSTOK

OUTER MONGOLIA

HARBIN

SMR

MUKDEN

SEA OF
JAPAN

KOREA

BEIJING

PORT ARTHUR

DALNII

CHINA

YELLOW
SEA

JAPAN

= CHINESE  EASTERN RR
= SOUTH   MANCHURIAN RR
= USSURI RR
= AMUR RR
= TRANSBAIKAL RR
= CIRCUMBAIKAL RR
= CENTRAL - SIBERIAN RR
= WESTERN - SIBERIAN RR
= URAL· MINING RR
= TRANSCASPIAN RR

state, in principle, can pursue no other goal than the common good of Russia. In the hands of the government of the tsar, who belongs to all social classes and to none, railroads cannot and will not ever consciously serve as the tool of estate or propertied privilege, or for the conscious maintenance or establishment of inequality; in a word, they can serve the interests of the Russian people alone, as a means of giving the people access to the highest blessings of culture.

Witte repeatedly expressed his admiration for Bismarck's economic policy, in particular for his nationalization of the German railroad network. He opposed Manchester liberalism and called himself a "realist" whose ideas were suited to Russian circumstances. He aimed to unify the nation and to end Russia's domination by European ideology and industry.[19] The new railroad policies would embody these political ideals.

The motives behind the protective import tariffs enacted under Alexander III were similarly political. As distinct from I. A. Vyshnegradskii, who recommended higher customs duties for fiscal reasons, most supporters of high tariffs wanted to preserve and expand Russia's dominance of its empire's industry and agriculture.[20] Influenced by the nationalism of the 1860s and 1870s, conservative intellectuals led by Katkov teamed up with Slavophile Russian merchants to lobby for limitations on business competition from abroad and from the non-Russian peoples of the borderlands—Poles, Jews, Tatars, and Greeks—who under Alexander II had begun to control a large percentage of Russia's trade. Alexander III was so swayed by their arguments that he continuously raised tariffs higher than the Ministry of Finance suggested.[21] Alexander's economic policy had become a means of implementing the ruling principle of his reign, "Russia for the Russians." It is only in this context that the decision to construct the Trans-Siberian Railroad can be understood.

19. S. Iu. Witte, *Printsipy*, ii, 83–84, 121–124, 126–127, 132–133, 219, 225–226, 234–236, 259. Witte proposed that the railroad network be nationalized only gradually, however, for he considered the tsarist bureaucracy not up to the task of running the system without help from private industry.

20. Shepelev, *Tsarizm*, 156; Anan'ich and Ganelin, "Vyshnegradskii i Witte," 31.

21. Alfred J. Rieber, *Merchants and Entrepreneurs in Imperial Russia* (Chapel Hill, N.C., 1982), 74–75, 77, 115–116, 118, 182–183, 197–198; Shepelev, *Tsarizm*, 143–144; Thomas C. Owen, *Capitalism and Politics in Russia: A Social History of the Moscow Merchants, 1855–1905* (Cambridge, 1981), passim.

# PART I

# IMPETUS

CHAPTER ONE

# A Weak and
# Distant Domain

In 1874 the future minister of transport K. N. Pos'et wrote that the stagnant and "semidesert" borderlands of Siberia and the Russian Far East stood in stark contrast to Japan and China, with their "millions-strong, compact population."[1] In the coming decades many others would echo the sentiment as the Orient showed signs of pulling out of the morass of inertia, leaving Asian Russia behind.[2] The most immediate reason for the government's decision to build a railroad through Siberia lay in the region's debility.

The state of affairs in the Russian territories east of the Urals—and especially beyond Lake Baikal—was indeed bleak. The quality of life there was so poor that visitors found the region demoralized. The railroad engineer L. N. Liubimov reported that

the growth of Vladivostok would have been far more significant, according to the general opinion of its inhabitants, had the conditions of life been somewhat different: here there is no beneficial climate, no splendid, poetic environment as in other borderlands of Russia, for instance in the Caucasus or Turkestan, no low cost of living; all is severe, and everywhere there are shortages and difficulties. The expenses are incredible. The reigning spirit of hard labor and exile crowns the oppres-

1. K. N. Pos'et, "Prekrashchenie ssylki v Sibir' (Zapiska K. N. Pos'eta)," *Russkaia starina* 99 (July 1899): 54.

2. See, for instance, "O velikom sibirskom puti," *ZhdD*, 1888, nos. 22–24: 170. The prospect of war with China during the Ili crisis in the late 1870s and early 1880s caused considerable uneasiness in St. Petersburg, especially after Eastern Siberian officials reported that Russia's military preparation in the region was plainly inadequate. See D. A. Miliutin, *Dnevnik D. A. Miliutina*, vol. 3 (Moscow, 1950), 239–240.

**13**

sion, and many long intensely to get out of here simply to liberate themselves from the daily contemplation of the dark side of the human soul.

The conditions of life wear especially hard on people of the "educated class" arriving here from European Russia, who yearn for their distant homeland. The oppressive feeling of solitude and dissatisfied spiritual needs, in conjunction with an unfamiliar climate, ruins the nervous system and engenders an irresistible desire to escape from the region once and for all. Add to that the almost daily murders, committed for the most part by fugitive hard-labor convicts, . . . and . . . the frequent funeral processions; . . . one can easily imagine that life for the Vladivostok resident is not sweet. For this reason, nowhere else, it seems, do they seek to drown their sorrows in spirits in such measure as in this dreary city. Here they drink to the utmost from morning until late at night and end up either suicides or insane.

Liubimov added that no butter was to be had in Vladivostok, only margarine, and that the meat was bad and expensive, as were vegetables, which had to be imported; "to make up for it all, there is an abundance of drinking houses, taverns, and houses of pleasure."[3]

The precariousness of life in Siberia and the Far East was brought about by a combination of interrelated factors, including a meager population, harsh climate, terrain unsuitable for agriculture, and poor means of communication.

### Population

Anton Chekhov wrote that even in the comparatively densely settled region of Siberia between Tiumen' and Tomsk, "as you travel, the only thing that reminds you of man are mileposts and telegraph wires humming in the wind."[4] Whereas the population density of the Russian Empire as a whole in 1888 was 5.7 people per square verst, the average for all of Siberia was 0.6 per square verst.[5] The Far East fell significantly below this average: Amur oblast had 61,000 Russian residents Amur oblast in 1888, and the Maritime oblast had fewer than

3. L. N. Liubimov, "Iz zhizni inzhenera putei soobshcheniia," *Russkaia starina* 156 (September 1913): 451–452, 454–455.

4. Anton Chekhov, "Across Siberia," in *The Unknown Chekhov: Stories and Other Writings Hitherto Untranslated*, trans. Avrahm Yarmolinsky (New York, 1954), 276.

5. "'O narodonaselenii Sibiri i o velikoi vostochnoi zheleznoi doroge' (Doklad professora E. Iu. Petri i beseda v VIII otdele IRTO)," *ZhdD*, 1888, nos. 33–34: 269. At that time Petersburg province had 42 people per square verst, Moscow province 74.7, and Warsaw province 108.

20,000.[6] In the Far East the population was largely restricted to the main river arteries and roadways, usually on the most productive soil. Aside from Vladivostok and the town of Pos'et, the few tiny villages of the South Ussuri uezds were located along the post road between Vladivostok and Lake Khanka. Settlers bypassed the North Ussuri region altogether until the late 1890s. In Amur oblast, settlement was restricted to the left bank of the Amur River and to the fertile valleys of the Zeia and Bureia rivers. There were only three insignificant settlements on the Bureia in 1884.[7]

The few people who did live in the Far East did not form a stable community. Roughly one-quarter of the population, and in some areas a large majority, consisted of soldiers—a non-productive element. Settlers from China and Korea made up a quarter of the urban population of both the Amur and Maritime oblasts by 1900, but most Russians regarded the Chinese as disloyal.[8]

Siberia had long been the destination of criminal exiles, and approximately 20,000 escaped convicts and vagrants roamed across the land, living in utter poverty. From within Siberia it was reported that "the exiles themselves, remaining idle and useless and with no means to make an honest living, lead disreputable lives, accompanied by drunkenness, debauchery, thievery, and other crimes, which, because of their large numbers in the towns, are almost impossible for the police to look after and prevent."[9] The exiles had a corrupting influence on the life of the region. They may not be fully responsible for the

6. I shall use "Priamur'e," as the Russians do, to refer to the Maritime and Amur oblasts together, which formed the Priamur general governorship. The term *oblast* may be translated as *region*, but so might *krai* be; to avoid confusion, I have not translated *oblast*. In imperial Russia, the krai was not an official administrative unit; when I refer to the North Ussuri, South Ussuri, or Ussuri region, I am replacing the word *krai*, which designates a geographical entity encompassing the territory of several uezds (districts) of an oblast. *Krai* can also refer to a broader region, such as the entire Russian Far East. "Transbaikal oblast" (Zabaikal'skaia oblast') is used interchangeably with "Transbaikalia" (Zabaikal'e), as in Russian sources. After mid-1884 Transbaikalia was an administrative division of the Priamur general governorship, so it may justifiably be referred to as part of the Russian Far East.

7. V. M. Kabuzan, *Dal'nevostochnyi krai v XVII–nachale XX vv. (1640–1917): Istoriko-demograficheskii ocherk* (Moscow, 1985), 99, 162 (table 3), 222 (table 12); A. Sil'nitskii, *Kul'turnoe vliianie ussuriiskoi zheleznoi dorogi na iuzhno-ussuriiskii krai* (Khabarovsk, 1901), 24; Robert Britton Valliant, "Japan and the Trans-Siberian Railroad, 1885–1905" (Ph.D. diss., University of Hawaii, 1974), 8; Evtiugin, 213–214.

8. P. Chikhachev, "Kaliforniia i ussuriiskii krai," *Vestnik Evropy*, June 1890, no. 6: 561; Valliant, "Japan," 7–9; Kabuzan, *Dal'nevostochnyi krai*, 127. In contrast to the migrant Chinese, Korean settlers came with their families, settled, converted to Orthodoxy, and attempted to assimilate (Kabuzan, *Dal'nevostochnyi krai*, 93–95).

9. N. M. Iadrintsev, *Sibir' kak koloniia v geograficheskom, etnograficheskom i istoricheskom otnoshenii*, 2d ed. (St. Petersburg, 1892), 125, 300.

high incidence of drunkenness throughout Siberia, but they surely contributed to the "dirty, slovenly, and poverty-stricken appearance of the peasant villages" which George Kennan found so striking.[10]

### Cossacks of the Far East

The hardships of the population of Transbaikalia and Priamur'e were epitomized by the experience of the Cossack settlers. As a military force, they faced the same problems that a regular army would face in the Far East. Cossacks had spearheaded the Russian exploration and conquest of Siberia and from the first they had played an important role in its defense. Before N. N. Murav'ev's appointment as governor general of Eastern Siberia,[11] few Cossack formations were located east of Lake Baikal. With an eye to their dual military and colonizing potential, Murav'ev ordered the formation of the Transbaikal Cossack host in 1851. Extreme measures were needed to augment their ranks. Murav'ev freed ex-convicts and enlisted them as serfs in the mines or enrolled them as Transbaikal Cossacks. He tried the same scheme with a few thousand soldiers from disciplinary battalions, but it was not successful: inscribed as "adopted sons" in Cossack and other households, they deserted their settlements and became drunken transients. In 1854 English activities in China led Murav'ev to propose the strengthening of the Transbaikal host and the transfer of some contingents to the Amur and Maritime oblasts. Out of these groups the separate Amur and Ussuri Cossack hosts were eventually formed.[12]

In the early years of colonization, their numbers were significant. From 1852 to 1897 Cossacks made up 30 percent of the population of Transbaikalia. In 1859 they formed between 60 and 85 percent of the

10. George Kennan, *Siberia and the Exile System*, vol. 1 (New York, 1891), 352–353. According to this American authority on Siberia, for every school there were thirty "rum shops" in Western Siberia and thirty-five in Eastern Siberia.

11. The general governorships of Eastern and Western Siberia are not to be confused with the more loosely delimited geographical regions of eastern and western Siberia.

12. O. I. Sergeev, *Kazachestvo na russkom Dal'nem Vostoke v XVII–XIX vv.* (Moscow, 1983), 46–47, 50, 55–56, 58–59, 62–63, 70; Peter Kropotkin, *Memoirs of a Revolutionist* (Cambridge, Mass., 1930), 185–187. See also N. I. Razumov, *Zabaikal'e* (St. Petersburg, 1899), 63–69. Kropotkin was attaché to the Eastern Siberian governor general for Cossack affairs. He writes that Murav'ev so desperately wanted to settle the region that he released 1,000 male hard-labor convicts, most of them robbers and murderers, and gave them land on the Amur. One hundred hard-labor women were then freed and married to the men of their choice.

population of the Far East, depending on the region. By 1869 they accounted for 43 percent. Even though new Cossack settlements were not created after 1862, Cossack settlers predominated among immigrants to the region throughout the years from 1858 to 1882, outnumbering peasants by 5,401 to 3,892 in the Maritime oblast, and in Amur oblast by 10,576 to 8,088.[13] With such percentages, clearly the quality of Cossack settlement would play a large role in forming the character of Russian colonization of the area.

Unfortunately, the combined use of the Cossacks for military duty and colonization of the province was a failure. In the eighteenth century it was difficult to provision Russian military personnel in eastern Siberia. Cossacks were given land and turned into farmer-soldiers so that they could support themselves, but they could not devote full time to either farming or soldiering and their circumstances were known to be difficult. Strapped with military and postal duties and given land inferior to that of the peasants, the Cossacks did not succeed at agriculture and many families were miserably poor. D. I. Subbotich, governor general of Priamur'e from 1902 to 1903, wrote that the Cossacks of the region had given up on agriculture. Some were engaged in fishing and hunting, "but mostly they lounge about near the steamship wharfs and postal stations." In defense, too, their success was minimal. The presence of the Ussuri host did not ease Russian military concerns about China during the Ili crisis (1871–1881); it seems that their greatest contribution was in chasing the Manchurian bandits who penetrated the Suchan area.[14]

The Cossacks were simply not equipped to cope with the environment:

> The motley crowd of Transbaikalian Cossacks, . . . settled in a hurry and often haphazardly along the banks of the Amur, certainly did not attain prosperity, especially in the lower parts of the river and on the Usuri

13. Sergeev, *Kazachestvo*, 79–80; Kabuzan, *Dal'nevostochnyi krai*, 67. By 1897 Cossacks formed only 10.3% of the Far East's population.

14. Sergeev, *Kazachestvo*, 36–37, 76–79, 90; Chikhachev, "Kaliforniia," 560; Kabuzan, *Dal'nevostochnyi krai*, 74, 79. The picture painted by Sergeev is distorted. He cites the many economic activities undertaken by the Cossacks, implying that this Russian underclass made a positive contribution to the settlement of the region. This view is contradicted by all other sources. See, e.g., Great Britain, Naval Intelligence Division, *Handbook of Siberia and Arctic Russia*, vol. 1 (London, n.d.), 81; D. I. Subbotich, *Amurskaia zheleznaia doroga i nasha politika na Dal'nem Vostoke* (St. Petersburg, 1908), 7. There were some pockets of prosperity in the Cossack settlements of the Far East, in particular among the "enterprising and sharp-witted" Cossacks of the Transbaikal host who were engaged in cattle breeding. See Grulev, 141; Kropotkin, *Memoirs*, 199.

[sic], where almost every square yard of land had to be won from a virgin . . . forest, . . . reducing whole populations to sheer despair and apathy.[15]

Others would have extricated themselves from such difficulties, but the Transbaikalians, Cossacks created by administrative order out of peasants, to a significant degree had lost the unyielding industriousness and the skills peculiar to those of their former calling. . . . Laziness and crime became ubiquitous (under the influence of the criminals settled among them), with the result that the government was forced to spend large sums to keep the Cossack settlements going.[16]

## Climate and Agriculture

The travails of the Cossacks mirrored those of the rest of the Russian population in the Far East. Their plight showed the deficiencies of Russia's system of colonization and defense as it existed before the construction of the Siberian Railroad. The problem was largely one of provisionment, an age-old challenge to the Russian administration of Eastern Siberia. If the settled population could barely eke out an existence, stationing the number of troops needed to guarantee defense of the region would be all the more difficult. For this reason Andrew Malozemoff alludes to the "failure of the original settlement."[17]

Agricultural self-sufficiency in the Russian Far East could not be achieved under the adverse climatic conditions. The region's climate is more continental than maritime, and although Vladivostok is farther south than Nice, its winters are colder than Leningrad's. Winters are very dry with little snowfall, spring and autumn are dry, and summers are hot. Summer brings the monsoon season, with its perpetual and often torrential rains, thick fog, and unbearable humidity. Cyclones are frequent in summer and winter, when precipitation can yield in twenty-four hours as much moisture as Moscow receives in six months.[18]

15. Kropotkin, *Memoirs*, 186.

16. Chikhachev, "Kaliforniia," 561.

17. Andrew Malozemoff, *Russian Far Eastern Policy, 1881–1904: With Special Emphasis on the Causes of the Russo-Japanese War* (Berkeley, 1958), 1 and passim. For the historical context, see also James R. Gibson, *Feeding the Russian Fur Trade: Provisionment of the Okhotsk Seaboard and the Kamchatka Peninsula, 1639–1856* (Madison, 1969).

18. S. P. Suslov, *Physical Geography of Asiatic Russia*, trans. Noah D. Gershevsky (San

The climate wreaked havoc on agriculture. In the north the hardiest grains would not flourish. Rice and soybeans might have grown in the south, but Russian settlers were unaccustomed to them. Grain planted in the valleys suffered from drought in the spring and from dampness and fungus disease in the summer. The rains turned the plains into swamps. The soil became unworkable and the flooding brought on by typhoons destroyed crops year after year. To avoid inundation, settlement was restricted to the elevated ridges, but the region's mountain ranges imposed obvious limitations on expansion.[19]

The early hopes entertained for both Transbaikalia and Priamur'e as the region's breadbaskets were soon dashed.[20] Local agriculture could not satisfy local food needs. According to the historical demographer V. M. Kabuzan, the small Russian population of Priamur'e had managed to provide the region with enough food by the late 1860s, but with the steady influx over the years of a disproportionate number of nonagricultural settlers, in particular gold miners and soldiers, peasants could no longer satisfy the demand for their products. With the exception of the South Ussuri region, which was somewhat more suited to agriculture, the Maritime oblast had always found itself in this desperate situation.[21]

In 1892 approximately 3.6 million puds of grain were required to feed the population of Priamur'e, including troops, civilians, prisoners, and gold miners, but only 2.75 million puds were harvested locally. In neighboring Transbaikalia, only one good harvest interrupted six years of hunger between 1884 and 1891. In both North and South Ussuri uezds, cultivation was minimal and local grains were scarce at the Khabarovsk and Vladivostok markets. The shortage of grain prevented the development of livestock husbandry, so meat was

---

Francisco, 1961), 333–336, 342–343; L. S. Berg, *Natural Regions of the USSR*, trans. Olga A. Titelbaum (New York, 1950), 60–61; E. B. Kovrigin, "The Soviet Far East," in *Soviet-American Horizons on the Pacific*, ed. John J. Stephan and V. P. Chichkanov (Honolulu, 1986), 7.

19. Suslov, *Physical Geography*, 334–337, 359, 363; Berg, *Natural Regions*, 62; Kropotkin, *Memoirs*, 186, and "The Great Siberian Railway," *Geographical Journal*, no. 5 (February, 1895): 153.

20. For an example of the exaggerated hopes, see N. Matiunin, "Nashi sosedy na Krainem Vostoke," *Vestnik Evropy*, July 1887, no. 7: 80, 82.

21. Kabuzan, *Dal'nevostochnyi krai*, 73–76, 80–81, 90–92, 127–128. By 1890 enough new peasant immigrants had arrived to reestablish a tenuous equilibrium, but it was short-lived. Kabuzan stresses this success of local agriculture in order to glorify the role of the Russian peasant settlers, and glosses over their inability to cope with the dire insufficiencies of the region, so vividly portrayed in most other sources.

expensive. Nor did the availability of grain guarantee that it could be used, for flour mills were scarce in the region. Similarly, although fish were plentiful in the rivers, a lack of both initiative and salt prevented all but local use of this food source.[22]

The government tried to alleviate the hardship first by providing supplies from European Russia to the army and settlers, then by taking measures to encourage local production. For a time it annually supplied salt, flour, and meat, carried on barges floated at high water from Chita through mountainous Transbaikalia. After 1880 the Volunteer Fleet carried Russian goods from Odessa. This overseas supply route shortened the journey from 320 to 65 days, lowered costs, and took some trade out of the hands of foreigners, a consistent ambition of the government. To save money and encourage local production, the military administration of eastern Siberia provided a limited number of agricultural implements to peasants in the Far East and constructed flour mills.[23]

The efforts of the military had little impact on the whole. The region remained dependent on imports, and foreigners dominated its trade. In the late 1880s the total volume of imports through Vladivostok was double that of exports.[24] Imports from China in the period 1863–1892 were five times as great as exports.[25] Russian peasants simply could

22. "Vopros o plavanii po r. Sungari," in General'nyi Shtab, *Sbornik po Azii*, vol. 55 (1894), 125; Grulev, 143; Sil'nitskii, *Kul'turnoe vliianie*, 1, 25; Valliant, "Japan," 8; K. A. Skal'kovskii, *Russkaia torgovlia v Tikhom okeane* (St. Petersburg, 1883), 30, 33; Chikhachev, "Kaliforniia," 562. Kennan mentions the high cost of forage and food in Eastern Siberia, in *Siberia and the Exile System*, 1:355. Still today the Russian Far East can supply only its own potatoes and eggs; the rest of its food must be imported. See V. P. Chichkanov and P. A. Minakir, "Economic Development of the Soviet Far East," in Stephan and Chichkanov, *Soviet-American Horizons*, 104.

23. Kropotkin, *Memoirs*, 186; Sil'nitskii, *Kul'turnoe vliianie*, 26–28; Skal'kovskii, *Russkaia torgovlia*, 31–32, 474.

24. A. P. Okladnikov et al., eds., *Istoriia Sibiri s drevneishikh vremen do nashikh dnei*, vol. 3 (Leningrad, 1968), 67. See also N. L. Shlyk, "The Soviet Far East and the International Economy," in Stephan and Chichkanov, *Soviet-American Horizons*, 115. Approximately 30% of Vladivostok's imports came from Germany, 25% from European Russia, 13% from England, 12% from China, 13% from Japan, 5% from the United States, and the remaining 2% from other nations, presumably Korea, Australia, France, and perhaps Belgium (Ministerstvo Finansov, Departament Torgovli i Manufaktur, *Sibir' i velikaia sibirskaia zheleznaia doroga*, ed. V. I. Kovalevskii and P. P. Semenov, 2d ed. [St. Petersburg, 1896], 222–223).

25. Value of imports: 415.5 million rubles; exports: 83.5 million rubles (Okladnikov et al., *Istoriia Sibiri*, 3:66). The treaty of Tientsin (1862) gave the Chinese the right to conduct duty-free trade in Transbaikalia and Priamur'e in a region extending fifty versts from the border with China, and gave Vladivostok and Nikolaevsk *porto-franco* status. The intention was to help feed the local population. Since it was not properly policed,

not compete with the Chinese farmers of Manchuria, whose grain was grown at less expense and was of better quality; the Chinese were familiar with working in such conditions, but Russian immigrants were not. Since the 1870s Manchuria had been a vital source of grain to the region. It made up for local shortages and flooded the market, leading many people to doubt that local Russian agriculture had a future. The Chinese were the exclusive suppliers of fresh fruits and vegetables in Blagoveshchensk, and Koreans controlled the economy in the South Ussuri town of Pos'et. Cattle were also imported from Manchuria and Korea, for cattle raising was undeveloped in the Far East and erratic in Transbaikalia because of the poor harvests.[26]

Under Alexander III, such a predominance of non-Russians was considered a threat in and of itself; it was all the more dangerous because it had a bearing on an important military issue: the inability of the region to feed the army in case of war. The Russian settlement of Priamur'e was so small and its agriculture so unstable that production was less than satisfactory in normal circumstances; how could the army be fed in wartime, especially if an enemy navy were to blockade the Amur?[27]

Transbaikalia could offer no relief. In the rare times of good harvest, peasants immediately sold their stocks of grain rather than build up reserves. At such a time, soldiers might still be able to depend on local sources, but the lack of mills and the small size of domestic stoves impeded their use of grain. The meat supply for approximately five hundred men would last one to two days, and not even that if the harvest was weak. Fodder, fuel, and water were also frequently unavailable. During the famine of 1888, the starving population of Transbaikalia refused to feed troops stationed there.[28]

---

the whole region was essentially a free-trade zone up to Lake Baikal, where the Russian tariff border began (M. I. Sladkovskii, *History of Economic Relations between Russia and China*, trans. M. Roublev [Jerusalem, 1966], 85; B. B. Glinskii, ed., *Prolog russko-iaponskoi voiny: Materialy iz arkhiva grafa S. Iu. Witte* [Petrograd, 1916], 236–237). These arrangements were apparently first suggested by Murav'ev-Amurskii. See E. L. Besprozvannykh, *Priamur'e v sisteme russko-kitaiskikh otnoshenii, XVII–seredina XIX v.* (Moscow, 1983), 166.

26. "Vopros o splavanii po r. Sungari," 125–126; Valliant, "Japan," 8–9; Charles and Barbara Jelavich, *Russia in the East, 1876–1880* (Leiden, 1959), 91n1; Skal'kovskii, *Russkaia torgovlia*, 66; Matiunin, "Nashi sosedy," 83.

27. Matiunin, "Nashi sosedy," 82; Evtiugin, 214.

28. Grulev, 143–145, 147–148; N. A. Voloshinov, "Sibirskaia zheleznaia doroga," *IIRGO* 27 (1891): 21–22.

## Transport

If natural causes were largely responsible for the deficiencies of the Far East, there was universal agreement that the condition of the roads hindered any progress that could be made. Mountainous Transbaikalia remained a barrier separating the Far East from the relative abundance of central Siberia.[29] K. A. Skal'kovskii stressed that "the reason for the weakness of the Russian population is remoteness and the difficulty of travel."[30]

"Remoteness and the difficulty of travel" were at the heart of the problem of defending the Far Eastern regions, and they were central features of the economic and political relations between Siberia and European Russia. The conditions of transport throughout Siberia had changed little since the eighteenth century. One writer considered Siberia to be poorer in overland routes than Mongolia.[31] The Treasury had built cart roads over the course of the eighteenth century, and with completion of the Moscow-Ekaterinburg highway in 1763 began construction of the Siberian highway.[32] Siberian peasants provided construction labor as part of their service obligation to the state. Villages of peasants and exiles were then settled along the road to maintain it and provide needed services; the government also encouraged this settlement as a means of establishing Russian control of the territory. The highway played a major role in developing the centers of Siberian economic and cultural life.[33]

29. Sil'nitskii, *Kul'turnoe vliianie*, passim; Valliant, "Japan," 9; Voloshinov, "Sibirskaia zheleznaia doroga," 20, 22.

30. Skal'kovskii, *Russkaia torgovlia*, 2.

31. M. N. Selikhov, "Sibir' pod vliianiem velikogo rel'sovogo puti," *Sibirskii torgovo-promyshlennyi i spravochnyi kalendar' na 1902 god*, otdel 2 (Tomsk, 1902), 17.

32. Its western route shifted southward as its capacity expanded over the next half century. In western and central Siberia it took the following path by 1838: Tiumen'-Ialutorovsk-Ishim-Tiukalinsk-Kainsk-Kolyvan'-Tomsk-Mariinsk-Krasnoiarsk-Nizhne-udinsk-Irkutsk. From there it branched off in two directions, one toward Lake Baikal, the other to Kiakhta. A post road also ran north to Iakutsk. See Okladnikov et al., *Istoriia Sibiri*, vol. 3, map between pp. 60 and 61; Selikhov, "Sibir' pod vliianiem," 17; Great Britain, Naval Intelligence Division, *Handbook of Siberia*, 1:319; Robert N. North, *Transport in Western Siberia: Tsarist and Soviet Development* (Vancouver, 1979), 17, 28; M. I. Pomus, *Zapadnaia Sibir' (Ekonomiko-geograficheskaia kharakteristika)* (Moscow, 1956), 106–107, 115; Slavinskii, "Russia and the Pacific to 1917," in Stephan and Chichkanov, *Soviet-American Horizons*, 36; Iadrintsev, *Sibir' kak koloniia*, 196. *Highway* is a translation of the Russian *trakt*, and refers to a major but unpaved road. I will use it interchangeably with *post road*. This particular road was also known as the "Great Siberian highway" and the "Moscow-Siberian highway."

33. Okladnikov et al., *Istoriia Sibiri*, 2:191, 273, 315. Road repairs were a heavy burden on the population: after two or three rains, the highway would be impassable and their

The Moscow-Siberian highway west of Lake Baikal sufficed for the cartage of more than 2 million puds of freight per year, and approximately one-fifth of the population along the route was engaged in servicing it as innkeepers, coachmen, carters, and craftsmen.[34] Yet it was a very bad, primitive road. In its western portions the highway was all of twenty-one feet wide. Alongside were stretches of clearing intended for grazing and telegraph lines, but they often became the main thoroughfare when the road itself was impassable for normal traffic. Coachmen frequently took their own routes, too, off the road along paths cutting through the taiga. Although some of the roads in Enisei province were hard-surfaced and were considered good, they were the exception. Everywhere else the highway was a sea of mud or clouded with dust in the spring and summer, and full of potholes in the winter. Its deep ruts made travel hazardous. Thousands upon thousands of carts dug the ruts deeper and deeper every day. In winter, according to Colonel N. A. Voloshinov of the General Staff, horses and carts would plunge into the potholes and literally disappear from view. During the summer rains travel was impossible. Bridges were of flimsy construction and often collapsed. Ferries carried travelers across the wider rivers.[35]

Kennan journeyed on the Siberian highway in a tarantass, and described it as an exhausting ordeal. The horses could barely make it up steep hills of liquid clay, across the often swamped road, or along its unrepaired corduroy sections. Sleep was impossible for days on end because of the jolting of the tarantass, the cold in winter, and the hordes of mosquitoes in summer. Frequently the only food available at way stations was bread and water. Meat and hot meals were unavailable.[36] Chekhov, too, made his way across Siberia by this route, and called it the "longest and . . . ugliest road in the whole world." He told of overflowing rivers that flooded the roads and described ending

work, valued by the state in the millions of rubles, would be undone (*TOSRPT*, vol. 18, otdel 1 [1887], 11).

34. *TOSRPT*, vol. 18, otdel 1 (1887), 14; Voloshinov, "Sibirskaia zheleznaia doroga," 20; Okladnikov et al., *Istoriia Sibiri*, 3:62–63. Kennan described passing caravans of 100 freight wagons at a time and counted 1,400 in one day on the western section of the tract (*Siberia and the Exile System*, 1:49). Freight consisted of grain, Altai metals, and Chinese goods, the latter including tea (North, *Transport*, 28).

35. Voloshinov, "Sibirskaia zheleznaia doroga," 19–20; Henry Lansdell, *Through Siberia*, vol. 1 (Boston, 1882), 139; M. Sobolev, "Puti soobshcheniia v Sibiri," *Sibir': Eia sovremennoe sostoianie i eia nuzhdy: Sbornik statei*, ed. I. S. Mel'nik (St. Petersburg, 1908), 36; Great Britain, Naval Intelligence Division, *Handbook of Siberia*, 1:323–326.

36. Kennan, *Siberia and the Exile System*, 1:73, 138–139, 356–357, 364.

up in pools of mud when, inevitably, the carriage tipped over. "The going is hard, very hard," he wrote,

> but what makes it worse is the thought that this foul strip of earth, this pock-marked horror, is practically the only artery connecting Europe with Siberia. And along this artery, we say, civilization flows into Siberia. So we say, we say a lot. If we were overheard by the drivers, the mailmen, or those wet, muddied peasants walking knee-deep in ooze beside their carts, which are loaded with tea for Europe, what would they think of Europe's candor?[37]

As if the physical features of the road were not bad enough, travelers also had to beware of nighttime attacks by escaped convicts. Iu. Ia. Solov'ev, a diplomat who returned from China along the highway, described the wooden crosses at the side of the road as "memorials to murdered travelers."[38] Under the circumstances, a cart on the Moscow-Kiakhta section of the road covered roughly fifty versts a day if conditions were favorable, thirty-five or less when the road was bad.[39]

River travel was perhaps a bit more reliable, but not by much. Although steamer traffic continued to grow throughout western and central Siberia, it was ill supplied: 73 steamships plied a fraction of the 8,000 versts of water routes in western Siberia. Personnel were scarce, too. Until the 1890s there were no passenger steamers: travel in Siberia was by tug or barge. Furthermore, the major rivers flowed from north to south. Although there was supposed to be a continuous east-west river route once the Ob'-Enisei canal was completed, it was too shallow to be of use. Frozen waters, fast-moving ice, floods, and rapids all limited navigation to only four months of the year, and even then to the middle stretches of most rivers.[40]

Siberian transportation west of Lake Baikal was bad, and east of the lake it got worse. That was the major reason that migration to the Far East (with the exception of the South Ussuri region, which was reached by the overseas route) remained insignificant.[41] Lake Baikal itself was a large part of the problem. The navigation period on the lake lasts eight months, from May through December; the rest of the

37. Chekhov, *Unknown Chekhov*, 284, 295–303.

38. Quoted in V. N. Kazimirov, *Velikii sibirskii put'* (Irkutsk, 1970), 6.

39. Okladnikov et al., *Istoriia Sibiri*, 3:62–63.

40. Zenone Volpicelli [Vladimir], *Russia on the Pacific and the Siberian Railway* (London, 1899), 277–283; Kropotkin, "Great Siberian Railway," 149; Okladnikov et al., *Istoriia Sibiri*, 3:64; North, *Transport*, 36, 38–39. For the estimated amounts needed to improve the Ob'-Enisei canal, see *TOSRPT*, vol. 18, otdel 1 (1887), 11–12.

41. Kabuzan, *Dal'nevostochnyi krai*, 99.

year the water is frozen. The lake is subject to violent storms, and ice in spring and fall often puts a halt to navigation. In good weather it took seven hours to cross from Listvianichnaia on the western shore to Mysovskaia on the eastern shore. An alternative was the Circum-baikal post road, winding from Irkutsk along the south shore of the lake to Verkhneudinsk, but it ran through wild terrain that was perilous for travelers and would have made the transport of troops more impractical than it already was.[42]

The post road built under Murav'ev-Amurskii through Trans-baikalia and Priamur'e could not be relied on as a commercial route, and in general it too was avoided because of the arduous terrain and severe weather.[43] The road along the shore of the Shilka and upper Amur became a narrow trail high in the cliffs. The last seven stations were so dangerous that they were known as the "Seven Mortal Sins."[44] Summer monsoons turned roads into impassable "slush" (rasputitsa).[45] The South Ussuri region had only one road to speak of, running from Kamen'-Rybolov on Lake Khanka to the village of Razdol'-noe, 140 versts to the south. It was often flooded year round. N. A. Voloshinov found the region east of Lake Khanka too swampy for travel by horse or foot; he suggested that freight haulers reroute from Vladivostok to the Amur by sea to Nikolaevsk. He was not optimistic about developing a local carrying trade.[46]

Travel by river was the preferred method east of Lake Baikal. The system consisting of the Selenga, Khilok, Ingoda, and Shilka rivers linked Baikal with the Amur River and placed all of Transbaikalia within reach by way of their branches. Several steamer lines carried passengers along the whole length of the Amur from Sretensk to Nikolaevsk, with service down the Ussuri River and up the Zeia and Bureia rivers to the gold camps.[47] Navigation in the region was not dependable, however. The Amur is frozen five to six months of the year, and sandbars blocked its mouth at that time. The Shilka was

42. Grulev, 131–132, 134; Volpicelli, *Russia on the Pacific*, 274; Suslov, *Physical Geography of Asiatic Russia*, 305–306.

43. Volpicelli, *Russia on the Pacific*, 274–275; Selikhov, "Sibir' pod vliianiem," 17. This despite the fact that, according to Grulev, the local inhabitants of Transbaikalia had a wealth of good horses and were eager to do carting (Grulev, 143).

44. Kropotkin, *Memoirs*, 189.

45. Suslov, *Physical Geography of Asiatic Russia*, 337.

46. Voloshinov, "Sibirskaia zheleznaia doroga," 24–25; Barabash, 165–166; Skal'-kovskii, *Russkaia torgovlia*, 56. Horses were quite expensive in the region and had to be imported from Tomsk or Transbaikalia (Matiunin, "Nashi sosedy," 83).

47. Grulev, 132–133; Volpicelli, *Russia on the Pacific*, 283. Along the Bureia were three widely separated small settlements, linked only by water (Evtiugin, 214n11).

clear of ice from mid-May to early October, but shallow water often made navigation treacherous after the first two months. Flooding from the hills made the waters even more unpredictable. The anarchist and geographer Prince Peter Kropotkin described the Amur during the monsoon season as swollen to a width of two to five miles in places, with waves of destructive height. The Amur, Ussuri, and Sungacha rivers, as well as Lake Khanka, became extremely shallow during the dry season, so that running aground on sandbars or in rapids was a frequent occurrence. At such times, Vladivostok could be reached only by sea.[48]

As the major commercial and naval port in the Russian Far East, Vladivostok was of vital importance to the communications of the region.[49] Whatever benefits it may have had as a commercial port, as a naval base it suffered from serious deficiencies, and still does. In this region the cold coastal seas cause the port to freeze over three months of the year. The sheer cliffs of the Sikhote-Alin Mountains line the coast of the Ussuri region, making Vladivostok inaccessible from this direction, and the straits guarding the Sea of Japan made open access to or from the Pacific Ocean doubtful in wartime. Vladivostok's location on a peninsula jutting into the bay opened it to attack from two sides, so that its defense was all the more difficult.[50]

Obviously transportation in all of Siberia was less than ideal. In the Far East all communications came to a halt for several months of the year, and except for an occasional caravan of camels over the frozen rivers, the region was cut off from the rest of Russia. The telegraph was unreliable, too, since repairs in remote flooded regions could not be made.[51]

---

48. Suslov, *Physical Geography of Asiatic Russia*, 338; Skal'kovskii, *Russkaia torgovlia*, 74–75; Grulev, 132, 138; John Albert White, *The Siberian Intervention* (Princeton, 1964), 26; Kropotkin, *Memoirs*, 190–191; Barabash, 166; Voloshinov, "Sibirskaia zheleznaia doroga," 24; Arthur John Barry, *Lecture on the Great Siberian Railway* (London, 1900), 18.

49. Vladivostok was a Russian military post in 1860 before the territory was officially ceded to Russia and in 1872–1873 became the main naval port on the Pacific, in place of Nikolaevsk-na-Amure. In 1880 Vladivostok became a separate administrative entity under a military governor; in 1888 it was reunified with the Maritime oblast, and in 1890 replaced Khabarovsk as its administrative center (Skal'kovskii, *Russkaia torgovlia*, 10; Erik Amburger, *Geschichte der Behördenorganisation Rußlands von Peter dem Großen bis 1917* [Leiden, 1966], 366, 407).

50. Suslov, *Physical Geography of Asiatic Russia*, 327, 333; Skal'kovskii, *Russkaia torgovlia*, 13–14; Matiunin, "Nashi sosedy," 81–82; Allen S. Whiting, *Siberian Development and East Asia: Threat or Promise?* (Stanford, 1981), 76. Matiunin suggested Pos'et, icefree and in a guarded location, as a more reasonable choice for a naval base. Whiting points out that the access problem still detracts from the Soviet naval base in Vladivostok.

51. Selikhov, "Sibir' pod vliianiem," 18; Skal'kovskii, *Russkaia torgovlia*, 60. On the use

The implications did not bode well for Russia's prospects of winning a war in the Far East. Of the 24,000 soldiers in 1891 under the command of Baron A. N. Korf, governor general of Priamur'e and ex officio commander of the Amur military okrug, only 60 percent were a viable force, and they were required to defend the border with China.[52] The British engineer Arthur John Barry estimated that Russia would need to put 100,000 men in the field if a serious war broke out; he did not think they could be supplied.[53] The General Staff was aware that the Chinese could interdict existing Russian lines of communication at any number of points, easily cutting off the rest of the Russian Far East. If the Chinese attacked the South Ussuri uezds in March, during the *rasputitsa*, it would take one and a half to two months for reinforcements from the Khabarovsk battalion to arrive; and Transbaikal Cossack units could not be mobilized for departure from Sretensk before May 1. Chinese troops could reach Pos'et from some points in Manchuria in as little as twelve to fifteen days.[54]

Officials in St. Petersburg and in Siberia understood as early as 1875 that poor communications were at the root of Russia's strategic weakness in the Far East. As a corrective measure, throughout the 1880's they discussed construction of a railroad across Siberia or at least from Vladivostok to the Amur River, especially as the race for territory in the Pacific heated up and war seemed increasingly likely.

---

of camels for transport and haulage, see Richardson Wright and Bassett Digby, *Through Siberia, an Empire in the Making* (New York, 1913), 187, and Kennan, *Siberia and the Exile System*, 2:418.

52. Valliant, "Japan," 10.

53. Barry, *Lecture*, 22. This figure was for Russian territories; significant additional numbers would also be needed to defend the Chinese-Eastern Railroad when it was built.

54. Barabash, 128, 134–135, 165–167; Evtiugin, 215. Whiting shows that the threat of interdiction remains alive today for the Siberian Railroad and restricts the military utility of the Baikal-Amur Main Line (BAM) (Whiting, *Siberian Development*, 92–93, 100–102, 108).

CHAPTER TWO

# An Appetite for Asia

The dire deficiencies of the Russian settlement in the Far East forced the imperial government to face its vulnerability to foreign aggression in the Pacific region. The defensive strategy it developed was to rely on a vigorous offense; the construction of a Siberian railroad was seen as a means to that end.

## Russia in the Pacific Rim

Russia's strategic position in the Far East had a dual dimension insofar as it was concerned with the extension of European rivalries in the area as well as local relationships, including the defense of the immense frontier with China. England and China were the two major threats to Russian interests and security in the region; the presence of other powers was slightly less worrisome until the mid-1890s.

Up till then the Russian government was not disturbed about the potential strength of its future antagonist, Japan. Russo-Japanese relations were by and large good, and St. Petersburg did not perceive Tokyo's activities as threatening. In the mid-1880s, Russian and Japanese interests in Korea even tended to complement each other: Russian specialists were of the opinion that Japan might act in Korea to block English gains. The only fear was that Japan would acquire ports on the mainland; but as long as Japan was confined to its islands, the Russian government did not consider it a problem.[1] One gets the

1. A. L. Narochnitskii, *Kolonial'naia politika kapitalisticheskikh derzhav na Dal'nem Vostoke, 1860–1895* (Moscow, 1956), 371, 373, 549–550; Andrew Malozemoff, *Russian Far*

sense that the Russian government, and even the military, viewed Japan's development with equanimity—at least for the time being.[2]

European and American activity in the northern Pacific, however, had distressed Siberian officials as early as the 1780s.[3] By the mid–nineteenth century, the fiercely competitive intervention of the Western powers in the affairs of East Asia had commenced. Britain had annexed territory throughout Southeast Asia in the eighteenth century, and in 1842, with the Treaty of Nanking and the end of the Opium Wars, it secured a foothold in China. France, Germany, and the United States were also active in the Pacific, either acquiring territories or working to open the region to their trade. By the treaties of Tientsin (1858), Chinese ports were opened to other European powers as well, including Russia.

Established on the Pacific since the seventeenth century, Russia began in the mid–nineteenth century to acquire new territories in the Far East: the Amur oblast by the treaty of Aigun in 1858 and the Maritime oblast by the treaty of Peking in 1860. Russia signed a trade treaty with Japan in 1855 immediately after Commodore Matthew Perry did so for the United States, and in 1875 Japan ceded Sakhalin Island to Russia in exchange for recognition of Japanese sovereignty over the central and northern Kurile Islands.

Technological developments sped the process and gave the advantage in communications with the Far East to Western Europe and America, despite Russia's geographical proximity. The development of efficient steamships in the 1840s and the completion of the Suez Canal in 1869 directed trade more rapidly through the Indian Ocean than the previous overseas route.[4] Along with the American transcon-

---

*Eastern Policy, 1881–1904* (Berkeley, 1958), 16–18. For more detailed background information on this period, see the introduction to George Alexander Lensen, *Balance of Intrigue: International Rivalry in Korea and Manchuria, 1884–1899* (Tallahassee, 1982), vol. 1.

2. Malozemoff speculates that Japanese naval expansion may have been a factor in the decision to build the Siberian Railroad, but notes that there is no direct evidence to that effect (*Russian Far Eastern Policy*, 34–35). For this period in Russo-Japanese relations in general, see also George Alexander Lensen, "Japan and Tsarist Russia—the Changing Relationships, 1875–1917," *Jahrbücher für Geschichte Osteuropas* 10, no. 3 (October 1962): 337–338. Two Soviet sources incorrectly claim that the growth of Japanese power compelled the Russian government to build the Trans-Siberian Railroad: A. V. Pataleev, *Istoriia stroitel'stva velikogo sibirskogo zheleznodorozhnogo puti* (Khabarovsk, 1951), 9, and "Zheleznye dorogi," in *Sibirskaia sovetskaia entsiklopediia*, vol. 1 (Novosibirsk, 1929), 909.

3. E. L. Besprozvannykh, *Priamur'e v sisteme russko-kitaiskikh otnoshenii XVII–seredina XIX v.* (Moscow, 1983), 119.

4. Daniel R. Headrick, *The Tools of Empire: Technology and European Imperialism in the Nineteenth Century* (New York, 1981), 142–156; "Budushchie zheleznye dorogi iz

tinental railroads and talk of a Central American canal, these advances were a source of great concern to members of the Imperial Russian Technological Society.[5] Russian trade and transport to Asia seemed insignificant, and the realization was made all the more galling by the fact that the greater part of Russian territory was in Asia.

Russia's trade position in the Pacific was decidedly weak. Germany, France, and England had all established rapid steamship service between their home ports and China and expanded their commercial representation there. By 1892 Hong Kong was almost as busy a port as London. English and German manufactures dominated the China market, and the United States was the main source of imported fish in China. Russia's trade with China soon made up less than 6 percent of the total. Foreigners dominated trade not only in China but in the Russian Far East itself. Russia's coastal trade virtually ceased to exist after the sale of Alaska, and the Chinese controlled the commerce in seaweed, the major export product from Vladivostok. Commercial fishing in Russia's Pacific waters was in the hands of the Japanese and Americans. German ships carried 70 percent of the freight arriving at Nikolaevsk-na-Amure. Foreigners, most of them from San Francisco, conducted an overwhelming proportion of the trade in Nikolaevsk.[6]

Russians could not help feeling that events were overtaking them. "The diverse interests of almost all European states, both Americas, China, and Japan are currently concentrated in the Pacific Ocean; the political center of gravity has shifted here from the Atlantic Ocean."[7] Russians did not intend to let their position in the area deteriorate further:

> In the Pacific Ocean a feast of industry and trade is taking place. Among the European, American, and Asian guests, we have been assigned one of

Evropeiskoi Rossii v Aziiu," *ZhdD*, 1885, no. 1: 2. According to Headrick, when electric lights were installed on ships after 1887, travel time was further reduced by half.

5. See, for instance, "'O velikom sibirskom puti v sviazi s pravitel'stvennymi izyskaniiami' (Doklad N. A. Sytenko i beseda v VIII otdele IRTO)," *ZhdD*, 1888, nos. 22–24: 170.

6. N. Matiunin, "Nashi sosedy na Krainem Vostoke," *Vestnik Evropy*, July 1887, no. 7: 79; Headrick, *Tools of Empire*, 168; K. A. Skal'kovskii, *Vneshniaia politika Rossii i polozhenie inostrannykh derzhav* (St. Petersburg, 1901), 545–546, and *Russkaia torgovlia v Tikhom okeane* (St. Petersburg, 1883), 17, 35, 71–72, 229, 237–240; P. Chikhachev, "Kaliforniia i ussuriiskii krai," *Vestnik Evropy*, June 1890, no. 6: 563; Great Britain, Naval Intelligence Division, *A Handbook of Siberia and Arctic Russia*, vol. 1 (London, n.d.), 78–79.

7. Matiunin, "Nashi sosedy," 80.

the prominent places. If at the moment we are sitting at the table but are not satisfying our appetites like the others, it does not necessarily imply that we are ready to excuse ourselves from the table.[8]

Asian experts on the General Staff clearly saw that the Russian position was precarious. The "promised land of European commerce" that was the Russian Far East was situated in so valuable a location that as foreign activity in the area expanded, the European countries gazed upon it with envy.[9] "Because of its location on the Pacific Ocean, where the vital interests of many nations are concentrated, Priamur'e has great value in their eyes."[10] Russia's interests in the region were therefore at risk: "For Russia it is all the more important in that it has no [access to the] open seas in Europe."[11]

Paradoxically, at the same time that the Russian General Staff saw Priamur'e as the source of Russia's weakness and ineffectiveness in the Far East, its members were under the impression that it gave Russia preeminence in the Pacific and made the rest of the world envious enough to plan its joint conquest.

### Russo-British Rivalry

England emerged as Russia's bete noire in the Pacific in the course of several incidents between 1850 and 1890, years of difficult, often hostile relations between the two powers in Europe and Asia. The threat was not limited to Russian interests in Asia; it was understood that if Russia found itself at war in Europe, its Far Eastern possessions would come under attack. Strength on the Pacific, therefore, meant strength in Europe.[12]

During the Crimean War, for instance, an Anglo-French naval force bombarded the Russian port of Petropavlovsk-na-Kamchatke and kept a presence afterward in the Sea of Okhotsk. The attack provided one motive for Murav'ev's annexation of the Amur territory: to defend the coast from the interior. Murav'ev recognized the importance of overland communications, and as part of his strategy against the

---

8. Barabash, 103–104.
9. Ibid., 103; N. A. Voloshinov, "Sibirskaia zheleznaia doroga," *IIRGO* 27 (1891): 26.
10. Barabash, 106.
11. Matiunin, "Nashi sosedy," 80.
12. Barabash, 106.

English he backed the proposal put forth in 1857–1858 by an American entrepreneur, P. M. Collins, for a railroad through Priamur'e. He lent his name to many other railroad schemes too, in the expectation that "for the naval powers it will be more threatening than one million troops and more dreadful than the unification of all the navies of Europe," as one of the engineers devising a railroad on the Pacific put it.[13]

From this point on, Russia and England were in constant competition for territory in Central Asia and the Far East.[14] During the Russo-Turkish War (1877–1878) they neared the brink of conflict. One element of England's proposed strategy was to blockade Russia's Pacific coast and strike at Vladivostok, using Chinese and Japanese ports as bases of operations. The Russians planned to counter with cruiser attacks on British merchant vessels, and for this purpose created the Volunteer Fleet in May 1878.[15] The Volunteer Fleet was to serve as a merchant fleet, a means of conveyance for settlers, and an auxiliary naval force; in the eyes of Alexander III it was the "main weapon in our struggle with England."[16] Once again the link between European relations and the Russian position in the Far East was made clear: "In 1877–1878, while clashing with Turkey, we had to prepare ourselves for war in Priamur'e."[17] The Volunteer Fleet was expected to foster military readiness, step up Russian activity in the area, and expedite Russian settlement of the territory.

The English threat continued to loom large in the next decade. Further Russian annexations in Central Asia, in particular the seizure of Merv in 1884, brought Russia threateningly close to Afghanistan, set up by the British in 1878–1879 as a protectorate to provide a buffer between India and an approaching Russia. Attempts to begin boundary negotiations failed and by February 1885 the two countries were again on the verge of war. The British especially feared Russian ac-

13. V. F. Borzunov, "Proekty stroitel'stva sibirskoi zheleznodorozhnoi magistrali pervoi poloviny XIX v. kak istoricheskii istochnik," in Akademiia Nauk SSSR, Sibirskoe Otdelenie, Dal'nevostochnyi Filial, *Trudy*, seriia istoricheskaia, vol. 5, ed. V. M. Vishnevskii et al. (Blagoveshchensk, 1963), 53, 58–62; Hugh Seton-Watson, *The Decline of Imperial Russia, 1855–1914* (New York, 1966), 83. For details of the attack on Petropavlovsk, see John Shelton Curtiss, *Russia's Crimean War* (Durham, N.C., 1979), 421–423.
14. C. J. H. Hayes portrays Russian expansion there as a major stimulus to British imperialism in Asia (*A Generation of Materialism, 1871–1900* [New York, 1941], 231).
15. Narochnitskii, *Kolonial'naia politika*, 221–223, 225; Skal'kovskii, *Russkaia torgovlia*, 466. The ships of the Volunteer Fleet were converted German mail boats.
16. D. A. Miliutin, *Dnevnik D. A. Miliutina*, vol. 3 (Moscow, 1950), 236–237.
17. Barabash, 106.

tions against Herat, which they considered the key to India. Russian and Afghan troops, the latter led by British officers, fought in the Penjdeh region.

Britain was limited, however, in its ability to respond militarily against Russia if a war were to break out: British ships were prevented from entering the Black Sea by the collusion of Germany and Turkey, the former acting as an adherent of the Three Emperors' League, the latter indignant at England's seizure of Egypt. Britain's only alternative was, again, to strike at Russia in the Far East. In April 1885 the order was given to occupy Port Hamilton off the coast of Korea, from which Vladivostok and Russia's Pacific coast could be attacked in the event of war. Russian forces were nominal and British ships were in position to destroy Russian ships before the latter could begin operations against British trade. In September 1884 England had already planned to offer Korea protectorate status and occupy Port Hamilton, and by April 1885 it was a de facto British coaling station. Totally unprepared for any military activities in the Far East, Russia turned to diplomacy in a desperate quest to remove the British from Korea.[18]

The situation was aggravated by the imminent completion of the Canadian-Pacific Railroad, which would cut the journey between England and Japan from the fifty-two days it took through the Suez Canal to thirty-seven days, and London expected to make use of it to concentrate its forces against Vladivostok.[19] Voloshinov wrote (distorting the truth) that England built and financed the Canadian-Pacific Railroad and in addition was subsidizing steamer transport on the Pacific Ocean. He and others regarded the Siberian Railroad as a means of countering these seemingly ominous developments.[20] It

18. Barbara Jelavich, *St. Petersburg and Moscow: Tsarist and Soviet Foreign Policy, 1814–1974* (Bloomington, Ind., 1975), 199–200; Michael Florinsky, *Russia: A History and an Interpretation*, vol. 2 (New York, 1960), 1128–1129; Dietrich Geyer, *Russian Imperialism: The Interaction of Domestic and Foreign Policy, 1860–1914*, trans. Bruce Little (New Haven, 1987), 114; Narochnitskii, *Kolonial'naia politika*, 370–371, 373, 376–381, 389.

19. "Tikhookeanskaia-kanadskaia i sibirskaia zheleznye dorogi," *ZhdD*, 1887, no. 19: 157; Narochnitskii, *Kolonial'naia politika*, 380.

20. N. A. Voloshinov [M. V——"], *Neskol'ko slov o sibirskoi zheleznoi doroge* (St. Petersburg, 1890), 20; *TIRTO*, 10:12. Voloshinov was incorrect about the financing of the Canadian-Pacific Railroad, which was paid for by a combination of Canadian government subsidies, the sale of land held by the Canadian Pacific Land Grant, and stocks issued in Canada, the United States, England, and France. See John Murray Gibbon, *Steel of Empire: The Romantic History of the Canadian Pacific* (New York, 1935), passim. While the British did plan to use the Canadian-Pacific for the rapid transfer of troops to Asia, it was Russia's talk of a trans-Siberian railroad that confirmed this need in the first place. Moreover, steamer service across the Pacific was intended primarily to supplement the railroad's income (Gibbon, *Steel*, 209–212, 300, 311–313).

was soon after the Afghan affair that the Committee of Ministers accepted the indispensability of the project.[21]

A strategy based on railroad construction had a recent precedent. In connection with the Afghan crisis, the tsar ordered General M. N. Annenkov in June 1885 to extend construction of the Transcaspian Railroad along the Afghan border, from Kizyl-Arvat through Merv to Chardzhou.[22] His hope was that the railroad, besides aiding in the subjugation of the native tribes, would also enable Russia to put pressure on English interests in India through Afghanistan. As A. G. Jomini, a chief aid to the Russian foreign minister, stated, the Transcaspian Railroad would "furnish [Russia] with a base of operations against England . . . should the British government, by the occupation of Herat, threaten our present position in Central Asia."[23]

Still another dimension to relations with the British involved China. Russia sensed that England and other Western powers were attempting to turn China against it. At the time of the Afghan crisis, British representatives in China actively sought to rally Chinese and Japanese diplomatic and military support against Russia. In exchange for acquiescence in the occupation of Port Hamilton, England offered China assistance in regaining from Russia the strategically important slice of territory fronting on Pos'et Bay, which gave Russia its border with Korea. There was also evidence that English and German influence was behind Chinese plans to build a strategic railroad through Manchuria to a point on the border of Russia's Ussuri region.[24] In Voloshinov's mind, the Chinese thus far seemed to have remained indifferent to foreign press reports that Russia was vulnerable in the Far East and that possession of the South Ussuri region would be advantageous to China. But he was certain that they would not resist temptation much longer. The Siberian Railroad, he asserted, was necessary to preserve the centuries-old friendship between China and Russia: Russian strength would give China the sense not to heed the "malicious counsels" of the Europeans.[25]

21. V. P. Potemkin, *Istoriia diplomatii*, vol. 2 (Moscow, 1945), 112; V. M. Khvostov, *Istoriia diplomatii*, vol. 2 (Moscow, 1963), 223–225.

22. This section was completed in 1887, and a further extension to Samarkand in 1888 (W. E. Wheeler, "The Control of Land Routes: Russian Railways in Central Asia," *Journal of the Royal Central Asian Society* 21 [October 1934]: 592–593; A. M. Solov'eva, *Zhelezno-dorozhnyi transport Rossii vo vtoroi polovine XIX v.* [Moscow, 1975], 196–197).

23. Quoted in Alexis Krausse, *Russia in Asia: A Record and a Study, 1558–1899* (New York, 1899), 204–205.

24. Narochnitskii, *Kolonial'naia politika*, 381–382, 391; "Man'chzhurskaia zheleznaia doroga," in General'nyi Shtab, *Sbornik po Azii*, vol. 53 (1893), 4.

25. Voloshinov, "Sibirskaia zheleznaia doroga," 26–27.

## Beyond the Chinese Border

To a large extent it was the presence of China that brought about the clamor for the Siberian Railroad within Russian military circles. For two centuries, from the beginning of Russo-Chinese relations, despite thousands of miles of shared border, relations between the two countries had remained peaceful and without major incident. Military demands elsewhere minimized the attention given Siberia by the Russian military. The number of troops was insignificant, only a few battalions in all of Siberia. Russia had given little thought to the defense of its border with China.[26]

Benign neglect was no longer possible after the Ili (or Kuldja) crisis. In 1864 a Muslim revolt in Sinkiang against Chinese rule came under the leadership of Yakub Beg, who, backed by the British, hoped to reunite Russian Turkestan with his newly proclaimed emirate. In 1871, when his troops threatened Kuldja, near the Russian border, Russian forces moved in and took control of the town and the surrounding Ili valley, assuring the Chinese government that the occupation would be only temporary. By 1878, after Yakub Beg was dead and the Chinese had repressed the rebellion, the territory still remained in the hands of the Russians, who in the unequal treaty of Livadia (1879) offered to return some of it for a huge payment and various trade concessions.[27]

The issue was eventually resolved through diplomacy to China's benefit, but only because the insulting treaty had led to an outcry for war against Russia in a China overly confident in the wake of its reforms and recent successes against internal rebellion. The Russians decided it would be in their best interest to accept the Chinese demands because, besides having their own domestic troubles, they viewed the prospect of victory over China as uncertain: the Russians exaggerated China's military strength, as did the rest of the world at the time.[28] Potential conflict was averted with the signing of the Treaty

26. A. N. Kuropatkin, *The Russian Army and the Japanese War*, trans. A. B. Lindsay, vol. 1 (London, 1909), 5, 68–69, 114–115; Skal'kovskii, *Vneshniaia politika*, 559.

27. Harry Schwartz, *Tsars, Mandarins, and Commissars: A History of Chinese-Russian Relations* (New York, 1973), 55–58. It is worthy of note that in 1878 A. N. Kuropatkin, then head of the Asian section of the General Staff, suggested that the Chinese pay 10 million pounds in gold as compensation for Russia's eight-year occupation of Ili, which the government could then put toward construction of the Siberian Railroad. Foreign Minister Giers and Minister of Finance Greig rejected this idea, though, and only 500,000 pounds was eventually demanded (Kuropatkin, *Russian Army*, 1:92–93).

28. Immanuel C. Y. Hsü, *The Ili Crisis: A Study of Sino-Russian Diplomacy, 1871–1881* (Oxford, 1965), 155–158, 189–191; Kuropatkin, *Russian Army*, 1:94. At least until the Sino-

of St. Petersburg in 1881 and the transfer of Ili to China in 1882. But the threat by China's war party stunned Russia's leaders into a sudden awareness of the strategic sensitivity of their border with China.

During the Ili crisis itself there was apprehension at the highest level that Vladivostok and the Maritime oblast were vulnerable to Chinese attack. The State Council, under its chairman, Grand Prince Konstantin Nikolaevich, discussed moving the naval base from Vladivostok further north to Ol'ga for security reasons, but War Minister D. A. Miliutin rejected the idea on the grounds that it would imply the abandonment of Vladivostok, which would have to be defended in any case.[29] In the wake of the crisis, the Russian military steadily increased the number of troops in the Far East, beginning a process that continued until 1917.[30] Still, the financial resources of the Treasury were overstretched and the military authorities felt the increased numbers were insufficient.[31]

Throughout the next decade events in China added to the concern of Russian officials, who theorized that even a weak power such as China could become a strong military threat in a short time. In the war between France and China (1884–1885) French naval victories forced the Chinese to recognize French control over Tonkin and Annam in Indochina. The defeat was humiliating for the overconfident Chinese, and the government drifted into torpor, leaving the nation unprepared to face the Japanese in 1894–1895. At the time, though, China's weakness was not apparent, and the fact that the Chinese forces had defeated the French on land distressed the Russians. The backers of reform in China, spearheaded by Li Hung-chang since the 1860s, saw the Franco-Chinese conflict as further justification of their desire to revamp the navy and reorganize the army on Prussian lines, as re-

---

Japanese War of 1894–1895, most observers in the United States and Great Britain considered the Chinese army to be superior to Japan's (Narochnitskii, *Kolonial'naia politika*, 421–422; A. Gal'perin, *Anglo-iaponskii soiuz, 1902–1921 gody* [Moscow, 1947], 26).

29. Miliutin, *Dnevnik*, 3:237.

30. Whereas in 1862 there were 6,900 regular troops in the Russian Far East, making up less than 1% of the total number of such troops in the Russian army, by 1882 there were 16,700, in 1891—24,800, and in 1895—32,100 (O. I. Sergeev, *Kazachestvo na russkom Dal'nem Vostoke v XVII–XIX vv.* [Moscow, 1983], 81–82). In the Maritime oblast, the number of troops increased from 6,813 in 1881 to 12,583 in 1892. In the South Ussuri region, the number rose from 1,753 in 1871 to 4,073 in 1881 (V. M. Kabuzan, *Dal'nevostochnyi krai v XVII–nachale XX vv. (1640–1917): Istoriko-demograficheskii ocherk* [Moscow, 1985], 127; 164, table 5).

31. Narochnitskii, *Kolonial'naia politika*, 357, 529.

ported by the Russian General Staff. Reform of the military was soon well under way. The Chinese brought in European instructors, set up military arsenals, established defense industries, and put up telegraph lines.[32] These endeavors troubled the governor general of Priamur'e, Baron Korf. In 1887 he cited the evidence of Chinese modernization as justifying construction of the Siberian Railroad, so that large numbers of troops could be sent to the Russian Far East.[33]

Chinese activity in Manchuria gathered steam at the same time, still further pressuring Russian defenses. The Chinese organized steamship traffic on the Sungari and Amur rivers as part of their program to settle the border region as rapidly as possible.[34] Contrary to longstanding policy, which was to leave Manchuria relatively unsettled to serve as an empty buffer between China and Russia, the government now promoted migration there. The Chinese were literally moving masses of settlers opposite Russian settlements in both oblasts of Priamur'e.[35] By 1890, according to one alarming (if embellished) military estimate, "in Manchuria there are more than 10 million while in all of the Maritime oblast there are fewer than 100,000."[36] It seemed that the Chinese right bank of the Amur would not long remain underpopulated.[37]

Colonel Ia. F. Barabash interpreted the situation to mean that the Chinese considered themselves strong and ready to confront Russia.[38] Hand in hand with the Manchurian settlers, he asserted, would come the Chinese military; as indeed they did. The Chinese reorganized and reinforced their Manchurian forces to the number of 85,000 men. They created the North China fleet and established the naval base soon to be named Port Arthur.[39] The newspaper *Novoe vremia* also reported that the Chinese government was directing the Chinese

32. Voloshinov, *Neskol'ko slov*, 18–19; Hsü, *Ili Crisis*, 192–193; Skal'kovskii, *Vneshniaia politika*, 559; "Reorganizatsiia kitaiskoi armii i flota," in General'nyi Shtab, *Sbornik po Azii*, vol. 24 (1886), 251, 254.

33. MPS, *Istoricheskii ocherk razvitiia zheleznykh dorog v Rossii s ikh osnovaniia po 1897 g. vkliuchitel'no*, comp. V. M. Verkhovskii (St. Petersburg, 1899), 460.

34. Ibid.

35. Malozemoff, *Russian Far Eastern Policy*, 22.

36. Voloshinov, "Sibirskaia zheleznaia doroga," 15. In the two provinces of northern Manchuria bordering on Russia, the estimated population in 1900 was more likely between 2 and 4 million, according to both David J. Dallin, *The Rise of Russia in Asia* (New Haven, 1949), 13–14, and a contemporary source, E. I. Martynov, *Rabota nashikh zheleznodorozhnykh del'tsov v Manchzhurii* (Moscow, 1914), 7.

37. Evtiugin, 214.

38. Barabash, 107–109.

39. Malozemoff, *Russian Far Eastern Policy*, 22–23.

robber bands known as the *hung hu tze* against Russian settlements to destabilize the region before troops were sent in to seize it.[40]

But if there was one thing that symbolized the multifarious Chinese threat to the Russians, it was plans to construct a railroad in Manchuria, which, as we have seen, had European backing. The Chinese began to build railroads in earnest in 1886. The Manchurian Railroad was conceived largely in response to Russia's deliberation over the Siberian Railroad and was planned to run in several branches through Mukden, Kirin, and Tsitsihar to points on the Russian border near Blagoveshchensk and Pos'et.[41] The Russian General Staff paid careful attention to the progress of these plans.[42] Foreign Minister N. K. Giers, in a letter of May 1891 to the finance minister, I. A. Vyshnegradskii, in which he stressed the importance of the Siberian Railroad for reasons of defense, expressed Russian sentiment about the Manchurian railroads: in collusion with a foreign power, China could conceivably use them to annex Russian Priamur'e.[43]

Giers's letter reflected the Russian attitude not only toward the Chinese railroads but toward China as a whole by the late 1880s and early 1890s. Northern Manchuria was blocked from the sea by Russian territory, and it would be senseless for the Chinese government to develop it without access to the oceans. Hence the logical conclusion, perhaps projected from Russian tactics onto the Chinese, was that the Chinese government would attempt to seize Pos'et and Vladivostok, then all of the territory gained by Russia in the Treaty of Peking; that is, everything "that constitutes the whole value of our Priamur possessions." Barabash wrote in 1883 that Chinese revanchism was a "black cloud on the horizon of relations with China."[44] Captain Evtiugin, writing in 1885, was of the "deep conviction that military conflict with

40. *Novoe vremia*, May 6, 1889, p. 2. The *hung hu tze* had their origins in both Manchuria and the Chinese settlements of Siberia. Robbers and murderers, they terrorized isolated Russian settlements and the Chinese population of the Ussuri region by gruesomely torturing their victims. See V. K. Arsen'ev (Wladimir K. Arsenjew), *Russen und Chinesen in Ostsibirien*, trans. Franz Daniel (Berlin, n.d.), 149–151, and John Albert White, *The Siberian Intervention* (Princeton, 1950), 46.

41. Robert Britton Valliant, "Japan and the Trans-Siberian Railroad, 1885–1905" (Ph.D. diss., University of Hawaii, 1974), 14–15; Skal'kovskii, *Vneshniaia politika*, 542; B. A. Romanov, *Russia in Manchuria (1892–1906)*, trans. Susan Wilbur Jones (New York, 1974), 40.

42. See, for example, Putiat, "Zapreshchenie kitaitsam selit'sia na man'chzhurskikh zemliakh: Zheleznye dorogi Tian'tszin-Tundzheo i Man'chzhurskaia," in General'nyi Shtab, *Sbornik po Azii*, vol. 42 (1890) (hereafter cited as Putiat), and "Man'chzhurskaia zheleznaia doroga," in ibid., vol. 53 (1893).

43. *Times*, May 30, 1891, p. 7.

44. Barabash, 111–116, 140.

China is inevitable and, what's more, in the not too distant future. We will be forced to this by necessity and, it goes without saying, we should always be prepared."[45] For Voloshinov, Chinese revanchism placed Russo-Chinese relations on unstable ground: "Just one spark is needed to blow up the whole powder magazine."[46]

There was some evidence to back such claims. The British had offered the Chinese support in seizing Russian territory, and the Russian ambassador to China, S. I. Popov, was told by a Chinese general that for reasons of security it was essential for Russia to cede the area around Pos'et to China. Nevertheless, Li Hung-chang's military reforms made only cosmetic improvements, and Chinese activities in Manchuria were aimed largely at gaining control of events in Korea rather than against Russia. On the whole, China tended to support Russia while mistrusting England and Japan.[47] It seems that Russian perceptions of a Chinese threat had little empirical foundation and were based on an unrealistic fear of numbers. In an era of heightened great-power rivalry, the presence of 300 million Chinese on the other side of Russia's unguarded Far Eastern frontier was difficult to disregard.[48]

### A Russian Railroad in the Far East

As military strategists throughout the 1880s discussed construction of a railroad across Siberia, or at the very least from Vladivostok to the Amur River, their ostensible intent was to enhance the defense of Russian territory; but official perceptions of the railroad presupposed that it would also be the means to an offensive, "forward" policy in China.

Some officers opposed construction of a railroad as wasteful or feared that it would benefit the military and economic activities of foreigners. Reflecting, for the time being, a lack of concern about Tokyo and its potential ability to restrict access to the Sea of Japan, they argued that a strong Pacific fleet based in Vladivostok, having free exit to the seas, would serve well to counter foreign threats and

45. Evtiugin, 218.
46. Voloshinov, "Sibirskaia zheleznaia doroga," 26–27.
47. Narochnitskii, *Kolonial'naia politika*, 386, 391, 421–422; Malozemoff, *Russian Far Eastern Policy*, 23.
48. " 'O narodonaselenii Sibiri i o velikoi vostochnoi zheleznoi doroge,' (Doklad professora E. Iu. Petri i beseda v VIII otdele IRTO)," *ZhdD*, 1888, nos. 33–34: 278.

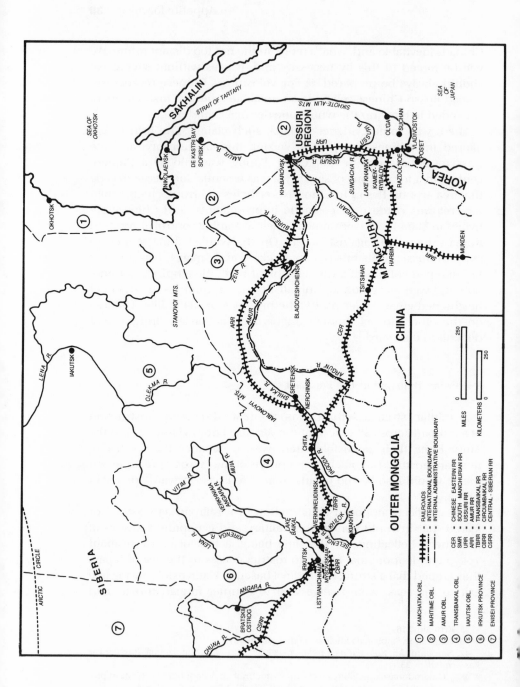

provision the troops. As for transport within Siberia, General I. I. Filipenko suggested that improvements in the existing water routes would be sufficient.[49]

The opponents of the railroad thus favored expansion of Russian naval power in the Pacific. They were in the minority, though, and the land-based strategy first implemented by Murav'ev-Amurskii predominated. The Russian military had learned from experience. The usefulness of Russian railroads in battle against Afghan troops in Central Asia proved their importance for the Far East. Past mistakes were also not forgotten. Inadequacies of the railroad network during the Russo-Turkish War had hindered the transport of troops and supplies.[50] Voloshinov repeated over and over that Russia should show it had learned the lesson of the Crimean War; lacking railroads, Vladivostok would be as exposed as Sevastopol' had been.[51]

By the mid-1880s, many government officials were clamoring for the Siberian Railroad as vital to the nation's strategic interests. Proponents of the railroad were well aware of the contemporary axiom that success in war comes to the side that most quickly concentrates the largest numbers in the field. Russia's inferiority in numbers could be corrected by construction of the Ussuri and Transbaikal railroads. Inextricably bound to the transport of troops was the need to provision them locally and end the region's dependence on Manchuria for grain. Only as part of a longer railroad stretching across the length of Siberia would the sections east of Lake Baikal accomplish these strategic tasks.[52]

Because the railroad would enable Russia to secure a firm foothold on the Pacific coast, the future foreign minister V. N. Lamzdorf was convinced of its necessity by 1890:

> Instead of colonies, which all other powers search for at the antipodes, we have one alongside us and do not know how to make use of it; . . . if the conviction that we are weak spreads and takes root on the distant borders [of the Far East], in the near future we will witness the rise of

49. Ibid., 281; " 'O naivygodneishem napravlenii magistral'noi i nepreryvnoi vserossiiskoi velikoi vostochnoi zheleznoi dorogi' (Soobshchenie kontr-admirala N. V. Kopytova na tekhnicheskoi besede v IRTO)," *ZhdD*, 1888, nos. 2–4: 28. See also Barabash, 104.

50. Kuropatkin, *Russian Army*, 1:27, 29, 86.

51. Voloshinov, "Sibirskaia zheleznaia doroga," 27, 36, and *Neskol'ko slov*, 4; *TIRTO*, 2:11–12.

52. S. V. Sabler and I. V. Sosnovskii, *Sibirskaia zheleznaia doroga v eia proshlom i nastoiashchem: Istoricheskii ocherk*, ed. A. N. Kulomzin (St. Petersburg, 1903), 34, 68–71, 73; MPS, *Istoricheskii ocherk*, 316, 443, 452–453, 457, 461, 464–467, 501; *ZhMPS*, official section, 1893, no. 2: 9, 12–13.

immense problems in the Orient, like waves in the ocean which engulf everything in their way.[53]

If the railroad was to bring strength to the Russian Far East, it was to do so by enhancing the region's defensive capabilities. It was a purely precautionary measure, according to Giers:

> The Chinese may not now have any hostile intentions against Russia, but Russia can never be certain that such ideas may not hereafter enter their heads, especially if we are brought into collision with any of the European naval powers. In this event the possessions of Russia in Eastern Siberia, cut off as they now are seven months out of the twelve every year, would be in an exceedingly precarious position.[54]

The railroad would create a strong defense but was not expected to alarm the Chinese. General D. G. Anuchin, governor general of Eastern Siberia from 1879 to 1885, explained that during the war scare in 1880, it became apparent that transporting troops to the Far East and maintaining them there would be difficult and expensive. At the same time, no one wanted a large contingent of Russian troops permanently stationed in the region, lest it intimidate the Chinese and threaten the peace. This reasoning led to the idea of building a railroad and improving water routes so that troops could be transported to the area on a temporary, emergency basis.[55]

If Anuchin's desire to preserve China's friendship had been sincere, within a few years the proclamations to this effect rang false. The reactionary newspaper *Grazhdanin* (Citizen) wrote that the Siberian Railroad would guarantee quiet with Russia's "menacing neighbor."[56] In the view of Admiral N. V. Kopytov, China's great and peaceful civilization was based on the family unit, which encouraged cooperation rather than hostility between individuals. Conversion to Christianity could make it an even greater nation, and to help bestow this benefit upon China he proposed the construction of a railroad through Chinese territory linking Abagaityi, on the Russo-Mongolian-Manchurian border, with Vladivostok. Manchuria was the most direct

53. V. N. Lamzdorf, *Dnevnik V. N. Lamzdorfa (1886–1890)* (Moscow/Leningrad, 1926), 182.
54. *Times*, May 30, 1891, p. 7.
55. *TIRTO*, 2:6.
56. Quoted in *Novoe vremia*, July 20, 1890, p. 1.

route, and, as he proclaimed, "great deeds befit great nations!"[57] His proposal is the direct forerunner of the Chinese-Eastern Railroad.

The idea that the Siberian Railroad should be built through Chinese territory was the logical culmination of strategic thinking about the Far East in the 1880s: the railroad was a key part of the vigorous offense that was the best defense. To thwart Chinese designs on the Russian Far East and preserve Russian political influence in Asia, Russia should get the upper hand by preparing to invade Manchuria.[58] Barabash, who had been promoted to general major and named commander of local forces and military governor of Transbaikal oblast, asserted that Manchuria's geographical location made it "our natural property."[59] Accordingly, he had studied in detail all potential operational lines for a Russian invasion of Manchuria.[60] Evtiugin advanced a similar proposal for the occupation of Mongolia.[61] The pro-government paper *Novoe vremia* suggested that when the Siberian Railroad was built, Russia could, if necessary, encourage the revolt of China's Mongol and Muslim populations.[62]

The advantages of using Chinese territory for Russian nonmilitary transport needs were also cited. To outdo Europe's advantage on the seas, a writer in *Zheleznodorozhnoe delo* (Railroad affairs) proposed

---

57. "O naivygodneishem napravlenii," *ZhdD*, 1888, nos. 2–4: 13–27. Kopytov put forth his plan for a Siberian railroad as an alternative to the official route developed in the Ministry of Transport. Its eastern portion would run through China (the route eventually adopted by the government); its western portion was to take a more southerly route. The major station stops, from west to east, were to be Orenburg, Orsk, Atbassar, Akmolinsk, Pavlodar, Biisk, Minusinsk, Nizhneudinsk, Irkutsk, Troitskosavsk, Abagaityi, Hailar, Tsitsihar, Kirin, Ningguta, Nikol'skoe, and Vladivostok. Kopytov's intention was to build a railroad not purely for the limited use of Siberia, but to serve all of northern Asia. This region, he asserted, had a far brighter future than did Siberia with its tundra, where even potatoes could not grow and for whose needs the rivers and post road would suffice.

58. Barabash, 115, 135, 169; Evtiugin, 216–217. Judging from the correspondence between the railroad magnate Poliakov and Pobedonostsev regarding a Russian railroad in Persia, it is clear that many people at the time saw railroad construction in neighboring countries as bringing foreign policy advantages. See K. Pobedonostsev, *L'Autocratie russe: Mémoires politiques, correspondance officielle et documents inédits relatifs à l'histoire du règne de l'empereur Alexandre III de Russie* (Paris, 1927), 364–369, 477–479.

59. "O naivygodneishem napravlenii," *ZhdD*, 1888, nos. 2–4: 28.

60. Barabash, 136–160.

61. Evtiugin, 217–218. His rationale would stand the test of time: "The Mongols are friendly toward us and await their liberation from Chinese rule, counting on being accepted as Russian citizens."

62. *Novoe vremia*, May 6, 1889, p. 2. This proposal is strikingly similar to the early Comintern strategy for Asia.

that Russia build a railroad from Moscow to Omsk to Kokpetinsk and from there through China to Shanghai.[63] K. A. Skal'kovskii, meanwhile, wrote that the best way to link the South Ussuri region with the Amur River by rail was across Chinese territory.[64] A Nerchinsk merchant named Butin saw annexation of a strip of Chinese territory as a means to facilitate travel on the Amur.[65]

Not all who endorsed a railroad through Siberia wanted to see it also go through China. Barabash felt that such a route would help England more than Russia. Anuchin argued that it would benefit Vladivostok to the detriment of the rest of the Russian Far East, and that it would require the Russians to fight the Chinese and turn their emperor into something akin to the emir of Bukhara.[66] N. Matiunin, border commissar in the Ussuri region, preferred to preserve the peace by forming an alliance with China.[67] Regardless of these voices of disapproval, the development of an offensive strategy made such a railroad all but inevitable, as did its obvious benefits for Russian communications. The only objection a high official in the Ministry of Transport had was that it could present diplomatic complications, but he accepted the principle.[68]

The consensus behind the construction of a Russian railroad through Chinese territory calls into question the passivity and moderation of Russian policy in the Far East in the mid- to late 1880s.[69] It must be taken into account in any assessment of the nature of the Chinese-Eastern Railroad and Russian involvement in Manchuria in the 1890s. Whatever the rhetoric about "peaceful penetration," the principle of taking Chinese territory for various strategic (and, to a lesser extent, economic) objectives had become an essential, if im-

---

63. "Budushchie zheleznye dorogi," *ZhdD*, 1885, no. 1: 4; no. 2: 9. Railroads to Kabul and Peshawar and through Central Asia were also proposed.

64. Skal'kovskii, *Russkaia torgovlia*, 56–57.

65. *TIRTO*, 10:9–10, 12.

66. Ibid., 6:6–7.

67. Matiunin, "Nashi sosedy," 83; Narochnitskii, *Kolonial'naia politika*, 393.

68. "O velikom sibirskom puti," *ZhdD*, 1888, nos. 22–24: 176–177. Others in the Russian Technical Society felt that the book should not be closed on the topic simply because of the diplomatic obstacle: a similar arrangement existed in the Balkans (presumably they were referring to the Berlin-Baghdad Railroad) and should be examined. See *TIRTO*, 21:4.

69. As portrayed by Malozemoff, *Russian Far Eastern Policy*, 16–19, 324. While this chapter serves as a contribution to the prehistory of the Chinese-Eastern Railroad, I shall not deal with this subject further except indirectly, as it is tangential to the development of Siberia per se and is currently receiving separate treatment by other scholars.

plicit, component of the Siberian Railroad project.[70] Indeed, there is evidence to suggest that Russian officials favored a cautious approach in the Far East only as a temporary expedient. When the Siberian Railroad was completed, Russia could then confront Chinese, British, and, later, Japanese forces from a position of strength. The government put its initiatives in Persia and the Bosphorous on hold as well so as not to risk entanglements that might jeopardize the Siberian Railroad project.[71]

The Siberian Railroad would enable the government to follow the unwritten formula it had applied from the earliest moments of the Russian presence across the Urals: lacking soldiers and colonists, the Russian empire would absorb the territory of a hostile race on its border as the best means of defense. Murav'ev realized immediately after he had annexed the territory on the left bank of the Amur River that it would be defenseless without the breastplate of the Ussuri region, so it too was taken. Similarly, Russia soon expanded to fill the power vacuum in Central Asia, in part as a means of defending Russia's adjacent territories.[72] The same traditional forms of expansionism were once again being set in motion with the Siberian Railroad.

But before advancing farther into Asia, in a departure from past practices, under Minister of Finance Sergei Witte's inspiration and guidance the state would attempt to strengthen its grip on Siberia and the Far East by systematically colonizing the area and stimulating its economy. For Russia's weakness in Siberia and the Far East was not only a factor in foreign policy; it also had threatening domestic implications for the government of Alexander III.

70. The Siberian regionalist newspaper *Vostochnoe obozrenie*, 1890, no. 39, pp. 1–2, opposing construction of the Siberian Railroad, pointed out that inevitably it would be used in an offensive war: each step Russia took to protect itself against its nonexistent enemy would be matched by China until the principles of Moltke would have to prevail and a preventive war launched.

71. "Proekt zakhvata Bosfora v 1896 g.," *Krasnyi arkhiv* 47–48 (1931): 51; "Pervye shagi russkogo imperializma na Dal'nem Vostoke (1888–1903 gg.)," ibid. 52 (1932): 79; Malozemoff, *Russian Far Eastern Policy*, 39; Valliant, "Japan," 13.

72. Krausse, *Russia in Asia*, 130; Besprozvannykh, *Priamur'e*, 175–176; and Geoffrey Wheeler, *The Modern History of Soviet Central Asia* (New York, 1964), 64.

CHAPTER   THREE

# Siberia Is for Russia

$M$any writers have portrayed the Siberian Railroad as serving exclusively the defense of Russia's Pacific shore and Far Eastern
border, but they have overlooked the domestic concerns that affected
the security of the empire and were ultimately as important as the
menace of foreign powers.[1] Economic policy as it evolved under
Alexander III was in part a response to internal threats to the order of
the realm, and it promoted a unified Russian polity through strong
government intervention, centralization, and Russification.[2] For these
reasons, too, the state embarked on the construction of this railroad
across some of the most uninviting terrain on the face of the earth.

### Siberia and the Empire before Alexander III

In the time of Catherine the Great, Siberia was viewed, accurately or
not, less as Russian territory than as part of a colonial empire. Cath-

1. Georg Cleinow, "Eisenbahnbauten und -pläne in Russisch-Asien," *Archiv für
Eisenbahnwesen* 51 (January–February 1928): 75; A. V. Pataleev, *Istoriia stroitel'stva
velikogo sibirskogo zheleznodorozhnogo puti* (Khabarovsk, 1951), 9; "Zheleznye dorogi," in *Sibirskaia sovetskaia entsiklopediia*, vol. 1 (Novosibirsk, 1929), 909–910; Robert
Britton Valliant, "Japan and the Trans-Siberian Railroad, 1885–1905" (Ph.D. diss., University of Hawaii, 1974), iv. Other writers saw—and worried about—the railroad's military
potential, but recognized a variety of motives in its construction: e.g., G. Krahmer,
*Sibirien und die große sibirische Eisenbahn* (Leipzig, 1897); and Arthur John Barry,
*Lecture on the Great Siberian Railway* (London, 1900).
2. This book uses the words *Russification* and *Russify* in accordance with the
definitions found in Edward C. Thaden, ed., *Russification in the Baltic Provinces and
Finland, 1855–1914* (Princeton, 1981), 7–9.

erine's lack of solid knowledge regarding Siberian conditions notwithstanding, she decreed a Siberian administration with forms adopted from European Russia, and then made efforts to colonize the territory and develop its economy. These measures were in keeping with her general policy in the borderlands, one component of which was economic development and colonization for the sake of the consolidation and expansion of imperial power.[3] Catherine's heirs reversed her strategy, but it would be revived under Alexander III.

During Catherine's reign a sense of Siberia's potential began to emerge. Catherine called it "our India, Mexico, or Peru," and such publicists as the radical A. N. Radishchev spoke of its wealth. This attitude was shared by Mikhail Speranskii, whose reform of 1822 aimed to "protect Siberia" by correcting persistent administrative abuses and preventing the possible separation of this "colony" from Russia. Siberia was to have essentially the same administrative structure as Russia proper, with some local forms retained. Speranskii rejected a federalist solution in favor of uniformity and centralization, disallowing local participation in decision making. His reform was bureaucratic and its goal was to Russify Siberia. This was the legacy he handed down to future central authorities.[4]

Soon comparisons between Siberia and the United States became popular, eventually to be expressed with a disconcerting enthusiasm by the revolutionaries Alexander Herzen and Mikhail Bakunin.[5] Despite almost three hundred years of Russian possession and a predominantly Russian population, a fear grew that the "colony" of Siberia would inevitably attempt to declare its independence, just as the American colonies had done.

During the reign of Nicholas I this concern became acute, for by

3. S. G. Svatikov, *Rossiia i Sibir' (K istorii sibirskogo oblastnichestva v XIX v.)* (Prague, 1930), 6; Marc Raeff, *Siberia and the Reforms of 1822* (Seattle, 1956), 5–8, 17; idem, *Imperial Russia, 1682–1825: The Coming of Age of Modern Russia* (New York, 1971), 64; idem, "In the Imperial Manner," in *Catherine the Great: A Profile,* ed. Raeff, 197–246 (New York, 1972). On the administration of Siberia under Catherine the Great, see also John P. LeDonne, *Ruling Russia: Politics and Administration in the Age of Absolutism, 1762–1796* (Princeton, 1984), 277–283.

4. Raeff, *Siberia,* xiv–xv, 6, 42–44, 46, 84, 114–115, 131, 133–134, and *Imperial Russia,* 65–67; Pataleev, *Istoriia stroitel'stva,* 2d ed. (Khabarovsk, 1962), 32; Svatikov, *Rossiia i Sibir',* 10, 12; N. M. Iadrintsev, *Sibir' kak koloniia v geograficheskom, etnograficheskom i istoricheskom otnoshenii,* 2d ed. (St. Petersburg, 1892), 508–509.

5. A. S. Kuznetsov, "Sibirskaia programma tsarizma 1852 g.," in Irkutskii Gosudarstvennyi Pedagogicheskii Institut, no. 2, *Ocherki istorii Sibiri,* ed. V. G. Tiukavkin (Irkutsk, 1971), 11–12, 14, 25. On the attitudes of Herzen and Bakunin toward Siberia, see Stephen Digby Watrous, "Russia's 'Land of the Future': Regionalism and the Awakening of Siberia, 1819–1894" (Ph.D. diss., University of Washington, 1970), 1:202–207, 214–215.

mid-century Siberia's real value was apparent. The Altai region ranked second to the Urals in Russian mining and metallurgy, producing 95 percent of Russia's silver and 80 percent of its lead. It held second place in copper production and fourth in gold, yielding 40 percent of the empire's total by 1850. Gold, discovered in Eastern Siberia in the 1830s, brought in settlers and stimulated an expansion of agriculture in the Enisei region as well as in Western Siberia. And as fur-bearing animals grew scarce in Western Siberia, the fur trade of Eastern Siberia grew in importance.[6]

Russia's interest in Siberia began to grow after 1830, somewhat in parallel with the discovery and increasing production of gold. Leading aristocratic families were represented among the owners of Siberian gold mines, and, according to a Soviet historian, their financial stake in Siberia was influential in the formation of government policy.[7] Nicholas I's finance minister, E. F. Kankrin, echoed Catherine when he called Siberia the Russian "Mexico and Peru." Others described it as "El Dorado," "California," or, less poetically, "a gold mine."[8] Hopes for Siberia began to soar in mid-century, not least with Murav'ev's annexations in the Far East. But this enthusiasm only heightened the fear of losing Siberia, compounded by an exaggerated suspicion of religious heretics, criminals, and political exiles, all of whom seemed to have the potential to spark a revolt. Even more disconcerting was the growing influence of foreign powers in Eastern Siberia, especially Britain and America.[9]

To grapple with such problems Nicholas I reconstituted the Siberian Committee in 1852. Its proposed solution, reflecting the outlook of the tsar, was to encourage gentry landholding in Siberia as a pillar of the Russian state and to maintain Siberia as an agricultural terri-

6. Robert N. North, *Transport in Western Siberia: Tsarist and Soviet Development* (Vancouver, 1979), 23, 27; A. P. Okladnikov et al., eds., *Istoriia Sibiri s drevneishikh vremen do nashikh dnei*, vol. 2 (Leningrad, 1968), 385–389, 393–404; V. Iu. Grigor'ev, *Peremeny v usloviiakh ekonomicheskoi zhizni naseleniia Sibiri (Eniseiskii krai)* (Krasnoiarsk, 1904), 25–26, 29–30, 34–35.

7. Kuznetsov, "Sibirskaia programma," 4–5.

8. Iadrintsev, *Sibir' kak koloniia*, 710; Svatikov, *Rossiia i Sibir'*, 27. Paradoxically, many people, including Siberian regionalists and reformers, portrayed it as a pitiable land crushed by the burden of the exile system and its use as a penal colony. Still others saw it as an empty and worthless territory, of no benefit to Russia (Iadrintsev, *Sibir' kak koloniia*, 533). Siberia is still described with hyperbole, positive and negative, today. See Allen S. Whiting, *Siberian Development and East Asia: Threat or Promise?* (Stanford, 1981), 19–21.

9. Kuznetsov, "Sibirskaia programma," 5–10; John J. Stephan, "Russian-American Economic Relations in the Pacific: A Historical Perspective," in *Soviet-American Horizons on the Pacific*, ed. John J. Stephan and V. P. Chichkanov (Honolulu, 1986), 67–70.

tory. Murav'ev, then governor general of Eastern Siberia, had proposed that Chinese territory in the Amur region be seized to ensure Russian dominance over Siberia. P. D. Gorchakov, governor general of Western Siberia, contended that Russian control over the mouth of the Amur would only bring Siberia into greater contact with foreigners, a dangerous proposition. Better, he argued, to maintain eastern Siberia as a "forest cordon," behind which Russian territory would be safe. Gorchakov's outlook prevailed in Nicholas I's Siberian Committee, which made a conscious decision to keep Siberia backward and underdeveloped as the best way of bringing about the "firm unification" and "complete amalgamation" of Siberia with central Russia.[10]

### Siberian Regionalism

The state of affairs had changed by the time Alexander III came to the throne in 1881. At this point, developments in Siberia clashed with the strident nationalism and repressive inclinations of the regime. The government's Siberian policy shifted in a direction that in many ways it continued to follow until the most recent times.

The beginning of Alexander's reign coincided with the celebration of the tercentenary of Ermak's invasion of Siberia. Literature on Siberia poured forth, Siberian regionalism was in full blossom, and the question of Siberia took on national importance. Siberian regionalism was a heterogeneous, amorphous movement of Siberian intellectuals who stood in the broadest sense for the interests of their region. Their thinking owed much to the Polish and Decembrist exiles, who had written of Siberia's freedom, glorified its peasants, and compared the region with America. The regionalists broadened the already prevalent view of the "separateness" of Siberia, based on its geography and history.[11]

10. Kuznetsov, "Sibirskaia programma," 10–11, 13, 16–18, 25–26; Iadrintsev, *Sibir' kak koloniia*, 708n1. "Forest cordon" is Kuznetsov's phrase. Fear of foreign influence led to the rejection of the proposals for a Siberian railroad backed by Murav'ev, as well as later proposals by foreigners. See Svatikov, *Rossiia i Sibir'*, 31; V. F. Borzunov, "Proekty stroitel'stva sibirskoi zheleznodorozhnoi magistrali pervoi poloviny XIX v. kak istoricheskii istochnik," in Akademiia Nauk SSSR, Sibirskoe Otdelenie, Dal'nevostochnyi Filial, *Trudy*, seriia istoricheskaia, vol. 5, ed. V. M. Vishnevskii et al. (Blagoveshchensk, 1963), passim.

11. Wolfgang Faust, *Rußlands goldener Boden: Der sibirische Regionalismus in der zweiten Hälfte des 19. Jahrhunderts* (Cologne, 1980), 414, 421; Watrous, "Russia's 'Land of the Future,'" 2:434; Svatikov, *Rossiia i Sibir'*, 3–5, 24–26.

The most important spokesman of Siberian regionalism was Nikolai Iadrintsev. Ethnographer, geographer, historian, archaeologist, journalist, and editor, he was the leading authority on Siberia. His *Sibir' kak koloniia* (Siberia as a colony), first published in 1882, was the bible of regionalism. Here he writes that Siberia is a colony, with interests opposed to those of European Russia, the "metropolis," and he asserts the existence of a Siberian population without reference to nationality. He posits the Siberian as a "unique ethnic type" born of the intermingling of Slavic and native populations. Iadrintsev dwells on the Siberians' special qualities, including adaptation to severe climate and a unique intestinal structure. He idealizes the Siberians' pristine primitivism in the taiga, which has endowed them with great potential and promise. Unlike the Russians, Siberians are individualists who know freedom. The Siberians have, in fact, already forgotten that they are ethnically and historically Russian: they regard European Russians as foreigners.[12]

After describing the uniqueness and purity of Siberia, Iadrintsev asserts that Siberia, as an agricultural colony, will become settled and a new nation will arise, an "independent branch" of the metropolis, as he euphemistically expresses it. Isolated from Russia but close to America, China, Japan, and the Pacific, Siberia will have an enlightened and prosperous future. But Siberia's potential has not been realized. Far from following the paths of America and Australia to prosperity, Siberia has been left in the tundra, the miserable result of arbitrary administration, dependence on the metropolis, and the central government's exploitive self-interest in Siberia as a penal colony and source of furs and minerals.[13]

Iadrintsev's views were common at the time, repeated in the established press and by authors as respected as Chekhov; there was a consensus that the distant Siberian "colony" would naturally sepa-

12. Iadrintsev, *Sibir' kak koloniia*, 3–4, 67, 83, 91–92, 94–101, 103–108, 111–112, 115, 117–118, 127, 129. Iadrintsev is critical of certain by-products of Siberia's individualism, especially such business practices as monopoly and profiteering (pp. 118–119, 122), but he believes that with proper institutions these faults would be corrected. Here an ambivalence about capitalist enterprise becomes apparent. Later the individualism he has praised as distinct from European Russian collectivism he denigrates as a largely urban-commercial phenomenon alien to the true Siberians—peasants—who put self-help and the interests of the commune above private property (pp. 143–145). This contradiction is also found in the thought of the legal populists, to which regionalism was close intellectually. See Arthur P. Mendel, *Dilemmas of Progress in Tsarist Russia: Legal Marxism and Legal Populism* (Cambridge, Mass., 1961).

13. Iadrintsev, *Sibir' kak koloniia*, 432, 523, 526–527, 700, 707–712.

rate from the "metropolis."[14] The reaction of conservatives to Siberian regionalism and its sympathizers was sometimes frenzied. Iadrintsev saw Siberia as an "emerging society in which . . . the bones and muscles of a living organism are forming."[15] If it was, defenders of a strong state viewed it as a limb attached to the Russian organism, and intended to ensure that it remained attached.

The influential reactionary journalist M. N. Katkov led the opposition. He vehemently resurrected the notion that Siberia's regionalists were striving for independence.[16] Konstantin Pobedonostsev, the "ideologist" of the regime, warned Alexander III of the "bad element" in Siberia and, together with State Secretary A. A. Polovtsov, opposed the opening of a university in Tomsk, long on the regionalist agenda.[17] Grand Prince Konstantin Nikolaevich denounced the central assertion of regionalism: "Siberia is not a colony, and the movement of Russians from European Russia to Siberia is only the settlement of the Russian tribe within the borders of its state." In Siberia itself a centralist camp around the Tomsk newspaper *Sibirskii vestnik* (Siberian herald) arose in opposition to regionalism. Its editor, V. P. Kartamyshev, announced its platform:

> Siberia is for Russia, for the Russian people; the whole future of Siberia consists in its close unity with the rest of Russia. . . . The wealth of Siberia is the wealth of Russia. Siberia is not a colony of Russia, but is Russia itself; not Russian America, but a Russian province, and should develop

14. Ibid., 698–699; Chekhov told Kuprin that "as soon as I get a little better, I will certainly travel to Siberia once again. I have been there before, when I went to Sakhalin. You simply cannot imagine, old fellow, what a wonderful land it is. It's a state completely unto itself. You know, I am convinced that Siberia will someday totally separate from Russia, just as America separated from its metropolis" (A. I. Kuprin, *Polnoe sobranie sochinenii*, vol. 7 [St. Petersburg, 1912], 127).

15. Iadrintsev, *Sibir' kak koloniia*, x.

16. I. I. Popov, *Minuvshee i perezhitoe: Vospominaniia za 50 let: Sibir' i emigratsiia* (Leningrad, 1924), 97; Svatikov, *Rossiia i Sibir'*, 78; Watrous, "Russia's 'Land of the Future,'" 2:546, 606, 620.

17. K. P. Pobedonostsev, *Pis'ma Pobedonostseva k Aleksandru III*, vol. 2 (Moscow, 1926), 99–100. Polovtsov wrote: "Au lieu d'ouvrir une université en Sibérie, je proposerais de faire construire une maison de glace sur la Néva, comme au temps de l'impératrice Anna Ioannovna. Cette bouffounerie froide coûterait moins cher et serait moins dangereuse." He did not, however, object to a technical school (K. P. Pobedonostsev, *L'Autocratie russe: Mémoires politiques, correspondance officielle et documents inédits relatifs à l'histoire du règne de l'empereur Alexandre III de Russie* [Paris, 1927], 352–353). Despite the opposition to it, the Imperial University of Tomsk was opened in 1888.

in the same way that the other borderlands of the "Russian state" have developed.[18]

The centralists and the authorities considered Iadrintsev's newspaper, *Vostochnoe obozrenie* (Eastern review), which was the organ of Siberian regionalism, to be the mouthpiece of separatism and revolution.[19] The police harassed Siberian circles and censors would not permit "Siberia" to be set in contradistinction to "Russia."[20] Even the tsar's rescript of March 17, 1891, announcing that Tsarevich Nicholas would take part in ground-breaking ceremonies for the Siberian Railroad at Vladivostok, was reworded to avoid reference to Siberia's "distance from the capital."[21]

The separatist threat combined with the ever-present danger of foreigners dominating eastern Siberia. Pobedonostsev wrote to the future Alexander III in 1879 that "the natives [of northeastern Siberia] will forget that they belong to Russia. And already now many Chukchi speak English."[22] To make matters worse, in their isolation the Russian peasants of Siberia seemed to be taking on native ways and losing consciousness of their ethnic identity. "The Russian Siberian," one disconcerted Russian observed, "is even beginning to eat like an Eskimo."[23] General A. N. Kuropatkin later clarified these attitudes when he expressed the fear that if Russia annexed Manchuria, "eastern Siberia would become quite un-Russian, and it must be remembered that it is the Russians alone who form, and will form in the future, the reliable element of the population"; eastern Siberia was for their sole benefit.[24]

One part of Alexander III's solution was to accelerate the "gradual

18. Quoted in Svatikov, *Rossiia i Sibir'*, 52, 89.

19. Popov, *Minuvshee i perezhitoe*, 239. Not all the authorities viewed it this way. Count A. P. Ignat'ev, governor general of Eastern Siberia (1885–1889), denied that regionalism was separatist and advocated full implementation of the Great Reforms in Siberia (Watrous, "Russia's 'Land of the Future,'" 2:622; Svatikov, *Rossiia i Sibir'*, 78).

20. Svatikov, *Rossiia i Sibir'*, 87–88, 91–92; Popov, *Minuvshee i perezhitoe*, 239.

21. *Tri poslednikh samoderzhtsa: Dnevnik A. V. Bogdanovich* (Moscow/Leningrad, 1924), 137 (Mar. 30, 1891). For the final text of the manifesto, see S. V. Sabler and I. V. Sosnovskii, *Sibirskaia zheleznaia doroga v eia proshlom i nastoiashchem: Istoricheskii ocherk*, ed. A. N. Kulomzin (St. Petersburg, 1903), 105–106.

22. Pobedonostsev, *Pis'ma Pobedonostseva k Aleksandru III*, 1:184. There may have been some grounds for concern: American whalers were introducing the natives of the coast to American popular music and selling them liquor, tobacco, and firearms (Stephan, "Russian-American Economic Relations," 67).

23. "'O narodonaselenii Sibiri i o velikoi vostochnoi zheleznoi doroge' (Doklad professora E. Iu. Petri i beseda v VIII otdele IRTO)," *ZhdD*, 1888, nos. 33–34: 278.

24. A. N. Kuropatkin, *The Russian Army and the Japanese War*, vol. 1 (London, 1909), 71.

abolition of any sign of the administrative separateness of Siberia and the destruction of its internal administrative unity," a process begun under Alexander II.[25] In 1882 the Western Siberian general governorship was divided into Tomsk and Tobol'sk provinces and the Steppe general governorship, the latter comprising Akmolinsk, Semipalatinsk, and Semirech'e oblasts. Likewise in 1884 the Priamur'e general governorship was formed, including Transbaikal, Amur, and Maritime oblasts and Sakhalin Island, split off from the Eastern Siberian general governorship. The latter was itself replaced in 1887 by the Irkutsk general governorship, consisting of Irkutsk and Enisei provinces and Iakutsk oblast. By 1887 the very name Siberia was no longer used as an administrative term. The region's partial reorganization along European Russian lines and the proliferation of the general governorships on its borders were to provide a framework for the Russification and integration of Siberia.[26]

Alexander intended to facilitate the assertion of central authority through the economic development of Siberia. The idea derived in part from a "memorandum on the discontinuance of the Siberian exile system" which Pos'et had written immediately before he became minister of transport in 1874. In it he urged the abolition of the exile system and the implementation of more humane forms of punishment, so that Siberia would not continue to be a "land of criminals." Throughout he stressed that this system was at the root of

25. Svatikov, *Rossiia i Sibir'*, 76.
26. On the reorganizations, see *PSZRI*, sobranie tret'e, vol. 2, 1882, no. 886; vol. 4, 1884, nos. 2233, 2324; vol. 7, 1887, no. 4517; vol. 11, 1891, no. 7574; Svatikov, *Rossiia i Sibir'*, 76–78; Iadrintsev, *Sibir' kak koloniia*, 535–538; Erik Amburger, *Geschichte der Behördenorganisation Rußlands von Peter dem Großen bis 1917* (Leiden, 1966), 408. It must be noted that the elimination of Siberia's administrative unity was not the only object of these changes. The tremendous size of Siberia had made administration difficult: Enisei province alone was larger than all of the United States east of the Mississippi, and Priamur'e was more than six times the size of France (George Kennan, *Siberia and the Exile System*, vol. 1 [New York, 1891], 57; Iadrintsev, *Sibir' kak koloniia*, 57). That smaller administrative units were clearly necessary and to the benefit of Siberia was recognized by K. A. Skal'kovskii, *Russkaia torgovlia v Tikhom okeane* (St. Petersburg, 1883), 63, and N. Matiunin, "Nashi sosedy na Krainem Vostoke," *Vestnik Evropy*, July 1887, no. 7: 80, 82. Concern about Russia's defensive capability also provided a motive for reorganization, in particular in the Far East. See Andrew Malozemoff, *Russian Far Eastern Policy 1881–1904*, (Berkeley, 1958), 25; O. I. Sergeev, *Kazachestvo na russkom Dal'nem Vostoke v XVII–XIX vv.* (Moscow, 1983), 61–62; D. A. Miliutin, *Dnevnik D. A. Miliutina*, vol. 3 (Moscow, 1950), 239–240. For this purpose a separate administration was eventually created (see *PSZRI*, vol. 17, 1897, no. 14818, and vol. 19, 1899, no. 17214). These factors were probably as important in the administrative reorganization of Siberia as those the regionalists emphasized. But the latter factors did have the intention and effect stated and are therefore more relevant to our discussion.

Russia's weakness there; to change course, he asserted, "it is now necessary to give Siberia too the chance to embark on the path of development."[27]

Alexander III adopted a similar attitude: he regretted "the government's neglect of such an immense and wealthy region," which he held "close to [his] heart." He desired the "peaceful prosperity" of Siberia and would build the Siberian Railroad, a "veritable affair of the people," to "assist in [its] settlement and industrial development." Repeatedly stating that Siberia was an "indivisible part of Russia," he expected his actions to link the region to the empire by rail and bring "glory to our dear Fatherland."[28] Thus Russification and the extension of political control to the region were to be gained through the construction of a railroad and economic development.[29] Alexander's brand of conservatism anticipated that of the twentieth century.[30]

27. K. N. Pos'et, "Prekrashchenie ssylki v Sibir'," *Russkaia starina*, 99 (July 1899): 54–59. As Kennan pointed out, the call to eliminate the exile system was also motivated by a twofold desire: to end widespread criticism of the system and to increase the productivity and hence the taxpaying capacity of the Siberian population (*Siberia and the Exile System*, 2:467).

28. Sabler and Sosnovskii, *Sibirskaia zheleznaia doroga*, 69, 106, 130; Svatikov, *Rossiia i Sibir'*, 76–78.

29. The Kazan' Railroad was to be built primarily for a similar purpose. According to the minister of the interior and the chief of the General Staff, "Kazan' province and the adjacent region constitute the main political center of the Tatar population, which not only has not yet become closely tied to the Russian population of the empire but, on the contrary, has in recent times begun to display the manifest aspiration of alienating itself from the Russian nationality and of drawing closer to the Muslim world. Such a state of affairs necessitates . . . that the government take appropriate measures to eliminate such harmful tendencies in this part of the population. One of the most effective measures in this regard would be the rapid establishment of a close link between the Kazan' region and the internal, Russian oblasts of the empire" (MPS, *Istoricheskii ocherk razvitiia zheleznykh dorog v Rossii s ikh osnovaniia po 1897 g. vkliuchitel'no*, comp. V. M. Verkhovskii, pt. 2 [St. Petersburg, 1899], 450–451). The intention to construct railroads in Finland was similarly motivated: they would bind the Finns to the empire. See Tuomo Polvinen, *Die finnischen Eisenbahnen in den militärischen und politischen Plänen Rußlands vor dem ersten Weltkrieg* (Helsinki, 1962).

30. Cf. Richard Pipes, "Russian Conservatism in the Second Half of the Nineteenth Century," *Slavic Review*, March 1971, no. 1: 121–128.

# PART II

# DEBATE AND DECISION

# CHAPTER FOUR

# Divergent Visions

The compelling strategic and political reasons for the construction of the Trans-Siberian Railroad only gradually became apparent. There was strong opposition to the very notion of a Siberian railroad, not to mention fierce contention over the route, and various elements in the government were slow to consent to either the railroad or the development of Siberia. Much later than has been thought, the bureaucracy remained largely traditionalist in economics, as it had been before the Crimean War, and was not convinced of the possibility of extensive state-inspired economic expansion, which would become the hallmark of the 1890s.

Traditionally the Crimean fiasco has been portrayed as a watershed in Russian economic policy, awakening the state to the need to develop the economy if it was not to lose its claim to great-power status. Yet long after the Crimean War the bureaucracy vigorously opposed the minority in the government that did advocate something along these lines, the technocrats in the Ministry of Transport. Even in a period of autocratic reaction, ideological dissension within the upper bureaucracy shaped the political landscape.[1] Along with the endemic ministerial conflict that it exacerbated, the battle of ideas was a determining factor in economic policy during the reigns of both Alexander

---

1. See Heide W. Whelan, *Alexander III and the State Council: Bureaucracy and Counter-reform in Late Imperial Russia* (New Brunswick, 1982), and Theodore Taranovski, "The Politics of Counter-reform: Autocracy and Bureaucracy in the Reign of Alexander III, 1881–1894" (Ph.D. diss., Harvard University, 1976).

II and Alexander III.[2] Its contours can be charted through the debate over the Siberian Railroad.

The first stage of debate, from 1861 to 1875, was concerned with railroads that were limited in function and relatively small in scale. The Trans-Siberian was an afterthought lodged somewhere in the back of the public mind until the reign of Alexander III, when, for political reasons, such a thing became expedient. The debates surrounding the smaller railroads ultimately gave rise to mention of the Trans-Siberian Railroad and defined the parameters for discussion of its route and function. The issues and tone of the debate over the Trans-Siberian itself first became clear here, prefiguring the issues to be fought at the highest levels of bureaucracy for years to come.[3]

### The First Trans-Ural Projects

Initially many "Siberian" railroads were discussed, one for the Far East and several Ural-Siberian railroads in the west, each to have a distinct function.[4] Proposals for the railroad in the Russian Far East were a by-product of the recent annexations along the Amur and Ussuri rivers and included many put forward by foreigners in search of profit and glory. The strategic component of the Siberian Railroad was central to these projects. But while strategic concerns may have impelled the government to begin construction in 1891, in previous

2. On ministerial rivalry, see George L. Yaney, *The Systematization of Russian Government: Social Evolution in the Domestic Administration of Imperial Russia, 1711–1905* (Urbana, Ill., 1973), 281–282, 299, 310; William C. Fuller, Jr., *Civil-Military Conflict in Imperial Russia, 1881–1914* (Princeton, 1985), xxii. Yaney and Fuller explain the phenomenon by a variety of factors: as a by-product of the administrative growth that took place after 1860 and the resulting loss of a certain amount of control by the tsar over his ministers; as a consequence of the belief that each ministry fulfilled a distinct function unrelated to that of any other; and because responsibility to the tsar was stressed over coordination of policy.

3. Many of the early proposals did include vague notions of railroads across Siberia, likely inspired by the American transcontinental. But little knowledge of or interest in Siberia was evinced, and the goal was by and large to reach Peking. See, e.g., Sofronov's proposal (1858–1859) in V. F. Borzunov, "Proekty stroitel'stva sibirskoi zheleznodorozhnoi magistrali pervoi poloviny XIX v. kak istoricheskii istochnik," in Akademiia Nauk SSSR, Sibirskoe Otdelenie, Dal'nevostochnyi Filial, *Trudy*, seriia istoricheskaia, vol. 5, ed. V. M. Vishnevskii et al. (Blagoveshchensk, 1963), 53–54. See also the critical survey of several of these projects, including one for a horse-drawn railroad enclosed in a covered gallery, in "Doklad A. K. Sidensnera 'O zheleznoi doroge v Sibiri,'" in *TOSRPT*, vol. 17, otdel 2 (1886), 158–162, 171.

4. V. F. Borzunov, "Istoriia sozdaniia transsibirskoi zheleznodorozhnoi magistrali XIX–nachala XX vv." (Ph.D. diss., Tomskii Gosudarstvennyi Universitet, 1972), 206.

decades the appearance of a railroad in the Amur lands would have undermined the state's policy of maintaining Siberia as a "forest cordon." The fear that a railroad would introduce foreign influence was also widespread and continued into the 1880s, so the government discouraged thoughts of building a railroad there.

As for the Ural-Siberian lines, they were to accomplish three separate, narrow objectives: to bring the European Russian network to the border of Siberia; to boost the stagnant mining and metallurgy of the Urals; and to expedite trade between Siberia and central Russia. Three alternative railroad projects competed for acceptance.[5]

The first line was conceived in 1861 by V. K. Rashet, the long-time director of the Demidovs' Nizhnii-Tagil factories, then director of the state Mining Department (1862–1873).[6] He planned his "northern route," as it was known, to link the Ural mining region with the Kama and Tobol rivers, on either side of the mountains dividing Europe and Asia. The route he proposed, from Perm' through Nizhnii-Tagil Zavod to Irbit and Tiumen' (on the Tura River, a branch of the Tobol), would bring coal to Ural iron factories from the deposits of the north-central Urals and give them access to navigable rivers, thus benefiting local industry.

The next line was drawn up for consideration in 1866 by E. V. Bogdanovich, an official whom Minister of the Interior P. A. Valuev had sent on special assignment to investigate the causes of famine in Viatka and Perm' provinces. He concluded that a transit railroad was the answer to grain shortages and suggested a more southerly route from Nizhnii-Novgorod to Kazan', Sarapul, and Ekaterinburg, with a terminus at Tiumen'. His railroad, he argued, would additionally stimulate trade with Siberia and Central Asia. Because of its topography and proximity to Moscow, he deemed it preferable to Rashet's route.[7]

5. For details on these proposals see E. M. Mil'man, *Istoriia pervoi zhelezno-dorozhnoi magistrali Urala (70–90-e gody XIX v.)* (Perm', 1975), 42–87; S. V. Sabler and I. V. Sosnovskii, comps., *Sibirskaia zheleznaia doroga v eia proshlom i nastoiashchem: Istoricheskii ocherk*, ed. A. N. Kulomzin (St. Petersburg, 1903), 9–23; Steven G. Marks, "The Trans-Siberian Railroad: State Enterprise and Economic Development in Imperial Russia" (Ph.D. diss., Harvard University, 1988), 156–167.

6. Mil'man, *Istoriia*, 42; Erik Amburger, *Geschichte der Behördenorganisation Rußlands von Peter dem Großen bis 1917* (Leiden, 1966), 234.

7. On Bogdanovich's route and its vocal supporters in this period, see *Materialy k istorii voprosa o sibirskoi zheleznoi doroge*, suppl., *ZhdD*, 1891, no. 16: 1–10. Bogdanovich was an adventurer and swindler who pocketed government money earmarked for surveys of his route. His actions anticipated the corruption of the future contractors, employees, and officials of the completed Siberian Railroad. On the allega-

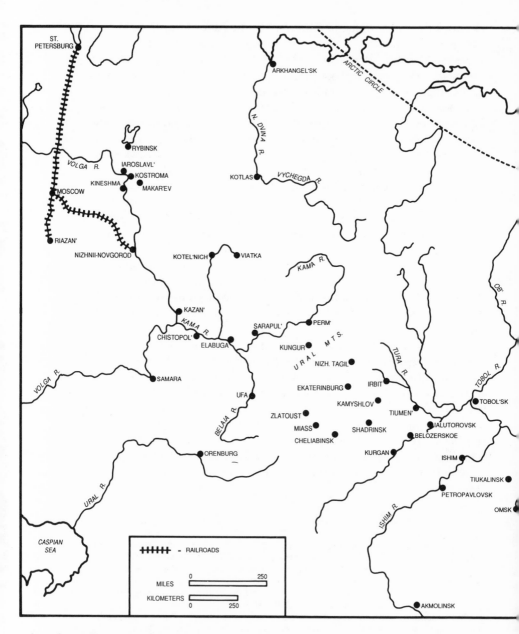

The Volga and Trans-Ural regions, 1862

I. Liubimov, an entrepreneur and mayor of Perm', was the originator of the third major route of this period.[8] After conducting his own
surveys, he asserted in 1869 that to satisfy the needs of both the
Siberian trade and the mining industry (but not to compete with his
own steamer company on the Kama) a railroad should be built from
Perm' to Kungur to Ekaterinburg and from there to Shadrinsk and
Belozerskaia Sloboda (now Belozerskoe), north of Kurgan on the Tobol River.

Simultaneous with a flurry of activity along the intended routes—
formation of committees, collection of statistics, surveying, publication of brochures, lobbying of regional officials—in 1870 both the
Imperial Russian Geographical Society and the Society for the Encouragement of Russian Industry and Trade convened lengthy sessions at which government officials, businessmen, engineers, and
representatives of the interested locales debated the issue. The pre-
ponderance of support was for Bogdanovich, because of the mercan-
tile stature of Moscow and Nizhnii-Novgorod.[9]

The government, though, had made its decision before the public
debates in the professional organizations even took place. Government commissions had found that both trade and mining needs
could not be satisfied by the same railroad; one required a winding
route between factories along the mountain range, the other the
shortest east-west crossing. Konstantin Skal'kovskii, then a representative of the Mining Department, expressed the government's point of
view: Russia could survive without Siberia's livestock but not without
metals. The United States and western European nations became
major powers thanks in large measure to their mining industries;
"without the Ural Mountains, Russia cannot maintain its current
position in Asia and in Europe, in the West and in the East."[10] Thus the
government adopted a shortened, altered version of Rashet's line with
its terminus at Ekaterinburg, in the Ural Mountains (that is, without its
transit link to Siberia), as the blueprint for a Ural Mining Railroad.[11]

---

tions of Bogdanovich's character and corruption, see Mil'man, *Istoriia*, 52, 60, and P. A.
Zaionchkovskii, *The Russian Autocracy in Crisis, 1878–1882*, trans. G. M. Hamburg (Gulf
Breeze, Fla., 1979), 119. On Siberian Railroad personnel, see chap. 9 below.

8. *O napravlenii sibirskoi zheleznoi dorogi (Publichnye preniia v obshchestve dlia
sodeistviia russkoi promyshlennosti i torgovle)* (St. Petersburg, 1870), 19.

9. See ibid., passim; *IIRGO* 6, no. 2 (1870): 61–63.

10. *O napravlenii*, 85–87.

11. Mil'man, *Istoriia*, 80, 82–84; Sabler and Sosnovskii, *Sibirskaia zheleznaia doroga*,
20–21, MPS, *ZhMPS*, official sec., 1893, no. 2: 1. By 1870 Rashet also agreed that Ekaterinburg was too important to bypass, as he had originally suggested, and that it should be

The question of a transit route was still open. The two lines in contest were Bogdanovich's "southern" route and Liubimov's "northern" route, the former focused on Moscow, the latter having been expanded to include construction to Viatka, Kostroma, Iaroslavl', and Rybinsk—in other words, to bring the Siberian line within reach of St. Petersburg.[12]

The backers of both routes wanted a railroad up to the border of Siberia rather than through it, for the purpose of reviving the trade with Siberia and Central Asia which had declined as transport costs rose.[13] Otherwise, from the same premises they reached different conclusions. The "southerners" claimed that Nizhnii-Novgorod and Kazan' provinces, through which their route ran, were both populous and productive, whereas the north was neither, and therefore a railroad there would not turn a profit. "Northerners" argued that for these very reasons they were in dire need of a railroad.[14]

The regional debate over northern and southern routes was overshadowed by rivalry between the interests of St. Petersburg and Moscow.[15] The major portion of the arguments was over the relative importance of these two cities in the Siberian trade. The defenders of St. Petersburg, potential beneficiary of the northern route, declared that the capital was the center of Russian life and civilization and must not be bypassed. Despite this plea, a direct route to St. Petersburg does not seem to have been absolutely necessary and would

---

the terminus of the Ural Mining Railroad (*O napravlenii*, 8–9). The railroad from Perm' to Ekaterinburg was not completed until 1878 (J. N. Westwood, *A History of Russian Railways* [London, 1964], 302).

12. Mil'man, *Istoriia*, 65, 68; *O napravlenii*, 15. Rybinsk was connected to St. Petersburg by rail via the Rybinsk-Bologoe Railroad, completed in 1870 (A. M. Solov'eva, *Zheleznodorozhnyi transport Rossii vo vtoroi polovine XIX v.* [Moscow, 1975], 296).

13. *O napravlenii*, 55–56, 69–70, 108; *Po povodu prenii o sibirskoi zheleznoi doroge v obshchestvakh sodeistviia russkoi torgovle i promyshlennosti* [sic] *i geograficheskom (Peredovye stat'i S.-Peterburgskikh vedomostei)* (St. Petersburg, 1870), 10; "Zaiavlenie chlena Obshchestva Gryf [sic] Iaksa Bykovskogo o zheleznoi doroge iz Rossii v Indiiu," *TOSRPT*, vol. 5, otdel 2 (1874), 6–14; "Doklad N. Shavrova o kitaiskoi i indiiskoi zheleznykh dorogakh," *TOSRPT*, vol. 9, otdel 2 (1876), 95–120; *Materialy k istorii*, 7; A. I. Chuprov, *Iz proshlogo russkikh zheleznykh dorog: Stat'i 1874–1895 godov* (Moscow, 1909), 158–160. In this period the sources show little interest in Far Eastern markets, a fact Pobedonostsev lamented, according to Robert F. Byrnes, *Pobedonostsev: His Life and Thought* (Bloomington, Ind., 1968), 134. The interest in Central Asia accords with the support among entrepreneurs for an annexationist policy there at the time. See Alfred J. Rieber, "The Moscow Entrepreneurial Group: The Emergence of a New Form in Autocratic Politics," pt. 2, *Jahrbücher für Geschichte Osteuropas* 25, no. 2 (1977): 192–193.

14. *O napravlenii*, 19–21, 59, 136; *Po povodu prenii*, 6–8; Chuprov, *Iz proshlogo*, 168–170.

15. Chuprov, *Iz proshlogo*, 166.

do little more than boost its prestige: since Moscow and St. Petersburg were themselves tied by rail, in either case the capital would be the final destination of a Siberian railroad.

The economist and railroad expert A. I. Chuprov, writing for *Russkie vedomosti* (Russian gazette), expressed the pro-Muscovite view: St. Petersburg might be important for the export trade, but its direct commercial dealings with Siberia were minimal and would not suffer if the railroad went to Moscow. The total amount of freight Siberia shipped to Petersburg in the late 1870s amounted to a meager 500,000 puds of tallow and lesser amounts of linseed, wool, and other animal hairs. Siberia's trade with the Moscow region was vastly greater in volume and importance; Siberian goods traffic "instinctively" flowed to Moscow via Kazan' and Nizhnii-Novgorod. Chuprov supported the southern route because it would create conditions for better internal and external markets and thereby stimulate manufacturing.[16]

The Moscow–St. Petersburg rift extended to the lobbying of other cities too. The Nizhnii-Novgorod fair committee was the most vocal supporter of the route from that city. It was dominated by representatives of high-value manufacturing, haberdashery, chandlery, and grocery interests, big merchants who came from Moscow and its allied towns along the Nizhnii-Novgorod route—Kazan', Chistopol', Elabuga, and Sarapul—to the exclusion of the providers of bulky, low-value metals and grain, livestock, and wood products, who were from less settled areas. Their petitions were therefore a biased extension of the Muscovite cause.[17]

Aside from these vested interests, the southern line continued to receive overwhelming support because of the importance of Moscow and the central industrial region. Contemporary theory held that along a given route all major industrial and commercial centers should be linked directly by rail. The understanding was that any alternative would break up this centuries-old trade route.[18] By way of contrast, the north was seen as barren. Even with construction of a railroad there, as one "southerner" had it, "$0 \times 0 = 0$."[19] A majority in the Committee of Ministers held these opinions too: as we shall see, in

16. For both sides of the argument, see ibid., 159–162, 166–167; *O napravlenii*, 11, 17, 53; *Po povodu prenii*, passim.

17. Chuprov, *Iz proshlogo*, 175–176.

18. Richard Mowbray Haywood, "The 'Ruler Legend': Tsar Nicholas I and the Route of the St. Petersburg–Moscow Railway, 1842–1843," *Slavic Review*, December 1978, no. 4: 641; Chuprov, *Iz proshlogo*, 167.

19. *O napravlenii*, 157.

1875 they rejected the minister of transport's plans for the northern route and resolved to build the railroad from Moscow to Nizhnii-Novgorod, Kazan', and Ekaterinburg.

## Pos'et's Proposal of 1875

On May 2–3, 1875, Admiral Konstantin Nikolaevich Pos'et, who had served as minister of transport for less than a year, presented his plans for a Siberian transit railroad before the Committee of Ministers. In many ways his arguments determined its nature when the state finally began construction.

After reviewing the alternative routes, Pos'et backed a version of the northern route—from Rybinsk (with its link to St. Petersburg) to Iaroslavl', Kostroma (with a branch to Kineshma), Makar'ev, Kotel'-nich (with a branch to Viatka), Perm', Nizhnii Tagil, Irbit, and finally Artamanov pier on the Tobol River. He examined the length and contour of each line and from this survey estimated the total cost. In the final analysis, he calculated that the northern route could be shortened to 1,623 versts, which would cost approximately 63 million rubles. The most reduced version of the southern route, at 1,427 versts, would be no less expensive. And if a connection to St. Petersburg and Arkhangel'sk were added, the length and cost of the southern route would be even greater.[20]

On these financial grounds alone, perhaps, he could have made his case, but Pos'et took a different tack. Looking beyond the narrow reason for the construction of this railroad—the eventual linkage of the Kama and Ob' river basins (that is, western Siberia and central Russia)—Pos'et proposed for the first time that this route serve as the starting point of a railroad from the Volga River to the Amur, running through Irkutsk to a possible terminus at Sretensk in Transbaikalia. The cost would exceed 250 million rubles and it could be managed only in the "distant future." This new trade route would bring Europe and Asia closer together and, he dreamed, compete with the Suez Canal.[21]

Pos'et rehearsed the advantages of the northern route, as its sup-

---

20. MPS, Upravlenie Zheleznykh Dorog, Tekhnichesko-Inspektorskii Komitet, "Pred-stavlenie v komitet ministrov MPS K. N. Pos'eta: 'O napravlenii tranzitnoi sibirskoi zheleznoi dorogi,'" May 2, 1875, no. 2319, pp. 1–5, 18–25, 42–43; Sabler and Sosnovskii, *Sibirskaia zheleznaia doroga*, 24–25, 28–30.

21. MPS, "Predstavlenie," no. 2319, pp. 25–27.

Konstantin Pos'et. From MPS, *Kratkii istoricheskii ocherk razvitiia i deiatel'nosti vedomstva putei soobshcheniia* (St. Petersburg, 1898).

porters set them forth: unlike the area between Nizhnii-Novgorod and Kazan', which had good means of communication roughly seven months out of the year, the Russian north was virtually isolated all the time, and a railroad would stimulate this neglected region.[22] He then

22. As Richard Mowbray Haywood has shown in "The Development of Steamboats on the Volga River and Its Tributaries," *Research in Economic History* 6 (1981), water routes between the Volga and the Baltic had been greatly improved in the 1840s and 1850s, and by 1872 railroads had been built to Rybinsk, Iaroslavl', and Vologda. This development detracts somewhat from Pos'et's argument that the north had no means of communications. Certainly, as will be seen, proponents of a given route were none too concerned about the accuracy of their claims regarding a given region. Nonetheless, in this case, except for the Northern Dvina River, water and rail routes largely skirted the edges of

stressed the relevance of the railroad across Siberia: "It is necessary to give Siberia too the chance to embark on the path of development; if it is justified [to say] that convenient means of transport are the foremost bearers of enlightenment and . . . development, then in Siberia this axiom should prove correct in the very largest measure." Furthermore, the railroad was bound to enhance Russia's position in the Far East, where political and trade relations were undergoing fast-paced change.[23]

Pos'et's proposition was far-reaching and innovative, involving the development of both northern Russia and Siberia. Above all, Pos'et intended to use railroads creatively, as a tool of progress, to bring prosperity to vast regions of Russia untouched by civilization; he had a nineteenth-century faith in technical progress unshared by many of his fellow bureaucrats. This veteran Far Eastern explorer's perception of unfolding events in Asia was prescient, while most of his contemporaries were indifferent to the region or just becoming aware of it.[24]

### The Rejection of Pos'et's Plan

The Committee of Ministers deliberated the matter on May 6 and 13, 1875, and the Council of Ministers did so the following December 18. Only three members of the Committee of Ministers supported Pos'et—significantly, former minister of transport General P. P. Mel'nikov and the engineers General E. I. Gerstfeld and K. I. Shernval'. The remaining twenty members came out for the southern route. As

---

the northern provinces, and navigational conditions hindered the use of steamers. As a result, the region remained isolated and undeveloped, a condition that Pos'et was hoping to overcome.

23. MPS, "Predstavlenie," no. 2319, pp. 35–36, 41–42.

24. Pos'et had many years of personal experience in Asia as explorer of the coastal waters of Russia's future Maritime oblast (for which activity a bay and town were given his name), as one of the negotiators of the first Russo-Japanese trade treaty, and as naval officer in the defense of Petropavlovsk-na-Kamchatke during the Crimean War. He played a role in Murav'ev-Amurskii's acquisition of Amur oblast and visited Siberia, China, Japan, the United States, and Canada. See A. I. Krushanov, "Nekotorye voprosy sotsial'no-ekonomicheskoi istorii Vladivostoka (1860–1916)," in Akademiia Nauk SSSR, Sibirskoe Otdelenie, Dal'nevostochnyi Filial, vol. 3, seriia istoricheskaia, *Trudy: Materialy po istorii Vladivostoka*, ed. V. G. Shcheben'kov et al. [Vladivostok, 1960], 21n16; K. N. Pos'et, "Prekrashchenie ssylki v Sibir' (Zapiska K. N. Pos'eta)," *Russkaia starina* 99 (July 1899): 52–53; G. I. Nevel'skoi, *Podvigi russkikh ofitserov na krainem vostoke Rossii, 1849–1855* (Moscow, 1947), 292, 321, 336, 341, 384n175; Andrew Malozemoff, *Russian Far Eastern Policy, 1881–1904* (Berkeley, 1958), 15; Brokgauz-Efron, *Entsiklopedicheskii slovar'*, vol. 48 (St. Petersburg, 1898), 718.

War Minister Miliutin put it, with satisfaction, Pos'et's proposal "failed in the face of attack by almost the whole committee."[25]

A. A. Abaza, at the time chairman of the State Council's Department of the State Economy, led the attack, in what Miliutin described as a "long and magnificent speech" that so "destroyed [Pos'et's] strange line of thought that the other members were left with little to add."[26] Abaza rejected the northern route on the grounds that it would fulfill a secondary objective rather than the primary one of constructing a transit route linking Siberia and central Russia: it would serve such secondary considerations as mining affairs, the needs of which were already satisfied by the Ural Mining Railroad; Arkhangel'sk port, which had been in steady decline since the eighteenth century; and the interests of St. Petersburg, at the sacrifice of those of the central industrial region. The southern route, on the other hand, would ease the transit trade between Siberia and its main markets, Nizhnii-Novgorod, Kazan', and Ekaterinburg.[27]

Underneath Abaza's support for the southern route lay his view of economics, one far different from Pos'et's. Abaza asserted that it was "impossible to expect improved living conditions for the population [of the northern region] with the construction of but one railroad in such a vast, sparsely populated area." Strongly (if subconsciously) echoing the Russian populists and Siberian regionalists, he suggested instead a reduction in the tax burden and other benefits. He saw advantage only in the building of a railroad through the more productive regions of the south, according to "that general economic law, that railroads are not able to create new sources of economic wealth, but rather can develop and strengthen agricultural and industrial activity to a significant degree only where it already exists."[28] With further populist overtones, Abaza held that "in the case of commerce, more than in other social realms, the success of artificial measures . . . is on the whole extremely dubious." Hence, since the southern route corresponded to the existing trade route, it should be the one selected. One could not alter trade ties and habits established for cen-

---

25. D. A. Miliutin, *Dnevnik D. A. Miliutina*, vol. 1 (Moscow, 1947), 196; Sabler and Sosnovskii, *Sibirskaia zheleznaia doroga*, 31. Those opposed included the chairman, P. N. Ignat'ev; Grand Prince Konstantin Nikolaevich; War Minister Miliutin; the former minister of the interior P. A. Valuev; Minister of Finance M. Kh. Reutern; S. A. Greig; the governor general of Western Siberia, N. G. Kaznakov; A. A. Abaza; and the engineer General S. V. Kerbedz.

26. Miliutin, *Dnevnik*, 1:196.

27. Sabler and Sosnovskii, *Sibirskaia zheleznaia doroga*, 31–32.

28. Ibid., 32.

turies and disrupt the attraction of local centers to one another without great shock. Experience in Russia and abroad showed that such disruptions resulted in significant trade crises, which should be strenuously avoided.[29]

On the basis of these arguments, the Committee of Ministers voted down Pos'et's proposal. On December 19, 1875, Tsar Alexander II approved the committee's decision to build the Siberian Railroad from Nizhnii-Novgorod along the right bank of the Volga to Kazan', thence to Ekaterinburg, Kamyshlov, and Tiumen'.

## The Contenders

The dispute between Abaza and Pos'et adumbrates the future course of the governmental controversy over the Siberian Railroad. In 1875, as in the following decade and a half, ideological, personal, and ministerial divisions, as well as financial exigencies, would keep the issue from being resolved one way or the other.

A primary distinction between the two antagonists was in outlook. Abaza, a former railroad concessioner, was minister of finance in the last months of Alexander II's reign (1880–1881), state comptroller from 1871 to 1874, and chairman of the Department of State Economy from 1874 to 1880 and again from 1884 to 1892. In these positions he wielded enormous influence, especially in the State Council, and if he opposed a budget request, there was little chance it would be approved. Abaza was one of the leading "liberals" of the period and would reject much of the course of policy in the 1880s, in particular the direct involvement of the government in the economy. Like other finance ministers of this period, he was mildly protectionist, and he was one of the few high government officials to show a concern for the lower classes by attempting to reduce their onerous tax burden. Abaza did favor government intervention in the nation's railroad affairs and as minister of finance initiated the purchase of private lines by the Treasury. His concern here, though, was not to fulfill his ideological conviction but rather to eliminate the waste of Treasury funds which the concessionary system of railroad building had occasioned. He acted, therefore, for practical reasons of fiscal economy.[30]

---

29. MPS, *Istoricheskii ocherk razvitiia zheleznykh dorog v Rossii s ikh osnovaniia po 1897 g. vkliuchitel'no*, comp. V. M. Verkhovskii, pt. 2 (St. Petersburg, 1899), 442.
30. K. A. Skal'kovskii, *Les Ministres des finances de la Russie, 1802–1890* (Paris, 1891),

It was this opposition to excessive state spending, along with an aversion to "social engineering" by the government, that motivated his opposition to Pos'et's projected northern route. Abaza's attitude harks back to Mikhail Speranskii's cautious approach to railroads in the 1830s. Like Speranskii, the great statesman of the early nineteenth century, he urged only the construction of lines that seemed certain to be financially successful, lest Russia's standing in public opinion and government credit suffer.[31] More interesting, in his belief that the national wealth was a fixed quantity and that new sources of it could not be created he is reminiscent of E. F. Kankrin, finance minister under Nicholas I.[32] Later Abaza was to rail against the theory that deficit spending could spur Russia's productive forces.[33] His caution and his desire to let events take their natural course indicates the persistence of the conservative economic views normally attributed to Nicholas I's reign.

Whereas Abaza was a traditionalist in economics, Pos'et represented a technocratic point of view that at the time had few adherents in the Russian government. In his disparate functions as admiral, bureaucrat, and head of the nation's engineers, he had assimilated the idea that it was part of his function actively to administer and organize society.[34] His outlook was voluntaristic, presupposing government intervention for the creation of progress from above. His aspiration to develop the provinces had its roots in the reign of Catherine the Great.[35] But he also echoed the cry of the eminent scientist D. I.

209–210, 228; Solov'eva, *Zheleznodorozhnyi transport*, 105, 107; Amburger, *Geschichte*, 69, 208, 221; L. E. Shepelev, *Tsarizm i burzhuaziia vo vtoroi polovine XIX veka: Problemy torgovo-promyshlennoi politiki* (Leningrad, 1981), 81, 116; Richard G. Robbins, Jr., *Famine in Russia, 1891–1892: The Imperial Government Responds to a Crisis* (New York, 1975), 66; Taranovski, "Politics of Counter-reform," 688; MPS, *Istoricheskii ocherk*, 293.

31. Richard M. Haywood, *The Beginnings of Railway Development in Russia in the Reign of Nicholas I, 1835–1842* (Durham, N.C., 1969), 84.

32. Walter M. Pintner, *Russian Economic Policy under Nicholas I* (Ithaca, N.Y., 1967), 6, 7, 21–22.

33. A. A. Polovtsov, *Dnevnik gosudarstvennogo sekretaria A. A. Polovtsova*, vol. 2 (Moscow, 1966), 253 (Dec. 28, 1889).

34. On engineers, see Donald W. Green, "Industrialization and the Engineering Ascendancy: A Comparative Study of American and Russian Engineering Elites, 1870–1920" (Ph.D. diss., University of California, Berkeley, 1972), 418–419. On bureaucratic attitudes, see Marc Raeff, *Michael Speransky: Statesman of Imperial Russia, 1772–1839* (The Hague, 1969), 362–365; also Donald Mackenzie Wallace, *Russia on the Eve of War and Revolution*, ed. Cyril E. Black (Princeton, 1984), 12.

35. Robert E. Jones, *Provincial Development in Russia: Catherine II and Jakob Sievers* (New Brunswick, 1984), 1, 3, 8; Marc Raeff, "In the Imperial Manner," in *Catherine the Great: A Profile*, ed. Raeff (New York, 1972), 199–200.

Mendeleev that attention be given to Russia's distant regions with their untapped sources of natural wealth.[36]

As minister of transport, Pos'et had imbibed the spirit of the French utopian Claude Henri de Saint-Simon, whose philosophy of development through great engineering works was taught at the Institute of Transport Engineers in St. Petersburg.[37] Pos'et followed in Mel'nikov's footsteps as a strong supporter of state railroad building, and like his predecessor he posited the capital-creating role of railroads, taken from the American view that expenditures on railroads would eventually be repaid in the form of revenues and an increase in national wealth.[38]

Pos'et, therefore did not consider that the decision to build the Siberian Railroad should be made on purely fiscal grounds. In contrast to his opponents, especially within the Ministry of Finance and the state comptroller's office, he asserted that the "socio-political and economic advantages" to be expected from the project "related mainly to a future time" and could not be justified or denied by any statistical data.[39] If state interest necessitated the construction of such a railroad, then it should be done regardless of normal economic considerations or private local interests.[40] It was on such a basis that Siberia and the remote territories of the country would eventually be developed. In his vision Pos'et was a forerunner of Sergei Witte and the Soviet devotees of large-scale development projects.

Further hampering progress in Russian railroad affairs and playing a large role in thwarting the Siberian Railroad project for more than a decade was a bitter rivalry between the ministries of finance and transport for control over the latter's area of responsibility. Abaza could not tolerate the outlook of the minister of transport and tried to rein him in. He demanded adherence to strict budgetary rules, with expenditures adjusted to the resources of the Treasury. Upon appointment as minister of finance, he laid down the following condition, referring to the ministries of both state domains and transport: "It is essential for the harmonious economic development of the

36. D. I. Mendeleev, "Ob issledovanii okrain Rossii," in *Problemy ekonomicheskogo razvitiia Rossii*, ed. V. P. Kirichenko (Moscow, 1960), 102–103.

37. W. H. G. Armytage, *The Rise of the Technocrats: A Social History* (London, 1965), 148. The Institut Inzhenerov Putei Soobshcheniia Imperatora Aleksandra I is today the Leningradskii Institut Inzhenerov Zheleznodorozhnogo Transporta imeni Obraztsova.

38. MPS, *Istoricheskii ocherk*, 291; Haywood, *Beginnings of Railway Development*, 203.

39. Sabler and Sosnovskii, *Sibirskaia zheleznaia doroga*, 59.

40. MPS, Upravlenie Zheleznykh Dorog, Tekhnichesko-Inspektorskii Komitet, "Predstavlenie v komitet ministrov MPS K. N. Pos'eta," June 1, 1884, no. 4751, p. 1.

nation that there be not only full unanimity of all departments with the Ministry of Finance, but a certain dependence in financial relations as well."[41]

The feud centered on control of large amounts of state funds. But it also grew out of the competition between the two ministries. Both considered themselves to be responsible for the nation's economic well-being and development, and they offered radically different and mutually exclusive solutions. Both struggled for years to dominate Russian railroad affairs, the keystone of economic development. This overlap of authority contributed to inefficient management of the state transport system.

The Baranov Commission (1876–1884) brought the dispute out in the open. Inspired in part by Minister of War Miliutin's criticism, it was created to examine insufficiencies in the railroad network which had come to light during the Russo-Turkish War. Pos'et naturally opposed many of the commission's proposals, because they would have limited his ministry's freedom of movement and because they were critical of his performance as minister.[42] His responsibility for the state of affairs within the Ministry of Transport has probably been exaggerated.[43] There is no doubt that problems plagued the ministry, but they should not be blamed on Pos'et. Skal'kovskii, a contemporary observer of officialdom, found that there was a huge difference between Pos'et's administration and those of previous ministers: there were abuses, but under Pos'et the ministry could no longer be called a bazaar.[44]

Individual hostility greatly amplified the interministerial conflict and affected the Siberian Railroad issue. Deputy Finance Minister F. G. Terner's opinion of Pos'et was typical. He considered the admiral a

41. Zaionchkovskii, *Autocracy*, 159.

42. Solov'eva, *Zheleznodorozhnyi transport*, 153–154, 156–157; Westwood, *History of Russian Railways*, 81–82; A. P. Pogrebinskii, "Stroitel'stvo zheleznykh dorog v poreformennoi Rossii i finansovaia politika tsarizma (60–90-e gody XIX v.)," *Istoricheskie zapiski* 47 (1954): 165–166.

43. For a characteristic view, see Solov'eva, *Zheleznodorozhnyi transport*, 156. Solov'eva relies on the testimony of Witte, who was involved with the Baranov Commission.

44. As K. A. Skal'kovskii pointed out, "under Pos'et, although the Augean stables were not fully cleaned—this being a task beyond the strength of an ordinary individual and even a whole generation—in many respects, order was achieved" (*Nashi gosudarstvennye i obshchestvennye deiateli* [St. Petersburg, 1890], 278–279). He mentions as Pos'et's other contributions the significant expansion and rationalization of railroad construction and a host of beneficial measures taken to improve water routes and ports. On these contributions see also the introduction to Pos'et, "Prekrashchenie ssylki," 53.

good "sailor" and of good personal character, but, apparently along with most of his contemporaries, he felt that Pos'et was an incompetent minister who "understood little of railroad affairs," with the result that Russia's railroad economy suffered and the Baranov Commission had to be called into being.[45] The evidence Skal'kovskii presented belies Terner's assertions. There is certainly little to justify A. A. Polovtsov's claim that Pos'et was "stupid" or Miliutin's that he was "obtuse"; these judgments reflect the vicious personal dislikes rife among the upper bureaucracy.[46]

Perhaps some of the scorn can additionally be attributed to the general low esteem in which engineers were held at the time.[47] Pos'et represented the interests of the engineers, many of whom were unemployed. There can be no doubt that the Siberian Railroad would put many of them back to work, and Pos'et's enthusiasm cannot be separated from this consideration.[48]

More certainly, the name-calling stemmed from a deep political division within the elite. In politics, as in economics, Abaza and Pos'et were on opposite sides, and the hostility between the two sides grew in the first few months of Alexander III's reign. Abaza belonged to a "democratic" faction that rallied around Grand Duke Konstantin Nikolaevich and included, among others, Minister of Finance Reutern, Miliutin (who was related by marriage to Abaza), and, tentatively, former minister of the interior Valuev. Abaza had close ties with the liberal general M. T. Loris-Melikov, who arranged his appointment as minister of finance. All of them advocated further reforms.[49]

Pos'et was a conservative Russian nationalist who opposed the aims of Loris-Melikov and his associates. He sided with Pobedonostsev and the new tsar at the meeting of the Council of Ministers called by Alexander III on March 7, 1881, to discuss Loris-Melikov's

45. F. G. Terner, *Vospominaniia zhizni*, vol. 2 (St. Petersburg, 1911), 78, 80.

46. Polovtsov, *Dnevnik*, 1:200 (Mar. 19, 1884); Miliutin, *Dnevnik*, 4:34–35.

47. For one example of this disdain, see Terner, *Vospominaniia zhizni*, 2:178. To some degree even American engineers had the same problem in the 1870s. See Judith A. Merkle, *Management and Ideology: The Legacy of the International Scientific Management Movement* (Berkeley, 1980), 38.

48. *Times*, May 16, 1883, p. 5. On Feb. 26, 1891, the *Times* reported that the Siberian Railroad "will be a great boon to thousands of engineers wanting employment, and great excitement prevails among this class."

49. Edward C. Thaden, ed., *Russification in the Baltic Provinces and Finland, 1855–1914* (Princeton, 1981), 26; Skal'kovskii, *Ministres des finances*, 212; Zaionchkovskii, *Russian Autocracy in Crisis*, 16, 135, 145, 147, 159. On Konstantin and Reutern, see Jacob W. Kipp, "M. Kh. Reutern on the Russian State and Economy: A Liberal Bureaucrat during the Crimean Era, 1854–60," *Journal of Modern History* 47 (September 1975): 438.

"constitution." He was clearly opposed to political change and even to limited participation by society in government, as advocated by Abaza, Loris-Melikov, and Miliutin.[50] Tellingly, Pos'et was one of the few ministers who remained in office under both Alexander II and Alexander III.

The many divisions reflected in the government's debate over the Siberian railroad plagued the project for more than a decade and a half. At bottom, the division was one of different world views: different approaches to government within the context of autocracy and different approaches to the economic development and well-being of Russia. Fed by personal and interministerial rivalry, the question of the Siberian Railroad, and, indeed, the general direction of Russian economic policy, would continue to be fervently contested along these lines.

50. Zaionchkovskii, *Russian Autocracy in Crisis*, 206–211; Miliutin, *Dnevnik*, 4:34–35.

# The Vital Nerve
# and the Tail End

The railroads that gave rise to the Committee of Ministers' decision of 1875 acted as foils to the Trans-Siberian Railroad. Those railroads were limited in scope and motive, projects conceived in civil society to serve the needs of trade and industry. The Trans-Siberian, by contrast, was an ambitious creation of the central government. The distinction is not only between railroad projects but between reigns—the momentary centrality of commercial interests and society under Alexander II and their loss of vitality under Alexander III. The spirit of the new reign would infuse Pos'et's Trans-Siberian proposals of the 1880s.

## Pos'et's Project of 1884

A crisis that might have worked against Pos'et's initial proposal of the northern route, had it been approved, instead knocked the wind out of the alternative. The Treasury's financial condition grew so grave that construction of the Siberian Railroad from Nizhnii-Novgorod to Tiumen' became impossible. Famine in Russia's southern provinces in 1875 and poor harvests in 1881–1882 and 1884–1885, combined with the lessening world demand for Russian grain and the consequent decline in export earnings, sent the ruble's exchange rate plummeting on international markets. Russian railroad indebtedness pushed the Treasury further into the red. In the mid-1870s, difficulties on foreign money markets made it so hard to place loans that the Treasury could no longer issue guaranteed railroad concessions.[1]

More damaging to the state's finances was the Russo-Turkish War (1877–1878). Before this war, between 1868 and 1875, Minister of Finance Reutern had stopped the downward fall of the ruble brought on in the late 1850s by the Crimean War, strengthened the currency, and largely brought its fluctuation under control. But the more recent conflict, during which the government spent more than a billion paper rubles, undid his accomplishment. By 1881 the country's deficit reached 80.5 million rubles, forcing the new government to proceed with the utmost caution in its spending.[2]

Because of the weakening of the Treasury's resources, Reutern had urged the Committee of Ministers as early as 1876 and 1877 to limit expenditures to the upkeep of existing railroads.[3] On similar grounds N. Kh. Bunge, minister of finance from 1881 to 1887, would justify delaying construction of the Siberian route approved by the Committee of Ministers in 1875. Russia's difficult financial condition led him to the conclusion that the finance minister's primary concern should be "balancing receipts with expenditures, by observing the strictest and most prudent economy." He laid down a railroad policy that followed suit.[4] In response to local petitions from interested parties in June 1880 he declared that "construction [of the Siberian Railroad] will be commenced when the means at the disposal of the State Treasury allow it; when existing railroads are finally put in order; and when those railroad lines that are truly necessary for the trade, industry, and agriculture of the Motherland are completed."[5] Bunge was clearly skeptical of the need for a Siberian railroad, whatever its location.

The victor of 1875 had lost momentum and the turn of events soon proved auspicious for Pos'et. By 1884, state finances, if not the econ-

---

1. K. A. Skal'kovskii, *Les Ministres des finances de la Russie, 1802–1890* (Paris, 1891), 247; L. E. Shepelev, *Tsarizm i burzhuaziia vo vtoroi polovine XIX veka: Problemy torgovo-promyshlennoi politiki* (Leningrad, 1981), 134; A. N. Kulomzin, *Le Transsibérien*, trans. Jules Legras (Paris, 1904), 18; S. V. Sabler and I. V. Sosnovskii, comps., *Sibirskaia zhe-leznaia doroga v eia proshlom i nastoiashchem: Istoricheskii ocherk*, ed. A. N. Kulomzin (St. Petersburg, 1903), 34–35; A. M. Solov'eva, *Zheleznodorozhnyi transport Rossii vo vtoroi polovine XIX v.* (Moscow, 1975), 117–118.
2. Olga Crisp, *Studies in the Russian Economy before 1914* (London, 1976), 96–97; Sabler and Sosnovskii, *Sibirskaia zheleznaia doroga*, 35.
3. Solov'eva, *Zheleznodorozhnyi transport*, 116.
4. Skal'kovskii, *Ministres des finances*, 235–236, 263.
5. Sabler and Sosnovskii, *Sibirskaia zheleznaia doroga*, 36.

omy, seemed to be improving gradually; the ruble's exchange rate was higher and foreign markets seemed to regain confidence in Russia.[6]

As the Russian transport network steadily advanced toward Siberia, the question of the Siberian Railroad became ineluctable. In 1877 the railroad system of European Russia reached Orenburg, at the southwestern border of Siberia. In 1878 the Ural Mining Railroad commenced operation. In 1880 the immense bridge called Imperator Aleksandr II, spanning the Volga near Syzran', opened, bringing central Russia even closer to Orenburg and the Siberian steppe. In 1882 work began on the Ob'-Enisei Canal, which would permit uninterrupted travel by river from Tiumen' to Irkutsk. Finally, between 1880 and 1882 the government decided to proceed with construction, at the Treasury's expense, of the Ekaterinburg-Tiumen' Railroad, running between the Volga and Ob' basins; work on it began in 1884. This road threatened to become the western section of the Trans-Siberian Railroad, and this prospect goaded Pos'et into action.[7]

After conducting new surveys and wrangling with the Committee of Ministers for several years, Pos'et presented his next proposal before that body on June 1, 1884.[8] For the first time he detailed his ambitious notion of a railroad through Siberia itself. The railroad would be built from Samara on the Volga to Ufa, then to Zlatoust in the Urals, whence it would emerge at Cheliabinsk and continue through western Siberia to Omsk. From there it was roughly to follow the existing post road through central Siberia—from Omsk to Kansk, Krasnoiarsk, Nizhneudinsk, and Irkutsk. East of Baikal the route was less certain, but until more detailed surveys were available, there too the best location for the railroad seemed to be close to the post road that went from Verkhneudinsk to Chita and Sretensk, then paralleled the Shilka and Amur rivers. Near Khabarovsk the railroad would turn south along the Ussuri River to Vladivostok.

The Samara-Ufa route was a rejection of both the previous routes,

6. Skal'kovskii, Ministres des finances, 252; Kulomzin, Le Transsibérien, 21.

7. MPS, Istoricheskii ocherk razvitiia zheleznykh dorog v Rossii s ikh osnovaniia po 1897 g. vkliuchitel'no, comp. V. M. Verkhovskii, pt. 2 (St. Petersburg, 1899), 303–309, 443; Robert J. Kerner, The Urge to the Sea: The Course of Russian History: The Role of Rivers, Portages, Ostrogs, Monasteries, and Furs (Berkeley, 1942), 96–97; Sabler and Sosnovskii, Sibirskaia zheleznaia doroga, 39–42; P. I. Roshchevskii, "K istorii proektirovaniia zheleznoi dorogi Ekaterinburg-Tiumen'," in Tiumenskii Gosudarstvennyi Pedagogicheskii Institut, Uchenye zapiski 5, no. 2 (1958): 179–202.

8. MPS, Istoricheskii ocherk, 318; ZhMPS, official sec., 1893, no. 2: 3; Sabler and Sosnovskii, Sibirskaia zheleznaia doroga, 42, 47–49. For routes surveyed, see MPS, Upravlenie Zheleznykh Dorog, Tekhnichesko-Inspektorskii Komitet, "Predstavlenie v komitet ministrov MPS K. N. Pos'eta," June 1, 1884, no. 4751, p. 1.

northern and southern. Pos'et castigated the "personal or local interests" behind the old southern route as not being of "decisive significance in so important a question as the joining of the two halves of the
Empire."[9] He portrayed the 1875 route, with its terminus in Tiumen',
as heading toward a nonproductive region of Siberia and as parallel to
rivers that might compete with the railroad.[10]

Pos'et reiterated the pioneer function of the railroad. Reflecting the
"turn inward" of Alexander III's reign, he had turned his attention to
the development of Siberia, where "all sides of life . . . were stagnant for
the almost exclusive reason of lack of convenient means of communication." It was clear that "under such conditions the population of
Siberia was developing separately and slowly, [and] that most of the
region's natural riches remained unproductive."[11] The railroad, he
said, would counteract this trend. He also provided a concrete example of the major changes in the economy that could be wrought by the
railroad if it were to follow the direction he had detailed. Linking the
grain-producing Cheliabinsk and Troitsk uezds with Orenburg province, it would take the grain trade out of the hands of the Kama grain
dealers, who, centered on the limited existing transit routes, forced
grain away from its natural destination to Ekaterinburg, where prices
were high.[12] Thus interventionist elements continued to be prominent in Pos'et's conception of railroads.

The Trans-Siberian Railroad was to serve a predominantly political
purpose. This is not to deny that there were good economic reasons
for Pos'et's choice of the Samara-Ufa route, but they were by no means
compelling. The established trade routes of western Siberia tended
north toward Tiumen' and Ekaterinburg in the central Urals, over the
land route from Central Asia, the Kazakh steppe, Petropavlovsk and
the grain-producing okrugs of Ishim, Kurgan, and Shadrinsk, and by
water via the Ob', Irtysh, Tobol, and Tura rivers. This northward
movement had been the natural tendency given the hostility of populations to the south, but circumstances had changed over the century.
Now only tradition and a monopoly on river traffic by four steamship
firms maintained the flow.[13]

9. MPS, "Predstavlenie," no. 4751, p. 14.
10. Sabler and Sosnovskii, *Sibirskaia zheleznaia doroga*, 44, 46–47.
11. Ibid., 43.
12. MPS, "Predstavlenie," no. 4751, p. 14.
13. *O napravlenii sibirskoi zheleznoi dorogi (Publichnye preniia v obshchestve dlia
sodeistviia russkoi promyshlennosti i torgovle)* (St. Petersburg, 1884), 25–26; M. Sobolev,
"Puti soobshcheniia v Sibiri," in *Sibir': Eia sovremennoe sostoianie i eia nuzhdy: Sbornik*

The post road had slowly moved south since the mid–eighteenth century, with the expansion of agriculture and Russian settlement. The recently completed Orenburg Railroad was attracting freight in this direction from the Ekaterinburg-Tiumen' highway, perhaps an indication of a new trend. Nizhnii-Novgorod, Ekaterinburg, and Tiumen' were once favorably located, but with a railroad line, freight originating in the south could be shipped along a better path.[14] And despite the arguments of the manufacturers who dominated the Nizhnii-Novgorod fair committee, it was obvious that the profitability of the Siberian Railroad would depend not on the transport of manufactures or clothing but on low-priced agricultural goods, for which savings on shipping costs would be considerable if the railroad were built between Omsk and Samara.[15]

The lands in this vicinity formed the center of the most productive agricultural and livestock region of Siberia and the trans-Urals: tallow was produced in Akmolinsk oblast and Shadrinsk, Kurgan, Ialutorovsk, Ishim, and Tiukalinsk uezds; cattle and their by-products— meat, hides, and butter—were brought all summer long from Akmolinsk and Semipalatinsk oblasts to the fair at Ozero Tainchi-Kul', near Petropavlovsk; grain was abundant in Cheliabinsk, Troitsk, Kurgan, Ialutorovsk, and Ishim uezds. The natural markets for these products were not only the Urals, Moscow, and St. Petersburg; the Samara-Ufa line would provide the shortest journeys to the southern Russian towns of Khar'kov, Odessa, and Rostov-na-Donu as well.[16]

For these reasons of trade and economics, the Samara-Ufa variant made sense. But there was a limit to the influence of such factors on the choice of the Ministry of Transport and, ultimately, the Russian state. On the whole, the commercial contribution of Siberia was not considered significant or vital, and there was little or no justification on economic grounds either for a railroad across Siberia or for the selection of Samara-Ufa as its initial section. In spite of the recent growth and obvious potential of Siberian agriculture, the government

---

*statei*, ed. I. S. Mel'nik (St. Petersburg, 1908), 33; Robert N. North, *Transport in Western Siberia: Tsarist and Soviet Development* (Vancouver, 1979), 20, 47.

14. North, *Transport*, 28, 34; M. I. Pomus, *Zapadnaia Sibir' (Ekonomiko-geograficheskaia kharakteristika)* (Moscow, 1956), 115; ZhMPS, official sec., 1893, no. 2: 2; N. Ostrovskii, *K voprosu o zheleznykh dorogakh v Sibiri* (Perm', 1880), 60–74, 83.

15. A. I. Chuprov, *Iz proshlogo russkikh zheleznykh dorog: Stat'i 1874–1895 godov* (Moscow, 1909), 178.

16. Ostrovskii, *K voprosu*, 12, 76–82; Chuprov, *Iz proshlogo*, 177. On the growth of agriculture and livestock husbandry in Siberia in this period, see also A. P. Okladnikov et al., eds., *Istoriia Sibiri s drevneishikh vremen do nashikh dnei*, vol. 3 (Leningrad, 1968), 27–32.

as yet gave no thought to exporting its products, either abroad or to European Russia: southern European Russia was the largest exporter of grain in the world at the time and the Urals were already receiving Siberian grain.[17]

The state of mining affairs also did not absolutely necessitate a railroad across Siberia. For various reasons mining and metallurgy in general declined on the Cabinet lands of Siberia after emancipation, with a 40 to 50 percent drop in the production of silver and nonferrous metals. Mining of gold, iron, and coal was stable or grew, but the strength of this sector seems to have fostered complacency, since the value of the mines, at least in the case of gold, compensated for the cost of extraction in remote areas. Nor was Siberian metallurgy deemed vital to European Russian industry: Russia began to be aware of Siberia's real reserve of metals only after construction of the railroad commenced, when geological research was first seriously undertaken.[18] Thus, while a railroad for these purposes would have been useful, it was not at all considered a necessity for economic reasons.

The idea of a railroad running through Siberia—a Trans-Siberian railroad—beginning with a stretch from Ufa to Omsk, did not originate within the government. Pos'et's adaptation of earlier private projects reveals the political function attributed to the Trans-Siberian by the state. The proposal of the Ministry of Transport had its roots in the work of V. I. Vagin and N. Ostrovskii. Vagin, a predecessor of the Siberian regionalists, had formulated his plan in 1858–1859 in the *Tomskie gubernskie vedomosti* (Tomsk provincial gazette).[19] Ostrovskii, a member of the Perm' statistical committee, published his in a lengthy pamphlet in 1880, which outlined a "South or Trans-Siberian railroad" from Ufa to Irkutsk along the route almost identical to the one eventually built.[20]

17. North, *Transport*, 45, 48, 68. As North also shows (p. 72), this underestimation of potential agricultural freight was a cause of the overload and inefficiency of the Siberian Railroad after operation began, so productive was Siberia in grain. See chap. 10 below.

18. Ibid., 42–44, 51. Gold mining in Enisei province declined precipitously between 1860 and 1890, according to V. Iu. Grigor'ev, *Peremeny v usloviiakh ekonomicheskoi zhizni naseleniia Sibiri (Eniseiskii krai)* (Krasnoiarsk, 1904), 62, but this loss was balanced by gains elsewhere in eastern Siberia and the Far East (Okladnikov et al., *Istoriia Sibiri*, 3:43–46).

19. V. F. Borzunov, "Proekty stroitel'stva sibirskoi zheleznodorozhnoi magistrali pervoi poloviny XIX v. kak istoricheskii istochnik," in Akademiia Nauk SSSR, Sibirskoe Otdelenie, Dal'nevostochnyi Filial, *Trudy*, seriia istoricheskaia, vol. 5, ed. V. M. Vishnevskii et al. (Blagoveshchensk, 1963), 51–52. The route he proposed was Ufa-Troitsk-Shadrinsk-Tomsk.

20. Ostrovskii, *K voprosu*, 96–108.

Both Ostrovskii and Vagin had in mind the gradual settlement and development of the region and a series of complementary measures that would improve the territory over a period of many years *before* construction of a cross-country railroad. A Trans-Siberian railroad was to appear only in the very distant future, once Siberia had gradually developed to a level sufficient to ensure the railroad's income. To achieve this level of development Ostrovskii suggested improving the means of communication in the short term by building three smaller railroads that would provide a lateral connection between Siberia's internal waterways.[21]

While these proposals may have laid some of the groundwork for the Ministry of Transport, its main recommendations were ignored: the ministry could not wait for Siberia's gradual development, given its desire to tether Siberia to European Russia as quickly as possible. The ministry (and it would soon have the full backing of the Russian state) was interested in economic development not for its own sake but rather to achieve its political objectives. To the enthusiastic editor of the *Zhurnal ministerstva putei soobshcheniia* (Journal of the Ministry of Transport), N. A. Sytenko, once the Trans-Siberian Railroad was completed "the ancient routes of the Huns and Mongols to Europe will be opened anew, but this time not for them; along these paths steam engines and railroad cars will whistle and dart, bringing life and culture to the land of bears, sable, and gold!"[22] "Life and culture" meant economic development to Russify this territory. As another writer put it, Russia needed to give Siberia a railroad, "this vital nerve of every nation," so that it would be "closely tied" to the motherland and to keep it from "completely alienating itself from the metropolis."[23] Pos'et clearly expressed this position before the Committee of Ministers in 1882:

> The task of unifying Siberia with European Russia by reorganizing its civil and social structure and granting it those improved administrative and juridical forms that are enjoyed in Russia will become feasible only when communications are rapid and unbroken, if possible, between all parts of the distant and vast borderlands and the center of government;

21. The lines he suggested were (1) Perm'-Tobol'sk (Kama-Irtysh railroad); (2) Tomsk-Krasnoiarsk (Ob'-Enisei railroad); and (3) Omsk-Barnaul (Irtysh-Ob' and future Russo-Chinese railroad).
22. "'O velikom sibirskom puti v sviazi s pravitel'stvennymi izyskaniiami': Doklad N. A. Sytenko i beseda v VIII otdele IRTO," *ZhdD*, 1888, nos. 22–24: 177.
23. "Zheleznye dorogi v Sibir'," *ZhdD*, 1883, no. 9: 101–102.

and until there is a railroad across all of Siberia, it will be estranged from the general system and political life of the state.[24]

Ironically, Pos'et recommended construction of a railroad through the geographical region that best suited commercial development, but for political reasons. To ensure the political success of this venture, the railroad would have to bring Russian settlers to colonize Siberia. The most suitable area for colonization would therefore determine the direction of the Siberian Railroad. West of Lake Baikal Pos'et chose the route Samara-Ufa-Zlatoust-Cheliabinsk-Kurgan-Petropavlovsk-Omsk-Kansk-Krasnoiarsk-Nizhneudinsk-Irkutsk over both the more northerly Tiumen' options and the more southerly variant from Orenburg to Omsk, which at the time some of the professional societies were actively promoting.[25] Samara-Ufa offered the most direct route to the European Russian rail network, it ran through the center of the Siberian Black Earth Zone, and it was close to coal and livestock regions. The potential for "cultural development" was greater along its path than in either the tundra, swamps, and taiga of the north, the uninhabited, desiccated Kazakh steppe to the south, or the impassable mountains to the southeast, along the Chinese border. "Omsk has national significance, and a railroad to it political importance": settlers went not north to Tobol'sk, but south to Biisk and Kuznetsk

24. *ZhMPS*, official sec., 1893, no. 2: 3. See also MPS, "Predstavlenie," no. 4751, pp. 2–3, where Pos'et states that "no other tool in the development of contemporary human societies may be compared with the power of the railroads in unifying the thoughts, mores, and affairs of people."

25. On the Orenburg proposal, see *TOSRPT*, vol. 12, otdel 1 (1881), 87–99; *Neskol'ko slov po voprosu o sibirskoi zheleznoi doroge*, 2d ed. (Moscow, 1882), 127–144; Imperatorskoe Russkoe Geograficheskoe Obshchestvo, Orenburgskii Otdel, *O preimushchestvakh orenburgo-omskogo napravleniia sibirskoi zheleznoi dorogi* (Orenburg, 1883). Two routes passing north of Lake Baikal, bypassing Irkutsk, were eventually surveyed and discussed, but on reexamination by an opponent they were shown to be longer and in more difficult terrain than the route through Irkutsk, near the south end of the lake ("O velikom sibirskom puti," 174; *Trudy kommissii* [sic] *imperatorskogo russkogo tekhnicheskogo obshchestva po voprosu o zheleznoi doroge cherez vsiu Sibir'*, vol. 21 [St. Petersburg, 1890], 1; N. A. Voloshinov, "Zhelezno-dorozhnaia razvedka mezhdu Angaroi i severnoiu okonechnost'iu Baikala," *Izvestiia vostochno-sibirskogo otdela imperatorskogo russkogo geograficheskogo obshchestva* 20, no. 5 [1889]: 1–14). The alternate routes were put forth by General Protsenko, governor of Turgai oblast, and N. P. Mezheninov, then chief of surveys for the Tomsk-Irkutsk section of the railroad. In its western reaches the route was to cross the Chuna River and head east for Bratskii Ostrog; it would cross the Angara, Lena, and Kirenga rivers, pass close to Lake Baikal, continue along the Verkhniaia Angara, and cross the Muia, Vitim, and Olekma rivers. Here are the unacknowledged origins of the recently completed Baikal-Amur Main Line (BAM).

okrug, by way of Omsk. Here is where four of the six million Siberian inhabitants lived, on either side of the post road, in a belt two to three hundred versts wide. Pos'et planned the railroad to go through the center of this population, following the line of the post road. He applied similar criteria in selecting the route east of Baikal. According to him, any other option was unthinkable.[26]

### Regional Bickering

The choice of Samara-Ufa-Cheliabinsk implied the rejection of the 1875 decision and would have bypassed Nizhnii-Novgorod, Kazan', Ekaterinburg, and Tiumen'. As soon as word was out that Pos'et was considering such an option, a new public debate began, more passionate and bitter than before. A vote in the Society for the Encouragement of Russian Industry and Trade showed that the membership was evenly divided on regional lines over the question.[27] Arguments on each side followed a familiar pattern: their route was objectively more important and more suited for the railroad; they were more in need of it; theirs was for the general good; the alternative would be wasteful.

Representatives of towns lying on the 1875 route asked which was better for Siberia, a railroad through the Bashkir steppe or through Kazan', Nizhnii-Novgorod, and Moscow? The latter was a populated region, the center of industry, the source of all Siberia's import needs, and the shortest route between European Russia and Siberian markets. Its proponents downplayed possible competition by the Volga by stressing the river's navigational difficulties, at the same time that they cited its heavy traffic as proof of the region's importance. Using arguments of the old northern route's supporters (which they had rejected when they themselves were the southern route), proponents of the Nizhnii-Novgorod line asserted the importance of the Baltic ports for Siberian export, as opposed to the Black Sea ports, more easily

26. Inzhener B., "K voprosu o sibirskoi zheleznoi doroge," *Inzhener* 11 (July 1887): 295; MPS, "Otchet o deiatel'nosti ministerstva putei soobshcheniia po stroitel'stvu sibirskoi zheleznoi dorogi za vremia s 30 marta 1889 g. po 17 ianvaria 1892 g." (TsGAOR, fond 677, opis' 1, delo 629), 23; *Otchet o zasedaniiakh obshchestva dlia sodeistviia russkoi promyshlennosti i torgovle, po voprosu o sibirskoi zheleznoi doroge* (St. Petersburg, 1884), 63; *ZhMPS*, official sec., 1893, no. 2: 3–6; North, *Transport*, 69; *TOSRPT*, vol. 18, otdel 1 (1887), 11–13. See also Georg Cleinow, "Eisenbahnbauten und -pläne in Russisch-Asien," *Archiv für Eisenbahnwesen* 51 (January–February 1928): 77.
27. *Otchet o zasedaniiakh*, 216.

reached via Samara. The difficulty of settlement in the south, its isolation, its lack of fuels, and its low level of development were reasons enough, according to them, not to put a railroad there.[28]

Katkov also defended the 1875 route, but on a loftier plane. Writing as editor of *Moskovskie vedomosti* (Moscow gazette), he had criticized the indecision of the government and the competition among regional interests. Yet he himself was a vocal opponent of the Samara-Ufa choice. For him, Moscow was the center of Russia, the heart of the state organism, and the "arteries of rail" should flow from there to provide a "living tie" to the "important parts of the state body." "There can be no justification for quarreling with history"; it would be dangerous to deviate from the established trade routes.[29] Moscow represented Russia to Katkov, and his justification of the 1875 route was a reflection of his nationalism as well as a mundane defense of Moscow's commercial interests.[30]

Petitioning for the new southern route were representatives from the zemstvos and towns of Ufa and Samara provinces, led by Mayor Volkov of Ufa. The "southerners" stressed the abundance of rich land in their region and the potential of their factories. From Samara and Ufa the Black Sea trade would benefit, as would all of southern Russia. The lower Volga for the first time would be supplied in times of famine; the north already had a source of grain, whereas here there was none because of the lack of proper transport. Why should Russia's interests revolve around Nizhnii-Novgorod and Kazan'? Kazan' had no ties to Siberia whatsoever and Nizhnii-Novgorod was not dependent on Siberian goods, which yielded only 7 percent of the fair's total. A railroad to the south would actually benefit Nizhnii-Novgorod, they

28. *Kanun desiatiletiia vysochaishe utverzhdennoi sibirskoi zheleznoi dorogi i agitatsiia protiv neia* (Kazan', 1884), passim; *Otchet o zasedaniiakh*, 19–21, 42, 44–45, 48–50, 52–53, 65–66, 80–82, 139–140; *TOSRPT*, vol. 15, otdel 1 (1885), 14–24.

29. M. N. Katkov, *Sobranie peredovykh statei moskovskikh vedomostei* (Moscow, 1898), *1882 god*, 625 (Nov. 25); *1884 god*, 127–128 (Mar. 6). See also *1882 god*, 623–624 (Nov. 25); *1884 god*, 125–126 (Mar. 5); 144–147 (Mar. 14); 168 (Mar. 23); 207–208 (Apr. 14); 622 (Dec. 1); 668–670 (Dec. 29).

30. See Martin Katz, *Mikhail N. Katkov: A Political Biography, 1818–1887* (The Hague, 1966), 14. For a similar attitude on the part of Moscow entrepreneurs, see Alfred J. Rieber, "The Moscow Entrepreneurial Group: The Emergence of a New Form in Autocratic Politics," pt. 2, *Jahrbücher für Geschichte Osteuropas* 25, no. 2 (1977): 191. It should also be noted that close personal and political ties between Katkov and Bogdanovich may have influenced Katkov's attitude toward the Moscow route. See George F. Kennan, *The Decline of Bismarck's European Order: Franco-Russian Relations, 1875–1890* (Princeton, 1979), 279, and P. A. Zaionchkovskii, *Rossiiskoe samoderzhavie v kontse XIX stoletiia (Politicheskaia reaktsiia 80-kh—nachala 90-kh godov)* (Moscow, 1970), 278.

explained, by preventing Moscow from exempting its entrepôt function. In any case, if its fair were so important, it would not collapse without this railroad, as the "northerners" feared.[31]

Meanwhile St. Petersburg commercial interests continued to speak out on their city's behalf, and Orenburgers were busy attempting to sell the extension of their railroad to Omsk as the most beneficial of the various possibilities.[32]

### The Reluctant Bureaucracy

The reaction of the Ministry of Transport to the resurgence of local competition over the route was negative, as was to be expected in a period when the government looked upon lobbying by regional interests with suspicion and regretted autonomous public participation in national decision making:

> The urgent solicitations of very opposing character arriving in great numbers for consideration by the government only impeded the calm and collected discussion of the important question of the Siberian road by the state institutions. And the nearer this question came to a final settlement, the stronger and more persistent became the concern expressed by the various interested parties.[33]

The government saw in the various petitions nothing more than the "egoism" of local European Russian trade interests and speculators.[34] Pos'et, by contrast, was envisioning a railroad that would serve the state's interests. Its route would not be determined by the commercial and financial considerations that governed other state and private railroads.[35] The problem of Siberia had fused with the temperament of

---

31. Volkov, *Zapiska upolnomochennogo ot ufimskogo gubernskogo zemstva i g. Ufy, ufimskogo gorodskogo golovy Volkova: K voprosu o napravlenii sibirskoi dorogi* (n.p., 1882), and *O napravlenii sibirskoi zheleznoi dorogi: Zapiska upolnomochennogo ot ufimskogo gubernskogo zemstva i goroda Ufy, ufimskogo gorodskogo golovy Volkova* (St. Petersburg, 1884); *Neskol'ko slov po voprosu,* 2d ed. (Moscow, 1882); *Otchet o zasedaniiakh,* 20–21, 24–25, 58–59, 63, 72–73, 76, 84–90, 140–144, 152, 164; *TOSRPT,* vol. 15, otdel 1 (1885), pp. 5–14, 23.

32. See, for instance, S.-Peterburgskii Birzhevyi Komitet, *Zametka k voprosu o sibirskoi zheleznoi doroge* (St. Petersburg, 1884), and above for the Orenburg-Omsk proposal.

33. *ZhMPS,* official sec., 1893, no. 2: 2.

34. As expressed by Chuprov, *Iz proshlogo,* 155.

35. According to Pos'et, "the answer to the question of unifying the two halves of the Empire [by means of a railroad] should not depend on whether the transport of various

Alexander III and the conviction of Pos'et to animate the traditional indisposition of the Russian government toward the private realm.

Many members of the bureaucratic elite continued to resist Pos'et, however, along the same lines as in 1875. The first to speak against his scheme in the Committee of Ministers, where the issue appeared on the agenda on December 18, 1884, and January 2, 1885, was the minister of state domains, M. N. Ostrovskii.[36] Ostrovskii was the "very closest confederate" of Katkov and one of the archreactionaries of Alexander III's reign, along with Pobedonostsev, Minister of the Interior Count D. A. Tolstoi, and Prince V. P. Meshcherskii. His allegiance had not always been with the right, though; he had been an ally of Loris-Melikov's when liberal ideas were in the ascendancy. Ostrovskii's shift of loyalties has been cited as evidence of his opportunism.[37] In economics, certainly, if no longer in politics, his outlook still reflected that of the liberal era and he remained close to Abaza. His views on railroad development were nonvoluntaristic, orthodox, and cautious.

Ostrovskii found Pos'et's reasoning fallacious and alien. "Siberia," Ostrovskii explained before the committee, "is not abundant in those very local products on whose sale in European Russia the various railroad projects so greatly pin their hopes; it is so unproductive that even the local market price of these products precludes any thought of their having large sales in Russia." Obviously ignorant of actual Siberian conditions, he rejected the "creative" or "pioneer" function of the railroad which Pos'et felt would develop Siberia's economy and modify its culture. Ostrovskii's doubts were seconded by the state comptroller, D. M. Sol'skii, and the then deputy comptroller, T. E. Filippov, a Pobedonostsev-style reactionary and ally of Ostrovskii's who produced a memorandum critical of Pos'et's plan.[38]

---

goods is convenient and cheap or whether it satisfies private local interests; rather, it must satisfy, above all, the needs of the central government" (MPS, "Predstavlenie," no. 4751, p. 1).

36. Sabler and Sosnovskii, *Sibirskaia zheleznaia doroga*, 55.

37. Zaionchkovskii, *Rossiiskoe samoderzhavie*, 83–84. The quote is Polovtsov's (p. 244).

38. Sabler and Sosnovskii, *Sibirskaia zheleznaia doroga*, 56–60; T. I. Filippov, "Zapiska gosudarstvennogo kontrolera upravliaiushchemu delami komiteta ministrov o proektirovavshemsia napravlenii sibirskoi zheleznoi dorogi," TsGAOR, fond 1099, opis' 1, delo 463; Brokgauz-Efron, *Entsiklopedicheskii slovar'*, vol. 70 (St. Petersburg, 1902), 759. Filippov was "invited" to work at the office of the state comptroller by Ostrovskii (K. A. Skal'kovskii, *Nashi gosudarstvennye i obshchestvennye deiateli* [St. Petersburg, 1890], 310). He would replace Sol'skii in 1889.

As an alternative to a Siberian trunk line, Ostrovskii suggested reliance on the Ekaterinburg-Tiumen' Railroad and several branch railroads to link the Volga and Ob' basins, as well as the possible extension of the Ural Mining Railroad south from Ekaterinburg to Ufa. He convinced the committee that this configuration, with the Ob'-Enisei Canal, would satisfy the low-level needs of the region for years to come.

If it was hesitant about the route through Siberia, however, the committee on the whole did make some movement in Pos'et's favor. Both Bunge and Abaza now agreed with Pos'et that of all the proposed routes *up to* Siberia, Samara-Ufa seemed to have the advantage over the 1875 line in its probable lower construction cost and potential long-term profitability. But the committee also felt that choosing Cheliabinsk as the terminus of this section would predetermine the route in Siberia itself, and this, again, was something it was not prepared to do. It ordered surveys for the Samara-Ufa branch, but in a location favorable to the construction of a connector from it to the Ekaterinburg-Tiumen' Railroad.[39]

### Regionalists and Reactionaries

On matters of fundamentals, the committee remained opposed to Pos'et and gave short shrift to economic development and the Far East, the issues at the heart of his project. But its hesitation did not last long. The perceived opposition to the railroad on the part of the Siberian intelligentsia extinguished the hostility of its detractors in both government and society and won most of them over to the side of the minister of transport.

The Siberian regionalists had qualms about the Trans-Siberian Railroad because of its political nature, and they expressed their feelings on the question with passion.[40] Though they are often categorized

39. Sabler and Sosnovskii, *Sibirskaia zheleznaia doroga*, 59–65; ZhMPS, official sec., 1893, no. 2: 7; MPS, *Istoricheskii ocherk*, 449–451.

40. Siberian regionalism can be compared with the Grange movement in the United States. The Grangers viewed the American South and West as colonial appendages of the industrial northeast and England, both of which they referred to as the "metropolis." Unlike the Siberians, they supported construction of a transcontinental railroad because they reasoned that it would, among other things, expand their potential markets, bring the country dominance in the world trading system, and rid it of its dependence on England. Their strategy was soon adopted by society at large. See Howard B. Schonberger, *Transportation to the Seaboard: The "Communication Revolution" and American Foreign Policy, 1860–1900* (Westport, Conn., 1971), xi–xii.

with the Russian populists, they held quite contrary political beliefs: their aim was political freedom. Their views were derived from the federalism of A. Shchapov, who described the Russian commune not as a bastion of socialism against capitalism, as the radicals saw it, but as a stronghold of local autonomy that stood in the way of Russian state centralization.[41] Economic issues—such as railroad construction—thus became for them issues of political importance.

Iadrintsev and G. N. Potanin, the "brains and heart" of Siberian regionalism, expanded Shchapov's theoretical, academic conceptions into the practical task of preserving the unity of Siberia as the sine qua non of their political existence.[42] The regionalists measured political and economic issues against concrete standards: Would they help or hurt Siberia? Would they facilitate or diminish "colonial" domination by the European Russian metropolis? Would they be a step toward or away from either political freedom or centralization? It was in accordance with this gauge of exploitation that the regionalists opposed the Siberian Railroad, both in its early conception to ward off the voraciousness of Moscow manufacturers and later to prevent the central government from putting a stranglehold on Siberia. In both cases, E. V. Bogdanovich's words regarding the Siberian Railroad seemed ominous: "Siberia is no longer. Henceforth this is Russia."[43]

The regionalists were afraid of the changes a railroad would bring to Siberia:

With the construction of the railroad, the old familiar Siberia will disappear forever and this will occur very quickly. A new Siberia will be formed

41. I. A. Iakushev, "Gr. N. Potanin (Ego politicheskie vzgliady i obshchestvenno-politicheskaia deiatel'nost')," in *Vol'naia Sibir'*, vol. 1 (Prague, 1927), 18–19; A. Walicki, *The Controversy over Capitalism: Studies in the Social Philosophy of the Russian Populists* (Oxford, 1969), 92–93n4. In this respect, the Siberian regionalists were more akin to Herzen or Bakunin than to the populists who were their contemporaries. Iadrintsev was suspicious that the populists were not committed to federalism, and there was a deep division between "centralist-Jacobins" and regionalists on the staff of the newspaper *Vostochnoe obozrenie* (S. G. Svatikov, *Rossiia i Sibir' [K istorii sibirskogo oblastnichestva v XIX v.]* [Prague, 1930], 73–74; I. I. Popov, *Minuvshee i perezhitoe: Vospominaniia za 50 let: Sibir' i emigratsiia* [Leningrad, 1924], 232). On the divergence between Siberian regionalism and populism, see also Franco Venturi, *Roots of Revolution: A History of the Populist and Socialist Movements in Nineteenth-Century Russia*, trans. Francis Haskell (Chicago, 1960), 320–321, and Abbott Gleason, *Young Russia: The Genesis of Russian Radicalism in the 1860s* (Chicago, 1980), 207, 223. Especially after Iadrintsev's death, *Vostochnoe obozrenie* came to be dominated by populists and featured Marxist writers, too, including Trotsky.
42. Iakushev, "Gr. N. Potanin," 17–18, 32.
43. *Materialy k istorii voprosa o sibirskoi zheleznoi doroge*, suppl. to *ZhdD*, no. 16 (1891): 98.

and it will unite those scattered and already weakened elements that make up Siberian society. Settlers and exiles, people of easy money, shady characters, swindlers—all of these types will find themselves new dealings just as soon as the first trains pass through. They and the mass of their kind will crop up from both ends of the empire, grabbing all trade and industry into their hands. The railroad will give birth to a period of speculation of the most roguish type ever to have a place in society. In contemporary Siberian society there is much confusion and disorder, but essentially it is vigorous. The healthy traits of Siberian life will be destroyed by the industrial fever of railroad promoters and other speculators.[44]

They dreaded the "invasion of a railroad civilization, grasping and greedy," and the dawn of "the rule of the Antichrist." To withstand the onslaught, the old Siberia would need to marshal all its civic strength.[45]

The regionalists lamented the probable end of Siberia's uniqueness because to them Siberia represented something pure and pristine, a hope and model for the future, which a railroad introducing alien Russian forms would destroy.[46] They were convinced that as Siberia's soul was destroyed, Russia would consolidate its position as exploiter. Absentee mining firms would ship Siberia's raw materials at low cost to European Russia and expensive manufactured goods would flood Siberian markets. The railroad would thus strengthen Siberia's dependence and worsen the oppression. There would be no one to protect its interests because of the continued lack of local participation in the administration of Siberia and because the Russian intelligentsia who would arrive with the railroad would soon outnumber Siberians.[47]

44. *Vostochnoe obozrenie*, 1890, no. 30:2. See also "'O narodonaselenii Sibiri i o velikoi vostochnoi zheleznoi doroge' (Doklad professora E. Iu. Petri i beseda v VIII otdele IRTO)," *ZhdD*, 1888, nos. 33–34: 269.
45. Stephen Digby Watrous, "Russia's 'Land of the Future': Regionalism and the Awakening of Siberia, 1819–1894" (Ph.D. diss., University of Washington, 1970), 2:678; Wolfgang Faust, *Rußlands goldener Boden: Der sibirische Regionalismus in der zweiten Hälfte des 19. Jahrhunderts* (Cologne, 1980), 486–487.
46. Faust finds this attitude analogous to D. Pisarev's and N. Shelgunov's opposition to competition from European industry in Russia (*Rußlands goldener Boden*, 396). Cf. also the attitude expressed by V. Vorontsov, N. G. Chernyshevskii, and Alexander Herzen, that the "latecomer" Russia had an advantage in its backwardness and would soon surpass Europe (Walicki, *Controversy over Capitalism*, 116–117). The regionalists had similar expectations of Siberia vis-à-vis Russia.
47. *Vostochnoe obozrenie*, 1884, no. 48: 3; N. M. Iadrintsev, *Sibir' kak koloniia v geograficheskom, etnograficheskom i istoricheskom otnoshenii*, 2d ed. (St. Petersburg, 1892), 364, 465; Faust, *Rußlands goldener Boden*, 341–342, 396–397.

The regionalists criticized what they viewed as the anti-Siberian bias in the public debates over the Siberian Railroad. As there were no zemstvos or other organs of local self-government in Siberia, its people had not been given a fair chance to participate in any of the discussions of the railroad. Siberian interests were secondary, although Kazan', Ufa, Orenburg, and the towns of the Urals all seemed to speak in Siberia's behalf. Though Siberia's agricultural and mineral wealth were the topics at hand, "there was not a single public discussion of this question" in Siberia itself.[48]

They found confirmation that non-Siberian interests alone were being served in the type of railroad favored by the government: though rapid construction with low technical standards might reduce the Treasury's initial outlay, it would require higher operating costs, which they predicted would be covered by taxes levied on the Siberian population. And who would bear the initial costs? Like the populists, they criticized the use of millions of the "people's means" when immediate returns were not guaranteed. There would be indirect costs too, but they would not be invisible: the railroad would almost surely eliminate innkeeping and cartage, which occupied up to one-quarter of the Siberian population in some provinces. This was too high a price to pay.[49]

It must be borne in mind that the regionalists' opposition to the railroad did not stem from a broad anticapitalist, anti-Western, or antiurban perspective; on a visit to the United States in 1893, Iadrintsev remarked with admiration, "This is Siberia in a thousand years."[50] Nor were they dogmatic revolutionaries unconditionally and irretrievably repudiating the government: they appreciated the state's efforts to break up monopolies and cartels in Siberia and praised highly those "enlightened" governors general of Siberia—all of whom were appointees of the central government and advocates of the Siberian Railroad—who had tried to improve conditions in Siberia.[51]

In fact, their opposition to the railroad was ambiguous and they never doubted its inevitability. Iadrintsev had at first, in the early 1870s, applauded the idea as a benefit to Siberian material life and as a means to ending its isolation.[52] Even later they saw much good in it.

48. *Vostochnoe obozrenie*, 1882, no. 5: 9; 1883, no. 9: 3; 1884, no. 18: 3.
49. Ibid., 1884, no. 28: 2; 1885, no. 4: 4; 1892, no. 39: 2; "Po povodu sibirskoi zheleznoi dorogi," *ZhdD*, 1893, nos. 27–28: 297.
50. Quoted in Faust, *Rußlands goldener Boden*, 547. Faust overstates the anticapitalist element in their thought (cf. pp. 117, 381–382, 395, 487).
51. Iadrintsev, *Sibir' kak koloniia*, 417, 538–542, 587, 660–661, 687.
52. Faust, *Rußlands goldener Boden*, 338–339.

Unlike Nikolai Chernyshevskii, who despised the Asian element in Russian culture, their task was to show Europe that Asia was not moribund but vital. Because of its location at the crossroads of Europe and Asia, Siberia would help to unify the two worlds. The Siberian Railroad, with branches to Turkestan and Peking, would bring the peoples of the world closer together.[53] With all the enthusiasm of the railroad age, Iadrintsev went further: when the Atlantic and Pacific oceans were linked by rail across Siberia, it would be the heir to the prosperity of Venice and the Cape of Good Hope; it would rival Egypt. Each in its time had served as way station between Europe and Asia; now it was Siberia's turn, and "the consequences of such a world event are really incalculable."[54]

The regionalists were therefore opposed not to a railroad per se, but rather to one that did not match their concept of it. They asserted that to prevent further exploitation by European Russian interests, Siberia's industry itself should be developed pending the introduction of a railroad. Siberia's raw material, rather than being stripped for export, should be worked locally, and an interregional trade serving local needs should be stimulated; the region would not otherwise give up its wealth. They called for the well-rounded, gradual, and full development of Siberia's productive forces, with a central role being given to cottage industries.[55]

Here again, on the face of it, we see some similarity to the outlook of contemporary populist economics: railroads should not be considered ends in themselves; they should not be built if they would not improve the lives of the people in a concrete way.[56] As Potanin wrote, "building a railway into Siberia means beginning the matter from the tail end first."[57] Siberia needed colonists, a denser population, and many factories before it needed the railroad. When it had the people and the factories, the railroad should serve them; they should not be introduced later solely to serve the railroad.[58] A railroad is one means

---

53. P. E. Skachkov, *Ocherki istorii russkogo kitaevedeniia* (Moscow, 1977), 239; Svatikov, *Rossiia i Sibir'*, 85; Iadrintsev, *Sibir' kak koloniia*, 719. On Chernyshevskii's attitude, see Andrzej Walicki, *A History of Russian Thought: From the Enlightenment to Marxism* (Stanford, 1979), 201.

54. "'Kul'turnoe i promyshlennoe sostoianie Sibiri,' (Doklad N. M. Iadrintseva)," in *TOSRPT*, vol. 14, (1884), 28–29.

55. *Vostochnoe obozrenie*, 1882, no. 5: 9–10; 1883, no. 9: 3; 1884, no. 20: 3; Iadrintsev, *Sibir' kak koloniia*, 350–351, 364, 373, 444–468; Iakushev, "Gr. N. Potanin," 35.

56. See Arthur P. Mendel, *Dilemmas of Progress in Tsarist Russia: Legal Marxism and Legal Populism* (Cambridge, Mass., 1961), 38–40.

57. Quoted in Watrous, "Russia's 'Land of the Future'" 2:675.

58. *Vostochnoe obozrenie*, 1892, no. 39: 2.

of introducing civilization, but only one—it is not a panacea for all
evils:

> Why is it that people who want to do good for Siberia and raise its
> cultural level, and who speak so heatedly of billions for a railroad, do not
> apply themselves to other equivalent and maybe more significant tools
> of civilization? Why is it not said: Strew people's schools and technical
> institutions across this region without sparing billions [of rubles] . . . ?
> But not a word is said about this. Why is it that nothing is said about
> raising the people's culture, developing education, etc. . . , to which
> Europe and other parts of the world are indebted no less, and maybe
> more, [than to railroads] for the luster of civilization and prosperity?
> Raise the culture and industry of the region, give full range to the
> development of life and to education with all its blessings, and railroads
> will appear by themselves as a result of this higher level.[59]

What the regionalists stood for was the protection of their autonomy and culture. Their attitude toward the Siberian Railroad was
integral to their clearly elucidated and pragmatic political program,
which called for the introduction of full civil rights at least to the
extent that European Russia enjoyed them, including the introduction of the courts, zemstvos, and other innovations of the Great Reforms which had been denied to Siberia, and the abolition of the exile
system.[60] This is hardly a program of utopians, as one historian calls
them; they are the demands of Siberian patriots, as they called themselves.[61] Their pragmatic, limited, realistic aims, unlike the goals of the
populists, anticipated those of the liberals of the Duma period.[62]
Then, too, the call to strengthen the country through education and
the granting of political rights would fall largely on deaf ears.

However ambivalent regionalist opposition to the Siberian Railroad
may have been, it seemed firm and threatening to conservatives. The
conservatives had themselves been less than enthusiastic about the

---

59. Ibid., 1884, no. 28: 2. See also 1883, no. 9: 3; 1884, no. 48: 3; 1886, no. 13: 4
60. See Iadrintsev, *Sibir' kak koloniia*, 225, 242, 296, 317, 349–351, 387, 432, 443, 463,
465–468, 709, 711–712, 715–716.
61. Faust, *Rußlands goldener Boden*, 590; Mikhail Lemke, *Nikolai Mikhailovich
Iadrintsev: Biograficheskii ocherk: K desiatiletiiu so dnia konchiny* (St. Petersburg, 1904),
197–198; Popov, *Minuvshee*, 207.
62. Indeed, a majority of regionalists joined the Kadet party after its formation in 1905,
and only a minority joined the S.R.s. Potanin himself ran for the First Duma—unsuc-
cessfully—as a Kadet in 1906, although he had hoped that the Kadets and S.R.s would
form one party (Gary Hanson, "Grigory Potanin, Siberian Regionalism, and the Russian
Revolution of 1905" [paper read at AAASS conference, Boston, Nov. 8, 1987], 16–17).

railroad; but when its political potential against the specter of a separatist Siberia dawned on them, they began to promote it.

Aside from regional loyalties, conservative opposition to the railroad was rooted in the traditional distrust of capitalist economic innovation as a disruptive force. Katkov warned against the use of the Siberian Railroad for the resettlement of landless peasants, in accord with his gentry-oriented conservatism. Russia was not Belgium, he argued; it was underpopulated, and the colonization of Siberia would lead to serious dislocations.[63] The reactionary editor of the newspaper *Grazhdanin*, Prince Meshcherskii, agreed with Katkov on these points and expressed his distaste for the fruits of modern technology: "civilization" and "progress" were not desirable for Russia, where they would confront "Russian sensibility" and "Russian integrity." Better to spend the Treasury's money on the spiritual realm to bolster Russia against the forces of modernity, represented by the Jews. "Today permit the construction of the Siberian Railroad—tomorrow Siberia will be given up forever to the Jews of the whole world, and in ten years it will be lost forever to Russia."[64]

Meshcherskii's "apocalyptic fear," as *Novoe vremia* put it, was not uncommon among tsarist officials in Siberia. One wrote that the railroad would unleash fierce competition between foreign and Russian merchants for control of Siberia's trade, ultimately bringing ruin on the Siberian peasant. The result would be chaos and the impossibility of "preserving order in the region."[65]

Soon enough this very concern for the authority of the state led conservatives to reverse themselves on the issue and enthusiastically champion the Siberian Railroad as a means of loosening what they perceived to be the grip of separatism or revolution on Siberia. Voloshinov pondered whether, after three hundred years of Russian rule, Siberia was truly under Russia's control. He could not answer in the affirmative.[66] For this reason, too, Meshcherskii shifted his ground suddenly: he saw taking place in Siberia

an unspoken, cerebral process of alienation from all things Russian, which one finds in the mother's milk as it nurtures the infant, in the

63. Katkov, *Sobranie: 1882 god*, 669 (Dec. 22).
64. Quoted in *Novoe vremia*, July 9, 1889, p. 1, and July 15, 1889, p. 1. See also July 5, 1889, p. 1.
65. Quoted in A. V. Pataleev, *Istoriia stroitel'stva velikogo sibirskogo zhelezno-dorozhnogo puti* (Khabarovsk, 1951), 8.
66. N. A. Voloshinov [M. V———"], *Neskol'ko slov o sibirskoi zheleznoi doroge* (St. Petersburg, 1890), 20.

mental attitude of the official, in the instincts of the popular masses, and in the world contemplations of the intellectual; [it is] in the air, so to speak, of all Siberia.[67]

The Siberian Railroad, they began to realize, would dissipate this miasma and was necessary for reasons of state.

Regionalist opposition only reaffirmed the widely held perception that the railroad would bind Siberia to Russia and, through development, Russify it.[68] Concerned with the preservation of Russian sovereignty over Siberia, many people overcame their doubts regarding the railroad, to confirm the insight of Albert Beveridge that "Russia considers nothing hers which she does not control in a visible, tangible, material way."[69] Many, that is, but not all overcame their doubts; though support was growing, the project still faced major obstacles.

---

67. Quoted in *Novoe vremia*, July 20, 1890, p. 1.

68. That the reactionaries were brought around to the government's point of view, rather than vice versa, is an indication that their power over decision making was not so great as it is often described. This conclusion supports the general contentions of Heidi W. Whelan, *Alexander III and the State Council: Bureaucracy and Counter-reform in Late Imperial Russia* (New Brunswick, N.J., 1982), and Theodore Taranovski, "The Politics of Counter-reform: Autocracy and Bureaucracy in the Reign of Alexander III, 1881–1894" (Ph.D. diss., Harvard University, 1976), regarding Katkov, Pobedonostsev, and Meshcherskii.

69. Quoted in Albert J. Beveridge, *The Russian Advance* (New York, 1904), 76.

# CHAPTER SIX

# Bureaucracy Prolix

In the last few years of Pos'et's ministry the Siberian Railroad project took on a new urgency within the government, but with its advancement came continuing dissension over both its financing and its supervision. In all its aspects, this discord was part of the broader conflict among ministries over prestige, distribution of funds, and ultimately predominance in the nation's economic policy making.

### Hostility of the Finance Ministry

Coming on the heels of growing apprehension about separatists in Siberia—real and imagined—the railroad issue was pushed to the fore by the "most humble reports" sent to the tsar in 1886 by two governors general, A. P. Ignat'ev of Irkutsk and Baron Korf of Pria-mur'e. Emphasizing the desperation of the provinces on the Chinese border and the strategic significance of the railroad, they had enormous impact, for they elicited the direct support of Alexander III. At the bottom of Ignat'ev's report the tsar commented: "I have already read so many reports of the governors general of Siberia, and it must be confessed with sadness and shame that up to now the government has done almost nothing to satisfy the needs of this rich but neglected region. And it is time, long since time." His message expressed his desire to prod the slow-moving, quibbling bureaucracy to action. Both the report and his resolution were read before the Committee of

Ministers on December 16, 1886; the tsar's backing made it a certainty that the railroad would be built.[1]

To resolve the issue rapidly the tsar formed four special conferences between late 1886 and mid-1887, at which ministers and other invited officials affirmed in principle the strategic necessity of a Siberian railroad. The conferences approved technical conditions worked out by the Ministry of Transport and ordered initial surveys for central-eastern Siberia between Tomsk and Sretensk, and for the Far East in the vicinity of Vladivostok.[2]

In spite of the tsar's resolution and the decisions of the special conferences, the minister of finance remained steadfastly opposed. The new minister was Ivan Alekseevich Vyshnegradskii. A former professor of mechanics, he was brought into office because of his practical business experience. While he served on the boards of two railroad companies, he reduced their expenses by millions of rubles. Although he had made many enemies in the process, he performed this difficult operation steadfastly and without favoritism. It was widely hoped that he would do the same for the administration of Russian state finances.[3]

Vyshnegradskii was given the position at the urging of Katkov and Pobedonostsev, who had waged a campaign against the more liberal Bunge.[4] Nonetheless, Vyshnegradskii did not represent a significant break from the traditionalism of his predecessors.[5] He enacted a

1. S. V. Sabler and I. V. Sosnovskii, comps., *Sibirskaia zheleznaia doroga v eia proshlom i nastoiashchem: Istoricheskii ocherk*, ed. A. N. Kulomzin (St. Petersburg, 1903), 69–70; MPS, *Istoricheskii ocherk razvitiia zheleznykh dorog v Rossii s ikh osnovaniia po 1897 g. vkliuchitel'no*, comp. V. M. Verkhovskii, pt. 2 (St. Petersburg, 1899), 451.

2. Sabler and Sosnovskii, *Sibirskaia zheleznaia doroga*, 71–78; MPS, "Otchet o deiatel'nosti ministerstva putei soobshcheniia po stroitel'stvu sibirskoi zheleznoi dorogi za vremia s 30 marta 1889 g. po 17 ianvaria 1892 g." (TsGAOR, fond 677, opis' 1, delo 629), 5–7; ZhMPS, official sec., 1893, no. 2: 8–12; MPS, *Istoricheskii ocherk*, 451–459.

3. K. A. Skal'kovskii, *Les Ministres des finances de la Russie, 1802–1890* (Paris, 1891), 273–274; Brokgauz-Efron, *Novyi entsiklopedicheskii slovar'*, vol. 12 (St. Petersburg, n.d.), 116. Vyshnegradskii sat on the boards of the Rybinsk-Bologoe and Southwestern railroads.

4. P. A. Zaionchkovskii, *Rossiiskoe samoderzhavie v kontse XIX stoletiia (Politicheskaia reaktsiia 80-kh—nachala 90-kh godov)* (Moscow, 1970), 142; B. V. Anan'ich, "The Economic Policy of the Tsarist Government and Enterprise in Russia from the End of the Nineteenth through the Beginning of the Twentieth Century," in *Entrepreneurship in Imperial Russia and the Soviet Union*, ed. Gregory Guroff and Fred V. Carstensen (Princeton, 1983), 130; L. E. Shepelev, *Tsarizm i burzhuaziia vo vtoroi polovine XIX veka: Problemy torgovo-promyshlennoi politiki* (Leningrad, 1981), 146–149.

5. Here I disagree with Anan'ich, who argues that Vyshnegradskii's policies were not directly inherited from Bunge, but were closely tied to Alexander III's politics ("Eco-

protective-tariff policy less to create a national, Russian-dominated industry than to bring money into the Treasury. He saw that putting Russia's monetary situation in order was a prerequisite for improving the health of the economic system.[6] At the very top of his agenda was the budget deficit, which he intended to eliminate by increasing state revenues and cutting expenditures.[7] He kept state disbursements for railroads to a minimum and "in principle" preferred that railroad construction be financed by private concessioners rather than the Treasury.[8] Concentrating solely on finances, he left development of the nation's resources to the side. Polovtsov declared with dismay, "This is a cashier, not a minister caring for the future development of the economic forces of the country."[9] It is not a coincidence that almost the identical comment had been made about Kankrin, Nicholas I's finance minister.[10]

Thus Vyshnegradskii's aversion to the Trans-Siberian Railroad was founded on fiscal and intellectual grounds. Primarily under his influence, the Committee of Ministers in 1887 repeatedly rejected or scaled down Pos'et's requests for funding of the railroad. In early 1887 Vyshnegradskii, then acting minister of finance, claimed that "extra-budgetary" expenditures could not be granted for surveys because he would be hard-pressed to find funds in the Treasury and foreign loans were not available. In reaction to Korf's continued messages of alarm from the Far East, however, the committee did accept the importance

nomic Policy," 130–132). See below and A. A. Polovtsov, *Dnevnik gosudarstvennogo sekretaria A. A. Polovtsova*, vol. 2 (Moscow, 1966), 209 (June 17, 1889), where Abaza is quoted as saying that Vyshnegradskii "simply continued the policies of his predecessors."

6. Shepelev, *Tsarizm*, 156, 166–167; Olga Crisp, *Studies in the Russian Economy before 1914* (London, 1976), 99–100.

7. I. F. Gindin, *Gosudarstvennyi bank i ekonomicheskaia politika tsarskogo pravitel'stva (1861–1892 god)* (Moscow, 1960), 62. The total state debt (foreign and domestic) had risen under Bunge from 6,046 million rubles in 1881 to 6,488 million in 1886; interest on the debt consumed more than a quarter of the state budget, more even than military expenditures. Thirty percent of the debt was owed to foreigners (George F. Kennan, *The Decline of Bismarck's European Order: Franco-Russian Relations, 1875–1890* [Princeton, 1979], 225).

8. N. A. Kislinskii, comp., *Nasha zheleznodorozhnaia politika po dokumentam arkhiva komiteta ministrov*, vol. 3 (St. Petersburg, 1902), 246; Sabler and Sosnovskii, *Sibirskaia zheleznaia doroga*, 99–100. During his administration, approximately 51.6 million rubles were spent on railroads annually (Crisp, *Studies*, 25–26).

9. Polovtsov, *Dnevnik*, 2:343 (Jan. 15, 1891); Crisp, *Studies*, 103–104.

10. By Prince Drutskii-Liubetskii, finance minister of Poland (1821–1830) and member of the Russian State Council (from 1832). Quoted in Walter McKenzie Pintner, *Russian Economic Policy under Nicholas I* (Ithaca, N.Y., 1967), 126.

Ivan Vyshnegradskii. From Ministerstvo Finansov, *Ministerstvo finansov, 1802–1902* (St. Petersburg, 1902).

of the proposed Ussuri Railroad from Vladivostok to Khabarovsk and split it off from the rest for more rapid consideration.[11]

Ostensibly Vyshnegradskii's opposition was based on his tight spending policy. But there were other reasons too. As he was closely tied to Katkov, especially while he was still acting minister, and a long time friend of Filippov's, it is likely that his personal connections played a role in his resistance to Pos'et's scheme.[12]

11. MPS, "Otchet o deiatel'nosti," 6–7, and *Istoricheskii ocherk*, 452, 460–461; Sabler and Sosnovskii, *Sibirskaia zheleznaia doroga*, 71–72, 78–80; ZhMPS, official sec., 1893, no. 2: 13.

12. On his relationship with Filippov, see K. A. Skal'kovskii, *Nashi gosudarstvennye i obshchestvennye deiateli* (St. Petersburg, 1890), 310.

The ongoing rivalry between the Ministry of Transport and the Ministry of Finance was definitely a central factor. Simultaneous conflict between the War Ministry and the Ministry of Finance arose out of their competition for limited fiscal resources, and this circumstance also explains much of the persistent difficulty between the two ministries.[13] In addition, they were grappling over the division of responsibilities in railroad affairs, which had traditionally been the exclusive realm of the Transport Ministry.

The conflict grew increasingly sharp as they struggled for control of both the extensive state railroad network and the new system of unified railroad tariffs. In 1887 the State Council asked the ministries of finance, transport, and state domains and the state comptroller to work together on a tariff law that would permit the state to regulate this critical economic ingredient in its own interest. Because of bitter disagreement between Vyshnegradskii and Pos'et, the issue would not be resolved until Pos'et resigned.[14] Vyshnegradskii apparently felt that if the unified tariff were left up to the engineers, it would never get done.[15] Pos'et, meanwhile, wanted tariff affairs centralized in his ministry rather than in the Ministry of Finance. According to N. N. Iznar, an official in the tariff institutions, "the controversy arose . . . because of individuals, i.e., . . . on the one side, Minister of Finance Vyshnegradskii with S. Iu. Witte behind him, and on the other K. N. Pos'et. Thus this reform . . . of great state importance was delayed as a result of a completely fortuitous circumstance."[16]

### The War Ministry's Desires

If Pos'et's responsibility for railroad affairs and the independent existence of his ministry were threatened by the Ministry of Finance, the Ministry of Transport's control over the Siberian Railroad project was threatened by the War Ministry, itself locked in struggle with the Ministry of Finance.[17]

13. See William C. Fuller, Jr., *Civil-Military Conflict in Imperial Russia, 1881–1914* (Princeton, 1985), xxii, 59, 61.
14. J. N. Westwood, *A History of Russian Railways* (London, 1964), 84; Shepelev, *Tsarizm*, 170. According to Polovtsov, their dispute over the question in the State Council reached the level of "rudeness" (*Dnevnik*, 2:96 [Mar. 26, 1888]).
15. F. G. Terner, *Vospominaniia zhizni*, vol. 2 (St. Petersburg, 1911), 178.
16. Quoted in Shepelev, *Tsarizm*, 162–163.
17. On the dispute between the finance and war ministries see Fuller, *Civil-Military Conflict*, 47–74.

"Because of the chiefly strategic character" of the Siberian Railroad, in June 1887 the special conferences had ordered the Siberian governors general to take charge of surveys for the railroad.[18] In effect the government was in the process of placing the project in the hands of the Ministry of War. Heading it would be General M. N. Annenkov, renowned for his rapid railroad building in Central Asia. Pos'et was so outraged that he threatened to resign.[19]

Again a personal element was present, Annenkov having been the originator of the idea to create the Baranov Commission, then its chief administrator.[20] In this capacity he was already a direct threat to Pos'et, and his strategic railroad building redounded to the credit of the War Ministry and detracted from the image of the Ministry of Transport. The London *Times* called Annenkov the "enemy" of Pos'et.[21]

Pos'et fought back. In his "most humble report" of June 12, 1887, to the tsar, he called attention to shortcomings in public works undertaken by the War Ministry and maintained that "construction of railroads could be accomplished with the most guaranteed success solely by that department within the governmental structure which was called into existence to direct the creation of state means of communication."[22] Both he and War Minister P. S. Vannovskii then went to the tsar at Peterhof to settle their dispute. The tsar refused to accept Pos'et's offer of resignation and "to give some satisfaction to the offended minister" ordered the governors general, who normally answered to the war minister, to be responsible to the minister of transport in the case of the Siberian Railroad. After the meeting, General Vannovskii departed for a leave of absence in the Caucasus; fortunately for Pos'et, illness made Vannovskii an ineffective minister.[23] For the time being, at least, the project was safe in the hands of Pos'et, but Annenkov was disappointed and more problems would occur later, when he and Vyshnegradskii would find common ground against a later minister of transport.

Pos'et resigned as minister on November 7, 1888, after a railroad

18. A. N. Kulomzin, *Le Transsibérien*, trans. Jules Legras (Paris, 1904), 31; Sabler and Sosnovskii, *Sibirskaia zheleznaia doroga*, 73, 75; MPS, *Istoricheskii ocherk*, 453, 455–456.

19. *Times*, June 25, 1887, p. 9.

20. Skal'kovskii, *Deiateli*, 74; Terner, *Vospominaniia zhizni*, 2:78. At the time, Annenkov was chief of the administration of military transport in the War Ministry (A. M. Solov'eva, *Zheleznodorozhnyi transport Rossii vo vtoroi polovine XIX v.* [Moscow, 1975], 155).

21. *Times*, July 1, 1887, p. 5.

22. MPS, *Istoricheskii ocherk*, 455–456.

23. *Times*, June 29, 1887, p. 5; July 1, 1887, p. 5; Fuller, *Civil-Military Conflict*, 66.

accident at Borki, in which the tsar and his family were lucky to escape injury. The incident worked to the advantage of Vyshnegradskii, who intrigued to have Lieutenant General G. E. Pauker appointed as transport minister.[24] Pauker died in March 1889 after only a few months in office. During his short, weak-willed tenure, Vyshnegradskii refused to release any funds for new railroads.[25] He and Witte now had an opportunity to cement the Ministry of Finance's position in railroad affairs, something Pos'et had fought to prevent. Pauker attended the meeting at which the new tariff administration was discussed and, according to Witte, he "agreed to everything. Of course, he agreed because of his close friendship with Vyshnegradskii."[26] In this way Vyshnegradskii and the Ministry of Finance gained the advantage over the Ministry of Transport, making things very difficult for the next minister, Giubbenet, and his attempts to build the Siberian Railroad.

## Giubbenet

Adol'f Iakovlevich Giubbenet had served for many years as an official of the State Treasury in various provinces and from 1880 to 1885 had been Pos'et's deputy minister. For four years (1854–1858) he had traveled throughout Western Siberia on special assignment for the province's governor general, and he considered himself especially well qualified to head the Siberian Railroad project.[27] In spite of his experience (as deputy minister of transport he had had more preparation for the position than any previous transport minister), he has been portrayed as an "illiterate" in railroad affairs.[28] Polovtsov, characteristically, called him stupid, as he had Pos'et.[29] These opinions, passed down to posterity by Giubbenet's opponents, are inaccurate. Indeed, one Soviet scholar has shown that it was Giubbenet who

24. According to Vannovskii, who had his own candidate for the spot (Polovtsov, *Dnevnik*, 2:124 [Dec. 8, 1888]).

25. Even an official railroad history complained of Pauker's lack of initiative (MPS, *Istoricheskii ocherk*, 342).

26. Shepelev, *Tsarizm*, 163, quoting S. Iu. Witte, *Vospominaniia*, vol. 1 (Moscow, 1960), 252–253.

27. Brokgauz-Efron, *Entsiklopedicheskii slovar'*, vol. 18 (St. Petersburg, 1893), 954; Erik Amburger, *Geschichte der Behördenorganisation Rußlands von Peter dem Großen bis 1917* (Leiden, 1966), 266; MPS, "Otchet o deiatel'nosti," 23.

28. Richard G. Robbins, Jr., *Famine in Russia, 1891–1892: The Imperial Government Responds to a Crisis* (New York, 1975), 8–9, 77–78, 212n9, quoting Witte.

29. Polovtsov, *Dnevnik*, 2:351 (Mar. 19, 1891).

developed the plan for the realization of the Siberian Railroad which Witte adopted as his own.[30] A more balanced judgment is provided by a relatively impartial observer, the future Russian foreign minister V. N. Lamzdorf, who, commenting on the occasion of Giubbenet's resignation, admitted that his abilities did not match his intentions, but nonetheless described him as "honest" and "impartial," with "personal convictions" that he upheld "resolutely" in opposition to Vyshnegradskii and his associates.[31] He would certainly have plenty of occasion to disagree with Vyshnegradskii.

What separated Vyshnegradskii and Giubbenet from the start was the unabating rivalry between their respective ministries and an intense personal hatred that was fuel to the fire. Compromise on policy issues, let alone implementation, was well-nigh impossible under these circumstances.

The adversarial relationship had much to do with the reorganization of railroad affairs in 1889. Genuine state intervention in railroad tariffs began in that year, with the promulgation of the "Temporary Regulation for Railroad Tariffs and Tariff Institutions."[32] While Pauker was minister of transport, Vyshnegradskii had been able to form the Department of Railroad Affairs in the Ministry of Finance and on March 8, 1889, named Witte, head of the Southwestern Railroad Company and participant in the preparation of the legislation, as its director.[33] The purpose of the new department was to reduce the state railroad deficit. Witte essentially tried to take control of Russian railroad finances and leave only technical responsibility to the Ministry of Transport. His ploy was largely successful, and his department's encroachment on the Transport Ministry's territory angered Giubbenet.[34] Witte's brazenness was compounded by the fact that he was not an engineer and had been promoted seven ranks at one step when he became head of the new department. In the Ministry of Transport he was seen as an outsider and an upstart.[35]

Moreover, along with his spending policy Vyshnegradskii encour-

30. V. F. Borzunov, "Istoriia sozdaniia transsibirskoi zheleznodorozhnoi magistrali XIX–nachala XX vv." (Ph.D. diss., Tomskii Gosudarstvennyi Universitet, 1972), 515–517.

31. V. N. Lamzdorf, *Dnevnik, 1891–1892* (Moscow/Leningrad, 1934), 239 (Jan. 18, 1892).

32. *PSZRI*, sobranie tret'e, vol. 9, 1889, nos. 5831 and 6236; Brokgauz-Efron, *Novyi entsiklopedicheskii slovar'*, 12:119–120.

33. Shepelev, *Tsarizm*, 171.

34. Robbins, *Famine*, 78.

35. S. M. von Propper, *Was nicht in die Zeitung kam: Erinnerungen des Chef-redakteurs der "Birschewyja Wedomosti"* (Frankfurt am Main, 1929), 160–161.

aged a new trend in railroad building, with private, as opposed to state, construction getting the edge.[36] He expected the new tariff rules to be sufficient to prevent the earlier abuses of the private railroad barons.[37] Giubbenet was firmly opposed to this limitation of railroad building by the Treasury, in principle and because it further reduced the role of his ministry.

The upshot was an intense animosity between Giubbenet on the one side and Vyshnegradskii and Witte on the other. The hatred reached such heights that it almost came to a duel between Witte and Giubbenet.[38] With Vyshnegradskii's backing, Witte attacked Giubbenet's performance in the pages of *Moskovskie vedomosti*, at the same time boasting of his own department's importance. Their campaign against Giubbenet was a major factor in his resignation.[39] Giubbenet expressed his resentment to Polovtsov, "calling [Vyshnegradskii] and Witte thieves and contending that in all aspects of railroad affairs there was no longer [concern for] the national interest, but the exclusive pursuit of private advantage."[40]

Giubbenet's end in government came with the famine of 1891–1892 and the ensuing crisis in railroad affairs, which had been made worse by the lack of cooperation between the ministries of finance and transport. Giubbenet resented the intrusion on his ministry's area of responsibility by those in charge of implementing the relief effort on the railroads. The incident gave Meshcherskii and Vyshnegradskii an opportunity to induce the tsar to remove him. Along with the subsequent appointment of Witte as minister of transport, this coup seems to indicate that Vyshnegradskii aimed to expand his ministry's control over the Transport Ministry.[41] Although the official history attributes Giubbenet's resignation to illness, the interministerial conflict was in fact responsible.[42]

36. Brokgauz-Efron, *Novyi entsiklopedicheskii slovar'*, 12:120. Vyshnegradskii's intentions were not, apparently, carried out: state railroad building continued to be on a par with private construction in this period. See Solov'eva, *Zheleznodorozhnyi transport*, 297–298.

37. MPS, *Istoricheskii ocherk*, 361.

38. Propper, *Was nicht in die Zeitung kam*, 162. Propper reported that Witte asked Minister of the Interior I. N. Durnovo and Prince Meshcherskii to be his seconds.

39. B. V. Anan'ich and R. Sh. Ganelin, "I. A. Vyshnegradskii i S. Iu. Witte—korrespondenty 'moskovskikh vedomostei,'" in *Problemy obshchestvennoi mysli i ekonomicheskaia politika Rossii XIX–XX vekov: Pamiati prof. S. B. Okunia*, ed. N. G. Sladkevich (Leningrad, 1972), 27–30, 33–34.

40. Polovtsov, *Dnevnik*, 2:351 (Mar. 19, 1891).

41. Robbins, *Famine in Russia*, 78–79, 90–91.

42. MPS, *Kratkii istoricheskii ocherk razvitiia i deiatel'nosti vedomstva putei soobshcheniia* (St. Petersburg, 1898), 183.

Adol'f Giubbenet. From MPS, *Kratkii istoricheskii ocherk razvitiia i deiatel'nosti vedomstva putei soobshcheniia* (St. Petersburg, 1898).

The antithetical ideological viewpoints of the two ministries join with the personal and political factors to explain the never-ending maneuvering over the Siberian Railroad issue. Throughout 1889 Vyshnegradskii tightened his fiscal stranglehold on the project. At the behest of the finance minister and with the backing of Abaza, the tsar decreed that for the five-year period 1890–1894 the government would put a ceiling on its total extraordinary expenses at 300 million rubles, or 60 million rubles per year. For 1890 the Ministry of Transport was to receive 49.5 million rubles, of which only 2.5 million were allocated for the construction of new lines; the rest was to go for improvements on existing lines.[43] This insignificant sum contrasted

43. To preclude the construction of pioneer railroads such as the Trans-Siberian this sum was designated solely for railroads "of economic significance" (MPS, *Istoricheskii ocherk*, 349).

with the 34 million rubles Giubbenet had requested for the construction of new state railroads. In May 1890 Giubbenet drastically reduced his requests, but once again the Committee of Ministers refused to release any additional funds.[44]

The committee's decisions brought urgent warnings in July 1890 from the Priamur governor general that the government must not delay construction of at least the Ussuri Railroad any longer. Alexander III agreed that "it is necessary to commence construction of this road very soon."[45] The tsar's demand left no alternative, even for Vyshnegradskii: the railroad could be blocked no longer.

Vyshnegradskii did attempt to reduce the damage as much as possible by asking the tsar to convene a special conference under Abaza to concentrate solely on the Siberian Railroad. The conference met on December 12, 1890, and discussed Vyshnegradskii's memorandum of August 16 and Giubbenet's memorandum of November 15 in rebuttal. The memoranda show the continuation of the ideational conflict that had been apparent since at least 1875. They represent the cautious traditionalism of the Ministry of Finance, obsessed by the state budget, and the grandiose strategy of development put forth by the Ministry of Transport.

Vyshnegradskii recommended that the Siberian Railroad be started in the west rather than at Vladivostok in the Far East and in sections across the portages between river routes rather than as a transit or through route, thereby reducing its length from 7,000 to 3,000 versts.[46] The income needed to pay for construction of the road and prevent the accumulation of debt once it was operational could be assured in no other way. He saw the Tomsk-Irkutsk section as being of first importance, whereas the Ussuri Railroad simply did not merit the expense. He warned that if the Ussuri road were built first, eastern Siberia would fall under the influence of North America, and the "stagnation" of the Chinese led him to discount the possibility that they would build a strategic railroad in Manchuria. He concluded that

44. MPS, *Istoricheskii ocherk*, 348–350, 464, and "Otchet o deiatel'nosti" 8–10; Sabler and Sosnovskii, *Sibirskaia zheleznaia doroga*, 83–85; *ZhMPS*, official sec., 1893, no. 2: 14–15.

45. MPS, *Istoricheskii ocherk*, 466, and "Otchet o deiatel'nosti," 12; Sabler and Sosnovskii, *Sibirskaia zheleznaia doroga*, 86.

46. Vyshnegradskii insisted on the same requirements for the proposed Trans-Persian Railroad, in a report of 1888 to Foreign Minister Giers. See Konstantin Pobedonostsev, *L'Autocratie russe: Mémoires politiques, correspondance officielle et documents inédits relatifs à l'histoire du règne de l'empereur Alexandre III de Russie* (Paris, 1927), 543–545.

"the construction of this road must proceed *gradually* . . . so that the local population, as well as the state, may derive some benefit from the matter." His criterion was the amount of income generated by each section, and the only possibility he admitted was construction of the central Siberian section.[47]

Giubbenet offered a plan characteristic for his ministry. Rather than decide the question on the basis of hypothetical cost estimates for the various sections of the railroad, he said, the government should "evaluate the enormous political, economic, and national significance of a continuous Siberian Railroad in the future." He roundly opposed the finance minister's proposal to build individual "portage lines" beginning from the west: without a direct line to the European Russian rail network, each section would be of little significance. Only a transit route built from both ends would benefit Russia. He estimated the total cost, which he compared with that of the Canadian-Pacific Railroad, at 362,479,258 rubles for 7,474 versts, including branch lines and bridges across major rivers.[48]

Giubbenet's opposition to Vyshnegradskii's mixed water-rail route was supported by the majority of engineers and businessmen in the professional societies, who argued that the cost of rail portages in time alone was high: trains would have to load and unload eight times, even those carrying soldiers to battle, and the line could operate only when the rivers were free of ice. They agreed with Giubbenet that the railroad was of more than economic importance: these distant, inseparable parts of the empire could be linked to "native Russia" only by a through route.[49]

47. Emphasis mine. Sabler and Sosnovskii, *Sibirskaia zheleznaia doroga*, 86–87; *ZhMPS*, official sec., 1893, no. 2: 17–18; MPS, "Otchet o deiatel'nosti," 12, and *Istoricheskii ocherk*, 468–469. For the exact route of Vyshnegradskii's portage railroad see *TOSRPT*, vol. 21, otdel 1 (St. Petersburg, 1892), 10. The minister of finance's proposal had its origins in Ostrovskii's project of 1880, as we saw in chap. 5, although the earliest proponent of a mixed water-rail route across Siberia appears to have been the minister of transport, P. P. Mel'nikov, in 1866. See M. I. Voronin and M. M. Voronina, *Pavel Petrovich Mel'nikov, 1804–1880* (Leningrad, 1977), 94.

48. MPS, *Istoricheskii ocherk*, 467–470, and "Otchet o deiatel'nosti," 13–19; Sabler and Sosnovskii, *Sibirskaia zheleznaia doroga*, 87–90.

49. See *TIRTO*, 2:8, 38:5; Sovet moskovskogo otdeleniia OSRPT, *Otkuda nachat' postroiku sibirskoi zheleznoi dorogi i v vide-li nepreryvnoi linii ili pereryvchatoi?* (Moscow, 1891), 4–5; *TOSRPT*, vol. 21, otdel 1 (1892), 9–14; "Zasedanie OSRPT po dokladu P. E. Gronskogo: 'Kak stroit' sibirskuiu dorogu?'" *TOSRPT*, vol. 21, otdel 2 (1892), 9, 23; "Tikhookeanskaia-kanadskaia i sibirskaia zheleznye dorogi," *ZhdD*, 1887, nos. 25–26: 192; "'O velikom sibirskom puti v sviazi s pravitel'stvennnymi izyskaniiami' (Doklad N. A. Sytenko i beseda v VIII otdele IRTO)," *ZhdD*, 1888, nos. 22–24: 180; N. A. Voloshinov, "Sibirskaia zheleznaia doroga," *IIRGO* 27 (1891): 32–33; A. I. Chuprov, *Iz proshlogo russkikh zheleznykh dorog: Stat'i 1874–1895 godov* (Moscow, 1909), 179–184.

In the end the conference decided nothing. It found that it could not exceed the 7-million-ruble limit for new railroads set for 1891 and that it was up to the Committee of Ministers to decide which new railroads should be built. Giubbenet accordingly took his memorandum there.

In its session of February 12, 1891, the committee acknowledged the primary importance to the government of building a transit route through Siberia. On February 15, 1891, the tsar approved the committee's resolution to build the Ussuri Railroad and in the near future the Trans-Siberian Railroad. For political and strategic reasons, the Committee of Ministers no longer concurred with the minister of finance. After seventeen years of discussion, it decided that the time was right for the railroad conceived by the Ministry of Transport and that it would be built by the state.[50]

Vyshnegradskii could not oppose the resolution, but he repeated his concern that construction of a railroad up to 7,500 versts in length at a cost of more than 300 million rubles would have an adverse effect on Russian securities and become a serious burden on the Treasury once it opened to traffic. He urged the state to proceed with the utmost caution. Abaza, wary as ever, stood behind him.[51]

Vyshnegradskii continued to stall the project by passing the buck to Abaza. Once the State Council approved credits for the Ussuri Railroad, Giubbenet felt confident enough to draw up a schedule for completion of the whole through route, in the form of a memorandum to Vyshnegradskii dated August 9, 1891. His plan extended over a twelve-year period, envisaging completion of the whole road from Cheliabinsk to Vladivostok by 1903. He inquired as to the source of the 350 million rubles he estimated construction would cost. Vyshnegradskii responded on September 13, 1891, that the transport minister's estimate of 47,000 rubles per verst seemed "very high." In any case, the assignment of credits for the Siberian Railroad would be up to the special conference under Abaza which would review extraordinary expenses for 1892.[52]

Abaza fixed the amount of credits for new railroad construction in 1892 at a mere 5.9 million rubles. After reviewing the proceedings of

50. Sabler and Sosnovskii, *Sibirskaia zheleznaia doroga*, 90–93; MPS, *Istoricheskii ocherk*, 356–357, 470–472, and "Otchet o deiatel'nosti," 22–24.

51. Sabler and Sosnovskii, *Sibirskaia zheleznaia doroga*, 92; MPS, *Istoricheskii ocherk*, 357.

52. MPS, *Istoricheskii ocherk*, 472, 479–482, and "Otchet o deiatel'nosti," 30–33; Sabler and Sosnovskii, *Sibirskaia zheleznaia doroga*, 92.

the special conference, the tsar augmented the sum by 1.1 million rubles to permit the extension of the Siberian line to Cheliabinsk and provide additional funds for the Ussuri Railroad, if nothing else.[53] Only with the tsar's intervention was the level of credits assigned to the project increased.

Again, though, Vyshnegradskii attempted to circumvent Giubbenet—and the Committee of Ministers—so that Treasury funds would not be used for railroad construction, in particular for the Siberian Railroad. Allied with him was Annenkov, who, in seeking French financing for the railroad, still aimed to win the project away from the Transport Ministry and place himself in charge.

### Financial Desperation

By late 1888 the Russian government's fiscal outlook had improved (at least on paper) to the point where it was possible for Vyshnegradskii to persuade French banking houses to convert the onerous German loans made during the Russo-Turkish War. This was the beginning of the financial relationship between France and Russia which became so extensive over the next two decades and preceded the formation of the Franco-Russian military alliance.[54]

The tsar was interested in using the French financial connection to make a political statement against Germany, but also, it seems, to secure financing for the Trans-Siberian Railroad.[55] Indeed, although Vyshnegradskii wanted to shift Russian borrowing from foreign to domestic sources, especially for railroad construction, for the Siberian Railroad he favored the use of French capital to prevent a drain on his ever-fragile budget.

The idea was proposed by General Annenkov, still angling for the lead role in building the railroad, and Vyshnegradskii found himself allied with him against the minister of transport.[56] Annenkov knew he

53. Kulomzin, *Le Transsibérien*, 40.

54. Skal'kovskii, *Ministres des finances*, 281; Kennan, *Decline*, 380–382, 387, 389. The condition of the Russian state budget was in fact tenuous at best at the moment, as it depended largely on the fortuitous circumstance of good harvests in 1887 and 1888 (Skal'kovskii, *Ministres des finances*, 283, 286, 289–292). On the conversion operations, see A. L. Sidorov, "Konversii vneshnikh zaimov Rossii v 1888–1890 gg.," *Istoricheskii arkhiv*, 1959, no. 3: 99–125. In *Dnevnik*, 2:344 (Jan. 24, 1891), Polovtsov claims that Vyshnegradskii profited personally from commissions on the renegotiated loans.

55. Herbert Feis, *Europe the World's Banker, 1870–1914* (New Haven, 1930), 214–215.

56. *Times*, Mar. 5, 1891, p. 5; Polovtsov, *Dnevnik*, 2:312 (Aug. 14, 1890).

would get Vyshnegradskii's support if he found funding outside of state coffers. Vyshnegradskii supported Annenkov out of concern for his budget and as a way of dealing another blow to Giubbenet. As the London *Times* reported, the issue of who would be in charge of the project, Annenkov or the minister of transport, still had not been settled decisively, regardless of the tsar's decisions of 1887. Giubbenet recognized the threat and insisted that he supervise construction of the railroad for the "prestige and *raison d'être*" of his ministry.[57]

But Annenkov was persistent. His initiative and drive alone had been responsible for surmounting the immense geographical and political obstacles in the way of the Transcaspian Railroad and for bringing it to completion. For this accomplishment he was awarded one of the highest honors of the Russian government, the Order of Alexander Nevskii with diamonds.[58] One is under the impression that Annenkov—like Ferdinand de Lesseps, with whom he shared many personal characteristics—was motivated by a quest for personal glory (and certainly financial gain) in attempting to take charge of what was at the time one of the greatest engineering projects ever attempted.[59]

Annenkov's energy and international recognition for the Transcaspian Railroad would help him in France, as would his personal French connection: his daughter was married to Viscount Eugène Melchior de Vogüé, former member of the French embassy in St. Petersburg, an authority on Russian affairs and literature, and habitué of the highest French political circles. Annenkov would use his acquaintance with French financiers and politicians to the fullest over the next few years. For their part, French capitalists were very interested in the Siberian Railroad project because of the expected expansion of industry it would bring, which promised a higher return on their other Russian investments.[60]

In early 1890, one of the French Rothschilds went with Annenkov to Merv in Turkestan. Annenkov received a promise of full financial support for the Siberian Railroad, but, according to Annenkov, only if he were placed in charge of the project. Vyshnegradskii pledged his support, but only after he inspected the Transcaspian Railroad to

57. *Times*, Sept. 6, 1889, p. 3; Feb. 26, 1891, p. 5.

58. Skal'kovskii, *Deiateli*, 73, 75–76.

59. On Lesseps, see David McCullough, *The Path between the Seas: The Creation of the Panama Canal, 1870–1914* (New York, 1977).

60. Kennan, *Decline*, 283–284; René Girault, "Les Relations économiques et financières entre la France et la Russie de 1887 à 1914" (Ph.D. diss., Université de Paris, 1971), 1:367. According to Girault, Vogüé was Annenkov's brother-in-law (*Emprunts russes et investissements français en Russie, 1887–1914* [Paris, 1973], 190).

assess Annenkov's performance. Annenkov went to Paris for talks with the Rothschilds on the Siberian Railroad, and it was widely thought that financing was guaranteed. By August 1890, as he left Paris, Annenkov felt confident that French bankers, in particular the Rothschilds, were ready to offer their financial support to his railroad project. With the blessing of Vyshnegradskii, the Rothschild firm seemed ready to play a leading role in the construction of the Siberian Railroad, as well as to gain dominance over Baku oil exporting.[61]

The Rothschilds offered 300 million rubles. Annenkov could work with this sum: he proposed to build the 7,000-verst railroad for 40,000 rubles per verst and still gain 20 million rubles for himself. He then assured the Committee of Ministers in January 1891 that he could complete the road across Siberia to Vladivostok in just three years.[62]

But it was not to be. Annenkov immediately suffered a string of setbacks in his quest for foreign funding. First, Vyshnegradskii came out against his proposals, perhaps because he foresaw that such rapid construction could not be accomplished without financial loss, which the Treasury would ultimately have to cover, or because of the unsatisfactory condition of the Transcaspian Railroad, for which Annenkov was responsible.[63]

Next, in February 1891 the Committee of Ministers announced that the Treasury would finance the building of the Siberian Railroad. Behind this decision had been Giubbenet, of course, but also Witte, who had argued strongly against any foreign involvement in the railroad as potentially harmful to the national interest, even if French financing should be solicited for the infrastructure necessary to complete the project. Finally, the Rothschilds withdrew from the picture altogether, severing financial ties with the Russian government largely to protest the expulsion of the Jews from Moscow in March 1891.[64]

61. Polovtsov, *Dnevnik*, 2:280 (May 3, 1890); Girault, *Emprunts russes*, 184, 190. In Paris Annenkov discussed a memorandum he had drawn up earlier that year for the war minister in which he suggested that foreign capital underwrite the company constructing the Siberian Railroad (Sabler and Sosnovskii, *Sibirskaia zheleznaia doroga*, 103; Polovtsov, *Dnevnik*, 2:499n26; V. F. Borzunov and A. N. Kalinin, "Bor'ba amerikanskogo i frantsuzskogo kapitala za zheleznodorozhnye kontsessii v Sibiri i na Dal'nem Vostoke v kontse XIX veka," in *Bakhrushinskie chteniia 1966 g.*, no. 2, *Sibir' perioda feodalizma i kapitalizma*, ed. A. P. Okladnikov et al. [Novosibirsk, 1968], 131–133).

62. Girault, "Relations économiques," 1:360–361; Polovtsov, *Dnevnik*, 2:343 (Jan. 15, 1891).

63. Polovtsov, *Dnevnik*, 2:343 (Jan. 15, 1891). On the condition of the Transcaspian Railroad, see *Tri poslednikh samoderzhtsa: Dnevnik A. V. Bogdanovich* (Moscow/Leningrad, 1924), 139 (July 4, 1891); and Westwood, *Russian Railways*, 125–127.

64. Girault, *Emprunts russes*, 180–190; Polovtsov, *Dnevnik*, 2:499n26.

Seemingly desperate for the job, Annenkov turned to an unnamed acquaintance who promised him that if he loaned 50,000 rubles to Duchess Zina, whose husband, the Duke of Leuchtenberg, was a relative of the tsar, he would be assured of getting his wish. Annenkov did so, borrowing the money from Polovtsov, who could not refuse because he wanted Annenkov to build a railroad of personal interest to himself, but nothing came of it.[65]

At the same time, Annenkov was approaching still more French financiers. In August 1890 Senator Charles Lesueur had formed a company to survey the possible conditions under which the Siberian Railroad might be constructed. Included in its membership were M. Duportal, director of French state railroads; Senator P. Decauville, director of the Decauville works and administrator of the Banque d'Escompte; and other prominent engineers who had been involved in the management of large enterprises, including the Suez and Panama canals. In August 1890 Duportal went to St. Petersburg to set up a branch of the company.[66] According to one source, Annenkov had attracted the group to St. Petersburg by promising to get them the construction contract if they would give him 200 million francs to bribe the relevant officials.[67] In March 1891, Giubbenet, with the implicit backing of Witte and the Committee of Ministers, turned down the company's proposal, on the grounds that "the government has not expressed any intention of turning to private enterprise in this matter."[68]

Annenkov still refused to quit, and when circumstances changed, he and the French financiers were given one final opportunity. The devastating harvests of 1890 and 1891 and the milestone famine of 1891–1892, whatever their causes, paralyzed the Russian economy and shattered the image of financial solidity the government wanted to present to the world.[69] When the fragility of state income was thus

65. Polovtsov, *Dnevnik*, 2:343 (Jan. 15, 1891). Polovtsov wanted Annenkov to build the Bogoslovskii Railroad in the Urals. Polovtsov's industrial interests in the northern Urals are discussed in chap. 8.

66. Girault, *Emprunts russes*, 231; Borzunov and Kalinin, "Bor'ba," 122; Sabler and Sosnovskii, *Sibirskaia zheleznaia doroga*, 102; Kulomzin *Le Transsibérien*, 38; MPS, *Istoricheskii ocherk*, 477.

67. *Tri poslednikh samoderzhtsa*, 227 (Jan. 12, 1899). Two days before this entry was written, Annenkov had swallowed poison and committed suicide to avoid court proceedings initiated by War Minister A. N. Kuropatkin for misappropriating 50,000 rubles from his ministry (Borzunov and Kalinin, "Bor ba," 135).

68. *Times*, Apr. 6, 1891, p. 6; Sabler and Sosnovskii, *Sibirskaia zheleznaia doroga*, 102–103; Kulomzin, *Le Transsibérien*, 38; MPS, *Istoricheskii ocherk*, 477–478.

69. On the famine, see Robbins, *Famine in Russia*. For the traditional interpretation— i.e., that Vyshnegradskii's policies bore primary responsibility for the famine—see

revealed, the governing elite panicked.[70] The demands on the Treasury were enormous, and to avoid excessive reliance on the printing press to supply the needed funds, Vyshnegradskii sent out feelers to reestablish ties with the Rothschilds and even German financial sources. Now even Witte, named minister of transport on February 27, 1892, realized that if the Siberian Railroad were to be started that year, foreign financing in some direct form would be essential.[71]

With this knowledge, Lesueur and Decauville renewed their proposal to the tsar, who received them at Tsarevich Nicholas's urging. Alexander explained the state's policy, but said he would review the matter and consult with Vyshnegradskii. At Polovtsov's suggestion they offered to place on the French market the 200 million rubles that Vyshnegradskii had hoped but failed to get through the Rothschilds. Vyshnegradskii agreed "*avec joie*," confident that the loan would go through. Decauville returned to Paris in March to organize the loan, but found no interest there. After one more bid by Lesueur in April, their attempts—and those of Annenkov—had reached an end.[72]

With the foreign money markets unwilling to assist, Witte and Vyshnegradskii had to come up with a solution. Witte "resigned himself" to proposing a domestic loan of 75 million rubles at 4.5 percent to finance the Siberian project. The public refused to come to the government's assistance, however, and subscriptions were not forthcoming: of 75 million rubles offered, only 15 million were placed.[73]

Vyshnegradskii despaired of finding financing at home or abroad.[74]

Theodore H. Von Laue, *Sergei Witte and the Industrialization of Russia* (New York, 1973), 30–31.

70. Brokgauz-Efron, *Entsiklopedicheskii slovar'*, 12:122; Skal'kovskii, *Ministres des finances*, 294.

71. Girault, *Emprunts russes*, 220, 229–233.

72. Polovtsov, *Dnevnik*, 2:421–424 (Feb. 15, 16, 18, 1892), 449 (Apr. 20, 1892); Girault, *Emprunts russes*, 230–231. In July 1892 Annenkov was apparently still soliciting foreign financiers. He contacted an American banker whom he had met in Paris in 1888, Wharton Barker of Philadelphia, and implied that the tsar desired to grant a concession for the Siberian Railroad to an American because of the difficulties experienced with the French. Annenkov hinted that for Barker, the guarantee offered by the government might be "1 to 1.5 percent more than to a Jew." See George Sherman Queen, *The United States and the Material Advance in Russia, 1881–1906* (New York, 1976), 180–183.

73. Girault, *Emprunts russes*, 231, 234. Other railroad loans issued by the government in 1891 and 1892 received little response as well because of the poor state credit. See Brokgauz-Efron, *Entsiklopedicheskii slovar'*, 12:120–121, and A. Ivashchenkov, *Kratkii obzor ispolneniia gosudarstvennykh rospisei (v sviazi s prochimi oborotami gosudarstvennogo kaznacheistva) za 1881–1899 g.g.* (St. Petersburg, 1901), table XXV.

74. Polovtsov, *Dnevnik*, 2:435 (Mar. 16, 1892). For the drastic drop in funding provided by loans between 1890 and 1891, see P. A. Khromov, *Ekonomicheskoe razvitie Rossii s drevneishikh vremen do velikoi oktiabr'skoi revoliutsii* (Moscow, 1967), table 25-b.

He learned, as S. M. von Propper put it, that "for Russia, as of old, it remains valid to claim that the only finance minister is Mother Harvest." Illness overtook him as he worked through the night during the crisis.[75] He went so far as to propose that Russia adopt a progressive income tax, then in the summer departed for a long leave in the Crimea.[76] In August Witte replaced him as finance minister.

This, then, was the situation Witte inherited, with the question of financing the Siberian Railroad still unresolved.


### The Divisive Government

It had taken more than a decade and a half for the imperial Russian government to decide to build the Siberian Railroad. The circumstances required for quick action did not exist, a fact that requires a reassessment of the notion of the state's preeminent ability to develop the country's economy. Tsarist economic policy, which has generally been portrayed as coherent and vigorous, in truth lacked consensus. The internecine conflicts among ministries and ministers made it virtually impossible for the various branches of the bureaucracy to work as one on economic issues, let alone compromise or accomplish anything.[77]

The autocratic system was responsible for much of the problem. As the supreme authority, the tsar was the ultimate arbiter of disputes within the bureaucracy.[78] Ministers thus competed to influence him in their favor, with the natural result that government was highly fractious.[79] As we have seen, the tsar's was the final word on the

75. Propper, *Was nicht in die Zeitung kam*, 138, 151.

76. Girault, *Emprunts russes*, 232.

77. This conclusion meshes with the findings of John P. McKay, who shows that the government's prevarication, bureaucratic rivalry, and inertia left the transportation problems of the Baku oil industry unsolved ("Baku Oil and Transcaucasian Pipelines, 1883–1891: A Study in Tsarist Economic Policy," *Slavic Review* 43 [1984]: 604–623). On this basis he disputes the assumption of "dynamic state leadership in Russian industrialization."

78. Contrary to the assertion of George L. Yaney that the tsar was a tool in his ministers' hands (*The Systematization of Russian Government: Social Evolution in the Domestic Administration of Imperial Russia, 1711–1905* [Urbana, Ill., 1973], 281–282). At the same time, Yaney (p. 299) somewhat contradictorily and equally incorrectly implies that Alexander III had improved coordination among ministries.

79. See Jacob W. Kipp and W. Bruce Lincoln, "Autocracy and Reform: Bureaucratic Absolutism and Political Modernization in Nineteenth-Century Russia," *Russian History* 6, pt. 1 (1979): 16; also Donald W. Green, "Industrialization and the Engineering

decision to build the Trans-Siberian, on who would control the project, and on the amount of funding to be devoted to it.

The government was hamstrung by ministerial strife. In economic policy, bitter disputes arose over how best to create a strong, viable nation out of weakness, and the solutions offered were mutually exclusive. Fiscal conservatism held sway in the Ministry of Finance as it trod softly on the thin ice of Russian finances. Such a solution was not solely a matter of exigency; it also reflected the ministry's basic distrust of innovation, a long-standing characteristic antedating the Crimean War. Before Witte's appointment as its head, the Ministry of Finance had little interest in economic development.[80]

Opposed to the pinchpenny complacency of the Ministry of Finance was the technocratic vision of the Ministry of Transport, which advocated active government intervention in the economy, in particular the development of the empire's vast unsettled territories. This was the only element in the government to have what Alexander Gerschenkron posited as the precondition for overcoming backwardness: a powerful, almost spiritual faith in economic development.[81] As such, it encountered only hostility and found itself isolated, even by those who may have shared its political views. The Transport Ministry's troubles with the Ministry of Finance over the Siberian Railroad were a symptom of the disagreements between them over these fundamental issues, one side preoccupied with the practical problem of balancing the budget, the other willing to risk deficit spending to realize its hopes for the future.

The Russian bureaucracy was not yet sure which road to follow until Witte took the decisive steps on the path first plotted by the Ministry of Transport. He would resolve, or perhaps circumvent, the

Ascendancy: A Comparative Study of American and Russian Engineering Elites, 1870–1920" (Ph.D. diss., University of California, Berkeley, 1972), 97–98.

80. Shepelev, *Tsarizm*, passim. This analysis refutes assertions that Reutern, Bunge, and Vyshnegradskii held the same views and were of the same mold as Witte. Cf. I. F. Gindin, "Russia's Industrialization under Capitalism as Seen by Theodor [sic] von Laue," *Soviet Studies in History* 11, no. 1 (1972): 6; Jacob W. Kipp, "M. Kh. Reutern on the Russian State and Economy: A Liberal Bureaucrat during the Crimean Era, 1854–60," *Journal of Modern History* 47 (September 1975).

81. Alexander Gerschenkron, *Economic Backwardness in Historical Perspective: A Book of Essays* (Cambridge, 1970), 24–25. Gerschenkron also argued that this element was central to Russian Marxism; Thomas C. Owen has asserted that a similar attitude developed among a small group of Moscow business leaders, in "Entrepreneurship and the Structure of Enterprise in Russia, 1800–1880," in Guroff and Carstensen, *Entrepreneurship*, 81.

disputes over the Siberian Railroad by removing his opponents and creating his own policy-making agency, the Committee of the Siberian Railroad. He therefore imposed consensus and, for several years at least, the state seemed to be of a single mind and perhaps capable of operating with verve. Yet this new modus operandi generated its own set of problems, and the subsequent history of the Siberian Railroad would vindicate Vyshnegradskii and its earlier opponents.

# PART III

# CREATION

# CHAPTER SEVEN

# A State
# within a State

The leading spirit and force behind the construction of the Trans-Siberian Railroad was Sergei Witte (1849–1915).[1] After his death, many people remembered him above all for this railroad, which they considered among his greatest accomplishments.[2] Yet its importance in his career has been given short shrift in the historical literature.

Upon becoming minister of finance, Witte saw the completion of the Siberian Railroad as his first priority. After Tsarevich Nicholas's trip to the Far East, it had become a very popular idea in Russia.[3] Immediately after Witte's appointment, Alexander III told him that he wanted more than anything else to see the railroad built, after ten years of bureaucratic delay.[4]

The tsar's backing contributed to Witte's success against the odds in bringing the Siberian Railroad to fruition. But he would still need to devote all his formidable energy and means to it. The methods he

1. He claimed so himself in S. Iu. Witte, *Vospominaniia*, vol. 1 (Moscow, 1960), 432–433: "I assiduously adhered to the idea of building the Great Siberian way; as much as previous ministers hindered the undertaking, I bore in mind the behests of Emperor Alexander III and tried as quickly as possible to accomplish it. . . . I would not be exaggerating if I were to say that this great undertaking was totally a result of my energy, of course backed up first by Emperor Alexander III and later by Emperor Nicholas II."

2. See the comments of contemporaries in B. B. Glinskii, "Graf Sergei Iul'evich Witte (Materialy dlia biografii)," *Istoricheskii vestnik* 140 (April 1915): 232–279.

3. F. G. Terner, *Vospominaniia zhizni*, vol. 2 (St. Petersburg, 1911), 222n1. The Soviet historian B. A. Romanov points out that until 1892, when he became transport minister, Witte showed no interest in the Far East, but from then on the Siberian Railroad was one of his main concerns (*Russia in Manchuria [1892–1906]*, trans. Susan Wilbur Jones [New York, 1974], 38).

4. Witte, *Vospominaniia*, 1:382, 432–433.

used were the same ones he would use throughout his career; his performance brings into focus both his successes and his failures over the long term of his public life, as well as the direction of Russian economic policy as a whole at the end of the nineteenth century.

## An Adventurer's Career

Witte's career was head-spinning. As one eulogist wrote, it was not out of the ordinary that in democratic America Abraham Lincoln had become president. But in imperial Russia it was unheard of for a railroad man with low official rank to achieve the political prominence Witte did. It is testimony to his extraordinary character and talents.[5]

Peter Struve pointed out that although Witte was an official most of his life, born and bred in that milieu, "he was not a functionary." His nature was through and through entrepreneurial; he was "an 'adventurer' in an official's uniform." In other centuries, in other places, he would have been a Spanish conquistador, an English or Dutch explorer.[6] Indeed, by virtue of his role in the development of Siberia, Witte should be considered one of the greatest colonizers in Russian history, in the tradition of Jakob Sievers, Grigorii Potemkin, Mikhail Speranskii, Murav'ev-Amurskii, and Konstantin Kaufman. He was active at a time when new empires were founded, continents settled, and nations unified. As he saw it, his life's task was similar in the vast, unsettled wilderness of Siberia, the largest land mass of the Russian empire.[7]

Witte's childhood and early professional career shaped his conception of the Siberian Railroad. His family was involved in the Russian colonization of the Caucasus, where his father and grandfather were colonial administrators. Here he was raised, and the frontier spirit of

5. A. E. Kaufman, "Cherty iz zhizni gr. S. Iu. Witte," *Istoricheskii vestnik* 140 (April 1915): 220. On the social obstacles he faced and Alexander III's steadfast confidence in him, see V. V. Shulgin, *The Years: Memoirs of a Member of the Russian Duma, 1906–1917,* trans. Tanya Davis (New York, 1984), 82.

6. Peter Struve, "Witte und Stolypin," in *Menschen die Geschichte Machten,* vol. 3, ed. Peter Richard Rohden and Georg Ostrogorsky (Vienna, 1931), 264.

7. According to Izvol'skii, Russian foreign minister from 1906 to 1910, Witte took Cecil Rhodes, the "empire builder," as his model. This account may have some relevance for Siberia, although strictly speaking Izvol'skii refers to Witte's activities in Manchuria (*Recollections of a Foreign Minister: Memoirs of Alexander Iswolsky,* trans. Charles Louis Seeger [New York, 1921], 121).

the region left a strong impression on him. It is no wonder that Witte turned to the colonization of Siberia: his fondest childhood memories, he wrote, were of the colonizers of the Caucasus.[8]

After receiving a degree in mathematics from Novorossiisk University, Witte entered railroad administration with the Odessa State Railroad, later reorganized into the Southwestern Railroad Company. He became its business manager and in 1886 its executive director. To increase the railroad's traffic, he strove to stimulate the economic activity of the region it served.[9] He took a position unique within Russia: that railroads could create wealth and have an impact on a wide geographical region, and he would apply these principles when he built the Siberian Railroad.

Witte's talent and energy overcame all obstacles to advancement. His contemporaries attested to his driving ambition, fighting spirit, and tireless capacity for work.[10] According to Struve, Witte possessed not so much insight as a supreme will to achieve. The Trans-Siberian Railroad, the gold standard, and the state spirits monopoly were not his ideas, but he *accomplished* them.[11]

His rapid and formidable leap from a local office to the highest level of government were also no doubt expedited by his flair for scheming. Witte made use of personal contacts, whatever their reputation, to form political alliances of convenience. He funded *Grazhdanin*, the paper of the reactionary Meshcherskii, with whom he lunched several times a week; he curried favor with Grand Prince Nikolai Nikolaevich; and, in an attempt late in life to stage a political comeback, he established contact with the empress's confidant, the debauched pseudo holy man Grigorii Rasputin.[12] He did not hesitate to ally himself with former antagonists, such as Bunge, if it was in his interest to do so.

At the same time, Witte was not scrupulous about turning on erstwhile benefactors, such as Vyshnegradskii. They first became acquainted while Vyshnegradskii was a director of the Southwestern

8. Witte, *Vospominaniia*, 1:48–58; Theodore H. Von Laue, *Sergei Witte and the Industrialization of Russia* (New York, 1973), 39–43.

9. Von Laue, *Sergei Witte*, 43–47.

10. See, for instance, V. I. Kovalevskii on Witte in L. E. Shepelev, *Tsarizm i burzhuaziia vo vtoroi polovine XIX veke: Problemy torgovo-promyshlennoi politiki* (Leningrad, 1981), 196.

11. Struve, "Witte und Stolypin," 265.

12. P. A. Zaionchkovskii, *Rossiiskoe samoderzhavie v kontse XIX stoletiia: Politicheskaia reaktsiia 80-kh–nachala 90-kh godov* (Moscow, 1970), 146; Ernst Seraphim, "Zar Nikolaus II. und Graf Witte: Eine historisch-psychologische Studie," *Historische Zeitschrift* 161, no. 2 (1940): 282.

Railroad Company in St. Petersburg.[13] They campaigned together
against their enemies in government, and the alliance brought its
rewards. As soon as Witte entered government, though, he began to
intrigue against his mentor. After he became transport minister and
Vyshnegradskii refused funds for the Siberian Railroad, their rivalry
flared up.[14] To predispose Alexander III against Vyshnegradskii, Witte
fed him untoward information about the finance minister's mental
condition after he fell ill, hoping to have Vyshnegradskii removed from
office and receive the appointment himself.[15]

Witte was also adroit at promoting himself and his various policies
and projects in the press. He surreptitiously advertised himself for the
position as head of the new Department of Railroad Affairs in *Moskovskie vedomosti*, just as later he propagandized on behalf of the Siberian Railroad.[16] His extensive use of domestic and foreign newspapers
was brilliant, if manipulative, and showed that he acted as a truly
modern political figure.[17] All of his tactics would be put to good effect
in the Ministry of Finance as well as in the Committee of the Siberian
Railroad.

## Political Beliefs

If Witte was ambitious personally, he was no less so for his country
and its autocratic form of government. He was a conservative bureaucrat whose Slavophilism, although it underwent permutation,
remained with him his whole life.[18] Raised in a religious family as a

13. Von Laue, *Sergei Witte*, 45–46.

14. According to Witte, this was the reason for their estrangement (Witte, *Vospominaniia*, 1:283).

15. On Witte's intrigues against Vyshnegradskii see Zaionchkovskii, *Rossiiskoe
samoderzhavie*, 146–147. According to Polovtsov, in *Dnevnik gosudarstvennogo sekretaria A. A. Polovtsova*, vol. 2, ed. P. A. Zaionchkovskii (Moscow, 1966), 448 (Apr. 17, 1892),
Witte said that Vyshnegradskii was not trustworthy.

16. B. V. Anan'ich and R. Sh. Ganelin, "I. A. Vyshnegradskii i S. Iu. Witte—korrespondenty 'Moskovskikh vedomostei,'" in *Problemy obshchestvennoi mysli i ekonomicheskaia politika Rossii XIX–XX vekov: Pamiati prof. S. B. Okunia*, ed. N. G. Sladkevich
(Leningrad, 1972), 21–22.

17. See, e.g., *Tri poslednikh samoderzhtsa: Dnevnik A. B. Bogdanovich* (Moscow/
Leningrad, 1924), 179 (Apr. 23, 1894); Anan'ich and Ganelin, "Vyshnegradskii i Witte."

18. Theodore Taranovski, "The Politics of Counter-reform: Autocracy and Bureaucracy in the Reign of Alexander III, 1881–1894" (Ph.D. diss., Harvard University,
1976), 681–682; cf. Von Laue, *Sergei Witte*, 5, where he is portrayed as enlightened,
liberal, and pro-Western. On Witte's ideological affection for the Slavophilism of his
uncle R. A. Fadeev, see B. V. Anan'ich and R. Sh. Ganelin, "R. A. Fadeev, S. Iu. Witte i
ideologicheskie iskaniia 'okhranitelei' v 1881–1883 gg.," in *Issledovaniia po sotsial'no-*

Sergei Witte. From Ministerstvo Finansov, *Ministerstvo finansov, 1802–1902* (St. Petersburg, 1902).

monarchist, he was a right-wing student who opposed his leftist peers.[19] He remained a fervent supporter of the autocracy throughout his career, as evidenced by his memorandum *Samoderzhavie i zemstvo* (Autocracy and zemstvo), written at a time when he is reputed to have been most liberal.[20] In it he writes of the necessity of centralized, bureaucratic government in Russia, urging the curtailment of local self-government. He echoed Pobedonostsev, calling con-

*politicheskoi istorii Rossii: Sbornik statei pamiati Borisa Aleksandrovicha Romanova*, ed. N. E. Nosov et al. (Leningrad, 1971), 326.

19. Witte, *Vospominaniia*, 1:68.

20. He was quoted as saying in 1894 that "Russia requires to be governed in a truly Russian sense" (Princess Catherine Radziwill, *Memories of Forty Years* [London, 1914], 243–244).

stitutions the "great lie of our times." Autocracy and administrative centralization, in his view, formed the essential basis of Russian government and unity.[21]

His devotion to the person of the monarch also remained strong, although Nicholas soon put it to the test.[22] His preferred form of government was one in which the tsar chose talented, qualified ministers and allowed them to do their work as they saw fit. Ideal for Russia was an autocrat like Alexander III, who supported the policies of his ministers. For Witte, bureaucracy was the guiding force of the government, and Nicholas II's interference frustrated him.[23]

Beyond these constants it is difficult to categorize Witte's political beliefs. Struve found that he had never been consistently liberal or conservative—at times he was reactionary, at other times progressive.[24] Far from being a doctrinaire political ideologue, he was above all a pragmatist. If there was a common denominator, it was that all his activities, however progressive they may have seemed, were devoted to strengthening the realm, preserving the autocratic system, and bringing glory to the monarch.[25]

## Economic Nationalism

His economic policies, like his political views, seemed to comprise several contradictory strains (nothing unusual, perhaps, in imperial

21. S. Iu. Witte, *Samoderzhavie i zemstvo: Konfidentsial'naia zapiska ministra finansov stats-sekretaria S. Iu. Witte (1899 g.),* 2d ed. (Stuttgart, 1903). The constitution quote is on p. 211.

22. Witte wrote in his financial report for 1900, "To a Russian no obstacle is insurmountable when his Czar commands" (quoted in Albert J. Beveridge, *The Russian Advance* [New York, 1904], 451n1). While Witte was addressing the tsar and the public, he was not necessarily mouthing platitudes. Attacks on his industrial policies by reactionaries, however, along with Nicholas II's indecisive leadership and bad treatment of him, caused his views to evolve somewhat (Taranovski, "Politics," 681–683; Von Laue, *Sergei Witte,* 128–129).

23. Howard D. Mehlinger and John M. Thompson, *Count Witte and the Tsarist Government in the 1905 Revolution* (Bloomington, Ind., 1972), 24–25; Shepelev, *Tsarizm,* 197; Stuart R. Tompkins, "Witte as Finance Minister, 1892–1903," *Slavonic and East European Review* 11 (April 1933): 601, 603–604; M. N. de Enden, "The Roots of Witte's Thought," *Russian Review* 29 (January 1970): 6, 12–13, 16–20. Enden is wrong to say that Witte was interested in the efficient running of the government but not in its *form.*

24. Peter Struve, "Graf S. Iu. Witte: Opyt' kharakteristiki," *Russkaia mysl'* 36 (March 1915): 130.

25. Cf. the similar impulse behind the modernization and reform efforts in nineteenth-century Japan and Germany, in David Landes, "Japan and Europe: Contrasts in Industrialization," in *The State and Economic Enterprise in Japan: Essays in the Political Economy of Growth,* ed. William W. Lockwood (Princeton, 1965), 133–136, 139.

Russia), but overall were just as firmly committed to bolstering the autocracy and preserving the distinctiveness of Russia. The Siberian Railroad was integral to the execution of his policies.

At first glance Witte seems, as B. H. Sumner and others describe him, to have been a westernizer, a "representative of the new financial, commercial, and industrial interests which were transforming Russia."[26] Another historian likewise asserts that Witte was a firm believer in private industry and an opponent of economic nationalism, as shown by his reliance on foreign capital.[27]

This characterization is disputable. Witte's policies may have strengthened capitalism and private industry in Russia, but he was not sympathetic to private enterprise or entrepreneurs and the interests he aspired to benefit were not theirs but the state's.[28] He did desire to stimulate private enterprise and initiative, which he knew were for the good of the economy, but, ever the Russian official, he saw limits and controls on them as mandatory. The representative organs of businessmen that he encouraged, for instance, were to have no more than an advisory function.[29] Late in his life Witte attacked the private railroad barons of the 1870s, whose strength "was incompatible with the historically formed state traditions of the great Russian empire," and to the very end he vociferously opposed the reestablishment of a private railroad network on a par with that of the state system.[30]

An early work of Witte's provides a key to his opinions: for historical reasons, Germans were economical and "meticulous," and Americans entrepreneurial, inquisitive, and individualistic. These qualities were lacking in the Russian character, which was based on spiritual faith, and the corresponding Western forms of economic development would not thrive on Russian soil. According to his "realist" outlook, as

26. B. H. Sumner, *Tsardom and Imperialism in the Far East and Middle East, 1880–1914* (1940; rpt. n.p., 1968), 8. The Marxist economist M. Tugan-Baranovskii remembered him for bringing Russia closer to the West. (See Glinskii, "Graf Sergei Iul'evich Witte," 270.)

27. John P. McKay, *Pioneers for Profit: Foreign Entrepreneurship and Russian Industrialization, 1885–1913* (Chicago, 1970), 8, 10, 25–27. McKay makes these assertions to dispute Von Laue's suggestion that Witte was a precursor of Stalin.

28. Gregory Guroff, "The Red-Expert Debate: Continuities in the State-Entrepreneur Tension," in *Entrepreneurship in Imperial Russia and the Soviet Union,* ed. Gregory Guroff and Fred V. Carstensen (Princeton, 1983), 206.

29. Boris V. Anan'ich, "The Economic Policy of the Tsarist Government and Enterprise in Russia from the End of the Nineteenth through the Beginning of the Twentieth Century," in Guroff and Carstensen, *Entrepreneurship,* 135–136.

30. S. Iu. Witte, "Nekotorye soobrazheniia o prichinakh defitsitnosti russkoi zheleznodorozhnoi seti," *ZhdD,* 1910, nos. 17–18: 89–91.

he classified it, government intervention and centralization were more appropriate for Russian conditions.[31]

Witte was no more comfortable with Russian integration into the European economy than he was with the introduction of European forms of capitalism. In a frequently cited document, he spoke of a choice for Russia: industrialize or be dominated by the advanced European powers.[32] As for foreign capital, although he would be obliged to make extensive use of it, his wariness of its dangers, expressed in 1893, never waned.[33] His goal was to maintain Russia's integrity vis-à-vis the West. Witte encouraged the creation of a Russian merchant fleet for this reason: to take Russia's overseas transport from foreign carriers and place it in Russian hands.[34] And yet he intended to borrow foreign capital to build the vessels for the new fleet.[35] Russia's reliance on foreign capital, as on foreign know-how, was for the short term only.

Witte was skeptical of free enterprise and he sought to achieve a modicum of economic self-sufficiency. His policies were imbued with nationalism and statism, in the Russian bureaucratic and historical tradition. Russia's strength and the preservation of state power and the autocracy were the desired ends; as Witte made clear in his secret memorandum of March 1899, Russia was in many ways like a colony of Europe, the metropolis. But there was a difference: Russia

> has the right and the strength not to want to be the eternal handmaiden of states that are more developed economically . . . she is proud of her great might, by which she jealously guards not only the political but also the economic independence of her empire. She wants to be a metropolis herself.[36]

31. Sergei Witte, *Printsipy zheleznodorozhnykh tarifov po perevozke gruzov*, 3d ed. (St. Petersburg, 1910), 123–126, 128–129, 236.
32. His February 1900 report to Nicholas II, "On the Condition of Our Industry," quoted in Von Laue, *Sergei Witte*, 1–4.
33. Anan'ich, "Economic Policy," 133. This is a paradox of Russian economic thought of the period. Russian businessmen held the like view that Russia needed foreign investment in order to become a "self-sufficient organism." See Ruth Amende Roosa, "Russian Industrialists Look to the Future: Thoughts on Economic Development, 1906–17," in *Essays in Russian and Soviet History: In Honor of Geroid Tanquary Robinson*, ed. John Shelton Curtiss (New York, 1963), 201–202.
34. See the identical reasoning of Pobedonostsev in M. Poggenpol, *Ocherk vozniknoveniia i deiatel'nosti dobrovol'nogo flota za vremia XXV-ti letniago ego sushchestvovaniia* (St. Petersburg, 1903), 29–32.
35. "Dnevnik A. N. Kuropatkina," *Krasnyi arkhiv* 2 (1922): 22–23 (Jan. 12, 1903).
36. "A Secret Memorandum of Sergei Witte on the Industrialization of Russia," trans. and ed. Theodore H. Von Laue, *Journal of Modern History* 26 (March 1954): 66.

## The Siberian Railroad

One of the cornerstones of Witte's economic policy throughout the 1890s was the Siberian Railroad, which not only served the obvious political needs of the state but also provided a foundation on which to build devotion and respect at home and abroad. Witte took great pains to promote the railroad abroad for the multiple purpose of attracting international traffic and impressing Europe and the world with Russia's abilities.[37] Aside from luring revenues and investment, Witte wanted to show that Russia was the equal of the great powers of Europe, in a quest to satisfy the amour-propre of his nation.[38] This explanation is more fruitful than the superficial notion that Witte's goal was to establish a Russian trade monopoly in the Far East, and much more accurate than the idea that in Siberia "S. Iu. Witte reflected the material interests of the gentry landlords and bourgeoisie . . . in the capitalist development of the country."[39]

37. For this purpose the Ministry of Finance, Committee of Ministers, and Committee of the Siberian Railroad funded a number of publications, including several to be issued simultaneously in Russian, French, English, and German editions, in conjunction with international exhibitions. The Committee of Ministers' *Great Siberian Railway* (St. Petersburg, 1900), published for the Universal Exposition at Paris, portrayed Siberia as virtually free of convicts and natives (pp. 4, 6). The Committee of the Siberian Railroad took part in that exhibition, and in the ones held in Chicago in 1893 and Glasgow in 1901. On the committee's publications and their funding, see ZhKSZhD, zas. 37, SP, June 27, 1901, pp. 8–9, cols. 1–2; p. 14, col. 1; zas. 31, SP, Apr. 29, 1898, p. 32, col. 1. For other official publications, see also P. P. Migulin, *Nasha noveishaia zheleznodorozhnaia politika i zheleznodorozhnye zaimy (1893–1902)* (Khar'kov, 1903), 306–307.

38. Cf. David Landes's suggestion that the amour propre of nations stimulated economic imperialism ("Some Thoughts on the Nature of Economic Imperialism," *Journal of Economic History* 21, no. 4 [1961]: 505). See also Dietrich Geyer, *Russian Imperialism: The Interaction of Domestic and Foreign Policy, 1860–1914*, trans. Bruce Little (New Haven, 1987), 147, for a similar understanding of Witte's Asian strategy.

39. For the trade monopoly assertion, see V. G. Malekhon'kov, "Ekonomicheskaia politika tsarizma na Dal'nem Vostoke v kontse XIX nachale XX v.," in Kustanaiskii Gosudarstvennyi Pedagogicheskii Institut, *Uchenye zapiski*, vol. 3, vypusk istoricheskii (Kustanai, 1959), 60–61; for the quote, see V. F. Borzunov, "Istoriia sozdaniia trans-sibirskoi zheleznodorozhnoi magistrali XIX–nachala XX vv." (Ph.D. diss., Tomskii Gosudarstvennyi Universitet, 1972), 494. The public and professional debates did show a rising interest in selling Russian manufactures in Far Eastern markets, as well as in the idea that Russia had a civilizing mission in Asia. In both cases, though, Russia's sense of inferiority vis-à-vis Europe was a central consideration: Russia was behind Europe in Asia and could now attempt to catch up; with its historical and geographical links to Asia, Russia would have the advantage over Europe; with the Siberian Railroad, Russia could turn its back on Europe and live off its Asian trade. One gets the sense that the desire for markets was on the whole less important than the need to compensate for a felt deficiency. See, e.g., "Doklad N. Shavrova o kitaiskoi i indiiskoi zheleznykh dorogakh," *TOSRPT*, vol. 9, otdel 2 (1876), 99–102; *Otchet o zasedaniiakh obshchestva dlia*

The optimism of the railroad age suffused Witte's conception of the Siberian Railroad, and he projected it, as he did Russia's industrial development, onto the world stage. As he explained, as if in response to Alfred T. Mahan, although the seas were important in world history, naval supremacy was not everything. Russia was poorly situated to become a naval power, but railroads would compensate for its inability to float a great navy. The Siberian Railroad would give Russia a great future by developing its economy and settling its remote border areas.[40] The Siberian Railroad, he declared, deserved "to occupy one of the first places in the ranks of the largest and most important undertakings of the nineteenth century, not only in our Motherland, but also in the whole world."[41]

The Siberian Railroad would add luster to the image of Russia by providing a direct link between Europe and the Pacific. Russia would gain new sources of wealth as it became an intermediary in the trade between the Asian East and European West and its role in the world market grew. The railroad would end the isolation of the East, with Russia acting as cultural mediator between Europe and Asia, regulating their relations to its own advantage.[42] The Trans-Siberian Railroad would open new horizons for world trade and Moscow would become the center of that trade:

> If Moscow is currently more of a Russian than a world market, in the future an exceedingly bigger role will probably fall upon it, made certain by the Great Siberian transit route. The silk, tea, and fur trade for Europe, and the manufacturing and other trade for the Far East, will likely be concentrated in Moscow, which will become the hub of the world's transit movement.[43]

Witte described the Trans-Siberian Railroad as placing Russia at the center of world trade and culture, in a modern equivalent of the medieval religious doctrine that proclaimed Moscow the "Third Rome." In a paradoxical twist, Witte had the modern symbol of materialism and industry, the railroad, achieving the most glorious of

---

sodeistviia russkoi promyshlennosti i torgovle, po voprosu o sibirskoi zheleznoi doroge (St. Petersburg, 1884), 55–56; TIRTO, 10:10–11.

40. S. Iu. Witte, Vorlesungen über Volks- und Staatswirtschaft, trans. Josef Melnik, vol. 1 (Stuttgart/Berlin, 1913), 69–71.

41. B. B. Glinskii, ed., Prolog russko-iaponskoi voiny: Materialy iz arkhiva grafa S. Iu. Witte (Petrograd, 1916), 10.

42. Ibid., 13, 190.

43. Witte, Vorlesungen, 1:176.

Slavophile spiritual dreams. At the very least, we see in autocratic Russia's attempt to modernize its economic structure its desire for a prominent place in the sun.


## Windfall Budgets

To turn his utopian ideal into reality, Witte used every means at his disposal, first overcoming the tremendous obstacles to financing the railroad and then creating a manipulable administrative structure to orchestrate its construction. In both realms his genius was clearly evident.

The financing of a project as vast as the Siberian Railroad would not be simple to arrange in financially strapped imperial Russia and it had already aroused much acrimony within the upper bureaucracy. Witte's solution, which later became a regular characteristic of his budgetary practices, entailed massive spending to create national wealth and impress foreign audiences.

As Witte embarked on his spending program, his relationship with Vyshnegradskii deteriorated. Early in his tenure as finance minister, Vyshnegradskii had told the tsar that Witte would be the best choice eventually to succeed him in the position. The tight-spending Vyshnegradskii soon regretted his recommendation. He was afraid that Witte would "make use of credit too widely and carelessly," and suggested that Witte would make a better minister of trade than minister of finance. Alexander III was not at all receptive to the idea.[44] For his part, Witte felt Vyshnegradskii was "small-minded," and "always interested . . . more in petty things than in large-scale, important ones." He himself was less cautious, "much broader and bolder."[45] Witte's description captures the differences between them in all matters, not least in that of the budget, the central preoccupation of the minister of finance.

The crux of the problem was that Vyshnegradskii stood in adamant opposition to Witte's plans for financing the Siberian Railroad. As acting minister of finance, in November 1892 Witte toyed with the idea of resorting to the printing press to cover the costs of construction by issuing special "Siberian credit rubles."[46] According to V. I. Gurko,

44. Terner, *Vospominaniia zhizni*, 2:178, 220–222; Shepelev, *Tsarizm*, 195–196.

45. Witte, *Vospominaniia*, 1:222, 284.

46. S. V. Sabler and I. V. Sosnovskii, comps., *Sibirskaia zheleznaia doroga v eia proshlom i nastoiashchem: Istoricheskii ocherk*, ed. A. N. Kulomzin (St. Petersburg, 1903),

Witte was appointed finance minister precisely because he intended to speed up the economy by issuing new banknotes to build the railroad; Alexander III expected him to get the job done quickly.[47]

Under the tutelage of Bunge, who began to instruct Witte in currency matters, he revised his plans, but in a way that was just as inflationary.[48] Rather than issue new money, Witte now proposed the recovery of currency that the Treasury by law had retired but not yet destroyed.[49] In a special conference on the matter Bunge and Vyshnegradskii argued that his scheme would destabilize the ruble and threaten monetary reform, but the majority voted in favor of Witte and the tsar concurred.[50] Witte had just taken his first step toward making the State Bank an arm of the Ministry of Finance, an indication that his talent for fiscal legerdemain was already well developed.[51]

In the event, this plan also fell by the wayside, and the Siberian Railroad was financed out of the surpluses of the ordinary budget which supposedly had accumulated, thanks to its "favorable implementation" in 1894 and yearly thereafter.[52]

---

111; Glinskii, *Prolog*, 9; B. V. Anan'ich, *Rossiia i mezhdunarodnyi kapital, 1897–1914* (Leningrad, 1970), 14–16; Terner, *Vospominaniia*, 2:222n1; P. P. Migulin, *Nasha bankovaia politika (1729–1903)* (Khar'kov, 1904), 245. The Siberian credit rubles were to be issued by the Treasury gradually as the work proceeded, and canceled over twenty-three years beginning in 1894 (MPS, *Istoricheskii ocherk razvitiia zheleznykh dorog v Rossii s ikh osnovaniia po 1897 g. vkliuchitel'no*, comp. V. M. Verkhovskii, pt. 2 [St. Petersburg, 1898, 1899], 484).

47. V. I. Gurko, *Features and Figures of the Past: Government and Opinion in the Reign of Nicholas II*, ed. J. E. W. Sterling et al., trans. L. Matveev (Stanford, 1939), 55; Shepelev, *Tsarizm*, 198.

48. On Bunge's role, see Witte, *Vospominaniia*, 1:361–364; Anan'ich, *Kapital*, 15. On Witte's revised plan, intended for the special conference of Nov. 21, 1892, see MPS, *Istoricheskii ocherk*, 485; Glinskii, *Prolog*, 10.

49. For a more detailed elucidation of the 1881 *ukaz* requiring the reduction of paper money in circulation and Witte's circumvention of it, see *PSZRI*, sobranie tret'e, vol. 12, 1892, nos. 9139 and 9140; Sabler and Sosnovskii, *Sibirskaia zheleznaia doroga*, 117–119; A. N. Kulomzin, *Le Transsibérien*, trans. Jules Legras (Paris, 1904), 46–48; Glinskii, *Prolog*, 15–16; *ZhMPS*, official sec.: "Sibirskaia zheleznaia doroga," 1893, no. 1: 2–3; Anan'ich, *Kapital*, 11–12; and I. F. Gindin, *Gosudarstvennyi bank i ekonomicheskaia politika tsarskogo pravitel'stva (1861–1892 goda)* (Moscow, 1960), 96–99.

50. Sabler and Sosnovskii, *Sibirskaia zheleznaia doroga*, 119–120, 122; Polovtsov, *Dnevnik*, 2:460, 517–518n63.

51. On the development of this relationship, see Gindin, *Pravitel'stvennyi bank*, 123, and Anan'ich, "Economic Policy," 134.

52. "Iz dnevnika A. A. Polovtseva [sic]," *Krasnyi arkhiv* 46 (1931): 128 (Apr. 14, 1900); Sabler and Sosnovskii, *Sibirskaia zheleznaia doroga*, 122–123; Glinskii, *Prolog*, 22; Ministerstvo Finansov, Departament Zheleznodorozhnykh Del, *Kratkii otchet o deiatel'nosti tarifnykh uchrezhdenii i departamenta zheleznodorozhnykh del za 1889–1913 gg.* (St. Petersburg, 1914), 94. The latter source states that it was difficult for the state to build any other railroads in the 1890s, as "all the residual, nondesignated funds [*svobodnaia*

It is difficult to determine exactly what form of income contributed to the construction of the Siberian Railroad (or for that matter any item of expenditure) because of the feature of the "common till" (*edinaia kassa*) in which all government revenues were pooled.[53] The steady improvement in Franco-Russian relations certainly placed the financing of the railroad on a more secure footing for Witte than for Vyshnegradskii. Paradoxically, foreign loans contributed to the "surplus" of the budget: because Witte considered loans a form of income, he could claim, after making other adjustments, that his budget was balanced and provided a surplus.[54] In fact, expenditures on railroads, largely on the Siberian, helped to keep the budget as a whole in deficit for most of the 1890s.[55] But it was important for foreign creditors, the stability of the ruble, and national prestige to keep the fiction of a surplus alive.

Witte's fiscal techniques became more sophisticated, but in essence there was little to distinguish them from his earlier "inflationist" strategy. This strategy was consistent with his views of government finance as they evolved over the 1890s, even after the country went on the gold standard: in both periods he intended to spend money in large amounts whether it was available or not.[56] He felt that Vyshne-

---

*nalichnost'*] of the State Treasury" were being used for the Siberian Railroad. For the yearly amounts of *svobodnaia nalichnost'* in the Treasury from 1891 through 1904, see N. Petrov, *Finansovoe polozhenie russkoi zheleznodorozhnoi seti i glavneishie prichiny ukhudsheniia ego v polednie gody* (St. Petersburg, 1909), vol. 5 of Trudy vysochaishe uchrezhdennoi osoboi komissii dlia vsestoronnego issledovaniia zheleznodorozhnogo dela v Rossii, 157.

53. Migulin, *Nasha noveishaia zheleznodorozhnaia politika*, 54–55.

54. Romanov, *Russia in Manchuria*, 41. On Witte and the French loans of the 1890s, see Anan'ich, *Kapital*, 12–14; B. V. Anan'ich et al., *Krizis samoderzhaviia v Rossii: 1895–1917* (Leningrad, 1984), 35. According to the Committee of the Siberian Railroad, though, by 1900 only 100 million rubles of Siberian Railroad expenditures had been covered by "extraordinary sources" (i.e., loans), the rest by "ordinary budget revenues" (ZhKSZhD, zas. 34, SP, Dec. 8, 1899, p. 22, col. 2). "Other adjustments" included placing ordinary expenditures in the extraordinary budget, which was always in deficit, and ignoring state payments on the railroad debt.

55. A. P. Pogrebinskii, *Ocherki istorii finansov dorevoliutsionnoi Rossii* (Moscow, 1954), 86–92, and "Stroitel'stvo zheleznykh dorog v poreformennoi Rossii i finansovaia politika tsarizma (60–90-e gody XIX v.)," *Istoricheskie zapiski* 47 (1954): 176–178; W. O. Henderson, *The Industrial Revolution in Europe: Germany, France, Russia, 1815–1914* (Chicago, 1968), 228; Peter I. Lyashchenko, *History of the National Economy of Russia to the 1917 Revolution*, trans. L. M. Herman (New York, 1949), 554–555; M. I. Bogolepov, "Gosudarstvennoe khoziaistvo (1892–1903)," in *Istoriia Rossii v XIX veke*, vol. 8 (St. Petersburg, n.d.), 3, 8–9.

56. Polovtsov's words, written in 1892, are just as valid for 1899: "The essence of his financial program [was] thus: no matter what the needs of the government, they should be satisfied" (*Dnevnik*, 2:463 [Dec. 28, 1892]).

gradskii's kind of thrift was foolish, and he told Princess Catherine Radziwill that "a minister cannot practice economy in the administration of a state; money can only be found by spending it lavishly."[57]

From this perspective Witte justified expenditures on the Siberian Railroad: it would bring "numerous benefits that were not subject to direct arithmetical calculation;" its significance should not be judged from a "narrow financial point of view."[58] In his first budget report to Alexander III as minister of finance, for 1893, Witte "held that for historic reasons Russian financial administration must overstep the conventional boundaries of public finance."[59] He downplayed the effect of the famine on the state budget and argued that the Siberian Railroad was too important to be delayed by haggling over its cost.[60] Still in 1900 he felt it was "better to lose money than prestige."[61] And for him the Siberian Railroad was above all a matter of prestige.

Witte's spending pushed the budget into deficit, forcing him to overtax the internal market and export to the maximum. All of these measures imposed a heavy burden on the population.[62] The Siberian Railroad certainly required large sacrifices on the part of the Russian population, a sad fact Witte more than once acknowledged.[63]

---

57. Radziwill, *Memories*, 244; Von Laue, *Sergei Witte*, 34–35, 76.

58. Quoted in L. Kleinbort, *Russkii imperializm v Azii* (St. Petersburg, 1906), 15; Sabler and Sosnovskii, *Sibirskaia zheleznaia doroga*, 112.

59. Michael T. Florinsky, *Russia: A History and an Interpretation*, vol. 2 (New York, 1960), 1111.

60. *Russkie vedomosti*, no. 2 (Jan. 3, 1893), p. 5. The overwhelming majority of participants in the debates over the Siberian Railroad in the Russian Technical Society, the Society for the Encouragement of Russian Industry and Trade, and the periodical press held the like view that expense was of no concern and explicitly urged the government to build the railroad whatever the cost. See Steven G. Marks, "The Trans-Siberian Railroad: State Enterprise and Economic Development in Imperial Russia" (Ph.D. diss., Harvard University, 1988), 185–187.

61. "Pis'ma S. Iu. Witte k D. S. Sipiagin," *Krasnyi arkhiv* 18 (1926): 32 (July 7, 1900).

62. Leo Pasvolsky and Harold G. Moulton, *Russian Debts and Russian Reconstruction* (New York, 1924), 47–51, 57–58, 102–103. Under Witte more than 37% of the whole Russian railroad network—state and private—was completed; i.e., more than half as much as in the previous fifty years (Lyashchenko, *History of the National Economy*, 533). According to A. M. Solov'eva, 68% of railroad construction in the 1890s was in Asian Russia, mostly at Treasury expense (*Zheleznodorozhnyi transport Rossii vo vtoroi polovine XIX v.* [Moscow, 1975], 254). According to Olga Crisp, 78% of state revenues were from indirect taxes (*Studies in the Russian Economy before 1914* [London, 1976], 27).

63. See Witte, *Samoderzhavie i zemstvo*, 219; Glinskii, *Prolog*, 191; *Vestnik finansov, promyshlennosti i torgovli*, no. 1 (Jan. 2, 1900): 4, 7; ZhKSZhD, zas. 34, SP, Dec. 8, 1899, p. 22, col. 2.

### The Committee of the Siberian Railroad

Once he had overcome the financial hurdles, Witte could concentrate on organizing what became one of the major development projects in the history of the world. In forming the Committee of the Siberian Railroad Witte imposed consensus on a bureaucracy bitterly divided over the economic policy of the nation. The episode throws considerable light on the way politics functioned in late imperial Russia.

Heide Whelan refers to the Committee of the Siberian Railroad as one of the "temporary supreme organs" that the government established to circumvent opposition toward certain policies and to ensure their speedy execution.[64] As Witte explained:

> In order to move along the matter of the Siberian road, when I became minister of finance I decided that it was necessary to form a special Committee of the Siberian Railroad. This committee would have significant powers, in order to avoid any delays in its various dealings with the ministers and to avoid various difficulties in both the Committee of Ministers and the State Council. . . . The committee would be given powers not only in the administration of the road's construction but also in decisions . . . of a legislative nature.[65]

The idea of creating a "special, central managerial body for the construction of the Siberian Railroad" lay with Minister of Transport Giubbenet rather than Witte.[66] But he hardly inherited the project "as a going concern and in almost final form."[67] The assessment of the railroad's Soviet historian is more accurate: "Witte concretized and developed the idea of a centralized administration for this grandiose state enterprise."[68] The scope and competence of the committee, as Witte intended, were to extend far beyond construction questions alone.

Witte's original formulation of the statute of the Committee of the

64. Heide W. Whelan, *Alexander III and the State Council: Bureaucracy and Counter-reform in Late Imperial Russia* (New Brunswick, N.J., 1982), 40–41.

65. Witte, *Vospominaniia*, 1:434.

66. See MPS, "Otchet o deiatel'nosti ministerstva putei soobshcheniia po stroitel'stvu sibirskoi zheleznoi dorogi za vremia s 30 marta 1889 g. po 17 ianvaria 1892 g." (TsGAOR, fond 677, opis' 1, delo 629), 21.

67. As claimed in Romanov, *Russia in Manchuria*, 38.

68. Borzunov, "Istoriia sozdaniia," 513.

Siberian Railroad was approved by a special conference on November 21, 1892. The committee was to be chaired by an appointee of the tsar and include the state comptroller and ministers of finance, interior, state domains, and transport. It was to be responsible for the construction of the railroad, the auxiliary enterprises that were to help stimulate the Siberian economy, and financial estimates and oversight. Expenditures for auxiliary enterprises were not subject to review by the State Council, and were therefore to be discussed by the committee alone, then sent for approval directly to the tsar. Other matters were to be handled according to normal ministerial procedure: resolutions were to be passed on, when necessary, to either the State Council or the Committee of Ministers for discussion and approval before being sent to the tsar. The special conference voted to approve these arrangements, but left it up to the committee itself to work out its own functions with greater specificity.[69]

Witte used this opportunity, with the help of his new ally Bunge, vice chairman of the Committee of the Siberian Railroad, to expand the committee's authority further. At its first session, on February 10, 1893, Witte and Bunge jointly urged the revision of the statute to allow for more rapid, efficient, and unified action by the committee. As it stood, without executive authority and dependent on the State Council and Committee of Ministers in matters of finance and the route (including land use), the committee would be severely restricted. So as not to narrow the responsibilities of the ministers or infringe on the principles of government, but to allow for the utmost speed of execution on important matters, they suggested a compromise arrangement, the establishment of a "special order" for the committee. Rather than refer new legislation to the State Council for deliberation, the committee would vote on it immediately in joint session with the relevant department of the State Council, or with the Committee of Ministers on questions pertaining to the route. Resolutions were then to be referred immediately to the tsar for approval, or for resolution if unanimous agreement was not reached. The committee did not have executive authority; ministers carried out decrees according to their responsibilities.[70]

The precedents for such an institution included the Committee for

69. *PSZRI*, sobranie tret'e, vol. 12, 1892, no. 9140; *ZhMPS*, official sec.: "Sibirskaia zheleznaia doroga," 1893, no. 1: 3–5.

70. ZhKSZhD, zas. 1, Feb. 10, 1893, pp. 4–5, col. 2; *PSZRI*, sobranie tret'e, vol. 13, 1893, no. 9248; *ZhMPS*, official sec.: "Sibirskaia zheleznaia doroga," 1893, no. 1: 5–7; Borzunov, "Istoriia sozdaniia," 536–537.

the Construction of the St. Petersburg–Moscow Railroad, established by Nicholas I in 1842 under the heir to the throne, the future Alexander II. It was created because of the opposition to railroads that existed in the Committee of Ministers, although its membership was largely drawn from that body.[71] But the scope of the Committee of the Siberian Railroad was far greater than that of its ancestor, for it was not limited to railroad construction. Its purview and ambitions continued to expand with Witte at the helm; through it he gained control of the Asian policy of the empire, at least for a time.[72]

### Mobilizing the Ministers

Witte ensured his own predominance in the committee, as in government on the whole, by manipulating official appointees.[73] Throughout his career he almost systematically maneuvered to remove his opponents, or those who might pose a threat, and replace them with weak, pliant, often inferior ministers who would be obedient to his will. He continued to do so until 1900, when his position in government deteriorated.

Indicative was his recommendation of A. S. Ermolov for the post of minister of state domains after the death of Ostrovskii. Although an intelligent man and a trained agronomist, Ermolov was a weak and ineffective minister. Witte, whose assistant he had been, knew that he was a "person without character," as he described him, and it was probably this feature that best qualified him for the post in Witte's eyes.[74] It was certainly important to Witte's plans for the Committee of the Siberian Railroad that he have some measure of control over the activities of the Ministry of State Domains, given its central importance in peasant resettlement.

Even more crucial was the selection of the minister of transport, whose jurisdiction Witte had been encroaching on from the begin-

71. See Richard M. Haywood, *The Beginnings of Railway Development in Russia in the Reign of Nicholas I, 1835–1842* (Durham, N.C., 1969), 227–228; Erik Amburger, *Geschichte der Behördenorganisation Rußlands von Peter dem Großen bis 1917* (Leiden, 1966), 124. The committee was dissolved in 1858.

72. Borzunov, "Istoriia sozdaniia," 537.

73. Witte's string-pulling in appointments was complemented by the finance minister's control of the imperial purse strings.

74. On Ermolov, see Shepelev, *Tsarizm*, 204; Donald W. Treadgold, *The Great Siberian Migration: Government and Peasant in Resettlement from Emancipation to the First World War* (Princeton, 1957), 111–112; Witte, *Vospominaniia*, 1:347–349.

ning of his official career. Witte helped expose the corruption of A. K. Krivoshein, who had been appointed minister at the behest of both Prince Meshcherskii and the minister of the interior, I. N. Durnovo. Krivoshein was unfamiliar with railroad affairs and proved to be incompetent.[75] Witte induced the tsar to replace Krivoshein with a transport minister he could dominate. His choice was Prince M. I. Khilkov, whose mediocrity Witte noted before nominating him. Khilkov had been a jack-of-all-trades on railroads in the United States, worked under Annenkov, and served briefly as minister of railroads in Bulgaria. In his official post he put in a nine-to-five day; Witte characterized him as a better "chief locomotive engineer" than minister. These were the qualities Witte, who worked sixteen-hour days, demanded in the committee members, and Khilkov remained in office for a good ten years, from 1895 to 1905.[76]

Perhaps no position posed a greater threat to Witte's domination of the Committee of the Siberian Railroad than that of chairman of the State Council's Department of State Economy. This department almost solely represented the State Council on the committee, and its chairman was therefore very influential. In forcing the selection of his candidate as its chairman, Witte for all practical purposes was able to bypass the State Council in matters concerning the Siberian Railroad. Its chairman since 1884 was the skillful and powerful Abaza, who was likely to remain independent of Witte. Witte therefore lost no time in pressing for Abaza's removal from office in 1892, in connection with a stock-market scandal. The tsar considered appointing Vyshnegradskii to the post, but Witte persuaded him not to do so, for fear of his continued opposition to the financial arrangements for the Siberian Railroad. He persuaded the tsar instead to appoint D. M. Sol'skii, a

75. On Krivoshein, see Von Laue, *Sergei Witte*, 200; Witte, *Vospominaniia*, 1:290–291; 2:19–21. For Witte's further successful attempts to expand his own ministry's influence at the expense of the Transport Ministry in the newly created Administration for the Construction of the Siberian Railroad (1893), see ZhKSZhD, osobyi zhurnal, SP, May 26, 1893; *PSZRI*, sobranie tret'e, vol. 13, 1893, no. 9728; Borzunov, "Istoriia sozdaniia," 538–544.

76. See "Iz dnevnika A. A. Polovtseva [sic]," *Krasnyi arkhiv* 67 (1934): 183 (Dec. 27, 1894); Witte, *Vospominaniia*, 2:24–27; Henry Reichman, "Tsarist Labor Policy and the Railroads, 1885–1914," *Russian Review* 42 (1983): 57; Harmon Tupper, *To the Great Ocean: Siberia and the Trans-Siberian Railway* (Boston, 1965), 192. For his various positions on American railroads, see *Railroad Gazette*, Sept. 4, 1896, p. 616. As chap. 10 will show, Khilkov's tireless efforts while he was ill to improve the carrying capacity of the Siberian Railroad during the Russo-Japanese War seem to belie the characterization of him here. But Witte's perception is as important as reality; furthermore, Khilkov was clearly subservient to Witte.

former state comptroller. An ally of the liberal Loris-Melikov, he was an intelligent man and a reformer in spirit. But he was indecisive and uncommitted to any position. He was the perfect choice for Witte.[77]

Witte was less successful with other ministries. He had been in conflict with Durnovo, the incapable minister of the interior. When Bunge died in 1895 and Durnovo was named to his post as chairman of the Committee of Ministers, Durnovo wanted V. K. Plehve, Witte's antagonist, to succeed him. The tsar's doubts about Plehve's conservative colors (he had gotten his start under Loris-Melikov) gave Witte the opportunity to have the reputed moderate I. L. Goremykin placed in the position. Witte expected the new interior minister to be grateful to him and therefore manageable. As it turned out, although incomparably lazy, he was no more loyal to Witte than Durnovo had been. In 1899 Witte arranged his removal and had him replaced with his loyal and intellectually limited friend D. S. Sipiagin. Sipiagin, however, was assassinated in 1902 and replaced by Plehve, who contributed to Witte's downfall.[78]

Witte was also unsuccessful in his competition with the military over the Committee of the Siberian Railroad. According to its original statute, prepared by Witte, the committee would completely exclude the war and naval ministers from its ranks. The tsar recognized the attempt to deny them a part in the project and at his intervention they were included as full members of the committee.[79] These were setbacks for Witte, albeit minor ones.

### Nicholas II

Witte's most important and fateful manipulation was to have the Grand Duke Nicholas Alexandrovich, twenty-three years old in 1891 and heir to the throne, appointed chairman of the Committee of the Siberian Railroad. Nicholas's chairmanship all but guaranteed the completion of the Siberian Railroad: the tsarevich would eventually

77. See Witte, *Vospominaniia*, 1:240–242; 2:16–17; Shepelev, *Tsarizm*, 203; Taranovski, "Politics," 701; Terner, *Vospominaniia zhizni*, 2:222n1; K. A. Skal'kovskii, *Nashi gosudarstvennye i obshchestvennye deiateli* (St. Petersburg, 1890), 296–300.

78. See Shepelev, *Tsarizm*, 203–204; Zaionchkovskii, *Rossiiskoe samoderzhavie*, 151–152; Anan'ich et al., *Krizis*, 28; Von Laue, *Sergei Witte*, 157, 162, 167, 201.

79. *ZhMPS*, official sec.: "Sibirskaia zheleznaia doroga," 1893, no. 1:4; ZhKSZhD, zas. 1, Feb. 10, 1893, p. 3, col. 1; *PSZRI*, sobranie tret'e, vol. 12, 1892, no. 9174. For the context of this conflict see William C. Fuller, Jr., *Civil-Military Conflict in Imperial Russia: 1881–1914* (Princeton, 1985).

become the unlimited autocrat whose decisions in the committee would automatically become law.[80]

The idea was clever, because Witte knew that he would need the backing of the new tsar if he were to achieve his goals; the appointment was a way of ingratiating himself with Nicholas.[81] Witte also proposed Nicholas's appointment as chairman to Alexander III to prevent him from naming Abaza, whom Durnovo was busy promoting. According to Witte, Alexander's initial reaction was astonishment. "After all," said the tsar, "he is still a boy; he has a child's judgment: how on earth can he be the chairman of a committee?" Witte explained that "this will be his first elementary school for the conduct of state affairs." He suggested that Nicholas's tutor, Bunge, be made vice chairman so that he could assist the tsarevich. Alexander was convinced and a week later agreed.[82]

There was justification on other grounds for appointing Nicholas to the chair, and they are worth examining for the clue they give to both the future of the railroad and the fate of Witte. Nicholas had traveled throughout Asia in 1890–1891; no other tsar had been there before, and Gurko called him a pioneer. On the return trip through Siberia, Nicholas participated in ground-breaking ceremonies at Vladivostok for the Ussuri section of the Siberian Railroad. The journey had a lasting influence on him, and in the first decade of his reign he dwelt on thoughts of Russian development in the Far East.[83]

For the young and impressionable crown prince, the idea of Russia's mission and glory in the Far East was strong liquor. He absorbed the ideology of the "Orientalists" (*Vostochniki*), who justified Russian expansion in Asia on historical and cultural grounds. He was especially influenced by Prince E. E. Ukhtomskii, who accompanied him to Asia and whose account of the journey, the classic expression of this

80. Witte, *Vospominaniia*, 1:436–437.

81. The suggestion that Witte sought to ingratiate himself with Nicholas by involving him in the Far East is made by Gurko, *Features and Figures*, 259.

82. Witte, *Vospominaniia*, 1:434–436. For the creation of the post of vice chairman, see *PSZRI*, sobranie tret'e, vol. 13, 1893, no. 9248. Polovtsov claimed that it was his idea that Nicholas should be made chairman of the Committee of the Siberian Railroad (at the time not yet formed), "because the tsarevich feels burdened with inactivity" (*Dnevnik*, 2: 424 [Feb. 18, 1892]).

83. See Gurko, *Features and Figures*, 256. For the official account of the trip, see Prince Esper Esperovich Ukhtomskii, *Puteshestvie na Vostok ego imperatorskogo vysochestva gosudaria naslednika tsesarevicha, 1890–1891*, 3 vols. (St. Petersburg, 1893–1897). On ground-breaking ceremonies at Vladivostok, see MPS, "Otchet o deiatel'nosti," 27; K. Korol'kov, *Zhizn' i tsarstvovanie imperatora Aleksandra III (1881–1894 gg.)* (Kiev, 1901), 194–195; *Times*, Feb. 26, 1891, p. 5; Tupper, *To the Great Ocean*, 84–85.

Nicholas II. From Ministerstvo Finansov, *Ministerstvo finansov, 1802–1902* (St. Petersburg, 1902).

ideology, Nicholas personally revised before publication.[84] Although a central element of this school of thought was the kinship of Russia and Asia as distinct from Europe, it amounted to little more than a justification of Russian chauvinism. The Orientalists condescended toward the Asian nations they intended to "civilize," and fear of the "yellow peril" played no little role in their thinking; they shared these elements with the European ideologists of imperialism from whom they dissociated themselves.[85] The Trans-Siberian Railroad would allow Russia to begin its work: "great Siberia is our vanguard."[86]

The ideology of the Orientalists had a European perspective and was a function of Russia's inferiority complex vis-à-vis the West. Even in their most extreme proclamations of oneness with Asia, they were expressing not the fact that Russia and Asia were equals, but resentment at Europe's humiliation of Russia.[87] This inferiority was at the psychological core of Witte's world view too, and he exulted with Nicholas over Russia's mission in Asia, which he felt was to export the basic autocratic and Orthodox Christian principles of the Russian world. Like contemporary French and British imperialists, Witte failed to see the inherent contradiction in making such an exclusivist ideology the basis for a civilizing mission. He understood Russia's mission to be "cultural-enlightening," as opposed to western Europe's alleged economic exploitation and injustice.[88] Witte's critique of European

84. Gurko, *Features and Figures*, 256–257; Witte, *Vospominaniia*, 1:438–440. According to Witte, after the disasters of the Russo-Japanese War and the 1905 revolution, it was popularly thought to have been a mistake for Nicholas to travel to the Far East rather than through Europe and European Russia, from whose affairs he remained aloof. On the ideology of the *Vostochniki*, see Andrew Malozemoff, *Russian Far Eastern Policy, 1881–1904* (Berkeley, 1958), 41–50; Gerhart von Schulze-Gävernitz, *Volkswirtschaftliche Studien aus Rußland* (Leipzig, 1899), 193, 234–236. On the almost religious zeal to make Asia Russian, see Beveridge, *Russian Advance*, 367–373.

85. See Ukhtomskii, *Puteshestvie*. See also Heinz Gollwitzer, *Europe in the Age of Imperialism, 1880–1914*, trans. David Adam and Stanley Baron (New York, 1969).

86. Ukhtomskii, *Puteshestvie*, vol. 2, pt. 4, p. 206.

87. Nicholas V. Riasanovsky, "Asia through Russian Eyes," in *Russia and Asia: Essays on the Influence of Russia on the Asian Peoples*, ed. Wayne S. Vucinich (Stanford, 1972).

88. Witte expressed his views on these matters in a memorandum to Alexander III which explained his support for a proposal of P. A. Badmaev (the Buriat medicine man, linguist, intriguer at the St. Petersburg court, and advocate of the Russian conquest of Mongolia, Tibet, and China) for construction of a branch of the Siberian Railroad through Mongolia to Lanzhou in western China. Alexander rejected the idea as "extraordinary and fanciful," but Nicholas, and Witte, would soon embrace it in the form of the Chinese-Eastern Railroad. See *Za kulisami tsarizma: Arkhiv tibetskogo vracha Badmaeva*, ed. V. P. Semennikov (Leningrad, 1925), 78–79. On Badmaev, see also Malozemoff, *Russian Far Eastern Policy*, 48–49. Geyer, in *Russian Imperialism*, 189, asserts that Witte used Badmaev's words to justify construction of the Siberian Railroad, but that com-

colonialism bears similarities to that of Marx and Lenin. But his conviction that Russia's machinery—especially the railroad—would be the salvation of China is identical to the attitudes of western Europe.[89]

Nicholas became absorbed in the affairs of the Committee of the Siberian Railroad and chose to retain the post of chairman after he became tsar. A quick learner, unlike his father, after the first few sessions he began to act as a true chairman. According to Witte, he was "not bad" and attentive, always aware of the issues at hand.[90] He was certainly not, as Gurko calls him, an "honorary" head of the committee, without influence on its decisions; his involvement in the minute details of the sessions and his informed decisions are reflected in the sources.[91]

Witte and Nicholas worked well together at first, the new tsar expressing confidence in his minister of finance.[92] But the relationship did not last long. Witte noted that the tsar was so involved in the Committee of the Siberian Railroad that Russian Far Eastern policy became, fatefully, an expression of his personality.[93] The same can be said of Witte, and their two unlike temperaments proved inharmonious. Struve found Witte's nature to have been more suited to that of an autocrat, whereas Nicholas was weak willed.[94] Witte had been compatible with Alexander III and respected his character and leadership. He felt he remained in office for eight years under Nicholas solely because Alexander III had approved of him.[95] In all other respects, Witte's relationship with Nicholas and his father paralleled that of Bismarck with Kaisers Wilhelm I and II. Nicholas felt he was a spectator at Witte's performance, especially in the Far East, where the minister's powerful presence seemed to thwart Nicholas's own ambi-

---

mercial considerations were closer to his heart. There is no reason to doubt, however, that he expressed his convictions in this private memorandum to Alexander III, for he must have known that the tsar would not be receptive to such ideas.

89. For a penetrating analysis of Europe's understanding of its civilizing mission in Africa and Asia, see Michael Adas, *Machines as the Measure of Men: Science, Technology, and Ideologies of Western Dominance* (Ithaca, N.Y., 1989), chap. 4.

90. Witte, *Vospominaniia*, 1:435–436, 440–441; "Iz dnevnika A. A. Polovtseva [sic]," *Krasnyi arkhiv* 67 (1934): 174 (Nov. 13, 1894).

91. Gurko, *Features and Figures*, 13; see ZhKSZhD, passim.

92. See, e.g., *Tri poslednikh samoderzhtsa: Dnevnik A. V. Bogdanovich* (Moscow/Leningrad, 1924), 175 (Jan. 2, 1894).

93. Witte, *Vospominaniia*, 1:437.

94. Struve, "Witte und Stolypin," 267.

95. Witte, *Vospominaniia*, vol. 1, passim; Von Laue, *Sergei Witte*, 67; Shepelev, *Tsarizm*, 195.

tions. Witte surpassed everyone, and Nicholas grew jealous and resentful.[96]

The committee was so closely associated with Witte that it did not long survive his fall from power. Witte was relieved of office on August 16, 1903. The Committee of the Siberian Railroad was formally abolished in 1905, ostensibly because the major portion of the railroad work was completed and the government had to be restructured after the October Manifesto was issued.[97] But its real demise had come two years earlier, with the downfall of Witte. According to A. N. Kulomzin's memoirs, it had succumbed to a power struggle with the Committee of the Far East, whose supporters in government had been in the forefront of the assault on Witte.[98]

In the meantime, though, the Committee of the Siberian Railroad was active with Witte at the helm. The extent of his activities in the committee is evidence of his far-reaching authority. In no other realm is Alexander Izvol'skii's claim that Witte was "*de facto*, if not *de jure*, the real head of the Russian Government" so apparent; he had created a "State within a State."[99]

96. Gurko, *Features and Figures*, 259. As the tsar said of Witte in 1903, "he is a very gifted person, but he gets easily carried away" ("Dnevnik A. N. Kuropatkina," *Krasnyi arkhiv* 2 [1922]: 37 (Mar. 8, 1903]).

97. See *PSZRI*, sobranie tret'e, vol. 25, 1905, no. 27044.

98. A. V. Remnev, "Komitet sibirskoi zheleznoi dorogi v vospominaniiakh A. N. Kulomzina," unpublished manuscript (Leningrad, n.d.), 19.

99. Izvol'skii, *Recollections of a Foreign Minister*, 112–113.

# CHAPTER EIGHT

# Witte and the Taming
# of the Wild East

The colonization of Siberia at the end of the nineteenth century has been portrayed as analogous to the American westward movement. Russian peasants are said to have set out for Siberia to make themselves a new life, *mutatis mutandis*, much the way their pioneer counterparts had done on the American frontier, spontaneously and with minimal supervision by the central government. The Russian state failed to halt the migration, and formulated its policy in reflex to the overwhelming force of numbers. The society the peasants created in Siberia was said to be freer and more prosperous than the one they left behind.[1]

There is an element of truth to this characterization: the movement did press on regardless of the government's efforts to decelerate it, and the living standards of the migrants were eventually higher than they had been in European Russia. But it leaves much out of the picture by implying that the role of the government was negligible. Peasant resettlement was but one, albeit a central, facet of a larger program intended to colonize—and thereby Russify—Siberia through economic development. For this reason the Committee of the Siberian Railroad in St. Petersburg planned, coordinated, and controlled colonization and development.[2]

1. See Donald W. Treadgold, *The Great Siberian Migration: Government and Peasant in Resettlement from Emancipation to the First World War* (Princeton, 1957). François-Xavier Coquin, *La Sibérie: Peuplement et immigration paysanne au XIXᵉ siècle* (Paris, 1969), 687–746 and passim, finds the peasant migrants to have been much less successful than Treadgold does, and he rejects the comparison between farmers on the American frontier and Russian peasants in Siberia.

2. The comprehensive planning undertaken by the Committee of the Siberian Railroad in the development of Siberia has been pointed out by J. N. Westwood, *A*

## Guiding Principles

The guiding principles of the Committee of the Siberian Railroad were set forth by Witte, whose outlook they reflected. The common understanding of Witte holds that by 1889 he had abandoned his Slavophile antipathy to modern capitalism. In its place stood a new devotion to the theory of national industrialization expounded by Friedrich List. Soon thereafter, Vyshnegradskii's policies were discredited in the wake of famine and the "industrializer" Witte was to try to implement a new "system."[3] According to this view, Witte quickly shelved agricultural reform in spite of the famine and, preoccupied with industrialization and the Siberian Railroad, left the wounds of the countryside to fester.[4]

Such a picture does not, however, correspond to the reality of Witte's attitude or actions. As we have seen, Witte's Slavophilism remained intact until his death, and it applied to his economic views as well as his political convictions. There is no evidence that he had elaborated his so-called system at this time, and his acceptance of List does not represent a departure from Slavophilism. He stressed the power and nationalist dimensions of industry, not political liberalism or capitalism.[5]

The Siberian Railroad, the major component of Witte's economic policy in his first years as minister of finance, combined both Slavophile and Listian economic ideas, in a manner Witte thought suitable for Russian conditions. Desiring to achieve economic self-reliance and impress the world with Russia's ability, Witte established the principle that the construction of the Siberian Railroad, this "great pursuit of the Russian nation," should rely solely on a Russian work force and use exclusively Russian materials and equipment.[6] He also

---

*History of Russian Railways* (London, 1964), 124, and *Endurance and Endeavour: Russian History, 1812–1986*, 3d ed. (Oxford, 1987), 138–139; and M. R. Sigalov and V. A. Lamin, *Zheleznodorozhnoe stroitel'stvo v praktike khoziaistvennogo osvoeniia Sibiri* (Novosibirsk, 1988), 16. Michael T. Florinsky's assessment, in *Russia: A History and Interpretation*, vol. 2 (New York, 1960), 1104, that the committee was "modelled after the boards of American railroad companies," is inaccurate, as this chapter and the next will show.

3. See Theodore Von Laue, *Sergei Witte and the Industrialization of Russia* (New York, 1973), 33, 54–63, 114–115; L. E. Shepelev, *Tsarizm i burzhuaziia vo vtoroi polovine XIX veke: Problemy torgovo-promyshlennoi politiki* (Leningrad, 1981), 193–194.

4. Richard Robbins, Jr., *Famine in Russia, 1891–1892: The Imperial Government Responds to a Crisis* (New York, 1975), 180.

5. See Von Laue, *Sergei Witte*, 62–63. Von Laue ignores the implications of this characterization in his own interpretation.

6. *Otchet po komitetu sibirskoi zheleznoi dorogi za 1893–1897 gg.* (n.p., n.d.), 19–20; G. K. Tsvetkov, "Ekonomicheskoe znachenie sibirskoi zheleznoi dorogi," *Vestnik*

called for the well-rounded development of Siberia, indicating that heavy industry would not be favored to the exclusion of cottage industry or farming, as might be supposed. Agriculture was not just an incidental responsibility—it was one of his top priorities. Witte consciously attempted to solve the Russian agricultural crisis by promoting peasant resettlement in Siberia. The assertion that he ignored the plight of the Russian peasantry is therefore unjust, although his solution did not prove to be sufficient in the end.[7]

Even the regionalist paper *Vostochnoe obozrenie* was impressed by the range of the Committee of the Siberian Railroad's activities: it admitted that they would "have an effect on the essential economic interests of Siberia."[8] But the approval was only grudging, for Witte's motives were antipathetic to the regionalists'. As Witte said,

> Up to now Siberia has not made significant progress in its economic growth, despite the abundance of its natural riches. After more than three hundred years of possession by the Russian state it remains at a low level of civil development and is sparsely inhabited, even in the regions with the most auspicious natural conditions. It has not yet succeeded in imparting to its aborigines the basic traits of Russian nationality, or even the least inclination to culture. Such an unfortunate situation has doubtless been brought about primarily by its disconnection from European Russia. Siberia, although a part of Russia, has not participated in the latter's civil, cultural, and economic progress, but somehow has hardened in its centuries-old immobility. To connect Siberia by means of the railroad with the European Russian rail network, in such a way as to bring it closer to European Russia—this is to give it access to Russian life and to bring about those very conditions of existence and development that are prevalent in the other parts of Russia, which are linked among themselves by the railroads, as well as with the vital centers of the country.[9]

Witte's words express a desire for centralization and Russification, and imply the destruction of the autonomy and uniqueness of Siberia which the regionalists so cherished. Their dictum was that "colonists

*moskovskogo universiteta*, 1946, no. 2: 116–117. The quote is from ZhKSZhD, zas. 10, Nov. 10, 1893, p. 14, col. 2.

7. According to Geroid Tanquary Robinson, "the natural increase of the rural population of the fifty *guberniias* [of European Russia] was nearly fourteen times as great as the net loss which these *guberniias* incurred through emigration to Siberia" from 1861 to 1905 (*Rural Russia under the Old Regime* [Berkeley, 1960], 109–110).

8. *Vostochnoe obozrenie*, 1893, nos. 13–14:2.

9. B. B. Glinskii, ed., *Prolog russko-iaponskoi voiny: Materialy iz arkhiva grafa S. Iu. Witte* (Petrograd, 1916), 11.

144    Creation

are not necessary for the railroad, but the other way around: the railroad is [solely] a convenient means of conveyance for them."[10] The state viewed the matter from the opposite perspective, and although the railroad committee seemed to be fulfilling the economic prescription of the regionalists with its concern for local needs and its program of comprehensive development, its priority was to serve the interests of state in building and operating the railroad.

Contrary to his portrayal by historians as a representative of commercial interests, Witte intended the Siberian Railroad to be built by the state and for the state. His skepticism toward private enterprise is evident in all aspects of the project. As he said, "the Siberian Railroad has an important advantage . . . [in being] built and operated by the government rather than by a private company. This circumstance allows for the application of measures that closely correspond to the state's interests and are necessary for the achievement of its . . . goals."[11]

To assist the railroad's construction and ensure its viability during operation, Witte had the committee establish a special fund for what were known as "auxiliary enterprises." As head of the special preparatory commission that administered it, Anatolii Kulomzin came to wield influence over all matters of colonization in Siberia.[12] The auxiliary enterprises were part of Witte's "detailed plan for the realization of the Siberian line," which he had inherited from Giubbenet and then refined.[13] The auxiliary enterprises included the improvement of Siberian water transport, the expansion of Siberian industry, and the

10. *Vostochnoe obozrenie*, 1892, no. 39: 2.
11. ZhKSZhD, osobyi zhurnal, Feb. 10 and 24, 1893, p. 3, col. 1.
12. V. F. Borzunov, "Istoriia sozdaniia transsibirskoi zheleznodorozhnoi magistrali XIX–nachala XX vv." (Ph.D. diss., Tomskii Gosudarstvennyi Universitet, 1972), 759; Glinskii, *Prolog*, 19–20. The fund was initially set at 14 million rubles but was enlarged in 1897 to 21.7 million. According to Borzunov, more than 32 million rubles were eventually spent on the auxiliary enterprises. Borzunov devotes little more than two pages (out of more than 1,800) directly to the topic of the auxiliary enterprises. Because of this major shortcoming his work fails to convey the nature and full significance of the Siberian Railroad project.
13. S. V. Sabler and I. V. Sosnovskii, comps., *Sibirskaia zheleznaia doroga v eia proshlom i nastoiashchem: Istoricheskii ocherk*, ed. A. N. Kulomzin (St. Petersburg, 1903), 111; Borzunov, "Istoriia sozdaniia," 517. Witte himself referred to the "planned construction of the Siberian road" in his *Vospominaniia*, vol. 1 (Moscow, 1960), 441. For Giubbenet's plan, see MPS, "Otchet o deiatel'nosti ministerstva putei soobshcheniia po stroitel'stvu sibirskoi zheleznoi dorogi za vremia s 30 marta 1889 g. po 17 ianvaria 1892 g." (TsGAOR, fond 677, opis' 1, delo 629), 19–21; ZhMPS, official sec., 1893, no. 2: 20–21. Aside from the auxiliary enterprises and the funding of construction, the "detailed plan" established a construction schedule for the railroad. See Sabler and Sosnovskii, *Sibirskaia zheleznaia doroga*, 116–117.

coordination of peasant resettlement. Taken together, they compose Witte's effort to colonize the lands beyond the Urals.

## Waterways

After the Siberian Railroad was constructed, the region's rivers played an increasingly important role in its economic life.[14] Their importance was due to the geographical fact that, unlike the railroad, they extended throughout Siberia, but it was just as much a result of the program of improvements implemented by the Committee of the Siberian Railroad. Witte spoke of connecting the great rivers of Siberia—the Ob', Enisei, Lena, and Amur—by rail, to encourage development of wide regions of Siberia beyond the direct range of the railroad. The committee thus recognized and sought to meet the demands of local transport independent of the railroad.[15]

But assistance to local river transport was also in the direct interest of the Siberian Railroad. When up to 40,000 kilometers of important rivers had access to the railroad, they would be natural feeders that could sustain its operation.[16] Furthermore, the immediate needs of rapid railroad construction, as opposed to the future use of the rivers, focused attention on the waterways as potential avenues for the supply of building materials, fuels, and food, all of which were either unavailable or difficult to transport overland in most of Siberia, and especially in Transbaikalia, accessible only by the often unnavigable Amur and Shilka rivers.[17] Railroad construction in Siberia was

14. Great Britain, Naval Intelligence Division, *A Handbook of Siberia and Arctic Russia*, vol. 1 (London, n.d.), 25–26.

15. *Vestnik finansov, promyshlennosti i torgovli*, no. 2, Jan. 10, 1893: 86; Glinskii, *Prolog*, 10–11; ZhKSZhD, osobyi zhurnal, June 14, 1893 (Ministr putei soobshcheniia), pp. 3–4, col. 1; osobyi zhurnal, Mar. 10, 1893, pp. 14–15, col. 1.

16. ZhKSZhD, osobyi zhurnal, Feb. 10 and 24, 1893, p. 11, col. 2; *Otchet po KSZhD za 1894 god* (n.d., n.p.), 5–6. Cf. the equivalent of the Committee of the Siberian Railroad's river-improvement scheme: the construction of additional track throughout the American Great Plains by the Union Pacific Company. The Union Pacific's auxiliary and branch lines were four times longer than the core system. If the railroad hoped to do anything but carry through traffic, it had to stimulate a wide territory beyond the reach of the trunk line. See Robert G. Athearn, *Union Pacific Country* (Lincoln, Neb., 1976), 16–18.

17. See ZhKSZhD, zas. 5, Mar. 15, 1893, SP, pp. 1–3, col. 1; osobyi zhurnal, SP, May 26, 1893 (Ministr putei soobshcheniia), pp. 2–3, col. 1; zas. 22, Mar. 8, 1895, pt. 2, SP, pp. 11–12; zas. 25, Nov. 29, 1895, SP, p. 4, col. 1; *TIRTO*, 14:6–8, 32:7; A. Pushechnikov, "O nedochetakh v dele postroiki zheleznykh dorog neposredstvennym rasporiazheniem kazny," *Inzhener*, April 1909, no. 4: 104; P. P. Migulin, *Nasha noveishaia zhelezno-*

dependent on water routes as the only means of supply despite their short navigation season.

Since most rivers were hazardous, the committee sought to implement an extensive program of improvements and initiated the systematic exploration of the vast Siberian water system. The auxiliary enterprises fund provided support for work on approximately 10,000 versts of major rivers in Siberia. The Water Routes Administration of the Ministry of Transport dredged and dammed rivers, deepening their navigation channels and strengthening their banks. It set up buoys and flood markers, established meteorological stations, prepared maps, studied navigational conditions, and surveyed the regions along the rivers. To ease the conveyance of materials to the railroad, the Ministry of Transport organized docking facilities at points where the railroad and rivers intersected and built numerous temporary lines from the main line to the river harbors. Rails could now be delivered to all sections.[18]

Lake Baikal received special attention to make it suitable for temporary steamer transport of supplies and, eventually, passengers. The Naval Ministry undertook surveys for port facilities and studied weather conditions, in particular ice formation. Of less immediate use, it commenced hydrographic surveys of the entire lake and the cataloging of the region's flora and fauna.[19]

Most ambitious of the committee's activities in improving water transport, if least fruitful at the time, was its attempt to use the Northern Sea route to supply rails to the heart of Siberia. Naval Minister N. M. Chikhachev proposed chartering steamers and barges in England to carry English rails to Krasnoiarsk in central Siberia. Although this arrangement violated the principle that construction materials be of Russian provenance, Witte lent his support because it would familiarize Russian sailors with the route and help them dis-

*dorozhnaia politika i zheleznodorozhnye zaimy (1893–1902)* (Khar'kov, 1903), 284; M. V. Braikevitch and I. R. Afonin, "The Railways of Siberia," *Russian Economist: Journal of the Russian Economic Association* 2 (October–December 1921): 1491.

18. ZhKSZhD, osobyi zhurnal, June 14, 1893 (Ministr putei soobshcheniia), p. 1–5, col. 1; zas. 10, Nov. 10, 1893, p. 6, col. 2; zas. 24, June 28, 1895, SP, pp. 21–22; zas. 26, Mar. 6, 1896, SP, pp. 6–7, col. 1; zas. 30, Dec. 10, 1897, SP, pp. 28–29, col. 1; *ZhMPS*, official sec.: "Sibirskaia zheleznaia doroga," 1894, no. 4: 10; TKIM, 3:16 and vols. 15–17; *TIRTO*, vols. 17 and 19; *Otchet po KSZhD za 1894*, 8–10; Braikevitch and Afonin, "Railways of Siberia," 1493.

19. ZhKSZhD, osobyi zhurnal, Feb. 10 and 24, 1893, pp. 6–7, col. 1; zas. 10, Nov. 10, 1893, p. 4, col. 1, and pp. 4–5, col. 2; zas. 11, Dec. 1, 1893, p. 7, cols. 1–2; zas. 22, Mar. 8, 1895, pt. 2, SP, pp. 9–11; zas. 28, Nov. 27, 1896, SP, p. 14, col. 1; zas. 30, Dec. 10, 1897, SP, p. 42, col. 1, and p. 31, col. 2; zas. 35, June 14, 1900, SP, p. 26, cols. 1–2. See also F. K. Drizhenko, "Rekognostsirovka Baikal'skogo ozera v 1896 godu," *IIRGO* 33, no. 2 (1897): 210–241.

place the foreigners, in particular the Norwegians, who were until then its primary navigators and explorers.

In the summer of 1893 the operation was carried out. Barges carried 1,500 tons of rails (6,000 individual pieces, or enough for 25 versts) from English factories through the Kara Sea to the mouth of the Enisei River and from there to the port of Krasnoiarsk. Several of the barges sank under the weight of their cargo, but most of the rails were retrieved. Improvements on internal waterways, the eventual construction of the railroad to Krasnoiarsk, and the reluctance to turn to foreign suppliers severely restricted demand for shipments via the Northern Sea route. The railroad committee was optimistic about its future, however, and the Naval Ministry continued to conduct studies of the Kara Sea and the rivers emptying into it. It had the full backing of *Vostochnoe obozrenie*.[20]

The same wariness of foreigners motivated Witte and the committee to create a Russian merchant marine. It was an opportune time to do so, with tens of millions of puds of railroad supplies requiring overseas transport to construction sites. After completion of the railroad Witte expected it to survive for general use and put an end to Russia's dependence on foreign merchant vessels. The committee expanded the Volunteer Fleet for this purpose and Witte gave it preferential treatment over competing private Russian shipping firms, another reflection of his ambivalence toward private enterprise.[21] To accommodate future expansion, the committee supervised the upgrading and expansion of the commercial port at Vladivostok and took over its administration.[22]

20. ZhKSZhD, osobyi zhurnal, Feb. 10 and 24, 1893, p. 11, col. 2; osobyi zhurnal, Feb. 24, 1893, pp. 1–4, cols. 1–2; osobyi zhurnal, Mar. 10, 1893, pp. 11–12, col. 1; zas. 7, June 2, 1893, pp. 8–9, col. 1, and p. 8, col. 2; zas. 8, June 14, 1893, p. 5, col. 1; zas. 10, Nov. 10, 1893, pp. 8–10, cols. 1–2; zas. 23, May 3, 1895, pt. 1, SP, pp. 23–24; zas. 25, Nov. 29, 1895, SP, pp. 19–20; *Otchet po KSZhD za 1894 god*, 43–44; *ZhMPS*, official sec.: "Sibirskaia zheleznaia doroga," 1894, no. 4: 45–47; Constantine Krypton, *The Northern Sea Route: Its Place in Russian Economic History before 1917* (New York, 1953), 79–92; Witte, *Vospominaniia*, 2:569–572; *Vostochnoe obozrenie*, 1894, no. 78: 2–3.

21. Borzunov, "Istoriia sozdaniia," 1429–1430, and "Bor'ba parokhodnykh kompanii za perevozki passazhirov i gruzov sibirskoi magistrali v kontse XIX v.," in Akademiia Nauk SSSR, Sibirskoe Otdelenie, Dal'nevostochnyi Filial, vol. 7, seriia istoricheskaia, *Trudy: Istoriia, arkheologiia i etnografiia Dal'nego Vostoka* (Vladivostok, 1967), 73, 79–80; ZhKSZhD, zas. 22, Mar. 8, 1895, pt. 2, SP, pp. 13–15. Even with higher shipping prices, the Volunteer Fleet was given twice as many orders as its largest competitor.

22. ZhKSZhD, passim; *Otchet po KSZhD za 1893 god* (n.d., n.p.), 43–46; *Otchet po KSZhD za 1894 god*, 44–46; *ZhMPS*, official sec.: "Sibirskaia zheleznaia doroga," 1894, no. 4: 18–19; Borzunov, "Istoriia sozdaniia," 1261; V. E. Timonov, "O glavneishikh vodnykh putiakh priamurskogo kraia v sviazi s voprosom ob izbranii mesta dlia tikhookeanskogo kommercheskogo porta sibirskoi zheleznoi dorogi," *IIRGO* 34, no. 3 (1898): 317–366.

The activities of the Committee of the Siberian Railroad in improving navigation on Siberian waterways, though initiated for the purpose of railroad construction, went beyond the task at hand and contributed to the exploration of Russian territory and waters. But the state's interests were primary, and local wants were satisfied only insofar as they contributed to the construction or operation of the railroad. In this way Russian sovereignty would be strengthened and the role and potential claims of foreigners reduced.

## Industrial Development

As part of its concern with the upgrading of Siberia's economic infrastructure, at least in principle the committee recognized the needs of the region independent of the railroad and hoped to serve them by stimulating Siberian industry. In accordance with the regionalists' program for the Siberian economy, as well as Witte's Slavophilism, heavy industry by no means monopolized the attention of the railroad committee; cottage industries and artels were also supported in the interests of the local economy.[23] To satisfy the future demand of the Siberian population for technical and commercial education, as well as the requirements of the railroad, the committee sponsored the opening of technical colleges in Tomsk and Khabarovsk. *Vostochnoe obozrenie* applauded this expansion of local educational opportunities.[24]

But despite the committee's talk of raising the cultural level of Siberia and introducing a high level of "technical perfection" to enliven its stagnant industry, its industrial policy was largely adapted to the priority of supplying the railroad with construction materials and fuels.[25] Although for the most part it intended to rely on private industry, it granted state subsidies in the form of loans and orders, and deemed factories and mines within Siberia worthy of support only if they were located close to the railroad. Once again the interests of the state set the course of Siberian industrial development. Indeed, the committee

23. *Vostochnoe obozrenie*, 1894, no. 75, p. 1; *Vestnik finansov*, no. 7, Feb. 16, 1897: 341–343, and no. 30, July 27, 1897: 139.

24. *Otchet po KSZhD za 1894 g.*, 13–14; *ZhMPS*, official sec.: "Sibirskaia zheleznaia doroga," 1894, no. 4: 44; Harley David Balzer, "Educating Engineers: Economic Politics and Technical Training in Tsarist Russia" (Ph.D. diss., University of Pennsylvania, 1980), 388–390; *Vostochnoe obozrenie*, 1894, no. 102: 1.

25. For an example of the committee's high aspirations, see *Vestnik finansov*, no. 2, Jan. 10, 1893: 92.

regarded Peter the Great's creation of the Ural iron industry as a successful precedent for its stimulation of Siberian industry.[26]

The committee conducted research into the viability of creating brick factories, sawmills, and cement factories for both long-term local uses and railroad construction, but most vital was the production of iron for rails, spikes, and bridges. The quantities needed would be enormous (more than 23 million puds for rails and spikes alone, making up two-thirds of the total production of pig iron in all of Russia for the years 1885–1889 and one-third for the years 1890–1894).[27] It was originally expected that the railroad would rely on the Siberian iron industry, so hopes for its expansion rose, but none of the three existing iron works in Siberia—the Gur'ev factory in Kuznetsk okrug, the Nikolaev factory near Bratskii Ostrog on the Angara, or the Abakan factory in the southwest of Enisei province—was capable of adapting to rail production, even with heavy state subsidies and large orders.[28]

Witte and his colleagues soon recognized that the Siberian Railroad would have to rely on the production of European Russia, in particular the Urals, for its rails and rolling stock. Thus the railroad would "raise the productive forces of our Motherland" and hold to the principle of building with Russian materials to the greatest extent possible. It would also keep to its construction schedule; Witte insisted that the schedule be kept, even though it would require the diversion of a very large part of the nation's rail production to Siberia.[29]

Eventually twenty-five Russian factories produced rails, joints, and spikes for the railroad, exceeding 23 million puds at a cost of more than 39 million rubles. Twelve European Russian and Polish factories contributed an additional 4 million puds of bridge iron. The Putilov Company and the Briansk Ironworks supplied the railroad with much

26. ZhKSZhD, osobyi zhurnal, Feb. 10 and 24, 1893, pp. 5–6, col. 1; pp. 7–9, col. 2. For the reference to Peter the Great, see TKIM 25:59.

27. ZhKSZhD, zas. 12, Dec. 22, 1893, pp. 14–15, cols. 1–2; zas. 23, May 3, 1895, pt. 1, SP, pp. 22–23; TKIM, vol. 10; A. V. Pataleev, *Istoriia stroitel'stva velikogo sibirskogo zhelezno-dorozhnogo puti* (Khabarovsk, 1951), 12. For the requirements of the Siberian Railroad, see Borzunov, "Istoriia sozdaniia," 817. For total Russian production figures, see M. E. Falkus, *The Industrialisation of Russia, 1700–1914* (London, 1972), 52.

28. *TOSRPT*, vol. 22, otdel 1 (1893), 38–40; TKIM, vol. 19; vol. 23, p. 1; ZhKSZhD, osobyi zhurnal, Feb. 10 and 24, 1893, p. 8, col. 2; osobyi zhurnal, June 14, 1893 (Ministr putei soobshcheniia, po delu dogovora s Polovtsovoi), pp. 1–2, col. 1; zas. 24, June 28, 1895, SP, pp. 14–15; zas. 26, Mar. 6, 1896, SP, pp. 13–14, cols. 1–2.

29. ZhKSZhD, osobyi zhurnal, May 26, 1893 (Ministr putei soobshcheniia), pp. 2–3, col. 1; zas. 10, Nov. 10, 1893, p. 12, col. 2; *Vestnik finansov*, no. 2, Jan. 10, 1893: 89. The quote is in Glinskii, *Prolog*, 190–191.

of its rolling stock. In 1893 alone, orders were placed for 148 eight-wheeled steam locomotives and 1,811 railroad cars and flatcars. By 1903, Russian factories had delivered 1,514 locomotives and 30,197 railroad cars. The cost of rolling stock made up one-sixth of the total construction expenditures of the railroad.[30]

One of the most important suppliers of rails was the Nadezhdinsk Iron and Steel Works in the Bogoslovskii mining district of the northern Urals, erected with a loan of 2.5 million rubles provided by the Committee of the Siberian Railroad in return for the shipment of 5 million puds of steel rails, and sustained thereafter by government subsidies. The factory's owner (and namesake) was Nadezhda Mikhailovna Polovtsova, the wife of A. A. Polovtsov, a state secretary and member of the State Council. Polovtsova was the daughter of the millionaire Baron M. Stieglitz, and she had made Polovtsov one of the wealthiest men in Russia.

The Bogoslovskii factories were of the first importance for Polovtsov, and he spared no effort to advance their cause. There can be no doubt that he used his influence at court and his position in the State Council to win the contract to supply rails to the Siberian Railroad. Witte was the most vocal defender of the contract in the Committee of the Siberian Railroad (against those who insisted on giving preference to Siberian industry) because he hoped Polovtsov would become a powerful ally on the State Council, which still regarded Witte with skepticism. The subsidy was the price of Polovtsov's support for Witte in the State Council. Supporting the Bogoslovskii factories with loans and contracts would tie Polovtsov to him and help grease the wheels of the bureaucracy in St. Petersburg, especially in regard to the Siberian Railroad. This consideration, as much as any other, determined the resolution of the problem of iron supplies for the railroad; the political customs of St. Petersburg molded the construction of the Siberian Railroad and Siberian economic development. The incident illuminates an important dimension of the state's stimulation of industry in Russia and calls into further question the quality of state-led industrialization under Witte.[31]

30. Borzunov, "Istoriia sozdaniia," 817, 980–981, 1068, 1069, 1143, 1145–1147, and "K voprosu ob ekonomicheskom znachenii sibirskoi zheleznoi dorogi v kontse XIX–nachale XX vv.," in *Voprosy istorii Sibiri i Dal'nego Vostoka*, ed. V. I. Shunkov et al. (Novosibirsk, 1961), 101; Sabler and Sosnovskii, *Sibirskaia zheleznaia doroga*, 275; ZhKSZhD, osobyi zhurnal, Mar. 15, 1893, pp. 3–4, col. 1. Wheel arrangements on these locomotives were either 2-4-4-0 or 00-8-0 (Westwood, *History*, 119).

31. On the relationship between the government and the Nadezhdinsk works, see Steven G. Marks, "The Trans-Siberian Railroad: State Enterprise and Economic Development in Imperial Russia" (Ph.D. diss., Harvard University, 1988), 259–263.

In the interests of rapid construction, it was often found convenient as well to turn to foreign manufacturers, if reluctantly. Some contractors on the Western Siberian Railroad made use of American-made steam shovels, and because of the relative proximity of the United States and the low cost of overseas shipping, American steel was imported to the Far Eastern sections of the railroad for twelve bridges. Other American contributions included an indeterminate number of steel rails and Baldwin locomotives.[32] None of these statistics justifies the claim that Witte ignored the principle of relying on Russian equipment or materials, or the assertion that the Trans-Siberian and Chinese-Eastern Railroads were "in all essentials" American-equipped.[33]

The committee gave preference to European Russian iron works, but it did not completely abandon its faith in a future for Siberian metallurgy. In 1888 the Kuznetsk basin had barely received mention in the Russian Technical Society debates as a potential source of coal.[34] By the mid-1890s, research had shown that iron deposits ex-

32. ZhKSZhD, zas. 10, Nov. 10, 1893, pp. 27–28, col. 1; George Sherman Queen, *The United States and the Material Advance in Russia, 1881–1906* (New York, 1976), 166–170, 175. Queen cites no evidence that more than 100,000 of 300,000 tons of rails ordered in the United States were ever delivered. It is equally unclear whether the number of locomotives he cites (500) were delivered to Russia and, if so, to which railroad. The Chinese-Eastern Railroad relied heavily on foreign steam engines, but it is unlikely that the Siberian Railroad did. Of the total number of locomotives that came into use on Russian railroads in the 1890s, fewer than 16% were made abroad. If all types of rolling stock were included, the percentage presumably would be even lower. See D. P. Il'inskii and V. P. Ivanitskii, *Ocherk istorii russkoi parovozostroitel'noi i vagonostroitel'noi promyshlennosti* (Moscow, 1929), 80. *The Railroad Gazette*, Mar. 22, 1895, p. 188, reported that some secondhand American locomotives were in use on the Ussuri Railroad in 1895, but that thereafter rolling stock and other iron equipment manufactured in the Baltic provinces were to be introduced. As for rails, Peter Gatrell, in *The Tsarist Economy, 1850–1917* (New York, 1986), 154, says that Russian imports did not exceed 1% in the 1890s. No rails purchased from the United States appear to have made their way for use anywhere outside of the Vladivostok terminus (*Railroad Gazette*, Mar. 17, 1899, p. 189).

33. The first claim is made by Borzunov, "Istoriia sozdaniia," 386. Other Soviet historians criticize Witte for relying too heavily on Russian factories, which were often far costlier than their foreign counterparts. This is closer to the truth, and Borzunov's figures back up this statement more than they do his own. See Peter I. Lyashchenko, *History of the National Economy of Russia to the 1917 Revolution*, trans. L. M. Herman (New York, 1949), 560, and G. K. Tsvetkov, "Khod stroitel'stva velikogo sibirskogo zheleznodorozhnogo puti," *Vestnik moskovskogo universiteta*, 1947, no. 2: 138. The second claim is by William Appleman Williams, *American-Russian Relations, 1781–1947* (New York, 1952), 83, cited in John J. Stephan, "Russian-American Economic Relations in the Pacific: A Historical Perspective," in *Soviet-American Horizons on the Pacific*, ed. John J. Stephan and V. P. Chichkanov (Honolulu, 1986), 72.

34. "O velikom sibirskom puti (Prodolzhenie besedy po dokladu N. A. Sytenko)," *ZhdD*, 1888, nos. 22–24: 197.

isted there close to rich veins of coking-quality coals and anthracite, a combination that would allow for the establishment of a Siberian iron industry in relative proximity to the Siberian Railroad. To plan its development, extensive geological research of the region was required.[35]

The desire to tap the apparent mineral wealth of the Kuznetsk basin pointed up the necessity of conducting geological surveys in all of Siberia. As one writer put it, the Committee of the Siberian Railroad made Siberia "a fashionable place for all types of research." In the two years 1894–1896 alone, according to his count, fifty-eight geological expeditions were sent to western Siberia and the Altai Mountains and forty-four to eastern Siberia and the Far East.[36] Before this time, surveying and exploration of Siberia had been desultory, limited to established mining regions and populated settlements.[37]

Characteristically, the committee limited geological expeditions to a zone bisected by the Siberian Railroad, for the purpose of charting the location of fuel and ore sources that would be of direct use to the railroad during construction and operation, or of indirect benefit through their exploitation by local industry. The Ministry of State Domains sent survey teams out yearly along the projected route in both eastern and western Siberia to catalog and map their resources. They discovered extensive deposits of coal, iron ore, copper ore, nephrite, graphite, lead, granite, and silver, as well as unidentified ores. They examined peat bogs for their fuel potential, conducted hydrographic studies in the Steppe oblast to find sources of water for the railroad, and sought salt in Priamur'e to permit the growth of a fishing industry, which it was felt might better sustain local settlement. They also searched for oil, but with very minimal success.[38]

35. "'O sposobakh obezpecheniia stroiushcheisia sibirskoi zheleznoi dorogi rel'sami i zheleznodorozhnymi prinadlezhnostiami' (Doklad A. A. Bogdanova)," *TOSRPT*, vol. 22, otdel 2 (1893), 458; ZhKSZhD, osobyi zhurnal, Feb. 10 and 24, 1893, pp. 5–6, col. 1, and pp. 8–9, col. 2; osobyi zhurnal, June 14, 1893 (Ministr putei soobshcheniia, po delu dogovora s Polovtsovoi), p. 2, col. 1; p. 3, col. 2; pp. 8–9, col. 2; zas. 10, pp. 11–12, col. 2; TKIM 23:17.

36. S. Nikitin, "Uspekhi geologicheskikh znanii za 1892–1893 goda," *Ezhegodnik imperatorskogo russkogo geograficheskogo obshchestva* 6 (1896): 61–62.

37. ZhKSZhD, osobyi zhurnal, Mar. 10, 1893, pp. 4–6, col. 1.

38. See ibid., passim; *Otchet po KSZhD za 1894 god*, 39–41; ZhMPS, official sec.: "Sibirskaia zheleznaia doroga," 1894, no. 4: 53, 55–58; "Sibirskaia zheleznaia doroga," *Inzhener* 20 (April 1896): 192. For the practical results of this research as regards coal, see E. Morskii, "Kachestvo sibirskikh uglei po dannym laboratorii sibirskoi zheleznoi dorogi," *Zhurnal obshchestva sibirskikh inzhenerov* 3 (March 1911): 79–86. According to Morskii, the Siberian Railroad was using more than 50 million puds of coal a year. The railroad's laboratories analyzed the output of each mine.

The committee's interest in gold mining is evidence of the prominent place held by the Siberian Railroad in Witte's economic policy. Witte was gradually won over to the idea of putting Russia on the gold standard; Siberia might provide the gold reserves this move required.[39] An increase in gold production would also bring revenues to the Siberian Railroad and was expected to enliven vast regions of Siberia and inject much-needed capital into the economy as a whole.

Witte called for a wide-ranging study of gold mining, financed by the auxiliary enterprises. For the first time, the potential for gold mining in the Far East and the Okhotsk-Kamchatka region was explored, with results that were greater than expected. The mining expeditions discovered and mapped rich gold fields throughout northeastern Siberia, in an area destined to be first worked on a large scale by forced labor in the Stalin period, under the administration of Dal'stroi (Far Eastern Construction Trust). The tsar ordered the government to open the new gold fields to private industry, but with close supervision to safeguard the interests of the state.[40]

As in all the auxiliary enterprises, the contours of the committee's work in the stimulation of mining and industry were shaped to fit the specific demands of the state in completing the railroad. But in its scope the committee contributed to the exploration and opening of the empire's distant Siberian lands, initiating a process of development that is still ongoing.

### Peasant Resettlement

The committee's promotion of the state's interests was most obvious in its detailed direction of the peasant colonization movement. This was the broad and diverse field of activity within the auxiliary enterprises which, next to railroad construction itself, received the bulk of the committee's attention and funding. Witte and others thought of it as their basic task and the most important of the auxiliary enterprises.[41]

39. B. V. Anan'ich, *Rossiia i mezhdunarodnyi kapital, 1897–1914* (Leningrad, 1970), 15.

40. *Otchet po KSZhD za 1894 god*, 41–42; ZhMPS, official sec.: "Sibirskaia zheleznaia doroga," 1894, no. 4: 53–54, 58–60; ZhKSZhD, zas. 23, May 3, 1895, pt. 1, SP, pp. 16–17; zas. 26, Mar. 6, 1896, SP, pp. 33–34, col. 1; zas. 29, Apr. 2, 1897, SP, pp. 41–43, col. 1, and pp. 41–42, col. 2; zas. 31, Apr. 29, 1898, SP, pp. 34–36, col. 1; zas. 32, Jan. 27, 1899, SP, pp. 25–26, col. 2; zas. 38, Dec. 5, 1901, SP, p. 11, col. 2; P. K. Iavorovskii, *Gornaia promyshlennost' Sibiri i sibirskaia zheleznaia doroga* (St. Petersburg, 1895), 1–2.

41. Witte, *Vospominaniia*, 1:441; *Otchet po KSZhD za 1893 god*, 26; ZhKSZhD, osobyi zhurnal, June 2, 1893, p. 14, col. 2. Of the more than 32 million rubles spent by the

Colonization would benefit the government in its efforts to build and operate the railroad. The committee intended to settle the region along either side of the railroad to provide a ready supply of passengers, freight, and repairmen.[42]

But the major reason for the controlled distribution of plots to immigrants was Russification. The specter of the "yellow peril" loomed before the committee and provided a compelling justification for state control of the migration: "For the sole purpose of strengthening the Russians' bulwark against the [inflowing] waves of the yellow race, all measures possible must be taken to increase the supply of lands where [Russian] peasants can be settled."[43] Rapid settlement by Russian peasants would secure the border.

In the interior the peril was no less strong. A survey undertaken by the committee showed that in the Amur region, many natives, in particular the Orochi and Manegry, still considered themselves subjects of the Chinese emperor rather than of the tsar.[44] Bunge counseled the reinforcement of the Russian element in Siberia and to this end Kulomzin commissioned a study of Bismarck's attempt to Germanize Prussia's Polish provinces through colonization. His methods became a model for the organized settlement of Siberia.[45]

The committee's program of resettlement was nothing short of demographic engineering on a mass scale. According to Witte, "landlessness" existed not because the empire was lacking in land but because its population was unevenly distributed.[46] The answer was to

---

auxiliary enterprises fund between 1893 and 1903, approximately 27 million went directly or indirectly for peasant resettlement. See Sabler and Sosnovskii, *Sibirskaia zheleznaia doroga*, app., table 2.

42. ZhKSZhD, osobyi zhurnal, Feb. 10 and 24, 1893, p. 4, col. 2; ibid., June 2, 1893, pp. 5–6, col. 1, and pp. 11–13, col. 2; ibid., June 14, 1893 (Ministr vnutrennykh del), pp. 2–3, col. 1; *Otchet po KSZhD za 1894 god*, 24–25, 29–30; TKIM(VP), vol. 21. Regardless of the dearth of water in the Barabinsk steppe, the committee prepared settler plots close to the railroad so as to guarantee that people would be available to clear the track of snow.

43. ZhKSZhD, osobyi zhurnal, June 14, 1893 (Ministr vnutrennykh del), p. 2, col. 1; zas. 10, Nov. 10, 1893, p. 19, cols. 1–2; zas. 22, Mar. 8, 1895, pt. 1, pp. 7–8; zas. 34, Dec. 8, 1899, SP, pp. 30–31, col. 2; zas. 35, June 14, 1900, SP, pp. 17–18, cols. 1–2, and pp. 19–20, col. 2; *Otchet po KSZhD za 1893–1897 gg.*, 21.

44. ZhKSZhD, zas. 27, Apr. 27, 1896, pt. 2, SP, p. 16, col. 1.

45. George E. Snow, ed. and trans., "The Years 1881–1894 in Russia: A Memorandum Found in the Papers of N. Kh. Bunge: A Translation and Commentary," *Transactions of the American Philosophical Society* 71, pt. 6 (1981): 66–67; N. P. Egunov, *Kolonial'naia politika tsarizma i pervyi etap natsional'nogo dvizheniia v Buriatii v epokhu imperializma* (Ulan-Ude, 1963), 142. On the attempt to colonize Germany's Polish provinces and its ultimate failure, see J. H. Clapham, *Economic Development of France and Germany, 1815–1914* (Cambridge, 1968), 229–231.

46. Sergei Witte, *Printsipy zheleznodorozhnykh tarifov po perevozke gruzov*, 3d ed. (St. Petersburg, 1910), 129.

Peasant migrants at railroad way station. From Pereselencheskoe Upravlenie, *Aziatskaia Rossiia* (St. Petersburg, 1914).

distribute it more evenly where it would satisfy the needs of the state. In his words, "The settlement of open lands . . . accords with the basic economic task of the state, namely, the colonization of its entire territory." Population density, he continued, "constitutes . . . an important condition of political power: the size of the army is determined by it, and on that depends the nation's internal and external security and the achievement of its political goals."[47] This statement explains the purpose of colonization. As a Ministry of Finance publication announced, the government was taking charge of the historic eastward movement of the Great Russian "tribe."[48] Between 1891 and 1914, approximately 5 million Russians, Ukrainians, and Belorussians settled in Siberia. Of this total, illegal migration from 1895 to 1910 fluctuated between 25 and 50 percent, although it climbed much

47. S. Iu. Witte, *Vorlesungen über Volks- und Staatswirtschaft*, trans. Josef Melnik, vol. 1 (Stuttgart/Berlin, 1913), 90, 99.
48. *Vestnik finansov*, no. 2, Jan. 10, 1893: 87–89.

higher during the Russo-Japanese War, when the military monopolized the railroad.[49]

When Western historians discuss the government's efforts to control the settlement of Siberia between 1861 and 1904, they emphasize its inability to stop the flow of migrants and portray it as legalizing its own broken rules in the wake of the fait accompli of illegal migration. Soviet historians, on the other hand, emphasize the restraints the government placed in the way of the peasants and its unwillingness to lend them more than minimal assistance.[50] While there is much truth to both of these interpretations, they fail to recognize how wholeheartedly the Committee of the Siberian Railroad promoted resettlement and concerned itself with the welfare of all the peasant migrants, all to channel the movement according to the state's requirements.

This is not to claim that there was unanimous agreement on the issue; there was not. At both the special conference of November 21, 1892, and the first session of the Committee of the Siberian Railroad, Witte broached the topic of resettling landless peasants in Siberia. The resettlement, according to him, would solve two problems simultaneously: the peopling of Siberia and the overpopulation of rural Russia, which had become a financial burden to the government. Especially the peasants of the western provinces who had not received land allotments would benefit from resettlement. The committee's task was to ascertain who should go, how to get them to Siberia, how to distribute lands, and how to administer the program.[51]

Minister of the Interior Durnovo initially expressed reservations as to details of Witte's proposal. He was concerned about the impact of

49. Treadgold, *Great Siberian Migration*, 33–34, 146; Coquin, *La Sibérie*, 723.

50. See Coquin, *La Sibérie*, 349–389, 466–494, 741–742; Treadgold, *Great Siberian Migration*, 67–81, 112–130; B. V. Anan'ich et al., *Krizis samoderzhaviia v Rossii, 1895–1917* (Leningrad, 1984), 46–69; E. M. Brusnikin, "Pereselencheskaia politika tsarizma v kontse XIX veka," *Voprosy istorii* 40 (January 1965): 28–38; M. S. Simonova, "Pereselencheskii vopros v agrarnoi politike samoderzhaviia v kontse XIX–nachale XX v.," in *Ezhegodnik po agrarnoi istorii vostochnoi Evropy 1965 g.*, ed. V. K. Iatsunskii et al. (Moscow, 1970), 424–434; B. V. Tikhonov, "Pereselencheskaia politika tsarskogo pravitel'stva v 1892–1897 godakh," *Istoriia SSSR*, January–February 1977, no. 1: 109–121. For the separate legislation and policy pertaining to the lands of the tsar's cabinet and the Russian Far East, see, respectively, G. P. Zhidkov, "Pereselencheskaia politika kabineta v 1865–1905 gg.," in *Voprosy istorii Sibiri dosovetskogo perioda (Bakhrushinskie chteniia, 1969)*, ed. A. P. Okladnikov et al. (Novosibirsk, 1973), 365–374; V. M. Kabuzan, *Dal'nevostochnyi krai v XVII–nachale XX vv. (1640–1917): Istoriko-demograficheskii ocherk* (Moscow, 1985), 50–135.

51. Glinskii, *Prolog*, 12; ZhKSZhD, osobyi zhurnal, Feb. 10 and 24, 1893, pp. 1–5, col. 1.

migration on the agriculture of the "old settler" peasants of Siberia. To safeguard their interests, he argued, surveys must determine the exact amount of land available. Not until all land was surveyed (and millions of acres were still unsurveyed) should it be opened to settlement. The government should then hold a lottery to distribute lands to a very limited number of European Russian peasants, specifically those with means; settlement of the poorest elements in the Ussuri region had been a costly failure. Furthermore, the western provinces should not be depopulated of their Russian peasants, so as not to take a step backward in the Russification of that region, and "foreign elements"— that is, non-Russians—must be prohibited from settling in Siberia.[52]

Ministers of the Interior Durnovo, Goremykin, Plehve, and even Sipiagin also continued to oppose Witte on the major issue of the peasant commune, which had a bearing on resettlement. Initially Witte was a staunch supporter of the commune as a bulwark of order and conservatism in the countryside. Under the influence of Bunge, he gradually came to understand that in stifling individual enterprise and the internal market, the commune was injurious to the health of the Treasury. Its responsibility for rural poverty contributed to political instability too. He advocated the reform of passport restrictions and joint responsibility for taxes, those features of the commune that most retarded initiative and acted to restrict the departure of peasants for Siberia. After many years of Interior Ministry resistance and obstruction, Witte eventually succeeded in bringing the issue before the government for discussion and achieved these limited changes, to the benefit of peasant mobility.[53]

The opposition of the ministers of the interior can be attributed more to their bureaucratic caution, suspicion of change, and wariness of individual initiative than to anything else. And although their resistance to the weakening of the commune is linked to the migration question, it was mostly a symptom of the growing incompatibility of

52. ZhKSZhD, osobyi zhurnal, Feb. 10 and 24, 1893, pp. 1–2, col. 2, and pp. 4–5, col. 2; osobyi zhurnal, June 2, 1893, pp. 4–7, col. 2.

53. For various aspects of this issue, see Boris V. Anan'ich, "The Economic Policy of the Tsarist Government and Enterprise in Russia from the End of the Nineteenth through the Beginning of the Twentieth Century," in *Entrepreneurship in Imperial Russia and the Soviet Union*, ed. Gregory Guroff and Fred V. Carstensen (Princeton, 1983), 131–133; Anan'ich et al., *Krizis*, 49–60; Von Laue, *Sergei Witte*, 222–229; Shepelev, *Tsarizm*, 199–200; M. S. Simonova, "Bor'ba techenii v pravitel'stvennom lagere po voprosam agrarnoi politiki v kontse XIX v.," *Istoriia SSSR*, January–February 1963, no. 1: 74–78.

their ministry with the Ministry of Finance, as well as personal conflict between Witte and themselves. Before open hostility set in at the turn of the century, the two ministries were in general agreement on most matters.[54] In regard to the problem of the Siberian migration, the objections of the Ministry of the Interior were only to minutiae.

Witte's memoirs contribute to the perception of an Interior Ministry in stubborn opposition to Siberian resettlement by deliberately misrepresenting its position. According to Witte, Durnovo led the resistance on behalf of the gentry landlords. The landlords opposed the migration for fear that it would hold land prices down, deplete the supply of cheap labor, and disrupt order and state authority.[55] Witte's account is deceptive, however, rooted as it is in the bad feelings of many years between the two ministries.

The truth is that by 1894, Durnovo accepted the committee's statistics showing that there was a surplus of agricultural labor in the European Russian Black Earth Zone, so that even if many peasants migrated, the gentry would suffer no shortage of laborers.[56] The following year, on the basis of the committee's study of peasant land holding, Durnovo acknowledged the poverty of the rural population and the virtues of resettlement: "To deny them the chance to improve their economic condition by migrating to provinces where land is plentiful can hardly be considered the government's aim."[57] He was in perfect agreement with Witte and the rest of the committee on the question.

Witte misrepresented his own position too. He wrote that the idea of resettlement was "extremely liberal and almost revolutionary," and that St. Petersburg regarded it as a dangerous heresy. But his plan was not in the least liberal or revolutionary, as the encouragement and support given it by both Alexander III and Nicholas II attest.[58] Witte never envisaged totally free settlement. Although he knew the Russian peasant was not an "adventure seeker," he agreed with Durnovo that in the interests of "social tranquility and order," the spontaneous (*samovol'noe*) migration of peasants was "highly undesirable from the government's point of view," and that the movement should be orga-

---

54. Theodore Taranovski, "The Politics of Counter-reform: Autocracy and Bureaucracy in the Reign of Alexander III, 1881–1894" (Ph.D. diss., Harvard University, 1976), 103–104.

55. Witte, *Vospominaniia*, 1:441–443; 2:512.

56. Simonova, "Pereselencheskii vopros," 431.

57. ZhKSZhD, zas. 22, Mar. 8, 1895, pt. 1, pp. 2–3.

58. See Witte, *Vospominaniia*, 1:442–443; 2:511–512.

nized and kept "in conformity with the law." Witte warned the committee against exciting the peasants to the point where they would get "carried away with dreams of new lands."[59]

Until the poor harvest of 1901 and the peasant revolts of 1902 forced some rethinking of Russian agricultural policy, only Bunge advocated the removal of restrictions and the opening of Siberia to all comers. And even this proposition was part of a formula Bunge had developed to combat socialism in Russia, not advocacy of a liberal migration policy for its own sake.[60]

Witte and the committee accepted the fact that large numbers of irregular settlers would join those who had received permission to leave Russia for Siberia according to law. The minister of the interior's initial inclination to take "repressive measures" and force their return to their villages was roundly opposed, not least by Nicholas. Having broken their ties to the commune, he argued, they were not likely to be welcomed back to the fold. Ermolov opined that it would be disruptive to allow them back into European Russia once their property had been liquidated. Certain that dislocation and disorder would follow their forcible return to European Russia, the committee found it preferable to settle them on state lands in Siberia. By 1896, Minister of the Interior Goremykin had come around to this point of view and expressed his willingness to extend loans to the irregulars on the same basis as for legal settlers. At the same time, he would work to discourage peasants from leaving their communes in the first place.[61]

Rather than struggle in vain to prevent the movement of peasants, the members of the committee opted to bring it under government control and direct it in such a way that it would assist their remaking

59. ZhKSZhD, osobyi zhurnal, Feb. 10 and 24, 1893, pp. 3–4, col. 1; zas. 22, Mar. 8, 1895, pt. 1, pp. 3–6; Glinskii, *Prolog*, 12.

60. ZhKSZhD, zas. 22, Mar. 8, 1895, pt. 1, pp. 7–8; Snow, "Years 1881–1894 in Russia." On June 6, 1904, a new resettlement law originally written in the Committee of the Siberian Railroad and backed by Plehve went into effect, which no longer required peasants to seek special permission to emigrate to Siberia. See Treadgold, *Great Siberian Migration*, 128–129; Anan'ich et al., *Krizis*, 65–66.

61. ZhKSZhD, zas. 22, Mar. 8, 1895, pt. 1, pp. 4–7; zas. 27, Apr. 27, 1896, pt. 1, pp. 7–8, col. 1. In a series of laws promulgated in 1896, illegal migrants were granted the right to settle on plots and receive state loans; by order of the tsar, the temporary laws of 1894 pertaining to regular migrants were extended for their benefit. Exemptions from military service were not given, however, and at the end of the year the committee, still hesitant to encourage spontaneous resettlement, discontinued transport loans to illegal settlers. The minister of the interior also had second thoughts about distributing state lands to irregulars. See ZhKSZhD, zas. 22, Mar. 8, 1895, pt. 1, p. 11; zas. 28, Nov. 27, 1896, SP, pp. 25–26, col. 1; Tikhonov, "Pereselencheskaia politika," 113–115, 117; Treadgold, *Great Siberian Migration*, 126–127.

of Siberia. To ensure state control the committee promulgated a series of regulations. Plots were to be distributed "with a view to satisfying the multifarious state needs in the land which might arise in the future."[62] It consciously avoided the land speculation that accompanied the settlement of the American West by limiting authorization for the sale of lands to local governors.[63] The government reserved full rights without exception, on both public and private land, to all minerals and precious stones in the soil. This policy too led to the opposite of the American western experience, where miners had the right to trespass on public lands.[64]

To watch over the lower classes, Witte envisioned the formation of private estates in Siberia on which to settle state officials and members of the gentry, many of whom were impoverished and landless themselves. In the end, however, few of this class showed any interest in resettlement to Siberia.[65]

The Committee of the Siberian Railroad attempted to organize basic

62. ZhKSZhD, osobyi zhurnal, June 2, 1893, p. 6, col. 1.

63. ZhKSZhD, zas. 23, May 3, 1895, SP, pt. 1, pp. 18–20. Voloshinov's fears, which led him to speak out against private landownership in Siberia, may have been reflected in this decision: "Our peasant, arriving . . . [in Siberia], is so inexperienced, so unfamiliar with local conditions, that it is impossible to think that he will be able to compete with the Jews, who are already picking their way to Transbaikal oblast." Within a few years, he predicted, if land were permitted to be sold or leased, the migrants would fall into the grip of the Jews, who would then be the ones to gain the benefits of colonization, at the railroad's expense (*TIRTO* 10:3). On the United States, see Frederick Merk, *History of the Westward Movement* (New York, 1978). The distinctions between land use in Siberia and in the United States bolster my argument that the two types of settlement were more dissimilar than alike.

64. ZhKSZhD, zas. 35, June 14, 1900, SP, pp. 11–12, col. 2; Merk, *History of the Westward Movement*, 414–417.

65. ZhKSZhD, osobyi zhurnal, Feb. 10 and 24, 1893, p. 3, col. 1, and p. 5, col. 1; zas. 27, Apr. 27, 1896, pt. 2, SP, pp. 13–14, cols. 1–2. This measure would have entailed the introduction of the private estate, a form of landholding alien to Siberia, with a few rare exceptions. To ensure that the gentry did not lose their Siberian lands as they were doing in European Russia, the conference on gentry affairs and the State Council advocated special privileges and exemptions that would maintain their agricultural competitiveness. However, the Committee of the Siberian Railroad, including Sipiagin, though in favor of granting lands to the gentry, preferred to establish private landholding on a nonstate basis, in order to raise productivity and encourage development by merchants. In the interests of peasant colonizers, furthermore, they wanted to restrict the size of plots designated for use by nonpeasants to between 60 and 100 desiatins (162 to 270 acres) per family, compared to 60 desiatins of land maximum for peasant homesteads. The committee in this case was overruled by the more conservative State Council, which, in the law of June 8, 1901, allowed for gentry estates of up to 3,000 desiatins (8,100 acres) and permitted the gentry alone to lease lands. See ZhKSZhD, osobyi zhurnal, Feb. 10 and 24, 1893, p. 7, col. 2; zas. 35, June 14, 1900, SP, p. 10, col. 1, and pp. 10–15, col. 2; *PSZRI*, sobranie tret'e, vol. 21, 1901, no. 20338; Iu. B. Solov'ev, *Samoderzhavie i dvorianstvo v kontse XIX veka* (Leningrad, 1973), 328–342.

aspects of the peasant migrants' lives, involving itself before their arrival in Siberia and continuing to do so long after they were settled. The state's active guidance of the peasant resettlement far exceeded Iadrintsev's call for the establishment of local peasant agencies and the extension of subsidies to migrants.[66] According to one authority, "the quality of systematization [*planomernost'*] was imparted to the very matter of resettlement and colonization."[67]

The administration of the migration received constant bureaucratic attention, and the number of officials in Siberia concerned with the resettlement increased dramatically.[68] Foreshadowing the creation of new urban complexes along the Baikal-Amur Main Line in the 1970s and 1980s, the committee hired an architect to determine where new towns might arise along the railroad and to work with local authorities to establish planned settlements on the sites.[69]

Surveyors attempted to keep pace with the migration. The Ministry of Agriculture (formerly the Ministry of State Domains) conducted surveys on arable land normally 200 versts on each side of the railroad. The War Ministry undertook a search for habitable land in Transbaikal oblast. As migrants continued to press into Siberia, plots in the Black Earth Zone grew scarce, and survey teams went to work preparing plots in the taiga of Tobol'sk and Tomsk provinces and the Irkutsk general governorship. The cost of this work increased tenfold from 1885 to 1901, from 40,000 to 400,000 rubles per year.[70] By 1899, the total amount of surveyed land exceeded 21 million acres.[71]

66. N. M. Iadrintsev, *Sibir' kak koloniia v geograficheskom, etnograficheskom i istoricheskom otnoshenii*, 2d ed. (St. Petersburg, 1892), 242.
67. I. I. Serebrennikov, *Sibirovedenie* (Harbin, 1920), 78.
68. ZhKSZhD. Whereas earlier each survey team had had no more than two dozen members, by 1899 their numbers had been increased to more than 200 (Brusnikin, "Pereselencheskaia politika," 34–35). Albert J. Beveridge, *The Russian Advance* (New York, 1904), 218–219, attests to the energy and enthusiasm of Russian officials overseeing peasant land distribution, rooted in their missionary-like commitment to the Russian colonization of Siberia and the Far East. He admits, though, that they were reputed to be inefficient.
69. ZhKSZhD, zas. 3, Feb. 24, 1893, p. 10, col. 2; zas. 24, June 28, 1895, SP, pp. 26–27; N. V. Slukhanov, "BAM stroit vsia strana," in *BAM: Pervoe desiatiletie*, ed. A. G. Aganbegian and A. A. Kin (Novosibirsk, 1985), 44–62.
70. ZhKSZhD, zas. 3, Feb. 24, 1893, pp. 3–5, col. 1; p. 8, col. 1; p. 11, col. 2; zas. 12, Dec. 22, 1893, pp. 2–3, col. 1; pp. 2–5, col. 2; pp. 11–12, col. 1; p. 9, col. 2; zas. 21, Jan. 4, 1895, pp. 4–5; zas. 22, Mar. 8, 1895, pt. 1, pp. 14–15; zas. 27, Apr. 27, 1896, pt. 1, pp. 8–13, col. 1; zas. 27, Apr. 27, 1896, pt. 2, SP, pp. 14–16, col. 1; *Otchet po KSZhD za 1894 god*, 24–25; Brusnikin, "Pereselencheskaia politika," 34.
71. ZhKSZhD, zas. 32, Jan. 27, 1899, SP, pp. 18–19, col. 2; zas. 34, Dec. 8, 1899, SP, p. 29, col. 2. This figure does not include plots carved out of forest lands.

The norm for a plot destined for one family was approximately 15 desiatins (40.5 acres), with access to forest and pasturage. As a rule, 100 individual plots were formed into one enclosure (*otrub*). Buildings in an enclosure were generally close together and formed a village. Although most settlers preferred this arrangement, many in the Tara region of Tobol'sk province, originally from western Russia, preferred individual homesteads (*khutora*). The committee established special survey teams for this purpose, too, and was preparing legislation to regularize this form of settlement. To attract skilled technical employees to work on the railroad, special plots along the right of way were formed. At a quarter desiatin (0.725 acres), they were large enough for a kitchen garden.[72]

To bring still more land under settlement, hydrotechnical teams drained swamps in Tomsk province and the Ussuri region and irrigated portions of the arid steppelands of Akmolinsk oblast, where existing sources of water were saline.[73] The committee designated more than 18 million acres of land belonging to the nomadic Kazakhs of Akmolinsk oblast as "superfluous" and made them available for distribution to peasants.[74] It also eyed for peasant resettlement the 42.4 million acres held by 10,000 Cossacks of the Ussuri host.[75]

The committee arranged and directed the transport of settlers well into Siberia. By the laws of April 15, 1896, family scouts (*khodoki*)

72. Treadgold, *Great Siberian Migration*, 119, 125; ZhKSZhD, zas. 24, June 28, 1895, SP, pp. 28–30; zas. 34, Dec. 8, 1899, SP, pp. 29–31, col. 2. Treadgold surmises that the *khutora* simply reflected a different preference for land use than the *otrub* arrangement, but that they remained a part of the village commune (*Great Siberian Migration*, 125–126).

73. ZhKSZhD, zas. 23, May 3, 1895, pt. 1, SP, pp. 15–16; zas. 26, Mar. 6, 1896, SP, pp. 23–24, col. 1; zas. 38, Dec. 5, 1901, SP, p. 16, col. 2.

74. Ibid., zas. 32, Jan. 27, 1899, SP, p. 20, col. 2. Kazakh iurts were also commandeered for use as migrant stations, then replaced with wooden structures in winter. The original residents were compensated in rubles (zas. 21, Jan. 4, 1895, pp. 6–7; zas. 24, June 28, 1895, SP, pp. 23–25; zas. 38, Dec. 5, 1901, SP, p. 17, col. 2). To encourage the Kazakhs to lead a settled existence, aside from taking their lands, the tsar proposed that they be given tax exemptions and other benefits similar to those of the Russian settlers (zas. 28, Nov. 27, 1896, SP, pp. 15–16, col. 2). According to Gurko, Siberian natives had few defenders in the government. "Everyone," he wrote, "coveted [their] lands," including the Peasant Resettlement Administration. See V. I. Gurko, *Features and Figures of the Past: Government and Opinion in the Reign of Nicholas II*, ed. J. E. W. Sterling et al., trans. L. Matveev (Stanford, 1939), 127, 147–148. As a consequence of these policies and attitudes, the impact of peasant colonization on the Kazakhs was devastating. By 1913 they had lost all their agricultural land to Russians. Their population and flocks were in decline and they had slid into poverty. See Manuel Sarkisyanz, "Russian Conquest in Central Asia: Transformation and Acculturation," in *Russia and Asia: Essays on the Influence of Russia on the Asian Peoples*, ed. Wayne S. Vucinich (Stanford, 1972), 251.

75. ZhKSZhD, zas. 34, Dec. 8, 1899, SP, p. 31, col. 2; zas. 39, June 6, 1902, SP, p. 22, cols. 1–2.

New village in the taiga, Tobol'sk province. From Pereselencheskoe Upravlenie, *Aziatskaia Rossiia* (St. Petersburg, 1914).

received cut-rate train fares to encourage them to travel to Siberia alone to select and reserve sites for their families. Advance preparations, it was hoped, would ease the transition of the family and eliminate some of the hazards of spontaneous migration. To familiarize prospective settlers with Siberian conditions and migration procedures, the committee printed and distributed hundreds of thousands of pamphlets. It subsidized travel to the Cheliabinsk resettlement point and into Siberia by making each family eligible for a loan of up to 50 rubles, or more if they intended to travel beyond Lake Baikal. The cost of a train ticket once the railroad opened was reduced for migrants to 25 percent of the regular third-class fare. Irregular migrants were offered free train tickets back to European Russia.[76]

Before the railroad was completed, migrants congregated at Tiumen' to await river transport to the interior. To ease the bottleneck of peasants that developed, the committee directed the sale of horses, wagons, and rafts, giving peasants the means to transport themselves by river or overland. For migration into the heart of the Amur oblast, the committee both subsidized the Volunteer Fleet to bring settlers overseas and provided migrants coming from the west with rafts on which to float their horses, cattle, and belongings down the Shilka and Amur rivers.[77]

Along the route of the railroad, on barges and steamers carrying migrants, on post roads, and in towns, stations were set up to dispense free medical assistance and hot tea to settlers. Food was available at low cost and free to children. In the Ussuri region, large barracks were put up (though not enough) to shelter peasants awaiting plots and to curtail the spread of disease.[78]

Once migrants arrived at their new settlements, the state gave a wide array of material assistance to help them establish themselves on the land. Special state stores provided lumber and other building materials and in Amur oblast sold livestock and grain to new arrivals. Interest-free loans were available for construction of a house, sowing, raising crops (on as much as two desiatins, or 5.4 acres), and general economic needs. Settlers could apply up to three years after their arrival. The loan ceiling per family was set in 1896 at 150 rubles in the Far East and 100 rubles elsewhere; later the ceiling was lowered, perhaps to limit peasant indebtedness. The same loans were available to migrants who chose to settle in the taiga; in addition, they were exempt from all taxation for ten years. By 1898, 88.2 percent of settler families in the regions west of Baikal had received loans, averaging 71.2 rubles per family. This amount often did not suffice, however, and

76. Ibid., zas. 26, Mar. 6, 1896, SP, app., pp. 51–52; zas. 28, Nov. 27, 1896, SP, pp. 25–26, col. 1; zas. 29, Apr. 2, 1897, SP, pp. 37–38, col. 1; Treadgold, *Great Siberian Migration*, 121–122; Migulin, *Nasha noveishaia zheleznodorozhnaia politika*, 302–303; Komitet Ministrov, *The Great Siberian Railway* (St. Petersburg, 1900), 11.

77. ZhKSZhD, osobyi zhurnal, June 14, 1893 (Ministr vnutrennykh del), pp. 2–3, col.1; zas. 21, Jan. 4, 1895, p. 8; zas. 26, Mar. 6, 1896, SP, p. 24, col. 1; zas. 34, Dec. 8, 1899, SP, p. 27, col. 2; zas. 36, Feb. 21, 1901, SP, pp. 20–21, col. 1; Beveridge, *The Russian Advance*, 219.

78. ZhKSZhD, passim; *Otchet po KSZhD za 1894 god*, 26–27; Komitet Ministrov, *The Great Siberian Railway*, 11; Beveridge, *Russian Advance*, 217.

applicants frequently had to wait up to a year for the money to come through.[79]

Once peasants were settled, the committee continued, directly and indirectly, to try to ensure them a livelihood. Its measures aimed at the creation, expansion, and sustenance of economic life in Siberia and the Far East, the precondition of permanent colonization.

The committee attempted to provide the infrastructure of daily life lacking in an unsettled region. It established a police administration for the western Siberian region, regulated water use, and steadily expanded postal services in the region of new settlement. It planned and constructed roads between villages, in the settled forest zone, to the gold mines of the Vitim region, and in Amur oblast and the Ussuri region. A pack road for the caravan trade between Biisk in the Altais and Mongolia and western China was also planned, which would have additional strategic utility by allowing Russian settlement on the Russo-Mongolian-Chinese border.[80] Witte surreptitiously subsidized Russian steamer transport on the Sungari River in Manchuria, also important for its dual commercial and military purpose, but prohibited by Chinese law.[81]

The survival of Russian settlement in the strategically vital but vastly underdeveloped Far East required special measures. The committee wanted to arrange the settlement of only the strongest elements by bringing to the Amur oblast 300 Cossack families of the Don and Orenburg hosts, which it considered the sturdiest and most purely Russian of the various hosts. In addition, 150 families of the Transbaikal host were to be transferred to the Ussuri region and enlisted in its host.[82]

The committee looked to introduce cottage industry to the Ussuri region, which was lacking in the essential elements of economic life. It brought scouts from the seafaring Baltic provinces to consider settling

79. ZhKSZhD, osobyi zhurnal, June 2, 1893, p. 7, col. 1, and pp. 9–10, col. 1; zas. 25, Nov. 29, 1895, SP, pp. 20–21; zas. 26, Mar. 6, 1896, SP, app., pp. 51–55; zas. 27, Apr. 27, 1896, pt. 1, pp. 8–13, col. 1; zas. 36, Feb. 21, 1901, SP, p. 18, col. 1, and pp. 18–19, col. 2; *Otchet po KSZhD za 1894 god*, 27–28; Coquin, *La Sibérie*, 477–479; Brusnikin, "Pereselencheskaia politika," 35.

80. ZhKSZhD, passim.

81. Ibid., osobyi zhurnal, Dec. 1, 1893 (Podgotovitel'naia komissiia), pp. 3–5, col. 2; zas. 26, Mar. 6, 1896, SP, pp. 17–18, col. 1, and pp. 18–19, col. 2. The farther a steamer was taken down the Sungari, the larger the subsidy to its owner.

82. Ibid., zas. 10, Nov. 10, 1893, pp. 19–21, cols. 1–2; osobyi zhurnal, June 14, 1893 (Ministr vnutrennykh del), p. 5, col. 1; *Otchet po KSZhD za 1894 god*, 35–36. See also O. I. Sergeev, *Kazachestvo na russkom Dal'nem Vostoke v XVII–XIX vv.* (Moscow, 1983), 72–73.

on the Tartary Strait and developing regional cabotage and a local fishing industry. Peasant craftsmen and peasant women were also encouraged to go. The government even offered North American Slavs immediate citizenship if they would immigrate to the Far East—but only those who were not "infected with socialist teachings."[83]

The committee took innovative measures to assist Siberian agriculture. Veterinarians were dispatched to inoculate cattle against Siberian anthrax and other epidemic diseases. Studs were sold for improved cattle breeding, and beekeeping and tobacco raising were encouraged and supported. Granaries went up along the railroad to store grain for transport and newly built state warehouses dispensed lumber and agricultural implements at low set prices. Their employees introduced the peasants to new implements and explained their use. The warehouses were a great financial success, and the tsar urged their introduction into European Russia.[84]

In a vivid example of the state intervention that characterized the project, the committee set the patterns of agricultural export. In June 1894, on Alexander III's command, Witte led an expedition to Arkhangel'sk and Murmansk in the Russian north to explore the possibilities of establishing an icefree naval base and creating an alternative to the Baltic ports. He found the proposition feasible, but since a port could be sustained only with the colonization of the northern provinces, and this was agriculturally unproductive territory, an outside source of grain was essential. At the same time, Siberian grain production was beginning to look like a threat to the gentry farmers of the Russian Black Earth Zone, where foreign competition was already forcing grain prices down. To avoid flooding the central Russian market and to provision the northern provinces of Olonets, Vologda, and Arkhangel'sk, Witte propounded the idea of building an extension of the Trans-Siberian in the old north, the Perm'-Kotlas Railroad. The Perm'-Kotlas would link Siberia with Arkhangel'sk via the

83. ZhKSZhD, zas. 31, Apr. 29, 1898, SP, pp. 26–28, cols. 1–2; zas. 32, Jan. 27, 1899, SP, pp. 26–27, col. 2; zas. 37, June 27, 1901, SP, p. 9, col. 2; zas. 38, Dec. 5, 1901, SP, p. 15, col. 2. The North American Slavs referred to were Galician Ruthenians (*Galichane*) and Hungarian Ruthenians (*Ugro-Russi*).

84. Ibid., zas. 24, June 28, 1895, SP, p. 25; zas. 26, Mar. 6, 1896, SP, pp. 32–33, col. 1; zas. 29, Apr. 2, 1897, SP, pp. 30, 33–34, col. 1, and pp. 28–29, col. 2; zas. 30, Dec. 10, 1897, SP, pp. 45–46, col. 1; zas. 34, Dec. 8, 1899, SP, pp. 27–28, col. 2; Brokgauz-Efron, *Entsiklopedicheskii slovar'*, vol. 29 (St. Petersburg, 1900), 739. The turnover of warehouses in 1899 on the sale of 17,000 plows (*plugi* and *sabany*), 450 reaping machines, 750 winnowing machines, 200 mowing machines, 200 threshing machines, etc., was approximately 500,000 rubles. Beveridge, *Russian Advance*, 213–214, notes that granaries lacked the capacity to hold the immense amounts of grain shipped on the railroad. Grain was often stored uncovered in sacks on the ground.

Ekaterinburg-Cheliabinsk Railroad, the Ural Mining Railroad, and the Northern Dvina basin. Construction under the auspices of the Committee of the Siberian Railroad was completed in 1899.[85]

The market for grain within Siberia was limited because of its relatively small urban population. It was clear that if Siberia was to prosper, it would have to export the bulk of its production, and the likeliest markets were in European Russia and the Baltic ports. To shift the flow of grain along the Perm'-Kotlas Railroad, either for sale in the Russian north or abroad via the port of Arkhangel'sk, the committee erected the Cheliabinsk tariff break in 1896. This measure raised the rate for the transport of a pud of grain along the Samara-Zlatoust section of the Siberian Railroad (and hence into central Russia or to the Baltic ports) by 5 to 9 kopecks, depending on its point of origin. Freight traveling on the Perm'-Kotlas Railroad was exempt from this additional charge. In 1900 a preferential rate lowered the cost of shipping grain from western Siberia to London via Arkhangel'sk by an additional 3 or 4 kopecks per pud.

Both contemporary observers and some Soviet historians have criticized the Cheliabinsk tariff break for isolating Siberia and retarding its full agricultural potential, in the class interests of the European Russian gentry.[86] More accurately, as T. M. Kitanina has shown, while protection of central Russian grain producers and the concern for Russia's foreign trade balance were components of the scheme, its main intentions were to colonize the old Russian north and to find domestic and foreign markets for Siberian grain.[87] It neither isolated

85. For discussion of the Perm'-Kotlas Railroad in the Committee of the Siberian Railroad, see ZhMPS, official sec.: "Sibirskaia zheleznaia doroga," 1894, no. 4: 33–36; ZhKSZhD, zas. 23, May 3, 1895, pt. 1, SP, pp. 2–8; zas. 29, Apr. 2, 1897, SP, p. 15, col. 2; zas. 32, Jan. 27, 1899, SP, pp. 14–15, cols. 1–2; zas. 35, June 14, 1900, SP, pp. 15–16, cols. 1–2, and p. 17, col. 1. On Witte's Murmansk expedition, see Witte, *Vospominaniia*, 1:391–403.

86. For example, S. V. Vostrotin, *Severnyi morskoi put' i cheliabinskii tarifnyi perelom v sviazi s kolonizatsiei Sibiri* (St. Petersburg, 1908), 29–33, and Borzunov, "K voprosu ob ekonomicheskom znachenii," 104–105.

87. T. M. Kitanina, "Programma ekonomicheskogo osvoeniia severa i tarifnaia politika S. Iu. Witte (K otsenke cheliabinskogo tarifa)," in *Problemy krest'ianskogo zemle-vladeniia i vnutrennei politiki Rossii: Dooktiabr'skii period*, ed. N. E. Nosov et al. (Leningrad, 1972), 191–210, and *Khlebnaia torgovlia Rossii v 1875–1914 gg. (Ocherki pravitel'stvennoi politiki)* (Leningrad, 1978), 184–191. The Perm'-Kotlas Railroad and Cheliabinsk tariff break were not wholly successful. Even if the flooding of the central Russian market with Siberian grain could have been prevented, the expansion of Siberian agriculture would have remained just as harmful: since the price of Russian grain was set by the foreign market, the export of Siberian grain would bring downward pressure on world (and hence European Russian) grain prices (*Railroad Gazette*, Sept. 28, 1894, p. 671). Furthermore, as Kitanina ("Programma," 206–207) points out, their effectiveness was hindered by the low operational efficiency of the Siberian Railroad, the high cost of long-distance hauls of grain within most of Siberia, and the revival of the Baltic ports under Nicholas II.

Schoolhouse in new village, Tobol'sk province. From Pereselencheskoe Upravlenie, *Aziatskaia Rossiia* (St. Petersburg, 1914).

Siberia nor hindered its development. The strategic and political
motives underlying it are clear, and Witte's manipulation of the internal economy in this fashion was unprecedented.

The state not only provided certain basic material needs to the
settlers; the committee also ministered to their spiritual needs,
through the Emperor Alexander III Fund, supervised by Procurator of
the Holy Synod Pobedonostsev. The fund received support from the
auxiliary enterprises, and also from the charitable contributions of
military officers, gentry assemblies, clerics, and members of the Chan-
cery of the Committee of Ministers. The purpose of the fund, as
Pobedonostsev pontificated before the Committee of the Siberian
Railroad, was to care for the spiritual and moral needs of railroad
workers, who would be bored and far from the constraints of civilization. Special railroad-car chapels, staffed by priests jointly appointed
by the Holy Synod and the Ministry of Transport, would follow
workers as construction progressed. The fund also supported the

construction of churches and schools near railroad stations and, to reduce costs, built combined church-schools elsewhere. It established charities and opened several orphanages.[88] These religious works were intended to lay the foundation of cultural life for the growing peasant population and to be a positive force in preventing "Iakutization" or "Buriatization," the Russian peasant's tendency to take on native ways and values. As part of this effort, the committee actively encouraged the conversion of Siberian natives.[89]

The use of religion to Russify and preserve social order is analogous to—indeed, is an antecedent of—Soviet ideological propaganda. It confirms the active, primary role of the state in directing the course of Siberian development. The extensive involvement of the government, its central planning, and the vast scope of its activity in water transport, industrial development, and agriculture gave the colonization of Siberia its unique color. There is no analogy in the American experience.[90] The colonization of Siberia is solidly in the Russian tradition; the Committee of the Siberian Railroad harks back to the Siberian *prikaz* of the Muscovite period and is a direct predecessor of Soviet development agencies.[91]

The settlement of Siberia was similar to a Soviet venture in still another respect. The success of colonization and development depended on the success of the railroad. But the performance of the state in railroad construction and management was less than impressive. The failings of this overly centralized bureaucratic operation cast a dark shadow over Witte's reputation.

88. ZhKSZhD, Feb. 16, 1893, SP, pp. 11–12, col. 2; zas. 24, June 28, 1895, SP, pp. 22–23 and passim; *Otchet po KSZhD za 1894 god*, 30–33. For descriptions, photographs, lists of churches and schools built by the fund, and contributors to it, see *Polozhenie tserkovnogo i shkol'nogo stroitel'stva v raione sibirskoi zheleznoi dorogi na sredstva fonda imeni imperatora Aleksandra III k 1 ianvaria 1900 goda* (St. Petersburg, 1900).

89. See M. A. Miropiev, *O polozhenii russkikh inorodtsev* (St. Petersburg, 1901), 343–344, a publication of the Holy Synod on the problem of the threateningly easy assimilation of Russians in Siberia to surrounding native cultures. See also Borzunov, "Istoriia sozdaniia," 1167–1168.

90. The role played by the U.S. government in the construction of the American transcontinental railroads cannot be denied (see Robert William Fogel, *The Union Pacific Railroad: A Case in Premature Enterprise* [Baltimore, 1960]). But the *degree* of government involvement in the United States was far less than that of the Russian government in Siberia.

91. The Siberian *prikaz* managed Siberia in the seventeenth century as a "huge business enterprise on the part of the Muscovite government," according to George V. Lantzeff, *Siberia in the Seventeenth Century: A Study of the Colonial Administration* (Berkeley, 1943), 200.

CHAPTER NINE

# Monument to Bungling

In the second half of the nineteenth century, American stockholders expected their railroad companies to generate a profit, and the continual quest for profits led management to devise innovative, modern forms of business organization and administration. The result, at least in the western and plains states, was an efficient, inexpensive railroad network that benefited the public, if not initial investors.[1] By contrast, the Russian government built and operated the Siberian Railroad in the political interests of the state, without being answerable to a multitude of owners concerned with profit and loss. Thus although the rugged and uninhabited terrain lay behind many of the setbacks that plagued the construction and operation of the railroad (as was the case, to a lesser degree, in the United States), they were exacerbated by human error resulting from the faulty organization of construction and inefficient management. Joseph Berliner's explanation for the lack of dynamism in Soviet industry applies equally to the Trans-Siberian Railroad: "Social ownership of productive property diminishes entrepreneurial effort by reducing the risk borne by entrepreneurs."[2] The very features of the project that were intended to bolster the state's control over Siberia—its centralization

1. See Alfred D. Chandler, Jr., and Stephen Salsbury, "The Railroads: Innovators in Modern Business Administration," in *The Railroad and the Space Program: An Exploration in Historical Analogy*, ed. Bruce Mazlish (Cambridge, Mass., 1965), 127–162; Julius Grodinsky, *Transcontinental Railway Strategy, 1869–1893: A Study of Businessmen* (Philadelphia, 1962).
2. Joseph S. Berliner, "Entrepreneurship in the Soviet Period: An Overview," in *Entrepreneurship in Imperial Russia and the Soviet Union*, ed. Gregory Guroff and Fred V. Carstensen (Princeton, 1983), 196.

and planning—jeopardized its control and sullied the reputation of state-led economic development. Both natural and manmade difficulties beset the project and imposed serious limitations on the railroad colonization of Siberia.

## Geographical Obstacles and the Engineering Response

The severe geographical conditions of Siberia and the Russian Far East presented the greatest challenge that Russian engineers had ever faced. The terrain was varied, extreme, and little conducive to the type of light construction envisaged by the railroad's designers.

The conditions under which construction proceeded on the Western Siberian Railroad (from Cheliabinsk to Ob') were most suitable, the terrain being level or undulating. Except when the tracks approached the region's many rivers, cuttings were not required, and embankments were shallow (3.5 feet maximum). Difficulties there were, however. The subsoil remained frozen until midsummer and for the most part navvies had access only to primitive tools. In the bogs of the steppe, the low level of the roadbed hindered proper drainage. Ditches were dug alongside the roadbed, but in effect they formed ponds that served as expanded breeding grounds for the swarms of mosquitoes and gnats that menaced railroad workers, employees, and settlers. All in all, the progress of construction was decidedly uneven.[3]

Leaving the low-lying, alluvial plains of western Siberia behind, the railroad progressed eastward in central Siberia, on the stretch between Ob' and Lake Baikal. Here work became more trying. Passing Krasnoiarsk, one enters the foothills of the Saian Mountains. Interspersed with level meadows and bogs, the hills were high, with steep, forested slopes whose trees had to be felled. Earthworks were delayed by the taiga's surface, which remained frozen until mid-July, two months longer than in western Siberia. Once thawed, the soil became a swamp, and laborers had to work in up to two feet of water. To avoid tunneling in the more mountainous sections approaching Lake

3. Arthur John Barry, *Lecture on the Great Siberian Railway* (London, 1900), 12; P. P. Migulin, *Nasha noveishaia zheleznodorozhnaia politika i zheleznodorozhnye zaimy (1893–1902)* (Khar'kov, 1903), 284; A. V. Pataleev, *Istoriia stroitel'stva velikogo sibirskogo zheleznodorozhnogo puti* (Khabarovsk, 1951), 11–12; *Railroad Gazette*, Feb. 17, 1893, p. 132; Harmon Tupper, *To the Great Ocean: Siberia and the Trans-Siberian Railway* (Boston, 1965), 106–107, 112.

Baikal, the railroad was built into the sides of the hills, with cuttings in rock, sharp curves, and heavy gradients. The embankments were steep and of substandard width. Each of the region's numerous wide, deep river valleys required the construction of a bridge; fifty wooden bridges went up across the various tributaries of the Angara alone, and the steel bridge across the Enisei was more than half a mile long.[4]

Lake Baikal presented a most extreme environmental challenge. The lake is a deep basin surrounded by steep, rugged mountains. The Committee of the Siberian Railroad had decided to postpone construction of the railroad on the southern shore of Baikal in view of the formidable difficulties it would entail. In its place, it made preparations for a steamer link to connect the two ends of the railroad being built to opposite shores.[5] Roughly equal to the length of the English Channel between Dover and Calais, the 66-verst crossing between Listvianichnaia on the western shore and Mysovskaia on the eastern was expected to save time over the 200-verst route round the lake. The committee then had to contend with winter conditions on the lake, which freezes to an average thickness of more than three and a half feet from mid-December to the end of April. The committee bought an English-made icebreaker, the *Baikal*, which could break through thirty-eight inches of ice with five inches of snow on top at a speed of 13 knots while carrying up to twenty-eight loaded freightcars. Unfortunately, at Mysovskaia harbor the lake freezes to a greater thickness than elsewhere and one of the icebreaker's propellers was disabled almost immediately, slowing its speed by half. A smaller steamer, the *Angara*, transported passengers, but it had to follow the *Baikal* as it broke the ice and was frequently in need of repairs itself.[6]

The problems of the steamer crossing, compounded by its rising cost, led to the eventual recommendation to undertake construction of the Circumbaikal Railroad; the transport of Russian troops to Manchuria during the Boxer Rebellion had confirmed the strategic impor-

4. Pataleev, *Istoriia*, 12; Barry, *Lecture*, 13, 15; *Railroad Gazette*, Oct. 23, 1896, p. 737; Tupper, *To the Great Ocean*, 116, 125–126, 128, 184; Brokgauz-Efron, *Entsiklopedicheskii slovar'*, vol. 29 (St. Petersburg, 1900), 732–733; Migulin, *Nasha noveishaia zheleznodorozhnaia politika*, 284.

5. See ZhKSZhD, osobyi zhurnal, Feb. 10 and 24, 1893, pp. 6–7, col. 1; zas. 10, Nov. 10, 1893, p. 4, col. 1, and pp. 4–5, col. 2; zas. 11, Dec. 1, 1893, p. 7, cols. 1–2.

6. Barry, *Lecture*, 15–16; Migulin, *Nasha noveishaia zheleznodorozhnaia politika*, 291; Tupper, *To the Great Ocean*, 226–230; ZhKSZhD, zas. 22, Mar. 8, 1895, pt. 2, SP, pp. 9–11; zas. 38, Dec. 5, 1901, SP, p. 7, col. 1; Zenone Volpicelli [Vladimir], *Russia on the Pacific and the Siberian Railway* (London, 1899), 300.

tance of uninterrupted rail transport to the Far East.[7] Work on the Circumbaikal section began in 1899 and it was completed for provisional use in August 1904, months after the outbreak of war with Japan. The difficulties were immense, as there were no natural terraces on which to build. The roadbed was hewn into the steep rock cliffs, often on the breast walls of the lake itself. Vaulted viaducts and two hundred bridges held the railroad over steep gorges and valleys, and the construction of thirty-three tunnels was unavoidable. Falling rock and landslides were common.[8]

The least forgiving region was Transbaikalia, whose fierceness was vastly underestimated. Following the Khilok, Ingoda, and Shilka rivers, the railroad crossed the thickly forested Iablonovyi Mountains, whose cliffs rose directly from the riverbeds. Here the Trans-Siberian was a mountain railroad on a narrow roadbed. Its curves were severe and gradients dangerously steep, the slopes dropping precipitously to the streams below. Earthworks in Transbaikalia were heavier than on any other section of the railroad, because of the region's permafrost, which was blasted away with dynamite. Water pipes froze and had to be installed in heated enclosures. The inexperience of engineers in building in this terrain was soon apparent: the irregular heaving and melting of the permafrost provided an unsure foundation for railroad track and buildings, not a few of which sank into the earth. The region was also visited by periodic droughts that destroyed the crops on which both laborers and draft horses depended. Regular outbreaks of Siberian boil plagues occurred, in one year destroying a great number of cattle and more than thirty men. The most serious danger to construction, though, was flooding. Fast-rising water and strong currents were characteristic of the rivers of Transbaikalia after torrential rains. In 1897 a flood washed away a 200-mile stretch of completed railroad west of Sretensk, taking with it fifteen bridges and stocks of lumber, and unleashing landslides that piled tons of earth on the remaining track.[9]

7. ZhKSZhD, zas. 25, Nov. 29, 1895, SP, pp. 7–8; zas. 36, Feb. 21, 1901, SP, pp. 4–6, col. 2; Migulin, *Nasha noveishaia zheleznodorozhnaia politika*, 291–292; V. F. Borzunov, "Istoriia sozdaniia transsibirskoi zheleznodorozhnoi magistrali XIX–nachala XX vv." (Ph.D. diss., Tomskii Gosudarstvennyi Universitet, 1972), 1362–1363.

8. Pataleev, *Istoriia*, 14–15; Tupper, *To the Great Ocean*, 338; S. V. Sabler and I. V. Sosnovskii, *Sibirskaia zheleznaia doroga v eia proshlom i nastoiashchem: Istoricheskii ocherk*, ed. A. N. Kulomzin (St. Petersburg, 1903), 216.

9. Barry, *Lecture*, 16–17; Brokgauz-Efron, *Entsiklopedicheskii slovar'* 29:733; Tupper, *To the Great Ocean*, 188–191, 250; Pataleev, *Istoriia*, 13–14; Erich Thiel, *The Soviet Far*

The easternmost section of the Trans-Siberian was the Ussuri Railroad. Originally the Maritime region was to be linked with Transbaikalia and the center of Russia by the Amur Railroad, but for technical and political reasons the government refrained from building this line and in its place substituted the Chinese-Eastern Railroad, which ran through Manchuria.[10] Stretching between Vladivostok and Khabarovsk, the Ussuri Railroad was thus a stump end, at least until the Amur Railroad was completed in 1916. The Ussuri section faced critical problems peculiar to its geography. Cholera struck in 1895, and other epidemic diseases broke out almost yearly. So did the Manchurian bandits who periodically infested the province. Work became bogged down as the region's heavy rains turned the land into a vast swamp and reduced the already short working season by fifty-five days per year on the average. It was not known during the first season of construction that the level of the Ussuri River rose thirty-five feet annually, although engineers became aware of it soon enough, and they were forced to re-lay the track on higher ground. The Iman River swelled to a width of three miles, also requiring an appropriate adjustment. Even without the flooding problem, the multitudinous tributaries of the Ussuri River called for extensive bridge building.[11]

### Design Flaws

Geographical severity was exacerbated by the light technical standards of the railroad. As a political railroad, the Trans-Siberian was not expected to yield positive financial results for many years of operation. For this reason and because the government saw its com-

---

*East: A Survey of Its Physical and Economic Geography*, trans. Annelie and Ralph M. Rookwood (New York, n.d.), 220; A. Pushechnikov, "O nedochetakh v dele postroiki zheleznykh dorog neposredstvennym rasporiazheniem kazny," *Inzhener*, June 1909, no. 6: 175–176; *Times*, June 8, 1900, p. 8; Alexis Krausse, *Russia in Asia: A Record and a Study, 1558–1899* (New York, 1899), 210. On the epidemic diseases of the region, see Great Britain, Naval Intelligence Division, *A Handbook of Siberia and Arctic Russia*, vol. 1 (London, n.d.), 228–229. On permafrost see Allen S. Whiting, *Siberian Development and East Asia: Threat or Promise?* (Stanford, 1981), 26–31.

10. On the construction of the Amur Railroad, see Steven G. Marks, "The Burden of Siberia: The Amur Railroad Question in Russia, 1906–1916" (paper read at AAASS conference, Honolulu, Nov. 19, 1988).

11. V. F. Borzunov, "Iz istorii formirovaniia sibirskoi burzhuazii v kontse XIX–nachale XX vekov," in *Iz istorii Sibiri i Altaia*, ed. A. P. Okladnikov et al. (Barnaul, 1968), 94–95; TKIM(VP), 2:1–2; 14:7; Tupper, *To the Great Ocean*, 178; Brokgauz-Efron, *Entsiklopedicheskii slovar'*, 29:733.

pletion as a pressing matter, both construction time and costs were to be reduced by building to light standards in the shortest possible direction. This decision had its critics in the professional societies, who asserted—reasonably—that future operating costs would be inversely proportional to the amount spent on construction; but the government's desire for speed of completion ensured that they were overruled.[12]

Government specifications called for a railroad of the simplest type, allowing for traffic of three pairs of trains between stations per twenty-four-hour period, with conversion possible to seven pairs of trains in wartime.[13] It would be single-tracked with light rails (18 pounds per foot on flat stretches, 20 on hilly sections); light ballast; wooden bridges over all but major rivers; a relatively narrow permanent way without provision in the width of the roadbed for double-tracking at a later date; a distance of fifty versts between stations; and on mountainous stretches very steep gradients and small, sharp curves.[14] These standards were lower than those prevailing on the Transcaspian Railroad, itself built with no frills and for a restricted purpose; indeed, it was pointed out later that such standards were justifiable only on spur tracks.[15]

Surveying was of a similar order. Expedition teams under instructions from the Ministry of Transport surveyed rapidly and superficially along a narrow four-verst belt straddling the future railroad line. Instead of a detailed examination of several potential routes, the ministry required only topographical surveys and leveling, to ensure that the railroad could be built along the path that was arbitrarily

12. Government engineers defended their position before the major technical societies of the country. See " 'Obshchii vzgliad na postroiku zheleznykh dorog i na ustroistvo sibirskoi zheleznoi dorogi i o nekotorykh merakh dlia uskoreniia po nei dvizheniia' (Stenograficheskii otchet po dokladu A. L. Sokolova i besede v VIII otdele IRTO)," *ZhdD*, 1905, no. 23: 266; " 'O velikom sibirskom puti v sviazi s pravitel'stvennymi izyskaniiami': Doklad N. A. Sytenko i beseda v VIII otdele IRTO," *ZhdD*, 1888, nos. 22–24: 178; *TOSRPT*, vol. 18, otdel 1 (1887), 13–15; "Zasedanie OSRPT po dokladu P. E. Gronskogo: 'Kak stroit' sibirskuiu dorogu?' " *TOSRPT*, vol. 21, otdel 2 (1892), 60, 62–64; *TIRTO*, 4:1–7; 10:12–14; 14:1–3, 7; A. I. Chuprov, *Iz proshlogo russkikh zheleznykh dorog: Stat'i 1874–1895 godov* (Moscow, 1909), 187–188.

13. A pair of trains means two trains, one in each direction.

14. *ZhMPS*, official sec., 1893, no. 2: 10–11; Migulin, *Nasha noveishaia zheleznodorozhnaia politika*, 283–284. For a contemporary study of the impact of curvature and gradient on operating costs, see Arthur M. Wellington, *The Economic Theory of the Location of Railways* (New York, 1877). See also A. C. O'Dell and P. S. Richards, *Railways and Geography* (London, 1971), 84–86, 88: "Rough track, sharp curves and steep gradients," the authors state, "are the bane of fast running."

15. *TIRTO*, 4:1–3; "Obshchii vzgliad na postroiku," 254.

determined in St. Petersburg as being the shortest and most direct between points. Some members of the Russian Technical Society suspected that even after construction had begun as much as half of the route had not been surveyed in any fashion. In Transbaikalia, surveys were inadequate at best, conducted with out-of-date instruments by a nonengineer accompanied by his two sons and a Mongolian-speaking guide. Needless to say, like much of the route, they were found to be unsatisfactory and required complete revision, at great expense, at the time of construction.

The Technical Society urged the government to undertake a wider and more detailed examination of the region, taking into account topographical, geographical, economic, hydrological, and climatic factors. Some members tried to disprove the claim of Transport Ministry engineers that the Canadian-Pacific Railway was built in similar conditions and could serve as a model for rapid, light construction. Nongovernmental experts pointed out that the Trans-Siberian would be the first railroad to have large sections built on permafrost, which was an unknown factor and needed a great deal more study than it had received. But their warnings were in vain: government engineers denied the incompleteness of their surveys and investigations. To build a perfect railroad, they asserted, would take one hundred years; its completion in ten was of the utmost importance.[16]

The fastest and most direct way to link Siberia with Russia was the prescription for fulfilling the state's political and military goals in the region. This desideratum determined the route and technical conditions of the Siberian Railroad. Little consideration was given to local interests, and many technical factors were disregarded. These charac-

16. The previous two paragraphs are based on the following: Sabler and Sosnovskii, *Sibirskaia zheleznaia doroga*, 77; A. N. Kulomzin, *Le Transsibérien*, trans. Jules Legras (Paris, 1904), 76; *TIRTO*, 2:2; 4:13; 10:10; 12:1–5, 15; 26:1–4; "Doklad A. K. Sidensnera 'O zheleznoi doroge v Sibiri,'" *TOSRPT*, vol. 17, otdel 2 (1886), 175–177; "Zasedanie po dokladu Gronskogo," 1–2, 12, 16–19; MPS, "Otchet o deiatel'nosti ministerstva putei soobshcheniia po stroitel'stvu sibirskoi zheleznoi dorogi za vremia s 30 marta 1889 g. po 17 ianvaria 1892 g." (TsGAOR, fond 677, opis' 1, delo 629), 11; *ZhMPS*, official sec., 1893, no. 2:9–12, 15–16; "O velikom sibirskom puti," 175, 178–179; "'O vazhnosti geologicheskikh razvedok i svedenii pri proizvodstve izyskanii dlia ustroistva zheleznykh dorog voobshche i dlia sibirskoi zheleznoi dorogi v osobennosti': Doklad L. A. Iachevskogo i D. L. Ivanova na besede v VIII otdele IRTO," *ZhdD*, 1888, nos. 27–28: 216–218, 225; A. Pushechnikov, "K voprosu o novykh zheleznykh dorogakh v Sibiri," *ZhdD*, 1908, no. 13: 90, and "O sovremennom polozhenii nekotorykh voprosov zheleznodorozhnogo dela v Rossii," *Inzhener* 29 (June 1910): 252–253; L. Iachevskii, "O vechno merzloi pochve v Sibiri," *IIRGO* 25 (1889): 341–355; L. Lugovskii, "Sibirskaia zheleznaia doroga," *Kalendar' tobol'skoi gubernii na 1892 god* (Tobol'sk, 1892), 2.

teristics accord with the authoritarian, centralizing purpose of the railroad.[17]

The government's strategy proved to be no match for the forces of nature. Construction was dangerously inadequate, and the attitude of the authorities encouraged further skimping. Embankments on the whole line, for instance, were often from four to six feet narrower than the already circumscribed width of sixteen and a half feet called for in the designs. As a consequence, they were insecure and susceptible to being washed away in storms. Many were sinking.

The permanent way was flimsy. Where ballast was not altogether lacking, it was so meager that the track often shifted to the side. Crossties were widely spaced and secured with a less than adequate number of spikes and bolts. They were made of untreated green wood, so that many began to rot after their first year of use, even on the sections that did not lie directly in marshes. The lightweight rails, made of poor-quality steel, were laid on the rounded side of the tie, fixed in notches and attached by spikes to the wood through holes in the flange without chairs. To stretch the iron supply, the rail joints were made exceedingly thin, but were placed so tightly that rail ends had no room to contract or expand, as they naturally did in reaction to changes in temperature. Coupled with the flimsiness of the rails, the placement of the joints led to ubiquitous buckling, which required constant adjustments to the rails en route.

The railroad also suffered from the sharp curves and steep inclines. Within one and a half months of initial use, the front and rear wheel flanges of a train would wear out from grating against the rails and joints, which themselves weakened. Engineers noted that this friction

17. To avoid deviation from this procedure, in 1892 Witte decided to bypass Tomsk, one of the major Siberian cities. Tomsk was situated in the taiga, surrounded by swamplands, at a wide stretch of the Ob' River which would have required an expensive bridge, and too far from the agricultural regions where most peasant migrants would head ("O velikom sibirskom puti," 173–174; *ZhMPS*, official sec., 1893, no. 2: 35–36; Sabler and Sosnovskii, *Sibirskaia zheleznaia doroga*, 109; A. Pushechnikov, "O nedochetakh v dele izyskanii i postroiki zheleznykh dorog v Sibiri," *ZhdD*, 1907, nos. 46–47: 524. For Tomsk's opposition, see V. P. Kartamyshev, *Doklad obshchemu sobraniiu chlenov OSRPT "O napravlenii magistral'noi linii sibirskoi zheleznoi dorogi na g. Tomsk ili v obkhod ego"* (n.p., 1892)). It was rumored at the time (and is accepted as fact by many Russians today) that Tomsk was bypassed because local worthies refused to pay the engineers the bribes they demanded. See Tupper, *To the Great Ocean*, 97–98. Tupper also accepts the rumor, but in light of the above explanation, there seems to be no truth to it. It should be noted that a branch line was eventually built to Tomsk, which became the headquarters of the Siberian Railroad administration.

Wooden bridge, Central Siberian Railroad. From *Velikii put': Vidy Sibiri i eia zheleznykh dorog* (Krasnoiarsk, 1899).

produced a significant layer of metallic dust along the tracks, and blamed it for innumerable derailments.

Sturdiness was to be found only on the large bridges, whose iron and steel girders and masonry piers were regarded as outstanding works of engineering; most were still standing in the 1960s. The vast majority of bridges, however, were ramshackle structures of soft pine, which rotted easily. The rapid and extreme fluctuations in temperature (in one twenty-four-hour period in Tomsk in the winter of 1902–1903, for instance, the thermometer went from −46° C to −8° C) caused the wooden bridges to distend and sag, not to mention their effect on other features of the track.[18]

The standards set for the railroad were patently unequal to the task at hand; better planning and design by St. Petersburg would have prevented many of the difficulties and saved time and money in the end.[19]

### Labor Force

The recruitment of a labor force for the Siberian Railroad demonstrated the geographical and demographic constraints on colonization and Russification. The Committee of the Siberian Railroad expected that the Western and Central Siberian lines, from Cheliabinsk to Irkutsk, would require 30,000 navvies for earthworks in the first three years and 50,000 skilled and unskilled laborers for all other types of work.[20] Siberia's low population, the unfamiliarity with railroad work, and the utter lack of skilled labor forced the committee to take extraordinary measures.

The problem did not actually exist in relatively populous western Siberia. There, 80 percent of unskilled heavy labor was provided by local peasants from the Cheliabinsk and Tobol'sk areas, with minimal reliance on contract laborers from European Russia. Local residents also supplied cartage, horses, and food, and a small number of local Kazakhs performed light work.[21]

Once construction reached the forest of the Central Siberian line, however, the difficulties became increasingly apparent. The sources

18. The preceding four paragraphs are based on Barry, *Lecture*, 11, 13–14; Tupper, *To the Great Ocean*, 107, 113–114, 246, 250; Krausse, *Russia in Asia*, 210–211; *Times*, June 8, 1900, p. 8, and Oct. 18, 1904, p. 9; "Obshchii vzgliad na postroiku," 254; L. N. Liubimov, "Vspuchivanie dereviannykh mostov na sibirskoi zheleznoi dorogi," *Inzhener* 27 (July 1903): 235–237; H. Claus, "Die klimatischen Verhältnisse Sibiriens und deren Einfluß auf die dort geplanten Eisenbahnen," *Archiv für Eisenbahnwesen*, 1889, no. 12: 901–904; A. N. Bukhman et al., *Doklad ob eksploatatsionnykh raskhodakh sibirskoi zheleznoi dorogi* (St. Petersburg, 1912), 7; Richardson L. Wright and Bassett Digby, *Through Siberia, an Empire in the Making* (New York, 1913), 15; J. N. Westwood, *A History of Russian Railways* (London, 1964), 118; *Railroad Gazette*, Feb. 17, 1893, p. 132, and Jan. 19, 1900, p. 41.

19. Cf. technical standards on the Union Pacific Railroad. From an engineering (if not financial) point of view this was a first-rate railroad, solidly built despite the speed of construction and the terrain over which it crossed. See Robert William Fogel, *The Union Pacific Railroad: A Case in Premature Enterprise* (Baltimore, 1960), 263–264.

20. ZhKSZhD, SP, Feb. 16, 1893, p. 8, col. 1.

21. Ibid., osobyi zhurnal, May 26, 1893, p. 2, col. 1; TKIM, 1:17–18.

of food and fodder were becoming more distant and, in spite of higher wages, workers resisted being transferred into the taiga, which they found dull and gloomy.[22] The local labor supply was smaller and less reliable. Drawing mostly from the peasantry, the railroad lost a large contingent of its workers during the harvest season. Except for carpenters, which were found locally, almost all skilled workers had to be imported, at great cost, from European Russia. They included in their ranks Kazan' Tatars. Of more than 2,000 stonemasons, 60 percent came from European Russia. An additional quarter were Italians. Few of these workers had anticipated local conditions, and found that they could not work up to their standards. Local natives and Cossacks were better equipped to deal with forest conditions, and they appeared more frequently, although there were few skilled craftsmen among them and their presence did little to alleviate the shortage of labor.[23]

In the distant and forbidding territories east of Lake Baikal, Russian settlement was still embryonic and could not supply even seasonal labor. Engineers on the Transbaikal section considered themselves fortunate in that it was still feasible to import some craftsmen from European Russia, Finland, and Italy, but they were few and it was a costly option. Local old settlers, many of whom were sober, industrious sectarians displaced from jobs in the goldfields, provided more than half the unskilled labor force. Local Cossacks were relied on for hauling, and, regardless of Russian suspicions about their loyalty, Buriat natives were found to be experienced and willing carpenters. For construction of the Ussuri Railroad, regional battalions assigned soldiers in great numbers from the start; they provided up to 3,300 men, or approximately one-fourth of the contingent of workers. Many of them—up to 2,800—also worked on the Transbaikal section after the Boxer Rebellion necessitated its early completion.[24]

22. M. V. Braikevitch and I. R. Afonin, "The Railways of Siberia," *Russian Economist: Journal of the Russian Economic Association* 2 (October–December 1921): 1491–1492.

23. ZhKSZhD, osobyi zhurnal, May 26, 1893, p. 3, col. 1; TKIM, 3:3, 5, 29; V. F. Borzunov, *Proletariat Sibiri i Dal'nego Vostoka nakanune pervoi russkoi revoliutsii* (Moscow, 1965), 26–27, 40–41; Henry Reichman, "The 1905 Revolution on the Siberian Railroad," *Russian Review* 47 (1988): 28.

24. Pushechnikov, "O nedochetakh v dele postroiki," *Inzhener*, May 1909, no. 5: 137–138, 141; Adrianov, "Estestvennye usloviia dlia zheleznoi dorogi v Zabaikal'e," *ZhdD*, 1895, no. 16: 143–144; TKIM(VP), 4:6; 17:1; Borzunov, *Proletariat*, 29–32, 36–37, and "Soldaty na stroitel'stve sibirskoi zheleznodorozhnoi magistrali (1891–1901 gg.)," in *Predposylki oktiabr'skoi revoliutsii v Sibiri*, ed. V. I. Dulov et al. (Novosibirsk, 1964), 117–135. Cf. the Baikal-Amur Main Line's reliance on soldiers as a major contingent of its work force, in Whiting, *Siberian Development*, 104.

The basic labor supply for the Ussuri section, and an important element on the Transbaikal Railroad, consisted of Japanese and Chinese migrant workers and the settled Korean population of the Ussuri region. The committee was at first reluctant to tap this source because officials regarded these people as physically unsuited for construction work and expected that they would spend their earnings on the Chinese market rather than in Russia. Moreover, except for the Koreans, they were not a resident work force; many did have to return to their homes to fight in the Sino-Japanese War. Nonetheless, 8,000 Asians were employed on the Ussuri Railroad, making up more than 60 percent of its work force (of 14,500) in 1897 and 14 percent of the entire railroad's work force in the same year. Their productivity, lower than that of any other category of laborers, only confirmed the impression that they were incapable, although this may well have been the result of the policy of paying them less than the others.[25]

Despite the recruitment of all these workers, still more were needed. Many could not be counted on to stay with the job till it was done. So the Committee of the Siberian Railroad turned to prison labor, solving Siberia's labor problem by decree.

The government had drafted prisoners for railroad construction since the 1860s, after Kulomzin suggested that it would be a convenient means of reducing costs, but never before on such a large scale.[26] In the spring of 1891 a shipload of 600 hard-labor convicts was rerouted from Odessa to Vladivostok for work on the Ussuri Railroad, rather than to Sakhalin Island, their original destination. Their work on the railroad was satisfactory, but their military guards were inexperienced. A number of violent criminals escaped into Vladivostok and other South Ussuri locales, where they raised havoc and were

25. Adrianov, "Estestvennye," 145; Pushechnikov, "O nedochetakh v dele postroiki," *Inzhener*, May 1909, no. 5: 140; ZhKSZhD, osobyi zhurnal, June 14, 1893 (MVD), pp. 2–3, col. 1; zas. 23, May 3, 1895, pt. 2, SP, p. 5; TKIM(VP), 4:6–7; 17:1–4; *Times*, Apr. 12, 1895, p. 3; Borzunov, *Proletariat*, 197, and "Rabochie sibirskoi zheleznodorozhnoi magistrali v 1891–1904 gg.," *Istoriia SSSR*, July–August 1959, no. 4: 117; ZhMPS, official sec., 1893, no. 2: 27–28. Asians received 85 kopecks per day on average, while free Russians were paid 1 ruble 50 kopecks, and soldiers 1 ruble. Until the pay of prisoners was raised, their productivity was comparable to that of the Asians. As the prisoners' rate of pay increased, so did their productivity; the same thing might have occurred with the Asians. Certainly the Chinese were regarded as satisfactory railroad workers in other parts of the world. On this point see O'Dell and Richards, *Railways and Geography*, 36.

26. See A. P. Pogrebinskii, "Stroitel'stvo zheleznykh dorog v poreformennoi Rossii i finansovaia politika tsarizma (60–90-e gody XIX v.)," *Istoricheskie zapiski* 47 (1954): 153. It is important to note Kulomzin's opinion at this early date, as it sheds light on the later rationale for the use of prison labor on the Siberian Railroad.

responsible for a rash of robberies.[27] The committee ironed out the wrinkles as it barred recidivists and long-term prisoners from working on the railroad.

The laws governing the use of prison labor on the Ussuri, Transbaikal, Circumbaikal, and Central Siberian lines gave local governors general charge of the prisoners, with power to determine their numbers and working conditions. Prisoners would either work directly for government engineers or be farmed out to contractors. They were to be compensated for their labor by a reduction in their sentence: one day of labor equaled two of prison time; one year equaled two years. Exiles received a reduction in the time of mandatory exile at the same ratio. Shackles were to be removed. Initially their wage was to be approximately 30 percent of the norm for free hired laborers, to be paid to the prison administration. Out of this sum came the costs of their transport, clothing, food, and military convoy; little or nothing was left over for the prisoners themselves. Eventually, in an effort to encourage "conscientious labor," they were paid at the same rate as free workers; after expenses were taken out, they were then left with between 8 and 18 rubles per month. Their productivity rose accordingly.[28]

The government was highly satisfied with the results. Several thousand prisoners and exiles worked on the railroad each year as a small but permanent and reliable labor force; their total numbers reached 9,000 prisoners and 4,500 exiles. By all accounts, the prisoners conducted themselves well, and there was little evidence of disobedience after the fitful start in the South Ussuri region. Disciplinary measures were rarely needed. Only 1 percent of prisoners escaped or attempted to do so.[29] The tsar was so pleased by the success of prison labor on

27. TKIM(VP), 18:1–4. For an account of their marauding in Kamen'-Rybolov and the angry reaction of a local resident, see *Vostochnoe obozrenie*, 1891, no. 40: 4.

28. *Otchet po komiteta sibirskoi zheleznoi dorogi za 1894 god* (n.p., n.d.), 7; ZhMPS, official sec.: "Sibirskaia zheleznaia doroga," 1894, no. 4: 20–22; ZhKSZhD, zas. 23, May 3, 1895, pt. 2, SP, pp. 3–4; TKIM, 21:2; TKIM(VP), 18:38; Borzunov, *Proletariat*, 33; *Times*, Sept. 3, 1895, 3; Pushechnikov, "O nedochetakh v dele postroiki," *Inzhener*, May 1909, no. 5: 138–139; *Tiuremnyi vestnik*, 1895, no. 3: 121.

29. Borzunov, *Proletariat*, 34–35, and "Rabochie," 117. Aside from the military convoy, infractions of the rules and escape were discouraged by the rule that the other members of the artel to which the offending prisoner belonged would suffer a reduction in pay after the first incident and a mandatory and permanent return to prison after the second (Borzunov, *Proletariat*, 62). On the comportment of prisoners and official satisfaction with it, see ZhKSZhD, zas. 22, Mar. 8, 1895, pt. 2, SP, pp. 8–9; zas. 31, Apr. 29, 1898, SP, pp. 21–22, col. 2; zas. 38, Dec. 5, 1901, SP, p. 8, col. 2; *Tiuremnyi vestnik*, 1894–1897, passim.

the Siberian Railroad that he proposed that it serve as a model for its organization in the rest of the empire.[30] Insofar as prison labor was viewed as a solution to a manpower shortage, its use on the Siberian Railroad was a direct antecedent of Soviet practices.[31]

The condition of prison laborers on the Siberian Railroad, however, was far better than the squalid and brutal slavery they were subjected to in Stalin's concentration camps.[32] Prisoners and exiles slept in wooden barracks, tents, or thatched huts much like those of other workers (not that these shelters were adequately ventilated or effectively shielded against the torrential rains or cold weather); those within a reasonable distance were returned to the prisons each night.[33] Prisoners' wages paid for clothing, regular breaks for tea or kvas, and two meals a day. The menu was listed in *Tiuremnyi vestnik* (Prison herald): lunch consisted of a hot dish with fish or meat flavored with pepper and bay leaf, and a vegetable portion; dinner was thin gruel with butter or lard and bread. A small amount of wine was dispensed on holidays.[34] The workday usually lasted more than

30. ZhKSZhD, zas. 38, Dec. 5, 1901, SP, p. 9, col. 2.

31. When the Committee of the Siberian Railroad discussed prison labor, F. G. Terner castigated the system for not fulfilling the humanitarian function of "correction and raising the moral standards . . . of the criminals." Minister of Justice N. V. Murav'ev responded that its purpose was economic, not corrective, and the tsar agreed that, with the desire to complete the railroad as rapidly as possible, rehabilitation had to be left to the side for the time being (ZhKSZhD, zas. 29, Apr. 2, 1897, SP, pp. 25–27, col. 1; pp. 24–25, col. 2). On the economic determinants of prison labor in the Soviet period, see S. Swianiewicz, *Forced Labor and Economic Development: An Enquiry into the Experience of Soviet Industrialization* (London, 1965).

32. See David J. Dallin and Boris I. Nicolaevsky, *Forced Labor in Soviet Russia* (New Haven, 1947), and Robert Conquest, *Kolyma: The Arctic Death Camps* (Oxford, 1979). The basic distinction between tsarist and Soviet prison labor, aside from living and working conditions, was that the Committee of the Siberian Railroad developed an incentive system whereby prisoners' wages were raised to encourage greater productivity. In Stalin's camps the reverse practice prevailed: threats of violence and deprivation of food were expected to induce more work. In the post-Stalin era, the terms of prison labor reverted to those employed on the Siberian Railroad. Prisoners employed by the Soviet authorities to make up for the shortage of labor in the Tiumen' oil fields were paid a wage and given a reduced sentence. See Violet Conolly, *Beyond the Urals* (Oxford, 1967), 261.

33. TKIM, 3:4; TKIM(VP), 15:2; *Tiuremnyi vestnik*, 1895, no. 3: 121. For the living arrangements of nonconvict laborers, see TKIM, 1:17, 51 (according to this source, some workers on the Western Siberian section also lived in railroad cars that moved with construction), and TKIM(VP), 15:1–2.

34. See *Tiuremnyi vestnik*, 1895, no. 3: 119, 121; 1897, no. 3: 130. Construction contractors sold food to free contract laborers at a set price (TKIM[VP], 15:4–5). According to TKIM(VP), an official source that did not hesitate to criticize the government's handling of the construction of the railroad, there were few complaints about the quality of the food on the Ussuri line. This was not the case, though, in the first season of con-

twelve hours, but construction was halted during rain and holidays. Sundays were days off.[35]

There is no denying that the work was hard, uncomfortable, and hazardous for prisoners and free laborers alike—construction was, of course, largely unmechanized, and horses were often unavailable for carting away rock and earth.[36] But sanitary conditions were considered good in general and work in the open air, with reasonable wages and inducements, was beneficial.[37] The sickness rate for prisoners was lower than in the central prisons of European Russia, at the Nerchinsk labor camp, or on Sakhalin Island, and only 1 percent of worktime was spent in the hospital.[38] The 2 percent death rate for both prisoners and free laborers certainly compared favorably with that of other large-scale construction projects around the world, such as the Panama Canal, where the death toll reached 25,000 and the sickness level more than 30 percent.[39] These facts contradict the claims of Soviet historians, following Lenin, that labor conditions were

---

struction, according to a report in *Vostochnoe obozrenie*, 1891, no. 33: 1: south Ussuri railroad workers were given rotten meat and stale bread that one European Russian worker claimed "his Nikol'sk pigs wouldn't eat!" When workers complained, they were treated as rebels and arrested. Poor food on the Transbaikal line was reported as late as 1900, but the situation clearly varied with the contractor; inedible food does not appear to have been the general rule (*Railroad Gazette*, May 18, 1900, p. 321). On clothing, see *Tiuremnyi vestnik*, 1896, no. 2: 142.

35. *Tiuremnyi vestnik*, 1895, no. 3: 120; 1896, no. 2: 141; 1897, no. 3: 129. Official working hours in peak season, May through August, were from 5:00 A.M. to 7:30 P.M. with a one-and-a-half-hour lunch break. Hours were reduced in winter, when most construction ceased. As today in the Soviet Union, when a holiday fell on a weekday, the work was made up the following Sunday.

36. TKIM(VP), 4:6; 15:1–3.

37. The wages of free contract laborers, according to Borzunov and Reichman, were less, in real terms, in Siberia than in European Russia because of the high cost of living in Siberia. See Borzunov, "Rabochie," 121 (sic; pagination is misprinted), and Reichman, "1905 Revolution," 30. While there may have been cause for labor unrest in declining purchasing power, it must be borne in mind that railroad wages were far higher than the norm in Siberia. Unskilled workers in western Siberia, for instance, earned up to eight times more on the Trans-Siberian than they normally had earned as farm hands in the employ of old settlers. See Braikevitch and Afonin, "Railways," 1498.

38. TKIM, 3:5; *Tiuremnyi vestnik*, 1895, no. 3: 142; 1897, no. 3: 130; *ZhMPS*, official sec.: "Sibirskaia zheleznaia doroga," 1894, no. 4: 23.

39. Borzunov, *Proletariat*, 144. Among the causes of death were run-ins with prison convoy guards. The Committee of the Siberian Railroad reported several incidents in which prisoners were shot to death by drunken guards (ZhKSZhD, zas. 38, Dec. 5, 1901, SP, p. 9, col. 1). The death rate cited for the Panama Canal refers to both French and American phases, the sickness rate only to the years of French activity (David McCullough, *The Path between the Seas: The Creation of the Panama Canal, 1870–1914* [New York, 1977], 173, 610). In Egypt, 15,000 workers died building the Mahmondieh Canal (W. O. Henderson, *The Industrial Revolution in Europe: Germany, France, Russia, 1815–1914* [Chicago, 1961], 150).

Unmechanized earthworks, Western Siberian line. From *Velikii put': Vidy Sibiri i eia zheleznykh dorog* (Krasnoiarsk, 1899).

"terrible" and constituted the "unprecedentedly harsh" exploitation and "militarization" of the work force.[40]

## Personnel

If recruitment of a labor force proved difficult, staffing for the critical tasks of operation and management proved even more so. It was difficult to find skilled or even unskilled employees after the road was

40. Borzunov, "Rabochie," 118–119, and *Proletariat*, 147; V. N. Kazimirov, *Velikii sibir-skii put'* (Irkutsk, 1970), 25.

completed, and it was rare for a post to remain occupied for long by anyone.[41] The turnover rate was at least 35 percent a year on some sections and up to 87 percent on others.[42] Partly responsible was the tedium of life in Siberia, with its hard work, low pay, high cost of living, scarcity of consumer goods, and unavailability of schooling. And its mercilessness—the extreme cold of winter and heat of summer, the swarms of infectious insects, the prevalence of disease, and the bad drinking water—did not contribute to permanence or stability.[43]

The railroad was unable to attract anything but the poorest-quality personnel. From European Russia came transients whose railroad careers had been wrecked and who could not be trusted in positions of responsibility. From its own small population Siberia offered a contingent of illiterate or half-educated exiles and former convicts whose criminal lives had not yet faded into the past. Almost 80 percent of personnel were in this category in 1904, among them 600 men who had been sentenced at one time for the gamut of violent crimes. A large percentage of night watchmen, responsible for the security of railroad freight, had been sent into Siberian exile for robbery. Murderers and rapists were employed as track security guards. In spite of rules restricting the employment of exiles after 1904, by 1912 they were still heavily represented.[44] As one authority described it, this milieu was not conducive to good work. Even the best

> master road builders deteriorate amazingly quickly, begin to get lazy, conduct their affairs carelessly, [and] become hard drinkers. . . . The more respectable ones quit, begging to be allowed back to Russia at much lower rates of pay than those they had received before their departure for Siberia; occasionally they leave on a moment's notice, without the hope of a new position.[45]

Here was fertile soil for corruption and crime, which seems to have been the rule rather than the exception. In the two years from 1910 to

41. L. N. Liubimov, "Opyt organizatsii i proizvodstva massovoi sploshnoi smeny rel'sov na sibirskoi zheleznoi doroge," *Inzhener* 27 (August–September 1903): 281. Liubimov reports that to upgrade the section between Kansk and Irkutsk "it was impossible to get workers at any price." See also Medem, 519.

42. Borzunov, *Proletariat*, 24–25; L. N. Liubimov, "Ocherk eksploatatsii sibirskoi zheleznoi dorogi v pervye tri goda posle soedineniia 'zapadnoi-sibirskogo' uchastka takovoi s 'sredne-sibirskim,'" *ISIPS*, 21, no. 10 (1904): 229–230.

43. Liubimov, "Ocherk eksploatatsii," *ISIPS*, 1904, no. 10: 229–231; Medem, 518.

44. Liubimov, "Ocherk eksploatatsiia," *ISIPS*, 1904, no. 10: 229, and "Opyt organizatsii," 280; Medem, 517–518.

45. Liubimov, "Opyt organizatsii," 280.

1912 alone the number of criminal prosecutions of railroad personnel approached 1,000, and few posts were immune.[46] Officials commonly stole railroad materials for their personal use. Over several months a telegraph chief named Leitneker, his assistant, Kats, and a shop steward named Liutynskii took shop materials to refurbish furniture, install a doorbell, and build casement windows and bookcases in Leitneker's home; to repair furniture and install indoor plumbing and window sashes in Kats's home; and to do a variety of work in the local cinema jointly owned by Kats's wife and Liutynskii.[47]

Employees in charge of storing and dispensing materials for the railroad—coal, firewood, cross-ties—stole or bought and sold them at cut-rate prices, then pocketed the proceeds. It was estimated that only 20 percent of the coal stored at the Omsk fuel depot of the Siberian Railroad found its way into use on the railroad; the rest was sold on the sly by railroad personnel in Omsk. The former locomotive engineer Prokofii Kulikov, who had contacts at the fuel depot, arranged a private contract for the delivery of 18,000 to 20,000 puds of the railroad's coal to the Women's School of the Omsk Eparchy. The city's government buildings were also heated with coal belonging to the railroad. During the revolution of 1905, the railroad, and thereby the State Treasury, lost hundreds of thousands of rubles in the organized "liberation" of freight and materials, an activity in which railroad personnel took part.[48]

The most common form of corruption was bribery, considered the only lubricant necessary for the operation of the Trans-Siberian. The railroad contractor I. N. Nikol'skii found that he had to pay off stationmasters to get anything accomplished. Bribes were demanded and given openly, usually with receipts indicating they had been paid. They were mandatory for hiring, for transfers, for raises, to prevent imposition of penalties, and for hauling freight. The testimony of Pavel Komarov, a small coal supplier, was typical. In 1909 he received an order for an amount of coal. Inspector Vladimir Teliatnikov delayed

46. Medem, 11–16. Stationmasters and track overseers figured prominently as targets of corruption proceedings. These were middle-level managers, who were responsible on American railroads for the efficient operation of the system. As the London *Times* put it, they did find an El Dorado in Siberia—and were quick to vanish with their fortunes (*Times*, Apr. 8, 1902, p. 3). One is tempted to compare them with Muscovite officials in Siberia, who saw their post as a way to make quick money, exploited it for what they could get, then left. See George V. Lantzeff, *Siberia in the Seventeenth Century: A Study of the Colonial Administration* (Berkeley, 1943), 32.

47. Medem, 36.

48. Ibid., 37–38, 40–42, 67–68, 84–86, 96–97.

the first shipment, but sent it off after six visits by Komarov. To speed the second shipment, though, he demanded "thanks" for the first. Komarov protested that he had no money at the time; Teliatnikov replied by pointing at his palm. Each time Komarov returned, he got the same answer: "When there is a payment, then there will be a shipment." Finally in July 1910 Komarov's coal was sent off while Teliatnikov was on vacation.[49]

The attitude that these methods were acceptable had deep roots. As an indicted siding chief named Bogdanovich explained to investigators, he "would take bribes even now if someone offered; . . . why not if they are given? There are two Russian proverbs on this: (1) if they give, take; if they beat, flee [*daiut—beri, b'iut—begi*] and (2) a fool gives, a clever one takes [*durak daet, umnyi beret*]." Engineer Khachatriants explained that he "took himself to Siberia to live on more than one income."[50] Inadequately supervised and inculcated with no sense of responsibility, personnel thus contributed significantly to the railroad's problems. Their corruption represented one more obstruction in the way of the state as it strove to build the railroad and control its distant territories.

## Contractors

The natural problems of geography and demography called for extraordinary expertise, but the organization of construction was so inadequate to the task that efficiency and cost control were virtually impossible.

Construction was organized in two ways. Chief engineers could either supervise their works directly or farm out the various tasks to contractors, depending on which method, in their opinion, would get the railroad finished most quickly. Most of the construction was done by private contractors.[51] In spite of rules to the contrary, as well as the admonishments of *Vostochnoe obozrenie*, large contractors or a few syndicates of contractors monopolized the contract work. Govern-

49. Ibid., 25–26, 28–29, 151–152.
50. Ibid., 25.
51. TKIM, 11:1; Borzunov, "Iz istorii formirovaniia," 89; Pushechnikov, "O nedochetakh v dele postroiki," *Inzhener*, May 1909, no. 5: 141. With the exception of the Circumbaikal section, which was built almost exclusively by contractors, the average amount of contract works on the Trans-Siberian as a whole was 55%. On the Transbaikal Railroad, it was only 20%, the remaining portion being done directly by the Building Administration. On the Tomsk branch, too, contractors played a lesser role.

ment engineers often gave them control of all the various tasks on a given section of the railroad in one contract.[52] Any contract worth more than 5,000 rubles required authorization, but that was no problem. One chief engineer who wanted to grant a monopoly on the supply of wood for a section of the Western Siberian Railroad to a single contractor, the merchant Brisker of Novgorod-Severskii, signed thirty-six separate contracts with him for a total value of 180,000 rubles. Since wood was freely available in Ufa, he also violated the stipulation that Siberian producers receive first preference.[53]

Regardless of the abuses associated with it, all the involved parties preferred this arrangement. For the state comptroller a lesser number of contractors eased the task of supervision. Construction chiefs were partial to it because it gave less opportunity for conflict with comptrollers and reduced burdensome correspondence. It got the job done quickly (regardless of costs) and relieved them of additional expenditures of time, direct responsibility for the labor force, and the detailed supervision of works (for which they often lacked the requisite specialized knowledge). The central administration in St. Petersburg was sympathetic because, in reducing the conflict between the builders and the comptrollers, the arrangement gave rise to fewer cases requiring time-consuming review and resolution.[54]

This form of construction led to widespread abuse. Their work essentially uncontrolled, contractors flouted all the rules. State engineers rarely publicized competitive bidding for contracts, as the Ministry of Transport had stipulated; contractors were chosen for arbitrary reasons. Estimates for a particular stretch of track were frequently based on the price asked by an individual contractor, who knew the government had not previously drawn up estimates. Having set his own high price, the contractor then called for even larger payments, and to keep him on the job the construction chief often approved the requests without higher authorization.[55]

52. *Vostochnoe obozrenie*, 1894, no. 75: 1; Borzunov, "Iz istorii formirovaniia," 90; Pushechnikov, "O nedochetakh v dele postroiki," *Inzhener*, no. 4 (Apr. 1909): 101. Borzunov shows that large contractors, with capital of from 50,000 to 500,000 rubles, did 98% of contract works. It is significant, as he also points out, that more than one-third of all contractors were of peasant origin. And judging by their low bankruptcy rate in comparison with other classes, they did comparatively well (pp. 90, 95).

53. TKIM, 11:4–5.

54. Pushechnikov, "O nedochetakh v dele postroiki," *Inzhener*, Apr. 1909, no. 4: 101; May 1909, no. 5: 133, 136–137, 139; ZhKSZhD, zas. 31, Apr. 29, 1898, SP, p. 3, col. 2; Gosudarstvennaia Duma, *Stenograficheskie otchety*, tretii sozyv, vol. 2, sessiia pervaia, zas. 46, Apr. 1, 1908, col. 1522 (all further references are to this session).

55. Gosudarstvennaia Duma, *Stenograficheskie otchety*, col. 1521; TKIM, 11:1–6, 21; 12:1–2, 4–5.

A particularly common, and costly, practice was to offer inducements and subsidies to contractors. A large proportion of their work was done without vouchers and they were given railroad equipment for their use at no cost, as well as, in many cases, tools, horses, food, forage, shelters, and a work force. Completion dates were delayed upon request. Most significant were advance payments. Such payments were lawful when they enabled the contractor to finish his work on schedule. Frequently, though, advances took the form of interest-free loans. Often in the tens or hundreds of thousands of rubles, they were paid to contractors and employees of the construction administration alike. Not surprisingly, the rate of repayment was low. In 1896 the amount of illegal advances exceeded 2.5 million rubles, and the practice showed no sign of contraction thereafter.[56]

Once a contract was in hand, the contractor sought to widen his profit margin by reducing construction costs. The technical standards established by the government were already low, and the contractor lowered them further. If regulations called for a formation of sixteen feet, for instance, it might be built at eleven feet. Or, since large contractors did not have the qualifications to undertake all forms of construction on a given route (several contractors on the Ussuri section were reputedly unqualified for any railroad work whatsoever), they would themselves farm out much of the work to subcontractors at the lowest price possible, the difference between the state contract and their own subcontracts forming their profit. The contractor thereby earned a handsome sum without risk or labor. Authorities estimated that while contractors made profits of 30 percent on the average, costs of construction and railroad supplies were inflated, with wide variation, up to 60 percent or more.[57] One peasant contractor from Smolensk province told A. Pushechnikov, chief construction engineer for the Transbaikal Railroad, "By recommending me for contract work on the Circumbaikal line, you have made me rich."[58]

56. TKIM, 12:1–4, 11–13; 13:4–6; Pushechnikov, "O nedochetakh v dele postroiki," *Inzhener*, May 1909, no. 5: 134.

57. Gosudarstvennaia Duma, *Stenograficheskie otchety*, cols. 1521–1523; Pushechnikov, "O nedochetakh v dele postroiki," *Inzhener*, Apr. 1909, no. 4: 102–104; TKIM(VP), 13:2–3; *Times*, May 25, 1901, p. 7; TKIM, 12:5–7. It was reported in the Committee of the Siberian Railroad that costs of materials on the Central Siberian Railroad rose from 26 to 91% over original estimates. See ZhKSZhD, zas. 32, Jan. 27, 1899, SP, p. 5, col. 1.

58. Pushechnikov, "O nedochetakh v dele postroiki," *Inzhener*, Apr. 1909, no. 4: 103–104.

## Management

A contemporary Russian railroad engineer called the project "a monument to Russian official bungling and laxity of administration."[59] The management of the Siberian Railroad during both construction and operation was bureaucratic and overly centralized, and the functions of its components were ill defined.

The Trans-Siberian was initially subdivided for purposes of construction and administration into four separate railroads corresponding to geographical divisions: the Western Siberian, Central Siberian, Transbaikal, and Ussuri railroads. In 1900 the Western Siberian and Central Siberian lines were unified into the "Siberian Railroad," with headquarters in Tomsk, a sop to that city for its location on a branch line. In 1906 the Siberian Railroad absorbed the Transbaikal Railroad and in the same year the Chinese-Eastern Railroad was given control of the Ussuri Railroad. Even before their amalgamation, the length of each section had made it difficult to supervise; afterward it was more so. It was impossible to carry out inspections more than twice a year, so that many problems were left undiscovered.[60]

Real authority over construction and operation lay not in Tomsk or Khabarovsk (headquarters of the Ussuri Railroad) but in distant St. Petersburg, in the Committee of the Siberian Railroad and the central organs of the Ministry of Transport—the Administration for the Construction of the Siberian Railroad and the Council for the Administration of the Siberian Railroad. A local administration would have been able to resolve problems effectively, without time-consuming correspondence with the capital. But St. Petersburg refused to delegate any of the authority it wielded so inefficiently.[61]

The railroad's management was centralized to an absurd degree.

59. Quoted in *Times*, Apr. 8, 1902, p. 3.

60. V. I. Kenge and N. D. Nakhtman, *Kratkii ocherk linii sibirskoi zheleznoi dorogi* (St. Petersburg, 1908), 7; Liubimov, "Ocherk eksploatatsii," *ISIPS*, 1904, no. 7: 141–142; Volpicelli, *Russia on the Pacific*, 294; Bukhman, *Doklad*, 6; *Sibirskaia sovetskaia entsiklopediia*, vol. 1 (Novosibirsk, 1929), s.v. "Zheleznye dorogi"; M. P. Fedorov, ed., *Doklady biudzhetnoi komissii vtoroi gosudarstvennoi dumy (ne razsmotrennye dumoi vsledstvie eia rospuska)* (St. Petersburg, 1907), 229.

61. OKIPP, 16; TKIM(VP), 2:1–2, 16:10; Migulin, *Nasha noveishaia zheleznodorozhnaia politika*, 282–283. See also A. Lavrov, "O korennykh nedostatkakh v organizatsii zheleznodorozhnogo dela v Rossii," *ISIPS*, 1917, no. 1: 11. A similar reluctance on the part of the central authorities of the Soviet Union to allocate authority over the Baikal-Amur Main Line to regional and local officials has been cited in Whiting, *Siberian Development*, 63, indicating continuity in the organization of economic development in the Russian Far East.

The tsar and his ministers reviewed each request for a grant of temporary monetary assistance made by an injured employee or a survivor
of an employee who had died in railroad service. Among numerous
others, the peasant Fedor Koniakin, permanently disabled while on
the Okhotsk-Kamchatka expedition, received 500 rubles after the
Committee of the Siberian Railroad considered his plight.[62] That the
tsar and his ministers, rather than local authorities, were responsible
for these decisions indicates the paternalism of "modern" economic
development in Russia and the persistence of a pattern developed in
the Muscovite period, when virtually every action of officials in Siberia
required written approval from Moscow.[63]

Muscovy did not always succeed in imposing its control over remote regions, and the knowledge of this failure engendered a lack of
responsibility on the part of officials. The state of affairs was no
different on the Siberian Railroad. Despite a centralized administrative structure, the state's instructions to the building administration
and construction chiefs were insufficiently detailed and unclearly
split responsibility among central authorities, local political authorities, and local railroad officials. Site managers and construction chiefs
bore no personal responsibility for a task entrusted to them, whether
they succeeded or failed. On the one hand, they were encouraged to
sidestep the law in order not to delay construction or implementation
of a policy that would improve operation. On the other hand, breaking
the rules would bring censure that was worse than the penalties for
allowing deficiencies in railroad operation; better, therefore, to leave
them uncorrected. Many questions that required speedy resolution
or could have best been resolved locally were up to central authorities
to deal with. Yet, at the same time that the central administration
could impose punitive measures on local railroad officials, it itself was
not answerable for the results of operation or construction, because of
the ambiguity of the instructions and the fact that it was not its task to
accomplish actual construction or operate the trains. In addition, for
the enormous amount of difficult work required, all officials involved
with the Siberian Railroad, from its central administrators to local
managers, were grossly underpaid.[64] The uncompromising central-

62. See ZhKSZhD, zas. 22, Mar. 8, 1895, pt. 2, SP, p. 6; zas. 23, May 3, 1895, pt. 1, SP, p. 2;
zas. 28, Nov. 27, 1896, SP, pp. 12–13, cols. 1–2; zas. 30, Dec. 10, 1897, SP, pp. 24–25, cols. 1–
2, and p. 26, col. 2; zas. 31, Apr. 29, 1898, SP, p. 34, cols. 1–2.

63. Cf. Basil Dmytryshyn et al., eds. and trans., *Russia's Conquest of Siberia: A Docu-
mentary Record, 1558–1700* (Portland, Oreg., 1985), passim.

64. ZhKSZhD, osobyi zhurnal, SP, May 26, 1893, pp. 6–10, col. 2; Sabler and Sosnovskii,

ism of formal control led to ambiguities and imperfections in actual administration that hampered the progress of the project no end.

The defects of managerial procedure were nowhere more apparent than in the procedures for financial control and accounting employed on the railroad. According to Witte, in a memorandum to Kulomzin, "in essence . . . the construction of the Siberian Railroad, an undertaking of such enormous importance requiring expenditures in the hundreds of millions of rubles, is virtually being carried out without any record of its costs." Faced with the fait accompli of overexpenditures, he continued, the Committee of the Siberian Railroad could do nothing; its approval of financing had been reduced to a formality.[65]

But in word and deed Witte and the committee had condoned the lack of financial discipline, in spite of some attempt to establish stricter standards and strengthen the authority of the state comptroller.[66] The Siberian Railroad was not held to the strict standards of financial reporting required of private railroads. Funding was never adequate for the preparation of such reports (or for administration on the whole), and the Ministry of Transport was permitted to postpone compilation of reports on construction for years after the railroad's completion.[67] The state comptroller, T. I. Filippov, was reputedly more absorbed in theological questions than in financial control, and many of his local representatives were incompetent and unfamiliar with railroad matters.[68] Prince Meshcherskii's opinion that the financial control of construction work would lead to higher costs and retard completion was shared by the Committee of the Siberian Railroad; especially after the Boxer Rebellion, it shunted financial control aside

*Sibirskaia zheleznaia doroga*, 136–137; Borzunov, "Istoriia sozdaniia," 544–546; OKIPP, 16; A. Pushechnikov, "O sovremennom polozhenii nekotorykh voprosov zheleznodorozhnogo dela v Rossii," *Inzhener* 29 (September 1910): 286; Bukhman, *Doklad*, 137–140, 182; Gosudarstvennaia Duma, *Stenograficheskie otchety*, col. 1524; Migulin, *Nasha noveishaia zheleznodorozhnaia politika*, 287.

65. Cited in Borzunov, "Istoriia sozdaniia," 1357–1358.

66. With promulgation of the "Temporary Laws on Control Operations for the Construction of the Siberian Railroad" in 1898. See Borzunov, "Istoriia sozdaniia," 1478; Sabler and Sosnovskii, *Sibirskaia zheleznaia doroga*, 137–139; ZhKSZhD, zas. 30, Dec. 10, 1897, SP, p. 2, cols. 1–2, and pp. 3–5, col. 2; zas. 34, Dec. 8, 1899, SP, p. 2, col. 2.

67. OKIPP, 23–25; Migulin, *Nasha noveishaia zheleznodorozhnaia politika*, 293. On the requirements for private railroads, see A. M. Solov'eva, *Zheleznodorozhnyi transport Rossii vo vtoroi polovine XIX v.* (Moscow, 1975), 160–161.

68. S. Iu. Witte, *Vospominaniia*, vol. 1 (Moscow, 1960), 307; K. A. Skal'kovskii, *Nashi gosudarstvennye i obshchestvennye deiateli* (St. Petersburg, 1890), 306–310; Pushechnikov, "O sovremennom polozhenii," *Inzhener*, September 1910, no. 9: 286–287.

and ordered engineers to finish the railroad at any cost.[69] The urgency of completing the railroad and the indifference of the state to matters of economy can ultimately be held responsible for many of the features of railroad management.

The establishment of cost estimates for the railroad was also faulty, so that adherence to formal procedure was almost impossible. Estimates were compiled in St. Petersburg before the building plans were completed, on the basis of surveys that were likely to be inaccurate. Anticipated costs were derived from the statistical assessment of previous European Russian railroad building, rather than of the very different conditions in Siberia. Representatives of the minister of finance and state comptroller often met in literal bargaining sessions to lower the cost estimates for various works, regardless of financial reality, so as to claim that they had made an attempt to reduce expenditures. The result was estimates that bore no relation to the actual costs of construction.[70]

The low priority given to cost considerations by almost everyone involved affected accounting on the railroad. Of course, the state of bookkeeping in Russia at large was primitive at the time: although merchants were legally obliged to keep books, many did not understand the reasons for doing so. Even some of the wealthiest kept no records at all and were unsure of the exact amounts involved in their current operations.[71] These attitudes were mirrored in the management of the Siberian Railroad.

The railroad's bookkeeping was in disarray. Accounting departments were underfunded and understaffed.[72] Accounting procedures varied with the section of the line: some were centralized under a chief bookkeeper; other sections maintained a separate bookkeeping department for each operating division. The form of books was distinct for each section and often varied from one division to the next within the same section. With rare exceptions, Italian double-entry

69. A. Koniaev, *Finansovyi kontrol' v dorevoliutsionnoi Rossii (Ocherk istorii)* (Moscow, 1959), 93; Pushechnikov, "O nedochetakh v dele postroiki," *Inzhener*, August 1909, no. 8: 249; Migulin, *Nasha noveishaia zheleznodorozhnaia politika*, 293.

70. A. Pushechnikov, "O nedochetakh v dele postroiki," *Inzhener*, Apr. 1909, no. 4: 99–100.

71. Alfred J. Rieber, *Merchants and Entrepreneurs in Imperial Russia* (Chapel Hill, N.C., 1982), 113.

72. Compare, in this regard, American railroads, which are thought to have employed in the nineteenth century more accountants and auditors than the federal government (Alfred D. Chandler, Jr., *The Visible Hand: The Managerial Revolution in American Business* [Cambridge, Mass., 1977], 110).

bookkeeping, a standard technique that originated in the late thirteenth century, was not employed on the Siberian Railroad. Often books were no more than a collection of receipts and other documents, in contradiction of the very notion of systematized bookkeeping. Data were imprecise, inconsistent, entered repeatedly, or missing altogether. The appearance of satisfactory performance was more important than a record reflecting the true position of the railroad. Management did not heed the standards set by the state comptroller for establishing an accounting system, so the data the railroad provided were often insufficient to permit the railroad's condition to be judged. The construction and operating administrations themselves often had no way to assess the financial position of the railroads under their control. An official investigative body noted the haphazard, chaotic bookkeeping of the Siberian Railroad during construction in the mid-1890s, but by the outbreak of World War I it had still not been corrected, and no figures concerning the railroad's operation could be regarded as wholly reliable.[73]

An infinite number of problems can be attributed to these deficiencies. The smallest details are important to the management of an enterprise as large and dynamic as a railroad. Inaccurate records and analysis hinder efficiency of operation and permit costs to skyrocket. American railroads devised new forms of accounting to cope with the complexities of operation and to digest the large flow of data that they generated. Furthermore, in the United States the lines of managerial responsibility were clearly drawn and authority was delegated to autonomous divisional managers to decentralize operations. Strict standards of control and evaluation were established as well.[74] But Russian attitudes and traditions, the bureaucratic approach to railroad management, and the political motivation of the Siberian Railroad brought about a very different configuration that jeopardized the whole venture.

73. TKIM, 13:1–3, 7–8; TKIM(VP), 16:1–2, 12–13; Bukhman, *Doklad*, 9–10, 154–155; Pushechnikov, "O nedochetakh v dele postroiki," *Inzhener*, June 1909, no. 6: 174–175.
74. See Chandler, *Visible Hand*, 94–121.

# CHAPTER TEN

# The Limits of Railroad Colonization

Improperly designed and poorly managed, the Trans-Siberian had inadequate capacity and its operation left much to be desired. It was not suited to accomplish the government's long-range goals in Siberia and the Russian Far East: it could not perform satisfactorily when it was called on for military service, it helped to strengthen the revolutionary element in Siberia, and its effectiveness in developing the Siberian economy was limited.

## Slow Motion

The condition of the track and roadbed did nothing to enhance the railroad's performance. The start of operation on the new stretch of road between Mariinsk and Achinsk was emblematic: the first locomotive to be driven on the line fell into a river below the tracks.[1] The Trans-Siberian had more accidents per verst traveled than the European Russian network. In 1901 alone, 93 people were killed and more than 500 injured in 924 wrecks.[2]

Technical problems forced trains to reduce their speed on the average to 20 versts per hour for passenger trains and 12 versts for

---

1. Harmon Tupper, *To the Great Ocean: Siberia and the Trans-Siberian Railway* (Boston, 1965), 117.

2. *Vestnik finansov, promyshlennosti i torgovli*, no. 47, Nov. 23, 1903: 333–334. In the same period there were 4,536 accidents in European Russia, with its much greater length of track. Details were kept from the public, much as in the USSR until recently. See *Railroad Gazette*, Sept. 21, 1900, p. 625.

freight trains—a rate that was below the norm for spurs. On some unsafe sections the trains were reduced to a crawl; if nothing else, the slow pace made "shaving . . . quite easy," according to a British newspaper correspondent. The trip by passenger train from Moscow to Port Arthur or Vladivostok, touted to take seven days, took twenty-eight days in the best of conditions, and for six months of the year the administration could not guarantee arrival in less than a month and a half.[3]

The railroad was capable of handling no more than three pairs of trains a day (that is, six trains, three in each direction) between stations, the size of trains varying with the terrain—conditions allowed for thirty-six cars per train on flat sections, sixteen in the hilliest regions.[4] Operating procedures were far from conducive to efficiency and contributed to the railroad's inability to provide good service:

> Trains were not dispatched but were handled on a station-to-station basis by the station masters. Timetables and printed train rules were non-existent while even watches were rare among the trainmen. Fueling was slow and handled in a primitive fashion. A given locomotive was driven exclusively by one engineer and went back and forth with him as he made his round-trip runs.[5]

The railroad's capacity was severely overtaxed by the growing demand of freight traffic. When the Western Siberian section opened in 1897, 3,000 cars were immediately backlogged. The situation worsened over the next few years, as tens of thousands of tons of goods awaited shipment for over three and a half months. Grain rotted on open platforms outside the stations. By 1901 the railroad administration gave notice that it could no longer be responsible for on-time delivery of freight.[6]

Shortages and deficiencies of rolling stock were both causes and effects of the overloaded system. The original orders for cars and

3. P. P. Migulin, *Nasha noveishaia zheleznodorozhnaia politika i zheleznodorozhnye zaimy (1893–1902)* (Khar'kov, 1903), 297; Tupper, *To the Great Ocean*, 245–246; *Times*, July 17, 1901, p. 5. For the report on shaving aboard the Central and Western Siberian lines, see *Times*, Oct. 22, 1898, p. 8.

4. Migulin, *Nasha noveishaia zheleznodorozhnaia politika*, 297; Medem, 421–422.

5. John Albert White, *The Siberian Intervention* (Princeton, 1950), 48.

6. *Railroad Gazette*, Oct. 21, 1898, p. 764; Robert Britton Valliant, "Japan and the Trans-Siberian Railroad, 1885–1905" (Ph.D. diss., University of Hawaii, 1974), 105–106, 109; A. P. Pogrebinskii, "Stroitel'stvo zheleznykh dorog v poreformennoi Rossii i finansovaia politika tsarizma (60–90-e gody XIX v.)," *Istoricheskie zapiski* 47 (1954): 173; *Times*, May 6, 1901, p. 6.

Taiga station, Central Siberian Railroad. From *Velikii put': Vidy Sibiri i eia zheleznykh dorog* (Krasnoiarsk, 1899).

engines were placed before the extent of traffic was known. Even then, orders far exceeded what Russian firms could produce, and the new equipment was often of poor quality because of the low technical level of the factories. Secondhand trains from the European Russian network provided the bulk of the railroad's rolling stock. In 1900, 20 percent of the rolling stock belonging to the Siberian Railroad was out of service because of defects brought about by age, overuse, and poor surface conditions. By 1914, the only reliable form of freight service was that provided for the export of fresh Siberian butter on special refrigerated cars.[7]

Passenger service suffered along with freight traffic. Station stops absorbed a large portion of running time, seemingly without rhyme or reason. An American passenger reported a seventeen-hour delay at one stop, irregular departures elsewhere, and travel in filthy, graffiti-covered cars.[8] Another traveler wrote:

> Our train would draw up at a wood pile and a log-house. The peasants would scramble out of the train, build their fires, cook their soup, boil their tea, and still the train would wait. There was usually no baggage to be taken on or put off, no passengers to join us, no passing train to wait for. . . . At last, for no particular reason, apparently, the station-master would ring a big dinner-bell. Five minutes later he would ring another. Then, soon after, the guard would blow his whistle, the engineer would respond with the engine whistle, the guard would blow again, the engineer would answer him once more, and, after this exchange of compliments, the train would move leisurely along, only to repeat the process two hours later at the next station.[9]

Improvements that increased the speed to 37 versts per hour and reduced travel time between St. Petersburg and Vladivostok to nine days were still not sufficient to attract foreigners to the express service, as the administration intended. There were other factors as well. Train agents rarely spoke a foreign language, and tourists were strictly forbidden to photograph even the most innocuous sights from the train or stations. The railroad's restaurant cars served meals by St. Petersburg time, oblivious of the seven time zones between the capital and Vladivostok. Despite the dearth of passengers, three express

---

7. V. F. Borzunov, "Istoriia sozdaniia transsibirskoi zheleznodorozhnoi magistrali XIX–nachala XX v." (Ph.D. diss., Tomskii Gosudarstvennyi Universitet, 1972), 1220–1222; MPS, *Istoricheskii ocherk raznykh otraslei zheleznodorozhnogo dela i razvitiia finansovo-ekonomicheskoi storony zheleznykh dorog v Rossii po 1897 g. vkliuchitel'no*, comp. V. M. Verkhovskii, pt. 6 (St. Petersburg, 1901), 114; A. M. Solov'eva, *Zheleznodorozhnyi transport Rossii vo vtoroi polovine XIX v.* (Moscow, 1975), 257–258; *Railroad Gazette*, Sept. 29, 1899, p. 677; J. N. Westwood, *A History of Russian Railways* (London, 1964), 122–123.

8. *Railroad Gazette*, Nov. 12, 1897, p. 798.

9. Quoted in Tupper, *To the Great Ocean*, 258–259. One might construe this anecdote as illustrating the contradictions that occur when a preindustrial society is in the process of adapting to the modern technology grafted onto it by the state.

trains ran throughout the year, often virtually empty and at great expense.[10]

Nor did the Siberian Railroad live up to expectations as a transit route shuttling trade between Western Europe and the Orient. Its international freight was insignificant (less than 10 percent), and it could not offer the competitive rates or service needed to lure passengers or freight from the sea routes. Although there was some growth in trade with Japan and China, it was of little importance.[11]

### The Russo-Japanese War

In its military capacity, too, the Siberian Railroad was deficient. After the Sino-Japanese War (1894–1895), Japan's involvement on the Asian continent for the first time became a factor in Russian Far Eastern policy. In the face of this menace, in 1896 the Committee of the Siberian Railroad increased the budgetary allocation to the railroad by 65 percent to speed its completion.[12] The operational defects of the railroad adversely affected Russia's ability to defend the region. In 1897 Kulomzin wrote in distress, "When the necessity of urgently transferring any significant number of troops to the Far East presents itself, complete disappointment will ensue and [the Trans-Siberian] will prove to be a toy railroad."[13]

The committee made an effort in January 1899 to increase the railroad's carrying capacity to seven pairs of trains per day by adopting the following measures, to be implemented over the next eight years at a cost of 84 million rubles: addition of sidings to shunt off trains, construction of new stations, replacement of light 18-pound

10. M. L. Fedorov, *Ekonomicheskoe polozhenie sibirskoi magistrali* (St. Petersburg, 1912), vol. 76 of *Trudy vysochaishe uchrezhdennoi osoboi vysshei komissii dlia vsestoronnego issledovaniia zheleznodorozhnogo dela v Rossii*, pp. 20–25.

11. "Znachenie sibirskoi zheleznoi dorogi kak ona vyiasniaetsia v nastoiashchee vremia," *ZhdD*, 1900, no. 33: 360; Migulin, *Nasha noveishaia zheleznodorozhnaia politika*, 301; Robert N. North, *Transport in Western Siberia: Tsarist and Soviet Development* (Vancouver, 1979), 67. On the disappointing trade relations between Russia and Japan, see the detailed account in Valliant, "Japan," chaps. 5 and 6. For the dimensions of Russo-Chinese trade in this period, see M. I. Sladkovskii, *Istoriia torgovo-ekonomicheskikh otnoshenii narodov Rossii s Kitaem (do 1917 g.)* (Moscow, 1974), 337–345. The total value of trade increased by 250% between 1895 and 1914, but in 1913 Russian exports to China were valued at approximately 29 million rubles and Chinese exports to Russia at 90 million. (Predominant among Russian exports were cotton fabrics; tea led imports from China by a wide margin.)

12. Valliant, "Japan," 104–105.

13. Quoted in Pogrebinskii, "Stroitel'stvo," 173.

(per foot) rails with 24-pound rails, thickening of ballast, widening of the roadbed, replacement of wooden bridges with steel ones, and a vast supplement of rolling stock, including new, larger locomotives, each with twelve (0-6-6-0) instead of eight wheels. The committee also attempted to improve commercial freight haulage, creating a trunk line from St. Petersburg to Siberia by building a branch off the Perm'-Kotlas Railroad from Viatka to Vologda and thence to the capital. This alternative route would allow a certain amount of traffic to bypass the western stretch of the Siberian Railroad (Samara-Zlatoust), which was congested because it had to share the only bridge over the Volga with the Orenburg Railroad.[14]

The events of the next few years should have confirmed the need for reconstruction. The backlog during the winter of 1898–1899 reached 7,000 carloads. In 1900, 120,000 soldiers were mobilized and transported on the Siberian Railroad to suppress the Boxer Rebellion and occupy Manchuria. For hundreds of versts, trains were slowed to 10 versts per hour. More than forty new Sormovo locomotives and tens of cars and flatcars were wrecked on the way. The railroad had failed its first real test, foreshadowing its performance in the Russo-Japanese War. Khilkov recommended a further increase in capacity to fourteen pairs of trains per day, and War Minister Kuropatkin urged that construction be completed on the Circumbaikal route so as to remove the impediment to troop transport presented by the lake. To relieve traffic, Admiral Chikhachev advised consideration of a railroad running either from Orenburg to Tashkent or through the southern Siberian steppe.[15]

Witte, who was personally identified with the railroad as it stood, at first adamantly opposed improvements, especially when they were urged by military officials, and he hesitated to approve the requested credits.[16] By 1903, however, after his own inspection tour to Siberia and the Far East, he reluctantly agreed. According to Polovtsov, Witte

14. ZhKSZhD, zas. 31, Apr. 29, 1898, SP, pp. 15–17, cols. 1–2; zas. 32, Jan. 27, 1899, SP, p. 2, col. 1; S. V. Sabler and I. V. Sosnovskii, *Sibirskaia zheleznaia doroga v eia proshlom i nastoiashchem: Istoricheskii ocherk,* ed. A. N. Kulomzin (St. Petersburg, 1903), 261–266; A. A. Bublikov, *K voprosu o spriamlenii peterburgo-sibirskoi tranzitnoi magistrali* (St. Petersburg, 1905), 5–6; North, *Transport,* 72. The St. Petersburg–Viatka line opened in 1905, but the low capacity of the Ural Railroads made it ineffective as a transit route.

15. Valliant, "Japan," 109; *Times,* Apr. 8, 1902, p. 3; ZhKSZhD, zas. 36, Feb. 21, 1901, SP, pp. 4–5, col. 2; zas. 39, June 6, 1902, SP, p. 4, col. 1, and pp. 5 and 7, col. 2. Chikhachev's proposed rail line through the steppe followed the western portion of the route earlier drawn up by his subordinate Admiral Kopytov.

16. ZhKSZhD, zas. 39, June 6, 1902, SP, pp. 8–9, col. 2; see also zas. 31, Apr. 29, 1898, SP, pp. 15–17, cols. 1–2.

announced to several members of the State Council that "a 780-verst section between Tomsk and Irkutsk is built in such a way that it must be entirely rebuilt, and that now even traveling on it presents a serious danger."[17] He told Kuropatkin that in his opinion the eastern sections of the railroad were so "badly traced it would have been better to stick with the centuries-old post road."[18]

By this time, it was too late to make a difference in war. Kuropatkin worked out his strategy for the Far Eastern theater in 1903, presupposing a carrying capacity of ten pairs of trains per day on the Siberian Railroad to allow for the accumulation of an overwhelming number of Russian troops against the Japanese. On January 18, 1904, just days before Admiral Togo's surprise attack on Port Arthur, a special conference convened at the war minister's demand, to discuss the capacity of the railroad. Kuropatkin asked the government to do everything it could to delay the inevitable war until the Siberian and Chinese-Eastern railroads were strengthened. Despite initial efforts to carry out the earlier recommendations and to smooth gradients by reconstructing mountainous sections of track, at the outbreak of war capacity stood at under four pairs of military trains per day. Adding an additional pair of trains would have meant closing the line to civilian traffic altogether. Japanese agents had informed their general staff of the railroad's capacity, and this information was used to calculate Russian strength in the region. Japanese divisions were increased proportionately and the war was initiated at the very moment when Russia was most vulnerable—when the ice on Lake Baikal had reached the depth at which the icebreakers could no longer function.[19]

During hostilities the efforts made to improve the railroad were impressive. The first priority was to organize transport across Baikal. Icebreakers could not operate on the lake for three and a half months, from late December to mid-April. Aside from expediting construction on the Circumbaikal Railroad, Khilkov devised and personally supervised a temporary way around this natural obstacle. Five hundred laborers laid more than 30,000 rails, or 42 versts of track, on the ice.

17. "Dnevnik A. A. Polovtseva (sic)," *Krasnyi arkhiv* 3 (1923): 167 (Jan. 1, 1903).

18. "Dnevnik A. N. Kuropatkina," *Krasnyi arkhiv* 2 (1922): 24 (Jan. 19, 1903).

19. P. A. Belov, "Zheleznodorozhnyi transport v russko-iaponskoi voine, 1904–1905 gg.," *Trudy akademii krasnoi armii*, 1940, no. 4: 108, 110–111; J. N. Westwood, *Russia against Japan, 1904–05: A New Look at the Russo-Japanese War* (Albany, 1986), 122; Valliant, "Japan," 146, 148, 265, 291; Sabler and Sosnovskii, *Sibirskaia zheleznaia doroga*, 267–269; Medem, 420–422; L. N. Liubimov, "Opyt organizatsii i proizvodstva massovoi sploshnoi smeny rel'sov na sibirskoi zheleznoi doroge," *Inzhener* 27 (August–September 1903): 278–279, 281–282.

Railroad cars were decoupled and pulled across the lake by horses, more than 3,000 of them. On either side of the track were sleigh routes for the transport of passengers. Soldiers marched across, guided at night by the electric lights and telephone wires set up parallel to the track; in severe weather they would march along the shore of the lake. Every six versts heated barracks were erected, and halfway across stood the station Seredina (Middle), with separate first-, second-, and third-class buffets. To service the track, which was subject to disturbance by cracking ice, the Ministry of Transport organized special artels. Construction of the route began on February 2, 1904, and it was opened to traffic on the 27th. In early March it was dismantled in time for navigation to recommence in April. Five military trains per day were able to cross in this fashion, with more than 16,000 passengers and 500,000 puds of freight. This total was comparable to the full capacity of steamers in summertime and exceeded that of the icebreakers.[20]

By late 1904 the capacity of the remainder of the line was increased twofold and by the end of the war to twelve pairs of trains, although the goal had been sixteen pairs or more. The authorities accomplished these improvements, at a cost of more than 46 million rubles, by upgrading the track, building additional sidings, improving the water supply (particularly crucial in Transbaikalia, where the rivers froze solid in winter), completing the Circumbaikal Railroad, transferring thousands of pieces of rolling stock from other railroads, and constructing additional depots and repair stations. Traffic control was improved and the eastern sections of the line were placed under martial law. Furthermore, plans now existed to double-track the whole route from Cheliabinsk to Irkutsk, which the tsar considered vital, but the work was not undertaken during the war. As a result of the improvements, by late 1904 over 200,000 soldiers were transported to the war zone and eventually over a million. Freight turnover, mostly connected with the military, increased by 75 percent over prewar figures.[21]

20. Belov, "Zheleznodorozhnyi transport," 108–109; N. K. Struk, "Zheleznye dorogi vostochnoi Sibiri v russko-iaponskuiu voinu, 1904–1905 gg.," in *Sibirskii istoricheskii sbornik (Sotsial'no-ekonomicheskoe i politicheskoe razvitie Sibiri)*, ed. I. I. Kuznetsov and N. K. Struk, vol. 1 (Irkutsk, 1973), 26–27; Bredt, "Baugeschichte und Bauausführung der großen sibirischen Eisenbahn," *Archiv für Eisenbahnwesen*, January–February 1906, no. 1: 109–111; "Put' i perevozka po ozeru Baikal (Izvlechenie iz vsepoddanneishego doklada MPS ot 26-go marta 1904 g.)," *ZhdD*, 1904, 249–251.

21. Belov, "Zheleznodorozhnyi transport," 112–114; Struk, "Zheleznye dorogi," 28–34; Medem, 422–423; G. M. Budagov, *O propusknoi sposobnosti sibirskoi zheleznoi dorogi*

Remarkable as they were, the improvements were too little too late; the statistics mask the serious shortcomings that remained. The effort to bolster the Siberian Railroad's performance in war interfered with the normal operation of the whole Russian railroad network. The diversion of rolling stock from southern Russia interrupted grain exports from that region in their peak period. Civilian passenger service and freight transport were virtually curtailed on the Siberian line. Troops were still transported at the slow commercial speed of 12 versts per hour. The increasing number of wounded soldiers were evacuated on trains moving westward, which, along with empty cars, clogged the line. Had Russian soldiers not had access to local food sources in Manchuria (as would have been the case if fighting had shifted onto Russian territory), the railroad, which carried almost exclusively men, horses, and ammunition, simply would not have been able to cope.[22]

As it was, by the time the railroad's capacity was augmented, the important battles had been lost. Although Japan's mobilization took four months longer than expected, Russia's was eight months behind schedule.[23] Kuropatkin pointed out that the transport of reinforcements took twice as long as was required in the first five months of the war, when their presence was most vital. And he was dissatisfied with the transport of supplies. As he reported to the tsar from the front in November 1904, "the inability of the [Siberian] line to cope with the necessities of war is the main reason for the slow and indecisive nature of the campaign. Our reinforcements arrive in driblets. Supplies dispatched in spring are still on the Siberian line." He wrote that the slowness of the railroad led to "paralysis" and estimated that to salvage the Russian army's position in the war, the railroad would need to be double-tracked and brought up to a capacity of forty-eight trains.[24]

(Moscow, 1905), 22; A. N. Kuropatkin, *The Russian Army and the Japanese War*, trans. A. B. Lindsay, vol. 1 (London, 1909), 249, 261–262; Westwood, *Russia against Japan*, 122–123. Westwood incorrectly states that capacity reached sixteen pairs of trains per day by war's end; as the other sources attest, the government did not attain this goal.

22. *Times*, Oct. 15, 1904, p. 5; Belov, "Zheleznodorozhnyi transport," 122, 124; Struk, "Zheleznye dorogi," 28; Westwood, *Russia against Japan*, 123.

23. Westwood, *Russia against Japan*, 122; Belov, "Zheleznodorozhnyi transport," 121.

24. Kuropatkin, *Russian Army*, 1:244–245, 261–263, 267–268. The situation could have been much worse. The Japanese command was mulling over plans to blow up sections of the Siberian Railroad, a deed that probably would have presented little difficulty. For unknown reasons, the operation was never put in motion. See Valliant, "Japan," 296–298.

After the war, Kuropatkin laid much of the blame for the Russian defeat on the Siberian Railroad: "Next to the absence of a Russian fleet, the most important factor to assist the Japanese in their offensive strategy and to impede us was the condition of the Siberian and Eastern Chinese railways."[25] Admittedly Kuropatkin was trying to shift responsiblity for defeat from his own failings, but he was not alone in his view: most railroad experts, and eventually even its creator, Witte, assumed that if the capacity of the Trans-Siberian had not been so low, the outcome of the war would have been different.[26]

After the war, the government continued to take steps to improve the operation of the railroad. It reconstructed most of the line and built new branches. Gradients were further reduced and the railroad was double-tracked except for the Cheliabinsk-Omsk section and the Circumbaikal Railroad. For the latter, ferry traffic on the lake was expanded. On the former, traffic was heavy enough to warrant construction of an additional single-tracked railroad from Tiumen' to Omsk, linking the Siberian Railroad directly with the Perm' Railroad and the northern ports. This line was completed in 1913. Moreover, construction of the Amur Railroad, which had originally been abandoned for the Chinese-Eastern Railroad, began in 1908 and was completed in 1916, linking the Ussuri region with the Transbaikal Railroad through Russian territory. Improvements to internal waterways, the Northern Sea route, and the Moscow-Siberian highway were also discussed as ways to relieve the overtaxed Siberian Railroad. Construction of the Orenburg-Tashkent Railroad began in this period partially for this reason, having received the backing of Witte in 1903.[27]

Plans for new railroads in all parts of Siberia proliferated after the war, including several predecessors of the Baikal-Amur Main Line, branches running throughout the steppe and mountains of southern

25. Kuropatkin, *Russian Army*, 1:242.

26. S. Iu. Witte, "Nekotorye soobrazheniia o prichinakh defitsitnosti russkoi zhelezno-dorozhnoi seti," *ZhdD*, 1910, nos. 17–18: 91; N. Petrov, *Doklad o razvitii russkoi zhe-leznodorozhnoi seti* (St. Petersburg, 1912), 6, cited in L. G. Beskrovnyi, *Armiia i flot Rossii v nachale XX v.: Ocherki voenno-ekonomicheskogo potentsiala* (Moscow, 1986), 116. This interpretation contradicts that put forth by Allen S. Whiting, in *Siberian Development and East Asia: Threat or Promise?* (Stanford, 1981), 99, who views the Siberian Railroad as having performed successfully in the war.

27. Struk, "Zheleznye dorogi," 38–40; Beskrovnyi, *Armiia*, 117; Pushechnikov, "K voprosu o novykh dorogakh v Sibiri," *ZhdD*, 1908, no. 13: 91; "Izvlechenie iz vsepoddan-neishego doklada ministra finansov o poezdke na Dal'nii Vostok," *Vestnik finansov*, no. 8, Feb. 23, 1903: 312; Medem, 423; *Sibirskaia sovetskaia entsiklopediia*, vol. 1 (Novosibirsk, 1929), s.v. "Zheleznye dorogi"; Gosudarstvennaia Duma, *Prilozheniia k stenografiche-skim otchetam*, 1907–1908 gg., vol. 2, no. 401, cols. 414–419.

Siberia, and a series of lines linking Central Asia with Siberia.[28] The government also gave its attention to a project for a railroad or combined highway-railroad to be built by an American-French consortium from some point on the Central Siberian Railroad northeastward to the Chukotsk Peninsula and, via a tunnel under the Bering Strait, through Alaska.[29] The so-called Siberia-Alaska Railroad never appeared because of its impracticality; many of the other proposed lines were eventually built by the Soviet government.

These measures notwithstanding, by World War I the Siberian Railroad still could not keep up with the ever-increasing demand thrust upon it by peasant migrants and the expanding production of Siberian grain. Light rails had not been replaced along the whole length of the road, and after reconstruction the Transbaikal section was no less hazardous than before. In the words of a member of the State Council, it continued "from time to time to give highly unpleasant surprises."[30] The system was overloaded and operating well beyond capacity. In 1905 one railroad authority found that the Nikolaevsk Railroad between St. Petersburg and Moscow—the first major railroad in Russia, built sixty years earlier—was capable of handling thirty times more traffic than the Trans-Siberian, which had just been completed.[31] The ratio was barely changed by 1917.

28. See Pushechnikov, "O nedochetakh v dele izyskanii i postroiki zheleznykh dorog v Sibiri," *ZhdD*, 1907, nos. 46–47: 527; various dispatches in *ZhdD*, 1909, nos. 21–22: 121–126; no. 24: 143–144; Migulin, *Nasha noveishaia zheleznodorozhnaia politika*, 302; *Sibirskaia sovetskaia entsiklopediia*, s.v. "Zheleznye dorogi"; Sibirskoe Biuro pri Sovete S"ezdov Predstavitelei Birzhevoi Torgovli i Sel'skogo Khoziaistva, *Plan zheleznodorozhnogo stroitel'stva v Sibiri na blizhaishee desiatiletie* (Petrograd, Jan. 1917), 9.

29. See "Khodataistva inostrannogo sindikata o Sibir'-Aliaskinoi zheleznoi doroge i zheleznye dorogi v Aliaske (Doklad g-na Loik-de-Lobelia v sobranii armii i flota 12 marta 1906 goda, v zasedanii VIII otdela I.R.G.O.)," *ZhdD*, 1908, nos. 15–16: 31D–49D; V. Lestushevskii, "Predpolozheniia o postroike vostochnoi sibirskoi zheleznoi dorogi ot Beringova proliva," *ZhdD*, 1912, nos. 27–28: 157–161; G. Vereshchagin, "N. N. Romanov i amerikanskaia kontsessiia na zheleznuiu dorogu Sibir'-Aliaska v 1905 g.," *Krasnyi arkhiv* 43 (1931): 173–176.

30. A. N. Bukhman et al., *Doklad ob eksploatatsionnykh raskhodakh sibirskoi zheleznoi dorogi* (St. Petersburg, 1912), 6, 144–145; Westwood, *History*, 119. The quote is by V. I. Denisov, in his *Rossiia na Dal'nem Vostoke* (n.p., 1913), 26–27.

31. "'Obshchii vzgliad na postroiku zheleznykh dorog i na ustroistvo sibirskoi zheleznoi dorogi i o nekotorykh merakh dlia uskoreniia po nei dvizheniia' (Stenograficheskii otchet po dokladu A. L. Sokolova i besede v VIII otdele IRTO)," *ZhdD*, 1905, no. 23: 255. See also North, *Transport*, 72; Sibirskoe Biuro, *Plan zheleznodorozhnogo stroitel'stva*, 10.

## Economic Impact

The Trans-Siberian's efficacy as an instrument of political consolidation was no greater than its strategic utility. The railroad had been intended to spur the Siberian economy, but though it did induce certain changes in the form of Siberian economic life, by and large it was unsuited to effect major transformations, and its overall impact was restricted.[32]

On the surface, the Siberian economy seems to have made important advances after the railroad was built. Its agriculture and its exploitation of natural resources were expanding. In the two decades 1897 to 1917, the amount of land under cultivation increased by 122 percent, from 14 million to 31 million acres.[33] The wheat harvest in the

32. This section cannot survey comprehensively the economic significance of the Siberian Railroad, a subject that merits a full-scale study of its own. There is already a significant body of literature on various aspects of the topic. Interestingly, in both of the phases through which this work has passed, Soviet and Western interpretations are in full agreement, once ideological wrappings are stripped away from the former. In the earlier phase, for different reasons, historians on both sides stressed the remarkable percentage increase in all sectors of the Siberian economy after construction of the Siberian Railroad. See Anatole Baikalov, "Siberia since 1894," *Slavonic and East European Review* 11 (Jan. 1933): 328–340, and G. K. Tsvetkov, "Ekonomicheskoe znachenie sibirskoi zheleznoi dorogi," *Vestnik moskovskogo universiteta*, 1946, no. 2: 113–118. In both cases, these works follow, consciously or unconsciously, the optimistic account established by such official publications as Sabler and Sosnovskii, *Sibirskaia zheleznaia doroga*, and A. N. Kulomzin, *Le Transsibérien*, trans. Jules Legras (Paris, 1904). The second, more recent phase in the historiography adds depth and detail and corrects the earlier interpretation by emphasizing the uneven, limited impact of the railroad. Historians have recently resurrected the views of critical observers who wrote between 1905 and 1921, including local and national government officials, railroad experts, and regionalists, many of whose works are cited in this book. The major secondary works in this category are Elena A. Baranov, "The Trans-Siberian and Urban Change in a Time-Space Framework, 1885–1913" (Ph.D. diss., University of Kansas, 1987); G. A. Bochanova, *Obrabatyvaiushchaia promyshlennost' zapadnoi Sibiri, konets XIX–nachalo XX v.* (Novosibirsk, 1978); V. F. Borzunov, "K voprosu ob ekonomicheskom znachenii zheleznoi dorogi v kontse XIX–nachale XX vv.," in *Voprosy istorii Sibiri i Dal'nego Vostoka*, ed. V. I. Shunkov et al. (Novosibirsk, 1961), 97–107, and "Vliianie transsibirskoi magistrali na razvitie sel'skogo khoziaistva Sibiri i Dal'nego Vostoka v nachale XX v. (1900–1914 gg.)," in *Osobennosti agrarnogo stroia Rossii v period imperializma*, ed. S. M. Dubrovskii et al. (Moscow, 1962), 160–186; L. M. Goriushkin, *Agrarnye otnosheniia v Sibiri perioda imperializma (1900–1917 gg.)* (Novosibirsk, 1976); A. A. Mukhin, "Vliianie sibirskoi zheleznoi dorogi na sotsial'no-ekonomicheskoe razvitie vostochnoi Sibiri (1897–1917 gg.)," in Shunkov et al., *Voprosy istorii Sibiri i Dal'nego Vostoka*, 109–118; North, *Transport*; Nikolaus Poppe, "The Economic and Cultural Development of Siberia," in *Russia Enters the Twentieth Century: 1894–1917*, ed. E. Oberländer et al. (New York, 1971), 138–151.

33. Baikalov, "Siberia since 1894," 331.

period 1910–1914 exceeded 3.2 million tons and the rye harvest 800,000 tons.[34] To an American consular representative, the heavy demand for agricultural machinery in Siberia was evidence of its vitality and economic growth.[35] Animal husbandry was growing even more vigorously; the total amount of livestock in Siberia more than tripled between 1904 and 1916, to over 38 million head. Cooperative creameries produced one of the most successful Siberian products, fresh butter. The creation of this industry was possible only with the rapid refrigerated transport offered by the railroad. The first cooperative was opened in 1896; by 1911 there were 1,318, out of a total of 3,102 creameries.[36] Grain exports exceeded 70 million puds per year. Siberian butter, which had represented less than 9 percent of Russian exports of that product in 1896, by 1907 made up 94 percent of the total export figures.[37] Between 1896 and 1913 freight traffic on the Siberian Railroad grew fivefold by weight, the major items being wheat, coal, and wood. Butter deserves to belong in this category by value.[38]

Urban life showed development too. In 1897 Sretensk, in Transbaikal oblast, had 1,700 residents; by 1900 it had 8,000. Novonikolaevsk, lying at the junction of the railroad and the Ob' River, grew from a tiny village to a major town of 16,000 by 1900.[39] Such growth rates were common in many of the towns through which the Trans-Siberian passed. They experienced a corresponding growth of trade and, on average for the period 1904–1910, a 100 percent increase in their budgets (compared to a 50 percent average increase for the empire as a whole).[40]

Finally, trade patterns were being transformed within Siberia, in many ways for the broader good of the region. Two developments suggest the benefits that the railroad brought to the region. First, large

34. Poppe, "Economic and Cultural Development," 146.

35. John H. Snodgrass, *Russia: A Handbook on Commercial and Industrial Conditions*, for Department of Commerce, Bureau of Foreign and Domestic Commerce, Special Consular Reports no. 61 (Washington, D.C., 1913), 218.

36. Poppe, "Economic and Cultural Development," 146–147. For more detail on the butter industry, see P. M. Golovachev, *Ekonomicheskaia geografiia Sibiri* (Moscow, 1914), chap. 8.

37. Golovachev, *Ekonomicheskaia geografiia*, 109, 120–121.

38. North, *Transport*, 67; for exact figures for the period 1900–1909, see MPS, Upravlenie Sibirskoi Zheleznoi Dorogi, Kommercheskaia Chast', *Obzor kommercheskoi deiatel'nosti sibirskoi zheleznoi dorogi (za 1909 god po sravneniiu s predydushimi godami desiatiletiia 1900–1909 gg.)* (Tomsk, 1910), 147, 152–153, 160, 198.

39. M. N. Selikhov, "Sibir' pod vliianiem velikogo rel'sovogo puti," *Sibirskii torgovo-promyshlennyi i spravochnyi kalendar' na 1902 god*, otdel 2 (Tomsk, 1902), 51.

40. See statistics in Golovachev, *Ekonomicheskaia geografiia*, 160–162.

wholesale merchants were forced to release their monopolistic grip on Siberia's commerce. Before the advent of the railroad, it had been difficult for small tradesmen to survive in business. Every year they had to journey to the fairs at Nizhnii-Novgorod and Irbit, and often as far as Moscow, to order their wares a year in advance. The cost of a year's worth of goods was high even before transport costs were calculated. Muscovite manufacturers, for their part, risked heavy losses in extending credit for goods to small Siberian merchants. The procedure was so complicated and costly that a few large wholesale firms came to monopolize most imports from European Russia, taking on the responsibility for credit and transport. They dispensed their goods from warehouses, most of them in Tomsk and Irkutsk. Their dominance of the market allowed them to dictate prices, and the regionalists portrayed them as the bane of Siberia's existence. The construction of the railroad put Moscow and the small traders in direct contact. There was no more risk of long-term credit, as creditors easily controlled their debtors by cutting off their supply of manufactures. Local merchants no longer needed large amounts of capital to buy and ship goods. The middlemen's reason for existence had disappeared and their operations collapsed.[41]

The second development was the appearance of patterns of inter-regional trade within the overall movement of freight on the railroad line. Initially exports constituted the bulk of Siberian Railroad freight traffic. By 1900, and increasingly by 1910, the trend was for local transport within Siberia to predominate at the expense of exports. The most significant items in this trade were grain, shipped to eastern Siberia and beyond, and coal, going in the opposite direction.[42] This movement signals a certain regional specialization within Siberia and, faintly, the region's increasing economic self-sufficiency. The importance of this trend should not be overemphasized, however, because the sum of Siberian exports and imports continued to exceed its local traffic.

In some respects the economic impact of the railroad was detrimental. Enisei and Irkutsk provinces did not benefit from rail communications as western Siberia did. These regions in the geographical center of Siberia lost their foreign and domestic markets as a result of

41. Gr. P——n (Potanin), *Ocherk proektov zheleznodorozhnogo stroitel'stva v Sibiri* (St. Petersburg, 1910), 5–6; M. N. Sobolev, *Ekonomicheskoe znachenie sibirskoi zheleznoi dorogi* (Tomsk, 1900), 23.

42. "Znachenie sibirskoi zheleznoi dorogi kak ona vyiasniaetsia," 360; MPS, *Obzor kommercheskoi deiatel'nosti*, 154; Bukhman, *Doklad*, 7.

the railroad. Their livestock industries, particularly buttermaking, could not compete with western Siberia's, which enjoyed lower shipping costs to western Europe. Foreign imports became more competitive than the products of these industries in Transbaikalia and the Ussuri region, which had formerly been their primary markets. Cheap, high-quality western Siberian agricultural goods were also making inroads into their local markets. Agricultural decline was the result in central and eastern Siberia.[43]

Specific industries and towns were affected similarly. The railroad made highway cartage redundant in its path, and whole villages lost their primary means of employment. Many haulers attempted to return to agriculture, but with the competition of new settlers and depressed conditions in all but western Siberia, it could not absorb most of them.[44] Cottage industries suffered somewhat from the influx of cheap European Russian manufactures, as did Siberia's ironworks. Most of the ironworks shut down after the railroad was built. Finally, the majority of the towns that the Trans-Siberian bypassed slid into torpor as their merchants shifted operations to locations on the railroad.[45] The regionalists had feared these developments. In one branch of industry, however, their predictions turned out to be false: the railroad gave a boost to hostelry and tavernkeeping.[46]

The railroad had an adverse effect on one of Siberia's most valuable natural resources as well—its forests. Whole oblasts of the Urals were deforested to supply the railroad with fuel and construction materials. In Siberia the process was exacerbated by colonists, who were also in need of lumber. Both the railroad and the settlers were blamed for frequent forest fires. Witte had mentioned the problem in 1903, but by 1915 little had been done to confront it, as the shortage of firewood in Tomsk, in the taiga zone, attests.[47]

43. P. Kolotilov, "Ocherk razvitiia sibirskoi torgovli i promyshlennosti," *Vestnik finansov*, no. 22, June 1, 1908: 359; V. Iu. Grigor'ev, *Peremeny v usloviiakh ekonomicheskoi zhizni naseleniia Sibiri (Eniseiskii krai)* (Krasnoiarsk, 1904), 75–79; A. Kaufman, "Zemel'nyi vopros i pereselenie," *Sibir': Eia sovremennoe sostoianie i eia nuzhdy: Sbornik statei*, ed. I. S. Mel'nik (St. Petersburg, 1908), 116–117. The latter two sources point out that the agricultural crisis in these provinces was also due to the independent decline of their gold industries, which had long been a source of demand for grain.
44. Kaufman, "Zemel'nyi vopros," 116; Gosudarstvennaia Duma, *Stenograficheskie otchety*, vtoroi sozyv, sessiia vtoraia, zas. May 18, 1907, col. 856.
45. Selikhov, "Sibir' pod vliianiem," 52; M. Sobolev, "Puti soobshcheniia v Sibiri," in Mel'nik, *Sibir': Eia sovremennoe sostoianie*, 28; R. S. Livshits, *Razmeshchenie promyshlennosti v dorevoliutsionnoi Rossii* (Moscow, 1955), 222.
46. L. Kleinbort, *Russkii imperializm v Azii* (St. Petersburg, 1906), 23–24.
47. "Izvlechenie iz vsepoddanneishego doklada ministra finansov," *Vestnik finansov*,

It can be argued that the railroad, far from stimulating the European Russian iron industry, as Witte and the Committee of the Siberian Railroad had expected, had a deleterious effect here, too. The committee's orders for rails and rolling stock tripled the production of the iron industry in the Urals and southern Russia, but with the completion of the main portions of the railroad and equivocation over the replacement of light rails, the boom came to a sudden end and output declined after 1899. By 1902, prices had fallen so low that production was often not possible.[48] The industry's reliance on government contracts also had an effect on the quality of the expansion. As the economist P. P. Migulin noted, rail mills and rolling stock factories grew like mushrooms after the rain, with fictitious capital and expectations of huge profits from the high prices they knew the state would pay to supply the Trans-Siberian. The factories were poorly but expensively equipped, and their employees were overpaid. Since the State Treasury was the buyer, they forced prices up to twice the market rate and collectively set artificially high rates when demand collapsed.[49] None of the developments that occurred in the Russian iron industry in connection with the Siberian Railroad can be considered desirable.

Many sectors of the Siberian economy were simply unaffected by the railroad. Siberian industry, for instance, by all accounts remained backward and undeveloped. Factory production was virtually nonexistent before the coming of the railroad and there was little change afterward. Most of the factories that found their way into the statistics were small cottage industries that employed family members to process the products of plants and domesticated animals for local consumption. Turnover was small and quality was poor. Distilleries, flour mills, and creameries were the most numerous "factories." East of Lake Baikal industries were few and far between; the Ussuri region did not see the founding of its first creameries until 1911. Towns grew along the Siberian line not as industrial centers but as distribution centers for Siberian raw materials. The scant business of the Omsk

---

no. 8, Feb. 23, 1903: 312; S. K. Fitingof, "Perspektivy ugol'noi promyshlennosti v zapadnoi Sibiri," *Zhurnal obshchestva sibirskikh inzhenerov*, Apr. 1915, no. 4: 98.

48. D. P. Il'inskii and V. P. Ivanitskii, *Ocherk istorii russkoi parovozostroitel'noi i vagonostroitel'noi promyshlennosti* (Moscow, 1929), 75, 83; M. N. Pokrovsky, *A Brief History of Russia*, trans. D. S. Mirsky, vol. 2 (Orono, Me., 1968), 43; Marshall Goldman, "The Relocation and Growth of the Prerevolutionary Russian Ferrous Metal Industry," *Explorations in Entrepreneurial History* 9 (Oct. 1956): 34.

49. Migulin, *Nasha noveishaia zheleznodorozhnaia politika*, 298n1.

stock market, located in a thriving commercial center of Siberia, is telling. A report blamed not only restrictive laws but also the fact that the conditions for the expansion of industry were not to be found in Siberia. Still lacking were capital, population density, and, despite the wishful thinking of Soviet historians, an industrial proletariat.[50]

The exploitation of natural resources was also largely unchanged by the railroad. The forest industry was still embryonic in 1912, although in the next five years it did experience some growth.[51] Despite publicity about Siberia's mineral wealth and the railroad's contribution to its discovery, mining was weakly developed. Gold was the most valuable commodity produced in all of Siberia, but it contributed little to the economy. As for coal, as late as 1915 coking coals from Kuznetsk were not yet being transported for use in the Ural iron industry. In the same year, of the more than 200 million puds of coal carried on the Siberian Railroad, 75 percent or more was for use on the railroad alone. Not long before, it had been 95 percent. Almost no other metal deposits were worked before World War I, and Russia continued to import iron, copper, zinc, lead, tin, and other minerals.[52]

Nor was Siberian agriculture as lustrous as its most successful branches made it seem. One must adjust calculations of the income from grain production to take into account the fact that much of the grain was consumed by its producers. And gains from the large amounts exported were somewhat diminished by the continued import of grain and other foodstuffs into the Far East from Manchuria, America, and Australia. Although there was a trend toward mechanization, for the most part Siberian farming was not advanced in its techniques.[53]

Such observations must not be allowed to obscure the fact that the bulk of peasants enjoyed a higher standard of living in Siberia than

50. Bukhman, *Doklad*, 7; *Sibirskii torgovo-promyshlennyi kalendar' na 1895 god*, 130–132, 156, 172–174, 207–209; *Sibirskii torgovo-promyshlennyi kalendar' na 1910 god*, otdel 1, pp. 44–48, 64–71; Golovachev, *Ekonomicheskaia geografiia*, 102, 105–106, 116, 163; Livshits, *Razmeshchenie*, 219–220; M. Sobolev, "Dobyvaiushchaia i obrabatyvaiushchaia promyshlennost' Sibiri," in Mel'nik, *Sibir': Eia sovremennoe sostoianie*, 164; Borzunov, "K voprosu ob ekonomicheskom znachenii," 98, 101, 105–106, and "Vliianie transsibirskoi magistrali," 180; *Vestnik finansov*, no. 38, Sept. 17, 1906: 437. The report on the Omsk stock market can be found in the latter source.
51. Fedorov, *Ekonomicheskoe polozhenie*, 14; Postoiannoe soveshchanie pri Narkomputi po Nadzoru i Otsenke Rabot Zheleznodorozhnogo, Vodnogo i Mestnogo Transporta, *Zheleznye dorogi sibirskogo okruga putei soobshcheniia* (Moscow, 1923), 76.
52. Fedorov, *Ekonomicheskoe polozhenie*, 11–14; Fitingof, "Perspektivy," 95–98; Sobolev, "Dobyvaiushchaia," 148–149.
53. Fedorov, *Ekonomicheskoe polozhenie*, 11; Borzunov, "K voprosu ob ekonomicheskom znachenii," 103–104.

they had in European Russia.[54] But it was probably not the railroad that was responsible for this prosperity. As Paul Cootner has argued, the natural ability of the land to produce has a greater effect on economic development than the introduction of transport innovations.[55] Indeed, Siberia outstripped the capacity of the railroad and was producing thousands of carloads of grain before it was even completed. For this reason Witte and the Committee of the Siberian Railroad still deserve a great deal of the credit for whatever development there was in the Siberian economy.[56] But to accomplish what they did it was not necessary to build the Trans-Siberian Railroad.

The economic development of Siberia was nonexistent or negligible beyond a swath of territory running 50 to 75 versts on either side of the tracks. The economic impact of the railroad was greatest in western Siberia and diminished as it continued eastward.[57] Against the original intentions of its planners, the Siberian Railroad did not achieve what the geographer Robert N. North refers to as "areal coverage": beyond the belt of the railroad's influence, life continued much as it had before.[58] More than ten years after the completion of the railroad, Transbaikalia and Priamur'e were as dependent as ever on foreign imports of meat, bread, flour, salt, sugar, coal, wood, iron, and bricks.[59] The words of Minister of Transport N. K. Schaffhausen in the State Duma in 1907 are reminiscent of observations from the 1880s: "The extreme poverty of communications in Siberia is sharply evident."[60]

54. See Poppe, "Economic and Cultural Development," 145–146; Lazar Volin, *A Century of Russian Agriculture: From Alexander II to Khrushchev* (Cambridge, Mass., 1970), 108–109. This comparison may not be valid, however, if Enisei and Irkutsk provinces and Transbaikal oblast are considered separately: the area of land cultivated in these regions by each household was, at 3.5 to 4 desiatins, smaller than in the "land-hungry" provinces of European Russia. See Alexis N. Antsiferov et al., *Russian Agriculture during the War* (1930; rpt. New York, 1968), 43.

55. Paul H. Cootner, "The Economic Impact of the Railroad Innovation," in *The Railroad and the Space Program: An Exploration in Historical Analogy*, ed. Bruce Mazlish (Cambridge, Mass., 1965), 109–110.

56. Most observers considered the auxiliary enterprises, administered by Kulomzin, to have been beneficial and reasonably priced at 32 million rubles. See Migulin, *Nasha noveishaia zheleznodorozhnaia politika*, 303–305.

57. Pushechnikov, "O nedochetakh v dele izyskanii," *ZhdD*, 1907, nos. 46–47: 527; Borzunov, "K voprosu ob ekonomicheskom znachenii," 100, 106; Fedorov, *Ekonomicheskoe polozhenie*, 61; Grigor'ev, *Peremeny*, pp. I–II.

58. North, *Transport*, 80–81.

59. Gr. P——n (Potanin), *Ocherk proektov*, 34–35; Fedorov, *Ekonomicheskaia polozhenie*, 28. The best description of conditions in Amur oblast is to be found in G.-M. Valuev, "Vsepoddanneishaia zapiska voennogo gubernatora G.-M. Valueva o sostoianii i nuzhdakh amurskoi oblasti za 1911 god" [Blagoveshchensk, 1912].

60. Gosudarstvennaia Duma, *Stenograficheskie otchety*, vtoroi sozyv, sessiia vtoraia, zas. May 18, 1907, col. 851.

The mixed results of economic development in Siberia speak to the nonachievement of the state's political goals there, to which the events of the 1905 revolution testify. The Trans-Siberian was a man-made conductor of revolutionary energy: its construction gave rise to the formation of a politically conscious work force and facilitated communication among revolutionaries operating in the urban centers of Siberia.[61] In view of the outcome, many people considered the tremendous cost of the railroad unjustified.

## The Cost

The relentless adversities of geography and climate, the imperfect managerial structure and organization of construction, and the state's nonchalant attitude toward economy and accountability all conspired to raise the cost of the Siberian Railroad far above original estimates.[62]

The state originally estimated that the Trans-Siberian Railroad, including all building materials and equipment, the Ekaterinburg-Cheliabinsk branch, the Amur section, and major bridges, would be constructed at a cost between 339,399,434 and 357,949,434 rubles, or between approximately 46,000 and 49,000 rubles per verst.[63] By early 1901, including cost overruns on construction, initial expenditures on inconsequential capacity improvements, and the deficits of its first three years of operation, the cost of the railroad, including the Chinese-Eastern Railroad (which was built in lieu of the longer Amur section), had reached 855,282,153 rubles, or, for a total length of 9,125 versts, 93,730 rubles per verst.[64] When the Chinese-Eastern Railroad is

61. See Patrick Robinson Taylor, "The Trans-Siberian Railroad and the Russian Revolution of 1905" (Ph.D. diss., University of Tennessee, 1969), and Henry Reichman, "The 1905 Revolution on the Siberian Railroad," *Russian Review* 47 (1988).

62. Because of the methods of financial control, no figures can be considered truly reliable. Here I have relied on the calculations of contemporary economists and government railroad experts, as well as the work of historians.

63. Migulin, *Nasha noveishaia zheleznodorozhnaia politika*, 284–285, 294–295. Migulin gives one figure in one place and the other in another, without explaining the difference. The Committee of the Siberian Railroad cited 357 million rubles as the 1892 maximum estimate (ZhKSZhD, zas. 34, SP, Dec. 8, 1899, p. 22, col. 2). Neither includes the estimates for the Perm'-Kotlas Railroad, which would require the addition of another 35 million. Minister of Transport Giubbenet's estimate was slightly higher, but changes were obviously made after it was compiled (see chap. 6).

64. ZhKSZhD, zas. 36, SP, Feb. 21, 1901, p. 13, col. 2. In 1906 an official publication noted that the railroad had cost more than 1 billion rubles (G. F. Kraevskii, "Amurskaia

excluded from consideration, the cost of the as-yet uncompleted Trans-Siberian exceeded 100,000 rubles per verst. This amount surpassed the original estimate of 357 million by almost 500 million rubles; in other words, the cost overrun at this time, before completion, amounted to almost 150 percent.[65]

According to Migulin, no previous railroad built in Russia by either the state or a private company had been as expensive as this one was. The Transcaspian Railroad had cost the Treasury less, and so had even the abuses of the railroad barons, which had initially motivated the state's intervention in railroad affairs. The per-verst cost of the Nikolaevsk Railroad from St. Petersburg to Moscow had been commensurate with that of the Siberian Railroad, but the Nikolaevsk was one of the first railroads in the world, it was built at a time when construction materials were not commonly manufactured, and the very highest technical standards were upheld in its construction.[66] The costs of construction were never widely publicized, of course, for the government had to take into account the sensitivities of foreign investors and an overtaxed populace.[67]

The cost of the railroad composed a significant proportion of the total state expenditures on railroads under Witte, which, according to A. P. Pogrebinskii, stood at 1.7 billion rubles.[68] If one accepts Arcadius Kahan's lower figure of 1 billion rubles for the 1880s and 1890s, the percentage was even larger.[69] In either case, the controversial assertion that government spending on the railroads had an insignificant effect on Russian economic development seems amply justified.[70]

---

zheleznaia doroga," *ZhMPS*, 1906, no. 4: 117–118). According to Borzunov, this figure had been reached by 1903; that is, before the additional expenditures on improvements during the Russo-Japanese War could have been figured in (Borzunov, "K voprosu ob ekonomicheskom znachenii," 102).

65. Migulin, *Nasha noveishaia zheleznodorozhnaia politika*, 295, 299.

66. Ibid., 295–296.

67. When Witte did publish the cost of the railroad, he understated it by up to 300 million rubles and emphasized the continued need of the nation to sacrifice for its completion. See "Izvlechenie iz vsepoddanneishego doklada ministra finansov," *Vestnik finansov*, no. 8, Feb. 23, 1903: 310.

68. Pogrebinskii, "Stroitel'stvo," 178.

69. Arcadius Kahan, "Government Policies and the Industrialization of Russia," *Journal of Economic History* 27 (December 1967): 466–467.

70. This contention appears to dovetail with the econometric studies of Jacob Metzer, who concludes that the direct impact of railroads on the Russian economy was insignificant. See Jacob Metzer, "Railroads in Tsarist Russia: Direct Gains and Implications," *Explorations in Economic History* 13, no. 1 (1976): 85–111, and *Some Economic Aspects of Railroad Development in Tsarist Russia* (New York, 1977). But circumstances were different in Siberia than in European Russia, where Metzer focuses his attention, and, as

The amounts indicated for construction of the Siberian Railroad
were unprecedented in the annals of Russian railroad affairs. Yet the
tale cannot be considered complete unless we take into account the
outlays from 1901 to 1914, which include the cost of the Amur Railroad (more than 390.5 million rubles) and the cost of additional reconstruction, double-tracking, and other improvements (between 117
million and 148.7 million rubles).[71] Investment costs must also be
included: official calculations for the Siberian Railroad excluded interest charges, as did government statistics for the state railroad network
at large (though private railroad companies were required by law to
include them in their accounts).[72] The total amount the state ex-
pended in this category has been estimated at 378 million rubles by
1914, exclusive of operating deficits of 432 million rubles; thanks to the
way it was constructed, the railroad was very much a steady drain on
the state's finances.[73] Finally, although no figures are available, it

Colin White and Paul Gregory have pointed out, Metzer ignores the indirect effects of
railroad development. See Paul R. Gregory, "Russian Industrialization and Economic
Growth: Results and Perspectives of Western Research," *Jahrbücher für Geschichte
Osteuropas* 25, no. 3 (1977): 213, and Colin White, "The Impact of Russian Railway
Construction on the Market for Grain in the 1860's and 1870's," in *Russian Transport: An
Historical and Geographical Survey*, ed. Leslie Symons and Colin White (London, 1975),
1–45. Further studies in Russian railroad history would contribute to the resolution of
this dispute.

71. For the cost of the Amur Railroad, see Steven G. Marks, "The Burden of Siberia: The
Amur Railroad Question in Russia, 1906–1916" (paper read at AAASS conference,
Honolulu, Nov. 19, 1988), 11. Cf. M. V. Braikevitch and I. R. Afonin, "The Railways of
Siberia," *Russian Economist: Journal of the Russian Economic Association* 2, no. 5
(October–December 1921): 1511, whose figure of 322 million rubles is too low. Regarding
the cost of additional improvements, the high figure in parentheses is found in Fedorov,
*Ekonomicheskoe polozhenie*, 16, the low in Braikevitch and Afonin, "Railways," 1506–
1507. It is unclear from the respective texts whether these figures include expenditures
made before and during the Russo-Japanese War, but since they definitely do not
include the cost of the Tiumen'-Omsk Railroad, neither is exaggerated.

72. Leo Pasvolsky and Harold Moulton, *Russian Debts and Russian Reconstruction: A
Study of the Relation of Russia's Foreign Debts to Her Economic Recovery* (New York,
1924), 54; Migulin, *Nasha noveishaia zheleznodorozhnaia politika*, 296.

73. Braikevitch and Afonin, "Railways," 1506–1513. These two numbers do not include expenditures on the Chinese-Eastern Railroad. The operating deficit of the
Siberian Railroad, even when the Chinese-Eastern Railroad is excluded, accounted for a
large portion of the indebtedness of the state railroad system on the whole. (See table in
Witte, "Nekotorye soobrazheniia," 90.) The incomes of all sections of the Siberian
Railroad, save for the Transbaikal section, were gradually on the rise, and in 1908–1909
receipts covered operating costs for the first time. (See MPS, *Obzor kommercheskoi
deiatel'nosti*, 257; M. M. Shmukker, *Finansy kazennoi seti zheleznykh dorog Rossii v
sviazi s biudzhetom [1890–1913 g.]* [Vol'sk, 1918], 16–17, 111, 119, 123.) However, this gain
was balanced by losses elsewhere. As an official government study made clear, only an
increase in shipments of tea pulled the railroad out of deficit. To attract these shipments the government had lowered customs duties on tea. The customs revenues lost

should not be forgotten that millions of acres of land were alienated and state-owned forests exploited for the Trans-Siberian. The prices of such resources, normally computed in the costs of private railroads, were ignored in this case; they were enormous.

The total cost of the Siberian Railroad by the outbreak of World War I (exclusive of the value of forests and alienated land) exceeded 1.47 billion rubles and may have reached higher than 2.06 billion rubles.[74] By contrast, the gross output of all Siberian industry in 1914 has been valued at roughly 90 million rubles.[75] To put the cost in clearer perspective, remember that the total yearly disbursements of the Russian state budget exceeded 3 billion rubles for the first time only in 1912. In 1903 it was 2.05 billion rubles, or roughly double the cost of the Trans-Siberian by that date.[76] As a percentage of the state debt, which according to one estimate was 8.8 billion at the end of 1913, it was also significant.[77]

The Trans-Siberian Railroad was the most expensive peaceful undertaking in modern history up to that time.[78] Mitigating its enormous costs somewhat was the immense amount of work involved in distant regions with severe terrain and climate: before 1903, 70,000 laborers were employed; among other feats, they raised 77 million cubic feet of

---

had far exceeded what the government earned by attracting tea to the railroad. (See Fedorov, *Ekonomicheskoe polozhenie*, 18–20.) In any case, despite the large amount of grain carried on the railroad, traffic was still below an economical level (Westwood, *History*, 139).

74. The first number is from Borzunov, "K voprosu ob ekonomicheskom znachenii," 102, and either excludes the cost of the Chinese-Eastern Railroad or, more likely, does not comprise investment costs and operating expenditures; Borzunov's text is unclear on these points. The second figure is from Braikevitch and Afonin, "Railways," 1513, and includes the Chinese-Eastern Railroad.

75. Borzunov, "K voprosu ob ekonomicheskom znachenii," 102. According to Borzunov, in 1904 the value of industrial output was only 50 million rubles.

76. Pasvolsky and Moulton, *Russian Debts*, 50.

77. This point is made in Braikevitch and Afonin, "Railways," 1514. For the state debt, see Pasvolsky and Moulton, *Russian Debts*, 177. According to Iu. N. Shebaldin, the total amount of state indebtedness on Jan. 1, 1914, was 12.745 billion rubles; see his "Gosudarstvennyi biudzhet tsarskoi Rossii v nachale XX v. (do mirovoi voiny)," *Istoricheskie zapiski* 65 (1959): 179.

78. My assertion is based on David McCullough's claim of the same honor for France's expenditure on its failed attempt to build the Panama Canal, which amounted to 1.435 billion francs, or $287 million. Even after the American contribution is added in, bringing the final cost of the canal in 1914 to $639 million at contemporary exchange rates (approximately 50 cents to the ruble in 1900), the Trans-Siberian was more expensive, although certainly not on a per-mile basis. It should also be kept in mind that the Panama Canal was technically "a masterpiece in design and construction" that has never required major repair. See David McCullough, *The Path between the Seas: The Creation of the Panama Canal, 1870–1914* (New York, 1977), 235, 610–611.

earthworks and cut down for railroad construction alone 108,000 acres of forest.[79] But these circumstances cannot have provided solace to those who knew, as one government authority wrote in 1912, that the railroad continued to be a drain on the nation's resources and would "for a long time yet require heavy sacrifices from the tax resources of the country."[80] A special conference under D. M. Sol'skii attributed the ultimate expense of the railroad to poor organization and management and least of all to the distant, difficult setting.[81] Economy had never been more than a secondary concern to the government builders and managers of the railroad. At the same time that its real cost dimensions were beginning to come to light, the Committee of the Siberian Railroad preened itself for the speed of the road's construction—faster than that of any other railroad in the world. The image and prestige of the Russian government in the nation and the world were always more important considerations.[82]

## An Explanation

How can we explain the failure of the Siberian Railroad to "tame the East"? Witte provided an answer in 1910:

> One can say without any exaggeration that if strategic and political considerations had not played such an enormous role in the configuration of our railroad network and in its management; if the development of railroad affairs in general in Russia had been subordinated solely to commercial and economic considerations, as is the case in America, for instance, then of course there would be no deficit, or at least the deficit would be moderate and incidental.[83]

79. Sabler and Sosnovskii, *Sibirskaia zheleznaia doroga*, 275.
80. Fedorov, *Ekonomicheskoe polozhenie*, 18.
81. ZhKSZhD, zas. 37, June 27, 1901, SP, p. 2, col. 1.
82. ZhKSZhD, zas. 32, Jan. 27, 1899, SP, p. 17, col. 2; zas. 36, Feb. 21, 1901, SP, p. 13, col. 2. Four hundred thirty-eight versts per year was the rate of construction for the Canadian-Pacific Railroad, hitherto the fastest railroad built. The Trans-Siberian progressed at an average of 651 versts per year (to 1901), although if one recognizes that work (e.g., the Amur Railroad and reconstruction) was still being done in 1914 to make it functional, it did not set any records.
83. Witte, "Nekotorye soobrazheniia," 91. Witte continues that these features of railroad construction were inevitable and unavoidable in Russia, and that it should not have been otherwise. *Railroad Gazette*, Jan. 1, 1897, p. 5, gives a similar assessment of the Trans-Siberian.

Witte's assessment is applicable not only to the railroad's finances but to every aspect of the project, including the state's efforts to develop the Siberian economy. Political inspiration and bureaucratic intervention were the dominant genes of Russian economic life as it evolved over the centuries. The Trans-Siberian, like many sectors of the Russian economy, was endowed with characteristics that were not conducive to efficient enterprise and that allowed the distortion of economic inputs. Both the Russian taxpayer and the government's own ability to attain its policy goals suffered accordingly. These characteristics go a long way toward explaining the uneven nature of imperial Russian industrial development, with its simultaneous advanced and backward features and the persistence of premodern techniques in modern forms.[84]

84. Cf. Olga Crisp, *Studies in the Russian Economy before 1914* (London, 1976), 40; Peter I. Lyashchenko, *History of the National Economy of Russia to the 1917 Revolution*, trans. L. M. Herman (New York, 1949), 421–422.

# Conclusion

The Trans-Siberian Railroad was an outgrowth of the historical urge of the Russian government to control its border territories through centralization and Russification. This urge had manifested itself continuously in Siberia since the time of Catherine II, and it became more forceful in the period of reaction under Alexander III and Nicholas II. The Siberian Railroad also represented a stage in the progression of Russian economic policy toward increasing state intervention. Most apparent in the vital railroad sector, this trend reflected the centralizing and chauvinistic proclivity of the last two tsars.

High-level bureaucrats, especially the ministers of finance before Witte, opposed the construction of the Trans-Siberian. Their views were formed in a wholly uncommon phase of Russian history, during which the government committed itself to a laissez-faire economic policy. Often (though not always) aligned with the politically liberal elements in the bureaucracy, they were skeptical of the efficacy of government involvement in the economy. Fiscally conservative and wary of risk-taking, they denied that the empire could be united through economic development. For all their political liberalism, their economic ideas were identical in their caution to those prevalent under Nicholas I. They refused to accept the argument that a nation's wealth was not static, but might expand, or that Russia's remote, hitherto unproductive borderlands could be made to bear fruit. They were especially hostile toward the technologists in the Ministry of Transport, where the vision of large-scale economic development first germinated. As the ministries of finance and transport battled for control of railroad affairs, the lines of ideological division hardened.

Many political conservatives also opposed the railroad, on the grounds that the new technology would introduce elements of modern industrial society that were alien to Russian traditions. Conscious of the declining position of the nobility in Russian life, they feared that the railroad would open Siberia to colonization and deplete the cheap labor force on which gentry agriculture in central Russia depended.

Opposition began to falter as strategic anxiety intensified in reaction to both the intrusion of the West in Asia and the supposed awakening of China. It was all too apparent that Russia's dominion in eastern Siberia and the Far East was made precarious by the poor means of communication and a population that had been unable to make a go of farming. The Trans-Siberian Railroad was proffered as a solution that would at a single stroke compensate for the lack of a Russian infrastructure in the region. The railroad would also implement the forward policy that Russian strategists believed would be the best defense on their Asian flank. The culmination of this belief was the construction of the Chinese-Eastern Railroad through northern Manchuria.

The sociopolitical situation in Siberia itself combined with strategic concerns to breach the wall of opposition to the railroad. Russian bureaucrats suspected the loyalty of the native population, saw the assimilation of local Russians to native ways as diluting Russian authority, and interpreted the development of a regionalist consciousness as the expression of revolutionary and secessionist sentiment. The government sought to cut away at Nicholas I's "forest cordon," the policy that had kept Siberia purposely undeveloped to inhibit social unrest and the influence of foreign powers. As Japan and Prussia had done, Russia embraced economic modernization and innovation not only to maintain its rank among the great powers but also to shore up the autocracy at home. This motive has too long been neglected by historians of imperial Russia.

Even then, the apprehension of many officials for the state of Russian finances and their hostility toward the schemes of the Ministry of Transport led them to support a more gradual pattern of development for Siberia. Along with some members of the professional societies, they proposed the construction of local railroads and the improvement of Siberian rivers to promote trade and industry until each region could provide enough revenue to sustain and make profitable its section of a Trans-Siberian trunk line. These views were shared by the regionalist intelligentsia, who voiced the hope that Siberia would thereby be able to withstand the onslaught of the centralizing metropolis against its unique culture.

In the end, although the bureaucratic opponents of the Siberian Railroad underrated the productive potential of Siberia, their objections seem to have been justified and their alternative blueprint more appropriate for Russian and Siberian conditions. The tracing, construction, and operation of the railroad were managed by the state along bureaucratic, centralized lines, which in many ways proved counterproductive. The economic advantages the railroad brought to Siberia were questionable and its cost was indefensible under the circumstances. In the strategic realm, the construction of a railroad theoretically capable of transporting troops to the Pacific and effecting the de facto annexation of northern Manchuria was a major contributing factor in the outbreak of war with Japan. In this conflict that its construction helped provoke, the railroad then failed to provide adequate logistical support to the Russian war effort. In the wake of its humiliating defeat at the hands of the Japanese, Russia was hurled into the turmoil of the 1905 revolution. In Siberia the artery of the revolution was the Trans-Siberian Railroad, whose appearance had energized the forces that wanted to destroy the regime.

In one area, the auxiliary enterprises of the Committee of the Siberian Railroad, the government was more successful. The state channeled the peasant resettlement movement, dispatched geological expeditions, improved water transport, and tried to stimulate local industry. Advancement was by and large limited to western Siberia, and to agriculture and water transport more than industrial development. But the systematic planning of the committee's activities made this pioneer venture unlike any other in the history of the world.

The unsatisfactory performance of the Siberian Railroad and the mixed results of the state-led economic reconstruction of Siberia can be attributed above all to the fact that these undertakings were motivated by politics. Considerations of profit and loss were given a relatively low priority. For the sake of reducing costs or completing the work rapidly the government often disregarded inefficiency and widespread corruption. It paid no heed to optimal economic or commercial conditions, and the folly of its policy became apparent soon after the trains began to run.

These factors lead me to conclusions that differ from those of other economic historians, who attempt to show that Russian modernization followed a well-trod European path with only slight deviation. I refer to the works of Alexander Gerschenkron and more recently Paul R. Gregory, who asserts that "Russia had begun to experience modern economic growth after 1880."[1] Statistical indices that demonstrate tremendous progress disguise the motivation and quality, indeed the very nature, of Russian economic development in the late imperial period.

The role of the state, substituting for a weakly developed bourgeoisie, appears in the historiography as vigorous and singularly effective in industrializing and developing the country. I do agree with Gerschenkron that the state was preeminent in the attempt to move the nation forward, although spontaneous or autonomous sources of growth probably would have sunk deeper roots given enough time after the 1905 revolution.[2] Nonetheless, this investigation of the Siberian Railroad affirms the conclusions of Arcadius Kahan that the state's economic policy hindered development even as it was trying to bring it about.[3]

All told, the results of the state's railroad construction program, as exemplified by the Siberian Railroad, were lackluster, not dynamic.[4] We must question the belief that in Russia "railroadization" was the most successful component of the state's industrialization drive and

1. Alexander Gerschenkron, *Economic Backwardness in Historical Perspective: A Book of Essays* (Cambridge, Mass., 1962), and *Europe in the Russian Mirror: Four Lectures in Economic History* (Cambridge, 1970); Paul R. Gregory, *Russian National Income, 1885–1913* (Cambridge, 1982), 161–162, 165 (quote), and passim.

2. Gregory (*Russian National Income*, 123–124) misstates Gerschenkron's argument in writing that, because of his emphasis on the role of the state, he categorizes Russian economic development of the postemancipation period as "Asiatic." Gerschenkron's point is that before the revolution, Russian industrialization followed a European pattern, with the state substituting for what private enterprise provided in Europe but could not do in Russia. It is only in the Soviet and Petrine periods that he finds a kinship to patterns of "Oriental despotism" (cf. Gerschenkron, *Europe in the Russian Mirror*, 117). As for the rise of a strong private sector after the 1905 revolution and the overthrow of Witte, statist attitudes were strong even then among entrepreneurs, who were proponents of centralized economic planning by the state. See Ruth Amende Roosa, "Russian Industrialists Look to the Future: Thoughts on Economic Development, 1906–17," in *Essays in Russian and Soviet History: In Honor of Geroid Tanquary Robinson*, ed. John Shelton Curtiss (New York, 1963), 198–218.

3. Arcadius Kahan, "Government Policies and the Industrialization of Russia," *Journal of Economic History* 27 (1967): 460–477.

4. The Siberian Railroad accounted for a large portion of the trackage built under Witte and set the standards for railroad management. Its methods of construction were adopted for the country at large after the Administration for the Construction of the Siberian Railroad was expanded into the nationwide Administration for Railroad Construction (Erik Amburger, *Geschichte der Behördenorganisation Rußlands von Peter dem Großen bis 1917* [Leiden, 1966], 265).

the precondition of its modernization.[5] The expanded transport net-work's very utility for efficient economic advancement was under-mined by the government's motives for developing the economy.

Perhaps equally at fault was Witte, whom historians generally por-tray as having given a virtuoso performance. Witte provided the lead-ership that was needed to accomplish the project, but his methods also contributed to its distortions. He excluded dissension and debate both by having weak, compliant individuals appointed to ministerial posts and by creating the Committee of the Siberian Railroad. As one critic put it, his was a "personal regime," standing above government and society.[6] His actions are symptomatic of the broader insufficien-cies inherent in an autocratic system that attempts to modernize from above largely to preserve and enhance the political power of the state.

The Russian economy at this time was by no means totally depen-dent on the state. The Witte "system" was discredited by the depres-sion at the turn of the century, and private enterprise continued to flourish until it was uprooted by the Bolshevik Revolution.[7] But we have seen that salient characteristics of tsarist enterprise anticipated familiar traits of a later era. The Olympian emphasis on speeding the railroad's construction; its gargantuan scale; the contempt for finan-cial control; the publicity given the railroad based on partial truths; and Witte's attachment of millenarian hopes to it—all came to be typical features of Soviet industrial enterprise, from Magnitogorsk in the 1930s to the Baikal-Amur Main Line in the 1980s. These projects also share the Trans-Siberian's technical and economic shortcom-ings, because they too were launched to achieve political objectives and were overseen by a central bureaucracy that acted at the behest of the political leadership.[8]

5. This is the view of Alexander Baykov, "The Economic Development of Russia," *Economic History Review* 7 (1954): 137–149; W. W. Rostow, "Leading Sectors and the Take-off," in *The Economics of Take-off into Sustained Growth*, ed. W. W. Rostow (London, 1963), 8; and Gregory, *Russian National Income*, 159–160.

6. V. S. Lavrov, "Dve politiki," *ISIPS*, 1915, no. 4: 72–73.

7. On the demise of the Witte system, see Peter Gatrell, *The Tsarist Economy, 1850–1917* (New York, 1986), 167–169, 172–173; Theodore H. Von Laue, *Sergei Witte and the Industrialization of Russia* (New York, 1973), 276–292.

8. See, e.g., John Scott, *Behind the Urals: An American Worker in Russia's City of Steel* (Cambridge, Mass., 1942); R. W. Davies, "Some Soviet Economic Controllers," pt. 3, *Soviet Studies* 12 (July 1960): 42–44; L. Iudovich, "Nedostroennyi BAM," *Novoe russkoe slovo*, Nov. 20, 1985, p. 3. Many of the problems cited by Iudovich in regard to the BAM—the "construction job of the century," as it was designated in the Brezhnev years—are identical to those I describe in chaps. 9 and 10 in regard to the Trans-Siberian before the revolution.

The Trans-Siberian project almost seems to belong more to the Soviet period than to the tsarist. Many of the projects the Soviets took up were first devised in the Committee of the Siberian Railroad, most notably the Ural-Kuznetsk combine, gold mining in the far northeast, the active use of the Northern Sea route, the creation of a merchant marine, and the promotion of mass Slavic resettlement in Asian Russia. The committee was also a pioneer in the governmental direction of applied scientific research and exploration of natural resources.[9]

One might say that the Soviet leadership (before Gorbachev) looked on the all-union economy as a field for development and political binding in the same way that Witte looked on Siberia. Both, of course, were motivated by political goals and dedicated to maintaining the state's power over its territory.[10] Although Witte's planning in the Committee of the Siberian Railroad was not nearly so comprehensive, did not rely at all on coercion, and did not forsake light industry, it was nonetheless akin to the Soviet five-year plans insofar as it embodied an act of will to remold the economy on lines deemed desirable by the state.[11] The Trans-Siberian "taught" Russia not managerial capitalism, as railroads did the United States, but rather the possibility of perfecting a centralized economy.[12] Although less centralized paths

9. Loren R. Graham, *The Soviet Academy of Sciences and the Communist Party, 1927–1932* (Princeton, 1967), 22–23, shows the influence of the Commission for the Study of Natural Productive Forces (KEPS) on Soviet applied research; I consider the Committee of the Siberian Railroad to be the forerunner of KEPS. For a survey of KEPS's activities, see B. A. Lindener, *Raboty rossiiskoi akademii nauk v oblasti issledovaniia prirodnykh bogatstv Rossii: Obzor deiatel'nosti KEPS za 1915–1921 gg.* (Petrograd, 1922). A recent study of Soviet railroad policy in Siberia looks to the Committee of the Siberian Railroad as a desirable model for the long-term development of the region. See M. R. Sigalov and V. A. Lamin, *Zheleznodorozhnoe stroitel'stvo v praktike khoziaistvennogo osvoeniia Sibiri* (Novosibirsk, 1988), 119.

10. According to the historian A. Lobanov-Rostovsky, the five-year plan "was conceived by the GOSPLAN in Moscow as making the Soviet Union into one economic whole, and making the component parts of the Union so interdependent as to kill their economic life if they segregate themselves from the greater body politic" (*Russia and Asia* [New York, 1933], 276). Trotsky had earlier expressed the clear political rationale behind industrial expansion in Siberia: "Backward Siberia became Soviet first and foremost by the force of modern technology. The power of the new technology has its most striking political effect on backward countries. If the factory furnaces were extinguished and the steam were let out of the boilers, in a very short time we would cease to exist as a united country. The dictatorship of the proletariat in a peasant country is in itself the political expression of the power of the new technology, which subdues not only nature but also inert modes of life" ("O Sibiri," *Severnaia Aziia* 3 [1927]: 7).

11. On this defining feature of Soviet planning, see Alexander Baykov, *The Development of the Soviet Economic System: An Essay on the Experience of Planning in the U.S.S.R.* (New York, 1947), 434.

12. On the impact of the railroads on business organization in the United States, see

of development still lay open to Russia before and after 1917, the Bolsheviks did find a ready-made tradition of state planning at their disposal when they came to power.

The Russian state's attempt to assert its control over a sprawling geographical realm through colonization has been a leitmotif of its history from the Muscovite grand princes to the Politburo. Through those centuries all Russian rulers have had to contend with their immense, often harsh, and seemingly threatened Asian territories. Similar complications resulting from the consequent reliance on over-centralization arose before and after October 1917. The revolution changed the face of Russia, but the continuity of certain patterns of economic development and economic enterprise is not difficult to see. And in both imperial Russia and the Soviet Union, the same complex of attitudes existed vis-à-vis the nation's territory. The history of the Trans-Siberian Railroad exemplifies the predilections of Russian rulers in the age of industrialization.

---

Alfred D. Chandler, Jr., *The Visible Hand: The Managerial Revolution in American Business* (Cambridge, Mass., 1977). In a book that influenced Lenin's economic thinking, V. I. Grinevetskii pointed to the Trans-Siberian as one of the few examples of prerevolutionary state planning for the broad purpose of economic development (*Poslevoennye perspektivy russkoi promyshlennosti*, 2d ed. [Moscow, 1922], 62).

# Bibliography of Primary Sources

### Periodicals

*Archiv für Eisenbahnwesen*
*Inzhener*
*Izvestiia imperatorskogo russkogo geograficheskogo obshchestva*
*Izvestiia sobraniia inzhenerov putei soobshcheniia*
*Krasnyi arkhiv*
*Novoe vremia*
*The Railroad Gazette*
*Sibirskii torgovo-promyshlennyi i spravochnyi kalendar'*
*The Times*
*Tiuremnyi vestnik*
*Vestnik finansov, promyshlennosti i torgovli*
*Vostochnoe obozrenie*
*Zheleznodorozhnoe delo*
*Zhurnal ministerstva putei soobshcheniia*
*Zhurnal obshchestva sibirskikh inzhenerov*

### Unpublished Works

Filippov, T. I. "Zapiska gosudarstvennogo kontrolera upravliaiushchemu delami komiteta ministrov o proektirovavshemsia napravlenii sibirskoi zheleznoi dorogi." TsGAOR, Moscow, fond 1099, opis' 1, delo 463.
Golokhvastov, A. D. "Zapiska A. D. Golokhvastova o torgovom znachenii obskoi zheleznoi dorogi." TsGAOR, Moscow, fond 677, opis' 1, delo 589.
"Otchet vysochaishe uchrezhdennoi komissii dlia issledovaniia prichin pere-

raskhodov po sooruzheniiu sibirskoi i perm'-kotlasskoi zheleznykh dorog."
[1900.] Saltykov-Shchedrin Library, Leningrad.
Russia, Komitet Sibirskoi Zheleznoi Dorogi. "Zhurnaly komiteta sibirskoi
zheleznoi dorogi." [1893, 1895–1902.] INION, Moscow.
Russia, Ministerstvo Putei Soobshcheniia, "Otchet o deiatel'nosti ministerstva
putei soobshcheniia po stroitel'stvu sibirskoi zheleznoi dorogi za vremia s
30 marta 1889 g. po 17 ianvaria 1892 g." TsGAOR, Moscow, fond 677, opis' 1,
delo 629.
———, Departament Zheleznykh Dorog. "O sposobe postroiki sibirskoi zheleznoi dorogi i o neotlagatel'nom pristupe k sooruzheniiu pervogo eia
uchastka Samara-Ufa." K. N. Pos'et, January 11, 1885, no. 266. LIIZhT,
Leningrad.
———, Upravlenie Zheleznykh Dorog, Tekhnichesko-Inspektorskii Komitet.
"Predstavlenie v komitet ministrov MPS K. N. Pos'eta: 'O napravlenii tranzitnoi sibirskoi zheleznoi dorogi.'" May 2, 1875, no. 2319. LIIZhT, Leningrad.
———. "Predstavlenie v komitet ministrov MPS K. N. Pos'eta." June 1, 1884, no.
4751. LIIZhT, Leningrad.
"Trudy vostochnoi podkomissii vysochaishe uchrezhdennoi komissii dlia
issledovaniia na meste dela sooruzheniia sibirskoi zheleznoi dorogi." 22
vols. [1895–1896.] LIIZhT, Leningrad.
"Trudy vysochaishe uchrezhdennoi komissii dlia issledovaniia na meste dela
sooruzheniia sibirskoi zheleznoi dorogi." 25 vols. [1895–1896.] LIIZhT,
Leningrad.
Valuev, G.-M. "Vsepoddanneishaia zapiska voennogo gubernatora G.-M. Valueva o sostoianii i nuzhdakh amurskoi oblasti za 1911 god." [1912.] Saltykov-Shchedrin Library, Leningrad.
"Vsepoddanneishii otchet o proizvedennoi s 30 maia 1910 goda po 29 fevralia
1912 goda po vysochaishemu poveleniiu senatorom grafom Medem revizii
material'noi sluzhby i khoziaistva sibirskoi zheleznoi dorogi." [1912.]
Saltykov-Shchedrin Library, Leningrad.

Published Works

"A. A. Auerbakh." Russkaia starina 156, no. 11 (1913): 396–418.
Barry, Arthur John. Lecture on the Great Siberian Railway. London, 1900.
Beveridge, Albert J. The Russian Advance. New York, 1904.
Bloch, Jan Gotlib [I. S. Bliokh]. Vliianie zheleznykh dorog na ekonomicheskoe
sostoianie Rossii. 5 vols. St. Petersburg, 1878.
Bublikov, A. A. K voprosu o spriamlenii peterburgo-sibirskoi tranzitnoi magi-
strali. St. Petersburg, 1905.
Budagov, G. M. O propusknoi sposobnosti sibirskoi zheleznoi dorogi. Moscow,
1905.
Bukhman, A. N., et al. Doklad ob eksploatatsionnykh raskhodakh sibirskoi
zheleznoi dorogi. St. Petersburg, 1912.

Chekhov, Anton. *The Unknown Chekhov: Stories and Other Writings Hitherto Untranslated*. Trans. Avrahm Yarmolinsky. New York: Noonday Press, 1954.

Chikhachev, P. "Kaliforniia i ussuriiskii krai." *Vestnik Evropy*, June 1890, no. 6: 545–568.

Chuprov, A. I. *Iz proshlogo russkikh zheleznykh dorog: Stat'i 1874–1895 godov*. Moscow, 1909.

Dement'ev, G. D. *Dokhody kazennykh zheleznykh dorog*. St. Petersburg, 1913.

Denisov, V. I. *Rossiia na Dal'nem Vostoke*. N.p., 1913.

Dmitriev-Mamonov, A. I., and A. F. Zdziarski, comps. *Guide to the Great Siberian Railway*. St. Petersburg, 1900.

———. *Wegweiser auf der großen sibirischen Eisenbahn*. St. Petersburg, 1901.

Fedorov, M. L. *Ekonomicheskoe polozhenie sibirskoi magistrali*. Trudy vysochaishe uchrezhdennoi osoboi vysshei komissii dlia vsestoronnego issledovaniia zheleznodorozhnogo dela v Rossii, vol. 76. St. Petersburg, 1912.

Fedorov, M. P., ed. *Doklady biudzhetnoi komissii vtoroi gosudarstvennoi dumy (ne razsmotrennye dumoi vsledstvie eia rospuska)*. St. Petersburg, 1907.

G., M. *Trudy kommissii* [sic] *imperatorskogo russkogo tekhnicheskogo obshchestva po voprosu o sibirskoi zheleznoi doroge i vopros o dal'neishikh izyskaniiakh i issledovaniiakh v Sibiri*. St. Petersburg, 1891.

Glinskii, B. B. "Graf Sergei Iulevich Witte (Materialy dlia biografii)." *Istoricheskii vestnik* 140 (April 1915): 232–279.

———, ed. *Prolog russko-iaponskoi voiny: Materialy iz arkhiva grafa S. Iu. Witte*. Petrograd, 1916.

Great Britain, Naval Intelligence Division. *A Handbook of Siberia and Arctic Russia*. Vol. 1. London, n.d.

Grigor'ev, V. Iu. *Peremeny v usloviiakh ekonomicheskoi zhizni naseleniia Sibiri (Eniseiskii krai)*. Krasnoiarsk, 1904.

Grinevetskii, V. I. *Poslevoennye perspektivy russkoi promyshlennosti*. 2d ed. Moscow, 1922.

Gurko, V. I. *Features and Figures of the Past: Government and Opinion in the Reign of Nicholas II*. Ed. J. E. W. Sterling et al. Trans. L. Matveev. Stanford: Stanford University Press, 1939.

Iadrintsev, N. M. *Sibir' kak koloniia v geograficheskom, etnograficheskom i istoricheskom otnoshenii*. 2d ed. St. Petersburg, 1892.

Iavorovskii, P. K. *Gornaia promyshlennost' Sibiri i sibirskaia zheleznaia doroga*. St. Petersburg, 1895.

Imperatorskoe Russkoe Geograficheskoe Obshchestvo, Orenburgskii Otdel. *O preimushchestvakh orenburgo-omskogo napravleniia sibirskoi zheleznoi dorogi*. Orenburg, 1883.

*Itogi mnenii po povodu napravleniia sibirskoi zheleznoi dorogi, podvedennye chlenom i korrespondentom raznykh sel'skokhoziaistvennykh obshchestv i komitetov*. St. Petersburg, 1875.

Ivashchenkov, A., comp. *Kratkii obzor ispolneniia gosudarstvennykh rospisei (v sviazi s prochimi oborotami gosudarstvennogo kaznacheistva) za 1881–1899 gg*. St. Petersburg, 1901.

Izvol'skii, Aleksandr. *Recollections of a Foreign Minister (Memoirs of Alexander Iswolsky)*. Trans. Charles Louis Seeger. Garden City, N.Y., 1921.

Kalmykow, Andrew D. *Memoirs of a Russian Diplomat: Outposts of the Empire, 1893–1917*. Ed. Alexandra Kalmykow. New Haven: Yale University Press, 1971.

*Kanun desiatiletie vysochaishe utverzhdennoi sibirskoi zheleznoi dorogi i agitatsiia protiv neia*. Kazan', 1884.

Kartamyshev, V. P. *Doklad obshchemu sobraniiu chlenov obshchestva sodeistviia russkoi promyshlennosti i torgovle: "O napravlenii magistral'noi linii sibirskoi zheleznoi dorogi na g. Tomsk ili v obkhod ego."* N.p., 1892.

Katkov, M. N. *Sobranie peredovykh statei moskovskikh vedomostei 1863–1887 gg.* 29 vols. Moscow, 1897–1898.

Kenge, V. I., and N. D. Nakhtman. *Kratkii ocherk linii sibirskoi zheleznoi dorogi*. St. Petersburg, 1908.

Kennan, George. *Siberia and the Exile System*. New York, 1891.

Kislinskii, N. A. *Nasha zheleznodorozhnaia politika po dokumentam arkhiva komiteta ministrov*. Ed. A. N. Kulomzin. 4 vols. St. Petersburg, 1902.

*Kitaiskaia vostochnaia zheleznaia doroga: Istoricheskii ocherk*. Vol. 1, 1896–1905 gg. St. Petersburg, 1914.

Kleinbort, L. *Russkii imperializm v Azii*. St. Petersburg, 1906.

Kokovtsov, V. N. *Out of My Past: The Memoirs of Count Kokovtsov*. Ed. H. H. Fisher. Trans. Laura Matveev. Stanford: Stanford University Press, 1935.

Korol'kov, K. *Zhizn' i tsarstvovanie imperatora Aleksandra III (1881–1894 gg.)*. Kiev, 1901.

Kraevskii, G. *Mirovaia-tranzitnaia sibirskaia zheleznaia doroga*. Irkutsk, 1898.

Krahmer, G. *Sibirien und die große sibirische Eisenbahn*. Leipzig, 1897.

Kropotkin, Peter. *Memoirs of a Revolutionist*. Cambridge, Mass., 1930.

Krzhizhanovskii, G. M., and P. S. Osadchii, eds. *Problema sibirskoi sverkhmagistrali*. Moscow, 1929.

Kulomzin, A. N. [A.-N. de Koulomzine]. *Le Transsibérien*. Trans. Jules Legras. Paris, 1904.

Kuprin, A. I. "Pamiati Chekhova." In *Polnoe sobranie sochinenii A. I. Kuprina*, vol. 7. St. Petersburg, 1912.

Kuropatkin, A. N. *The Russian Army and the Japanese War*. Ed. E. D. Swinton. Trans. A. B. Lindsay. Vol. 1. London, 1909.

Lamzdorf, V. N. *Dnevnik, 1891–1892*. Moscow/Leningrad, 1934.

———. *Dnevnik V. N. Lamzdorfa (1886–1890)*. Moscow/Leningrad, 1926.

Lansdell, Henry. *Through Siberia*. Vol. 1. Boston, 1882.

Legras, Jules. *En Sibérie*. Paris, 1899.

Lindener, B. A. *Raboty rossiiskoi akademii nauk v oblasti issledovaniia prirodnykh bogatstv Rossii: Obzor deiatel'nosti KEPS za 1915–1921 gg.* Petrograd, 1922.

Liubimov, L. N. "Iz zhizni inzhenera putei soobshcheniia." *Russkaia starina* 156 (September and December 1913): 448–463, 651–679.

Lugovskii, L. "Sibirskaia zheleznaia doroga." In *Kalendar' tobol'skoi gubernii na 1892 god*. Tobol'sk, 1892.

Martynov, E. I. *Rabota nashikh zheleznodorozhnykh del'tsov v Manchzhurii.* Moscow, 1914.

*Materialy k istorii voprosa o sibirskoi zheleznoi doroge.* Supplement to *Zheleznodorozhnoe delo,* 1891, no. 16.

Matiunin, N. "Nashi sosedy na krainem Vostoke." *Vestnik Evropy,* July 1887, no. 7: 64–88.

Mel'nik, I. S., ed. *Sibir': Eia sovremennoe sostoianie i eia nuzhdy: Sbornik statei.* St. Petersburg, 1908.

Mendeleev, D. I. *Problemy ekonomicheskogo razvitiia Rossii.* Ed. V. P. Kirichenko. Moscow: Izdatel'stvo Sotsial'no-ekonomicheskoi Literatury, 1960.

——, ed. *Ural'skaia zheleznaia promyshlennost' v 1899 g.* St. Petersburg, 1900.

Miliutin, D. A. *Dnevnik D. A. Miliutina.* 4 vols. Moscow, 1947–1950.

Miropiev, M. A. *O polozhenii russkikh inorodtsev.* St. Petersburg: Sinodal'naia Tipografiia, 1901.

*Neskol'ko slov po voprosu o sibirskoi zheleznoi doroge.* 2d ed. Moscow, 1882.

Nikitin, S. "Uspekhi geologicheskikh znanii za 1892–1893 goda." *Ezhegodnik imperatorskogo russkogo geograficheskogo obshchestva,* 1896, no. 6: 1–68.

*O napravlenii sibirskoi zheleznoi dorogi (Publichnye preniia v obshchestve dlia sodeistviia russkoi promyshlennosti i torgovle).* St. Petersburg, 1870.

Ostrovskii, N. *K voprosu o zheleznykh dorogakh v Sibiri.* Perm', 1880.

*Otchet o zasedaniiakh obshchestva dlia sodeistviia russkoi promyshlennosti i torgovle, po voprosu o sibirskoi zheleznoi doroge.* St. Petersburg, 1884.

Petrov, N. *Finansovoe polozhenie russkoi zheleznodorozhnoi seti i glavneishie prichiny ukhudsheniia ego v poslednie gody.* Trudy vysochaishe uchrezhdennoi osoboi vysshei komissii dlia vsestoronnego issledovaniia zheleznodorozhnogo dela v Rossii, vol. 5. St. Petersburg, 1909.

Pobedonostsev, K. P. *L'Autocratie russe: Mémoires politiques, correspondance officielle et documents inédits relatifs à l'histoire du règne de l'empereur Alexandre III de Russie.* Paris, 1927.

——. *Pis'ma Pobedonostseva k Aleksandru III.* 2 vols. Moscow, 1925, 1926.

Poggenpol, M. *Ocherk vozniknoveniia i deiatel'nosti dobrovol'nogo flota za vremia XXV–ti letniago ego sushchestvovaniia.* St. Petersburg, 1903.

Polovtsov, A. A. *Dnevnik gosudarstvennogo sekretaria A. A. Polovtsova.* 2 vols. Moscow: Nauka, 1966.

*Polozhenie tserkovnogo i shkol'nogo stroitel'stva v raione sibirskoi zheleznoi dorogi na sredstva fonda imeni imperatora Aleksandra III k 1 ianvaria 1900 goda.* St. Petersburg, 1900.

Popov, I. I. *Minuvshee i perezhitoe: Vospominaniia za 50 let: Sibir' i emigratsiia.* Leningrad: Kolos, 1924.

*Po povodu prenii o sibirskoi zheleznoi doroge v obshchestvakh sodeistviia russkoi torgovle i promyshlennosti [sic] i geograficheskom (Peredovye stat'i S.-Peterburgskikh vedomostei).* St. Petersburg, 1870.

Pos'et, K. N. "Prekrashchenie ssylki v Sibir' (Zapiska K. N. Pos'eta)." *Russkaia starina* 99 (July 1899): 51–59.

Potanin, G. N. [Gr. P——n]. *Ocherk proektov zheleznodorozhnogo stroitel'stva v Sibiri.* St. Petersburg, 1910.

Propper, S. M. von. *Was nicht in die Zeitung kam: Erinnerungen des Chef-redakteurs der "Birszhewyja Wedomosti."* Frankfurt am Main, 1929.

Radziwill, Catherine. *Memories of Forty Years.* London, 1914.

Razumov, N. I. *Zabaikal'e: Svod materialov vysochaishe uchrezhdennoi komissii dlia issledovaniia mestnogo zemlevladeniia i zemlepol'zovaniia, pod predsedatel'stvom stats-sekretaria Kulomzina.* St. Petersburg, 1899.

Russia. *Polnoe sobranie zakonov rossiiskoi imperii.* Sobranie tret'e, 1881–1913. St. Petersburg, 1885–1916.

Russia, General'nyi Shtab. *Sbornik geograficheskikh, topograficheskikh i statisticheskikh materialov po Azii.* 64 vols. Moscow/St. Petersburg, 1883–1896.

Russia, Gosudarstvennaia Duma. *Prilozheniia k stenograficheskim otchetam.* Tretii sozyv. Sessiia 1–4. St. Petersburg, 1908–1911.

——. *Stenograficheskie otchety.* Vtoroi sozyv. 2 vols. St. Petersburg, 1907.

——. *Stenograficheskie otchety.* Tretii sozyv. Sessiia pervaia. 3 vols. St. Petersburg, 1908.

Russia, Komitet Ministrov. *Aperçu de l'histoire de la colonisation en Sibérie.* Paris, 1900.

——. *The Great Siberian Railway.* St. Petersburg, 1900.

Russia, Komitet Sibirskoi Zheleznoi Dorogi. *Otchety po komitetu sibirskoi zheleznoi dorogi.* [St. Petersburg, 1893–1897.] BAN, Leningrad.

Russia, Ministerstvo Finansov. *Ministerstvo finansov, 1802–1902.* 2 vols. St. Petersburg, 1902.

——, Departament Torgovli i Manufaktur. *Sibir' i velikaia sibirskaia zheleznaia doroga.* Ed. V. I. Kovalevskii and P. P. Semenov. 2d ed. St. Petersburg, 1896.

——, Departament Zheleznodorozhnykh Del. *Kratkii otchet o deiatel'nosti tarifnykh uchrezhdenii i departamenta zheleznodorozhnykh del za 1889–1913 gg.* St. Petersburg, 1914.

Russia, Ministerstvo Putei Soobshcheniia. *Istoricheskii ocherk raznykh otraslei zheleznodorozhnogo dela i razvitiia finansovo-ekonomicheskoi storony zheleznykh dorog v Rossii po 1897 g. vkliuchitel'no.* Comp. V. M. Verkhovskii. St. Petersburg, 1901.

——. *Istoricheskii ocherk razvitiia zheleznykh dorog v Rossii s ikh osnovaniia po 1897 g. vkliuchitel'no.* Comp. V. M. Verkhovskii. 2 pts. St. Petersburg, 1898, 1899.

——. *Kratkii istoricheskii ocherk razvitiia i deiatel'nosti vedomstva putei soobshcheniia za sto let ego sushchestvovaniia (1798–1898 gg.).* St. Petersburg, 1898.

——. *Sooruzhenie sredne-sibirskoi zheleznoi dorogi, 1893–1898 g.: Sbornik tekhnicheskikh uslovii, instruktsii i poiasnitel'nykh zapisok.* St. Petersburg, 1901. LIIZhT, Leningrad.

——, Otdel Statistiki i Kartografii. *Rechnoi flot (parovoi i neparovoi) aziatskoi Rossii.* St. Petersburg, 1901.

——, Upravlenie Sibirskoi Zheleznoi Dorogi, Kommercheskaia Chast'. *Obzor kommercheskoi deiatel'nosti sibirskoi zheleznoi dorogi (za 1909 god po sravneniiu s predydushchimi godami desiatiletiia 1900–1909 gg.).* Tomsk, 1910.

Russia, Narodnyi Komissariat Putei Soobshcheniia, Postoiannoe Soveshchanie po Nadzoru i Otsenke Rabot Zheleznodorozhnogo, Vodnogo i Mestnogo Transporta. *Zheleznye dorogi sibirskogo okruga putei soobshcheniia.* Moscow, 1923.

Russia, Pereselencheskoe Upravlenie. *Aziatskaia Rossiia.* 3 vols. St. Petersburg, 1914.

*The Russian Government's Plan of Future Railroad Construction.* New York: Youroveta Home & Foreign Trade Co., 1918.

*Russkie vedomosti.* No. 2 (January 3, 1893).

Sabler, S. V., and I. V. Sosnovskii, comps. *Sibirskaia zheleznaia doroga v eia proshlom i nastoiashchem: Istoricheskii ocherk.* Ed. A. N. Kulomzin. St. Petersburg, 1903.

S.-Peterburgskii Birzhevyi Komitet. *Zametka k voprosu o sibirskoi zheleznoi doroge.* St. Petersburg, 1884.

Scott, John. *Behind the Urals: An American Worker in Russia's City of Steel.* Cambridge, Mass., 1942.

Semennikov, V. P., ed. *Za kulisami tsarizma: Arkhiv tibetskogo vracha Badmaeva.* Leningrad, 1925.

Shmukker, M. M. *Finansy kazennoi seti zheleznykh dorog Rossii v sviazi s biudzhetom (1890–1913 g.)* Vol'sk, 1918.

———. *Ocherki finansov i ekonomiki zheleznodorozhnogo transporta Rossii za 1913–1922 gody.* Moscow, 1923.

Shul'gin, V. V. *The Years: Memoirs of a Member of the Russian Duma, 1906–1917.* Trans. Tanya Davis. New York: Hippocrene Books, 1984.

Sibirskoe Biuro pri Sovete S"ezdov Predstavitelei Birzhevoi Torgovli i Sel'skogo Khoziaistva. *Plan zheleznodorozhnogo stroitel'stva v Sibiri na blizhaishee desiatiletie.* Petrograd, January 1917.

Sil'nitskii, A. *Kul'turnoe vliianie ussuriiskoi zheleznoi dorogi na iuzhno-ussuriiskii krai.* Khabarovsk, 1901.

Skal'kovskii, K. A. *Les Ministres des finances de la Russie, 1802–1890.* Paris, 1891.

———. *Nashi gosudarstvennye i obshchestvennye deiateli.* St. Petersburg, 1890.

———. *Russkaia torgovlia v Tikhom okeane.* St. Petersburg, 1883.

———. *Vneshniaia politika Rossii i polozhenie inostrannykh derzhav.* 2d ed. St. Petersburg, 1901.

Snodgrass, John H. *Russia: A Handbook on Commercial and Industrial Conditions.* Department of Commerce, Bureau of Foreign and Domestic Commerce, Special Consular Reports, no. 61. Washington, D.C., 1913.

Snow, George E., ed. and trans. "The Years 1881–1894 in Russia: A Memorandum Found in the Papers of N. Kh. Bunge. A Translation and Commentary." *Transactions of the American Philosophical Society* 71, pt. 6 (1981).

Sobolev, M. N. *Ekonomicheskoe znachenie sibirskoi zheleznoi dorogi.* Tomsk, 1900.

234 Bibliography of Primary Sources

Sovet Moskovskogo Otdeleniia Obshchestva dlia Sodeistviia Russkoi Promysh-lennosti i Torgovle. *Otkuda nachat' postroiku sibirskoi zheleznoi dorogi i v vide-li nepreryvnoi linii ili pereryvchatoi?* Moscow, 1891.

*The Status of the Private Railroad Business in Russia.* New York: Youroveta Home & Foreign Trade Co., 1918.

Subbotich, D. I. *Amurskaia zheleznaia doroga i nasha politika na Dal'nem Vostoke.* St. Petersburg, 1908.

Tanera, Karl. *Zur Kriegszeit auf der sibirischen Bahn und durch Rußland.* Berlin, 1905.

Terner, F. G. *Vospominaniia zhizni.* 2 vols. St. Petersburg, 1910, 1911.

*Tri poslednikh samoderzhtsa: Dnevnik A. V. Bogdanovich.* Moscow/Leningrad, 1924.

Trotsky, L. D. "O Sibiri." *Severnaia Aziia* 3 (1927): 5–17.

*Trudy kommissii [sic] imperatorskogo russkogo tekhnicheskogo obshchestva po voprosu o zheleznoi doroge cherez vsiu Sibir', 1889–1890 gg.* 41 vols. St. Petersburg, 1890.

*Trudy obshchestva dlia sodeistviia russkoi promyshlennosti i torgovle.*

Ukhtomskii, Esper Esperovich. *Puteshestvie na Vostok ego imperatorskogo vysochestva gosudaria naslednika tsesarevicha, 1890–1891.* 3 vols., 6 pts. St. Petersburg, 1893–1897.

United States, Department of the Treasury, Bureau of Statistics. *The Russian Empire and the Trans-Siberian Railway.* Washington, D.C., 1899.

Unterberger, P. F. *Primorskaia oblast', 1856–1898 g.g.* Zapiski imperatorskogo russkogo geograficheskogo obshchestva po otdeleniiu statistiki, vol. 8, no. 2. St. Petersburg, 1900.

*Velikii put': Vidy Sibiri i eia zheleznykh dorog.* Krasnoiarsk, 1899.

Volkov, *O napravlenii sibirskoi zheleznoi dorogi: Zapiska upolnomochennogo ot ufimskogo gubernskogo zemstva i goroda Ufy, ufimskogo gorodskogo golovy Volkova.* St. Petersburg, 1884.

———. *Zapiska upolnomochennogo ot ufimskogo gubernskogo zemstva i g. Ufy, ufimskogo gorodskogo golovy Volkova: K voprosu o napravlenii sibirskoi dorogi.* N.p., 1882.

Voloshinov, N. A. [M. V—"], *Neskol'ko slov o sibirskoi zheleznoi doroge.* St. Petersburg, 1890.

———. "Zhelezno-dorozhnaia razvedka mezhdu Angaroi i severnoiu okonech-nost'iu Baikala." *Izvestiia vostochno-sibirskogo otdela imperatorskogo russkogo geograficheskogo obshchestva* 20, no. 5 (1889): 1–14.

Volpicelli, Zenone [Vladimir]. *Russia on the Pacific and the Siberian Railway.* London, 1899.

Vostrotin, S. V. *Severnyi morskoi put' i cheliabinskii tarifnyi perelom v sviazi s kolonizatsiei Sibiri.* St. Petersburg, 1908.

Wallace, Donald Mackenzie. *Russia on the Eve of War and Revolution.* Ed. Cyril E. Black. Princeton: Princeton University Press, 1984.

Wellington, Arthur M. *The Economic Theory of the Location of Railways.* New York, 1877.

Witte, S. Iu. *Printsipy zheleznodorozhnykh tarifov po perevozke gruzov.* 3d ed. St. Petersburg, 1910.

———. *Samoderzhavie i zemstvo: Konfidentsial'naia zapiska ministra finansov stats-sekretaria S. Iu. Witte (1899 g.).* 2d ed. Stuttgart, 1903.

———. "A Secret Memorandum of Sergei Witte on the Industrialization of Russia." Ed. and trans. Theodore H. Von Laue. *Journal of Modern History* 26 (March 1954): 60–74.

———. *Vorlesungen über Volks- und Staatswirtschaft.* Trans. Josef Melnik. 2 vols. Stuttgart/Berlin, 1913.

———. *Vospominaniia.* 3 vols. Moscow: Izdatel'stvo Sotsial'no-ekonomicheskoi Literatury, 1960.

Wright, Richardson C., and Bassett Digby. *Through Siberia, an Empire in the Making.* New York, 1913.

# Index